Professional ASP.NET Server Controls

Building Custom Controls with C#

Matt Butler
Daniel Cazzulino
Mike Clark
Angelo Kastroulis
Matt Milner
Jan Narkiewicz
Ryan O'Keefe
Thiru Thangarathinam

Wrox Press Ltd. ®

Professional ASP.NET Server Controls

Building Custom Controls with C#

First Printed in Feburary 2002

Published by Wrox Press Ltd,
Arden House, 1102 Warwick Road, Acocks Green,
Birmingham, B27 6BH, UK
Printed in the United States
ISBN 1-861005-64-4

Trademark Acknowledgements

Credits

Authors
Matt Butler
Daniel Cazzulino
Mike Clark
Angelo Kastroulis
Matt Milner
Jan Narkiewicz
Ryan O'Keefe
Thiru Thangarathinam

Additional Material
Brian Francis
Chris Goode

Technical Architect
Chris Goode

Technical Editors
Ewan Buckingham
Gerard Maguire

Index
Michael Brinkman
Andrew Criddle

Production Coordinator
Tom Bartlett

Cover
Chris Morris

Author Agents
Avril Corbin
Nicola Phillips

Project Manager
Emma Batch

Project Adminstrator
Cathy Succamore

Technical Reviewers
Rob Birdwell
Maxime Bombardier
Andreas Christensen
Cristian Darie
Robin Dewson
Cristof Falk
Brian Francis
Damien Foggon
Jeff Gabriel
Mark Horner
Gary Johnson
Don Lee
Mark Mamone
Paul D. Murphy
Johan Normén
Phil Powers De George
Sumit Pal
Larry Schoeneman
Mark H. Simkin
Srinivasa Sivakumar
Konstantinos Vlassis

Proof Reader
Chris Smith

Category Manager
Steve Farncombe

Managing Editors
Viv Emery
Louay Fatoohi

About the Authors

Matt (.MAtt) Butler

Matt Butler is an independent contractor who specializes in Windows DNA, .NET, and Java.

.MAtt went from being a homeless, starving jazz musician to a programmer holding numerous certifications, including MCSD, Sun Java Certified Programmer, BEA Certified Programmer (Java/Weblogic), and a few other miscellaneous certifications. Rode the wave of the .COM craze working on sizable profile-based search engines and transactional e-commerce applications using the Windows DNA architecture in return for 'stock options' and pizza.

.MAtt's interests include all things computer-oriented (especially .NET and security), math, science, physics, spoken word, composing, and improvising introspective music.

Thanks to Daisey for being a loyal, supportive life-partner and muse and thanks to Morgan for being a wonderful daughter and talented friend. Thanks to the SA crew (Angelo, Joe, Brad, Engle, Tim, and Terry) for being hip, open minded, and visionary. Thanks to Angelo for being a great mentor and Gary for being a great friend and learning partner (and the great cover photo). Thanks to my family, and the people at Wrox (Chris, Gerard, Ewan) for being so good at what they do. Thanks to Matt and the Left Ear Design crew and, ultimately, thanks to all of the musicians whom I have had the chance to associate with and learn from – the Joes', Dennis B., Julie M, Greg I., Daisey, Ed R., Bunky G., Bill W., Kevin B., Akiva F., Super Greg, Kerpal, the Johns', Ken N., Tim S., Sean T., Dan B., the Chris', Roy D., Pete C., etc. It is with you all that I developed the discipline and focus that I have now applied in another direction… So I can EAT!

You can reach .MAtt at matt@biodigitalmusic.com.

Daniel Cazzulino

Daniel Cazzulino is a senior developer who discovered C# and the .NET Framework early its beta process. He has had many years experience developing distributed solutions based on Windows DNA, COM/COM+, and VB, but has now left this behind him to dedicate himself full time to the new platform. He's been tempted to work with Delphi and Java, but finally found his home in MS's new developer tools, and has done work related to XML, XSLT/XPath/XQuery, WebServices, .NET Security, ASP.NET, and others.

He runs his own company, DEVerest, in Buenos Aires, Argentina, and loves movies and music (ranging all the way from Pink Floyd to Shakira and Megadeth :-).

Mike Clark

Mike is currently working solely on Research and Development around Web Services and ASP.NET technologies. He is solely responsible for www.salcentral.com the World's first web services brokerage.

All his spare time is taken up with his wife and two kids, though it is seldom enough to stop the feelings of guilt for the time spent "playing in the attic" as the kids say.

You can contact Mike Clark at mikec@lucin.com.

Angelo Kastroulis

Angelo focuses his expertise on the design and development of software applications using Microsoft Windows DNA and .NET technologies. He has particular proven field experience in software architecture, database design, and development. Having served in the capacity of Lead Developer, Project Manager, Director of Software Development, and CTO, he is intimately familiar with technology, logistics, and business.

Matt Milner

Matt Milner works as a Technical Architect for BORN in Minneapolis where he designs and builds Microsoft solutions for clients in a variety of industries. Matt's primary focus has been using Windows DNA architecture and he is excited about the move to .NET and all the powerful new features.

When Matt is not working at the computer, he spends his time in his woodshop, reading, or enjoying the many great natural resources of Minnesota.

Jan Narkiewicz

Jan D. Narkiewicz is Chief Technical Officer at Software Pronto, Inc (jann@softwarepronto.com).

Over the years Jan has managed to work on an e-mail system that resided on seventeen million desktops, helped automate factories that make the blue jeans you have in your closet (yes, you own this brand), transmitted television programming to millions of homes all over the world, and kept the skies over the Emirate of Abu Dhabi safe from enemy aircraft. All this was achieved using technology such as COM/DCOM, COM+, C#, VB, C++, SQL Server, Oracle, DB2, ASP.NET, ADO.NET, Java, Linux, and XML.

In his spare time Jan is Academic Coordinator for the Windows curriculum at U.C. Berkeley Extension, he teaches at U.C. Santa Cruz Extension, writes for *ASPToday*, and *C#Today*.

Ryan O'Keefe

Ryan manages eBusiness for a medium-sized distribution company in the Dallas/Fort Worth area within the great state of Texas. Since starting on Unix platforms writing PERL CGI scripts, his work now concentrates on B2B and B2C e-commerce applications using C#, ASP and ASP.NET, Cold Fusion, and XML. Ryan is also a licensed private pilot with time logged in Cessna, Piper, and Grumman single engine aircraft.

"While my best friend was set on being a game developer, my intent in IT was to be a network bum. Decent pay, bermuda shorts, and lazy days playing network DOOM! Seemed too good to pass up. Alas though, one day many years ago my Father-In-Law advised me he had written a web page. Not to be out done, I quickly immersed myself in the ways of animated `.gif`*s and complex HTML such as the* `<frame>` *tag and thus, a paradigm shift had occurred."*

Dedication

First, I would like to dedicate my work in this title to my Father-In-Law. Thank you Allen for everything you have done for me, knowingly and unknowingly.

Second, I would like to thank my Wife Christine for her unwavering support and love. Our journey together is by far my proudest evolving achievement in life, I love you!

Third, to the wonderful hard working people at Wrox Press. Especially Chris Goode, Ewan Buckingham, Emma Batch, and the reviewers of my work. It is an honor to be a part of the wonderful work Wrox provides the programming community for the second time in my career.

Finally, thank you to the readers of this work for allowing my co-authors and me into your busy schedules. I hope we have achieved a text that will challenge you and help you through your journey with the new .NET Framework.

God Bless,

–Ryan O'Keefe

Thiru Thangarathinam

Thiru works as a Consultant at Spherion Technology Architects, an international technology consuting company, in Phoenix, Arizona. He is an MCSD, and during the last two years, he has been developing distributed n-tier architecture solutions for various companies using the latest technologies such as VB, ASP, XML, XSL, COM+, and SQL Server.

When not sitting in front of his computer and writing .NET code, Thiru can be seen chatting with his family, listening to Tamil songs and, of course, reading books. He can be reached via e-mail at ThiruThangarathinam@spherion.com.

He would like to dedicate his work in this book to his family who take so much of pride in his accomplishments.

Table of Contents

Introduction   **1**

    What does this Book Cover?   **2**

    Who is this Book For?   **3**

    What do you Need to Use this Book?   **3**

    Conventions   **4**

    Customer Support   **5**
        How to Download the Sample Code for the Book   5
        Errata   5
        E-mail Support   5
        p2p.wrox.com   6

Chapter 1: Introducing a Server Control Based Architecture   **9**

    ASP.NET Architecture   **10**

    What Are Server Controls?   **12**
        Types of Server Controls   13

    The Server Control Model   **15**
        The Life-Cycle of an ASP.NET Server Control   16

    When Should We Create Our Own Controls?   **18**
        User Controls Versus Server Controls   18
        Performance Considerations   19

    Creating a User Control   **20**

    Creating a Custom Server Control   **26**
        Using the Control in a Page   30

    Creating a Composite Control   **32**

    Summary   **39**

Table of Contents

Chapter 2: Rendering Server Controls   41

What is Rendering?   **42**
HtmlTextWriter Class   42

Server Control Creation   **43**
Writing the Markup Content Directly   43
Using the Utility Methods of the HtmlTextWriter Class   45
Exposing Attributes as Properties   48
Using the WebControl Class for Control Creation   51
A Complex Control Creation Example   56
Applications of the HtmlTextWriter Class   61

Custom Mobile Controls   **61**
Device Detection and Customized Rendering   62

Validation Controls   **64**
Limitations of Current Validation Techniques (Client-Side and Server-Side)   64
Plumbing Provided by the Validation Controls   65

Detecting Browser Capabilities   **66**
HttpBrowserCapabilities Class   66
Using ClientTarget Property to Affect the Output of a Server Control   68

Summary   **73**

Chapter 3: Events and Event Handling   75

Events in the .NET Framework   **75**
Delegates   76
Defining an Event   77
Consuming an Event   77
Event Sample   78
Custom EventArgs and Delegates   80
A Word About Naming   82

Events in ASP.NET Controls   **83**
Postback – Responding to Events and Data   83

Inheritance and Containment   **92**
Handling Events in Base Controls   92
Events in Contained Controls   93
Bubbling Events   96

Shopping Cart Loader   **98**

Summary   **105**

Chapter 4: Managing State   107

Introduction to ViewState   108
Mechanics of ViewState   109
ViewState with Simple Controls   112
ViewState with Composite Controls   116
Control Class Properties and Methods Affecting ViewState   124
ViewState and Performance   125
ViewState and Security   127

Accessing Application and Session State Variables   130
Exposing Application State Variables to a Server Control   131
Exposing Session State Variables to a Server Control   134

Summary   136

Chapter 5: Templated Controls and Styles   139

Templated Controls   140
Creating Templated Controls   144
Basic Templated Controls   147
Advanced Templated Control   156
Dynamic Templates   167
Event Bubbling and More   174

Styles   174
Working with Styles   175
Exposing Styles as Properties   177
Exposing Style Elements as Top-Level Properties   181
Creating a Custom Style Class   184
Bits and Pieces   187

Summary   188

Chapter 6: Controls that Work with Data   191

Using Databound Controls   192
A Word About Setup   194

Databinding Essentials   198

Creating a Simple Templated Databound Control   206

Creating a Simple Databound Control   214

Creating an Advanced Templated Databound Control   223

Summary   234

Table of Contents

Chapter 7: Custom Control Builders   237

ControlBuilder Overview   239
A Simple Example using AllowWhitespaceLiterals   240

ControlBuilder and Page Parser Interaction   243
AppendLiteralString and More Parsing Detail   248
HasBody   251
CloseControl Method and ControlBuilder Properties   252

Classes Derived from ControlBuilder   254
Classes Overriding HtmlDecodeLiterals   255
Classes Overriding AppendSubBuilder   258

NeedsTagInnerText and SetTagInnerText   261

GetChildControlType   265

OnAppendToParentBuilder   268

CreateBuilderFromType   269

Summary   269

Chapter 8: Building Controls Using Visual Studio .NET   273

What is the VS .NET IDE?   274

Features of the VS .NET IDE   275
Shared Development Environment   277
Look and Feel   277
Customizing the VS .NET IDE Using Template Policy   278
Multi-Language Debugging   281
Project Management   281

Non-Language-Centric Features   281
Solution Explorer   282
Document Window   285
Toolbox   285
Dynamic Help and Search   287
Task List   288
Server Explorer   290

Language-Centric Features   291
IntelliSense   291
Error Trapping   292
Syntax Checking   293
Debugging   293
Watching   294
Dynamic Help   294
Resource Checking   294

Server Control IDE Features Example   **297**

News Desk Server Control   297
Cross-Language Debugging   298
Overview of Design   299
Creating the News Web Site (VB .NET)   299
XML News Feed Server Control (C# .NET) – XMLNewsFeed   304
XML News Display Server Control (C# .NET) – XMLNewsDisplay   308
Completing the Web XML News Web Site   311
Debugging the XML News Web Site   312
Reviewing the Code   313

Summary   **314**

Chapter 9: Design-Time Support   **317**

What Does Design-Time Support Mean?   **318**

A Sample Control   318

Overview of the Design-Time Architecture   **320**

Basic   321
Intermediate   327
Advanced   345

Summary   **369**

Chapter 10: Deploying and Licensing Server Controls   **371**

Deploying Server Controls   **371**

Working with the Global Assembly Cache   372
Introducing Strong-Named Assemblies   373
Adding a Control to the GAC   377

Introduction to Licensing   **379**

Understanding Licensing   379
Licensing Models   381
Using Licensing in .NET   381

Summary   **391**

Table of Contents

Chapter 11: Case Study   393

Enter the Code-Behind Model   394

To Custom Control or to User Control? That is the Question...   395

Case Study: Wrox Travel – An Overview   395
Architectural Decisions   395
Login Custom Control   396
Login User Control   403
Hit Counter Custom Control   408
Context Menu Custom Control   411

Putting It All Together   421

Summary   423

Index   425

Professional ASP .NET Server Controls

Introduction

February 16th 2002 is a date a lot of people will remember as the day that .NET finally arrived. After literally years of waiting, a new era had finally arrived. The limitations of traditional ASP had finally been overcome, and the biggest buzz-word in the web development community was ASP.NET.

With ASP.NET came the world of the server control – a simple example of encapsulation in this new object-oriented paradigm. We've been given the ability to make use of complex user interface functionality by entering a single line of code in an ASPX page, and react with this control using code written in any .NET language to react to events, programmatically work with data and user input, and much more. This ground-breaking technology stands ready to revolutionize the way we create web sites.

The "out-of-the-box" controls that Microsoft has provided are already fairly powerful – all ASP.NET controls inherit a lot of basic functionality out of the box from their mother class. The `Control` class (`System.Web.UI.Control`) contains all the basic functionality that all custom controls inherit, providing us with a powerful template on which we can build. Our controls can then be designed to render output that's a simple as a single line of HTML on a web page, to a complex table full of data that adapts to the type of browser that is trying to display it.

What does this Book Cover?

Here is a quick breakdown of what you will find within the chapters of this book:

- ❑ **Chapter 1: Introducing a Server Control Based Architecture** – We'll start with a basic discussion of how Server Controls work, discussing the control-based architecture of ASP.NET. This will introduce the classes our controls need to inherit from and the interfaces they may need to implement. We'll move on to discussing the situations when we find the need to create our own controls, and look at the differences between custom controls and user controls. We will then move on to creating a User Control, custom Server Control, and a basic Composite Control.

- ❑ **Chapter 2: Rendering Server Controls** – This chapter will expand on our knowledge of Server Controls by taking an in-depth look at their rendering process. We'll look at the properties, methods, and features of the `HtmlTextWriter` class and consider how to use `HtmlTextWriter` class to create dynamic, and flexible Server Controls. We'll then move on to look at custom Mobile Controls and understand how rendering plays an important role in creating cross-device compatible applications. Finally we will take a look at the built-in validation controls supplied by ASP.NET and discuss their benefits in the context of generating browser-independent output.

- ❑ **Chapter 3: Events and Event Handling** – In this chapter, we will discuss how the event model in the .NET Framework operates, and apply that knowledge to building custom Server Controls for ASP.NET. We will be discussing how to define and create our own events, and important concepts such as how to manage events when working with contained controls including when to "bubble" those events to parent controls and how to expose them as events on our own class. In addition, the handling of postback events and data will be examined in the context of managing our control to know when to raise events.

- ❑ **Chapter 4: Managing State** – In this chapter, we are going to explore two ways that a Server Control can access state information. First, we will see how to use view state to persist state data across postback events, including the mechanics of view state, view state with Simple Controls, view state with Composite Controls, Control Class Properties and Methods Affecting view state, view state and Performance, and view state and Security. We'll then move on to looking at at accessing state data held within the web form application it may be running in.

- ❑ **Chapter 5: Templated Controls and Styles** – In this chapter we will be covering several topics that allow us to create Server Controls that give the consumer the ability to specify the layout. We will be covering templates and how we can allow the consumer to specify the positioning of the control contents as well as examining how to apply styles to our controls and expose specific or general style properties to allow the user to further control the presentation.

- ❑ **Chapter 6: Controls that Work with Data** – This chapter will look at creating controls that implement databinding and creating templates that are bound to a data source to retrieve property values. We'll look at how to consume controls that use or expose data, understanding the internals of databinding and how to make more advanced and dynamic controls, before looking at examples of how to create a variety of databound controls.

❑ **Chapter 7: Custom Control Builders** – this chapter will cover the `ControlBuilder` class, which can be used to modify how a control is parsed by the page parser. We'll look at how we can modify how the page parser behaves, including how it handles white space and how it treats encoded HTML text, as well as how we can modify the child controls of the parent control being parsed and the attributes of these child controls. We'll also look at how we can modify the attributes associated with the custom control being parsed, how we can disable certain functionality of the `ControlBuilder`, how we can dictate what data is provided to the `ControlBuilder` instance by the page parser, as well as how we can modify the literal HTML contained within the custom control.

❑ **Chapter 8: Building Controls with Visual Studio .NET** – In this chapter we will look at the Visual Studio .NET IDE, before moving on to discuss how we can build Server Controls within the VS .NET environment.

❑ **Chapter 9: Design-Time Support** – In this chapter we will discuss how to use various classes that enhance the design-time support provided by our controls to developers when working with Visual Studio .NET.

❑ **Chapter 10: Deploying and Licencing Server Controls** – We'll look at how we can deploy our server controls both by using the familiar drag-and-drop XCOPY deployment model, and by adding our control to the Global Assembly Cache. In order to do this, we'll also look at how to give our assemblies a strong name. We'll then move on to taking a brief look at how we can license our controls.

❑ **Chapter 11: Case Study** – Here we will see all of the elements we discussed in the book come together within a working application that will allow us to see how much these controls can benefit an application and the development process.

Who is this Book For?

The natural starting point for this book is anyone who has a good working knowledge of ASP.NET and wants to look into creating their own controls. We recommend reading *Professional ASP.NET* or a similar title prior to reading through this book. Readers should be familiar with the pre-existing controls built into ASP.NET, but if they are in need of a refresher on this topic, then they should refer to *Professional ASP.NET*, ISBN 1-861007-03-5. This book is aimed at the developer who thinks ahead and develops controls that can be reused in future projects, or even at the developer who is looking to develop and sell their controls to other developers.

What do you Need to Use this Book?

The main prerequisite for this book is to have a machine with the .NET Framework installed. In order to run ASP.NET pages, you need either Windows 2000 Professional or higher, or Windows XP Professional, with at least the minimum installation of .NET running on the machine. .NET currently comes in two "flavors":

❑ The .NET Framework Redistributable – the full framework on its own. Includes everything you need to run any .NET application. Approximate size: 20Mb.

❑ The .NET Framework SDK (Software Development Kit) – the full framework plus samples and tutorials that you can refer to in order to learn more about .NET. Approximate size: 130Mb.

Both of these are available for free download from http://www.asp.net/.

For the later chapters in this book, a copy of Visual Studio .NET Professional or higher is recommended. Visual Studio .NET is available to MSDN subscribers as part of the MSDN Professional or higher subscriptions, or available to purchase online.

The majority of this book is editor-neutral, so anyone who does not own a copy of Visual Studio .NET should still find that the majority of the content in this book is useful.

Conventions

We've used a number of different styles of text and layout in this book to help differentiate between the different kinds of information. Here are examples of the styles we used and an explanation of what they mean.

Code has several fonts. If it's a word that we're talking about in the text – for example, when discussing a For...Next loop, it's in this font. If it's a block of code that can be typed as a program and run, then it's also in a gray box:

```
<asp:Textbox id="MyTextBox" runat="server"/>
```

Sometimes we'll see code in a mixture of styles, like this:

```
private void MyButton_Click(object sender, System.EventArgs e){
  //Incredibly useful code here...
  Response.Write(MyButton.Text);
}
```

In cases like this, the code with a white background is code we are already familiar with; the line highlighted in gray is a new addition to the code since we last looked at it.

Advice, hints, and background information comes in this type of font.

> **Important pieces of information come in boxes like this.**

Bullets appear indented, with each new bullet marked as follows:

❑   **Important Words** are in a bold type font

❑   Words that appear on the screen, or in menus like the Open or Close, are in a similar font to the one you would see on a Windows desktop

❑   Keys that you press on the keyboard like *Ctrl* and *Enter*, are in italics

Customer Support

We always value hearing from our readers, and we want to know what you think about this book: what you liked, what you didn't like, and what you think we can do better next time. You can send us your comments, either by returning the reply card in the back of the book, or by e-mail to feedback@wrox.com. Please be sure to mention the book title in your message.

How to Download the Sample Code for the Book

When you visit the Wrox site, http://www.wrox.com/, simply locate the title through our Search facility or by using one of the title lists. Click on Download in the Code column, or on Download Code on the book's detail page.

The files that are available for download from our site have been archived using WinZip. When you have saved the attachments to a folder on your hard-drive, you need to extract the files using a de-compression program such as WinZip or PKUnzip. When you extract the files, the code is usually extracted into chapter folders. When you start the extraction process, ensure your software (WinZip, PKUnzip, etc.) is set to use folder names.

Errata

We've made every effort to make sure that there are no errors in the text or in the code. However, no one is perfect and mistakes do occur. If you find an error in one of our books, like a spelling mistake or a faulty piece of code, we would be very grateful for feedback. By sending in errata you may save another reader hours of frustration, and of course, you will be helping us provide even higher quality information. Simply e-mail the information to support@wrox.com; your information will be checked and if correct, posted to the errata page for that title, or used in subsequent editions of the book.

To find errata on the web site, go to http://www.wrox.com/, and simply locate the title through our Advanced Search or title list. Click on the Book Errata link, which is below the cover graphic on the book's detail page.

E-mail Support

If you wish to directly query a problem in the book with an expert who knows the book in detail then e-mail support@wrox.com, with the title of the book and the last four numbers of the ISBN in the subject field of the e-mail. A typical e-mail should include the following things:

❑   The **title of the book**, **last four digits of the ISBN**, and **page number** of the problem in the Subject field

❑   Your **name**, **contact information**, and the **problem** in the body of the message.

We won't send you junk mail. We need the details to save your time and ours. When you send an e-mail message, it will go through the following chain of support:

❏ Customer Support – Your message is delivered to our customer support staff, who are the first people to read it. They have files on most frequently asked questions and will answer anything general about the book or the web site immediately.

❏ Editorial – Deeper queries are forwarded to the technical editor responsible for that book. They have experience with the programming language or particular product, and are able to answer detailed technical questions on the subject.

❏ The Authors – Finally, in the unlikely event that the editor cannot answer your problem, they will forward the request to the author. We do try to protect the author from any distractions to their writing; however, we are quite happy to forward specific requests to them. All Wrox authors help with the support on their books. They will e-mail the customer and the editor with their response, and again all readers should benefit.

The Wrox Support process can only offer support to issues that are directly pertinent to the content of our published title. Support for questions that fall outside the scope of normal book support is provided via the community lists of our http://p2p.wrox.com/ forum.

p2p.wrox.com

For author and peer discussion join the P2P mailing lists. Our unique system provides **programmer to programmer**™ contact on mailing lists, forums, and newsgroups, all in addition to our one-to-one e-mail support system. If you post a query to P2P, you can be confident that it is being examined by the many Wrox authors and other industry experts who are present on our mailing lists. At p2p.wrox.com you will find a number of different lists that will help you, not only while you read this book, but also as you develop your own applications. Particularly appropriate to this book are the pro_windows_forms and the vs_dotnet lists.

To subscribe to a mailing list just follow these steps:

1. Go to http://p2p.wrox.com/

2. Choose the appropriate category from the left menu bar

3. Click on the mailing list you wish to join

4. Follow the instructions to subscribe and fill in your e-mail address and password

5. Reply to the confirmation e-mail you receive

6. Use the subscription manager to join more lists and set your e-mail preferences

Why this System Offers the Best Support

You can choose to join the mailing lists or you can receive them as a weekly digest. If you don't have the time, or facility, to receive the mailing list, then you can search our online archives. Junk and spam mails are deleted, and your own e-mail address is protected by the unique Lyris system. Queries about joining or leaving lists, and any other general queries about lists, should be sent to listsupport@p2p.wrox.com.

Professional ASP .NET Server Controls

Introducing a Server Control Based Architecture

If you're the sort of person who's spent hours looking at some spaghetti-like ASP code that someone else has written, wishing that there was a cleaner way of putting together web pages, you'll have been extremely relieved when ASP.NET was announced to the world as having a completely different architecture, that is designed to make encapsulation and code-reuse the way of life. Arguably the most powerful tool in the ASP.NET developer's toolbox is the Server Control, which epitomizes everything that ASP.NET stands for. You have the ability to create fully-functional pages with a minimum of code fuss, creating complex pages consisting of a few lines of HTML-style tags, and some C# or VB.NET code "glue" sitting either in a `<script>` block, or in a code-behind page. Gone are the days of `<%...%>` appearing scattered throughout a page, as we now have a compiled, object-oriented, event-driven paradigm.

Although ASP.NET comes with some great controls out of the box, the functionality exists for, and indeed promotes, the creation of custom Server Controls. These controls can contain a great deal of code that can produce complex user interfaces, and yet they are deployed on an ASP.NET page with a single tag, and possibly some code within a `<script>` block, or on a code-behind page, to manipulate the contents of the control at runtime.

In this chapter we will set the stage for the detailed development of the ASP.NET Server Controls that we will be covering throughout this book. We will begin by briefly reviewing ASP.NET's architecture and then look at the entry points for ASP.NET Server Control developers. We'll examine how Server Controls work within the ASP.NET framework, and discuss the base classes that controls inherit from, `System.Web.UI.Control` and `System.Web.UI.WebControls.WebControl`, before moving on to look at some specific examples of different controls in action. We will also briefly look at the design-time support that Visual Studio .NET provides.

The specific points that we will touch on are:

- ❏ ASP.NET's architecture

- ❏ What is a Server Control?

- ❏ Why and when would we need to create a Custom Server Control?

- ❏ User Controls vs. Server Controls

- ❏ Creating ASP.NET Server Controls

- ❏ Creating a User Control

- ❏ Creating a Custom Server Control

- ❏ Creating a Composite Control

We will look at a User Control that has a drop-down menu that directs the user to the selected site. We will also talk about what it takes to convert an existing .aspx page into a User Control. We will then look at how to create a basic Server Control and then see an example of how this control is put to use in a host ASPX page and manipulated programmatically. We will finish up the chapter with a walk through of how to create a Composite Control that consists of the elements necessary to create a basic search UI for a mythical job site. We will talk about the things .NET provides for us when we create a control like this and the requirements this type of control must meet in order to function properly.

> *This book assumes that you have prior knowledge of ASP.NET, and are comfortable with its basic use. Because of this, we won't be delving too deeply into its operation; instead we'll be covering these topics in just enough detail to refresh your memory. If you have any need for further clarification please see* Professional ASP.NET *ISBN 1-861007-03-5, also from Wrox Press.*

One thing to note about the examples that will be found throughout the book is that in order to keep code examples shorter and more readable, most of them are not written using the 'code-behind' method. They are, instead, written to contain the code directly in the ASPX page itself. In real-life situations we would, of course, use code-behind in order to keep a clean separation between the presentation code and programmatic logic.

ASP.NET Architecture

The ambitious goal of ASP.NET is to finally bring together all of the tools and functionality that developers need in order to be able to create enterprise-class applications without resorting to a solution that looks 'hacked' together. For years, we faced new challenges that have been the by-product of the evolution of business, but the programmatic environment that we used did not evolve as quickly, and so we were left finding ways to overcome the limitations. In some ways this initial period was necessary. It made developers tap deeper into the creative recesses of their minds on a regular basis. One example of this was developers feverishly trying to imitate the event-driven environment of the desktop.

Now that ASP.NET is here, that extra creative energy and focus can be directed towards the architecture of the application and solving the business needs instead of having some of it diverted to compensating for the limitations of old. For developers experienced with the Windows DNA paradigm, getting to grips with ASP.NET should be a relatively short process, as many of the changes to the programming style are things that may well have been on the wish list, which will make the potential pain of learning it more like the relief of having a tooth pulled after a weekend toothache! We also find that the DNA framework upon which we built applications is much the same. We will still find ourselves using trusty DNA staples such as MSMQ, breaking our applications into tiers, and, frequently running within a transaction.

ASP.NET is not 'traditional ASP with a few minor changes'; it's brand new, with a completely new codebase underneath. ASP.NET was designed to make migrating traditional ASP applications as easy as possible, so, in most cases it is as simple as changing the ASP extension to ASPX and making a few alterations to the code, though the application will not benefit from the new features, it will simply run. If the application is not going to be ported to take advantage of the full range of ASP.NET's features, it may make more sense to just allow the application to run along side ASP.NET in its own, native environment.

Some of what ASP.NET provides for us is:

❑ An event driven programming model via Web Forms (Server Controls) – this delivers on the promise that Visual Basic 6 seemed to be making with its IIS (remember when "Web Class" was the word to impress your friends with) and DHTML application types; the Visual Basic/Delphi/FoxPro IDE feel.

❑ When the JIT compiler processes the ASPX page, the result is compiled code. This allows early binding, strong typing, and improved performance. Application configuration is stored in human-readable XML files. This will allow greater ease of migration between platforms and configuration of the respective web servers.

❑ There is easy-to-use authentication and state management functionality built in to the .NET Framework.

❑ XML Web Services, which facilitates cross platform application-to-application communication using standard web protocols such as HTTP, XML, and SOAP.

❑ The ability to separate programming logic from presentation code at design time cleanly using the code-behind model. Using the code-behind model we are able to break the presentation layer into two files: one page containing markup code and the other containing the logic needed to respond to any data that code on the server sends in, to create a response to the user's actions.

❑ Support for authoring custom controls to encapsulate reusable code (we will be dealing with aspects of this within this book).

It would be a digression for us to cover ASP.NET in much more detail than this. For those of you that need a more detailed reference, you could refer back to Wrox's *Professional ASP.NET*. The crux of ASP.NET's programming model is Web Forms, which are built on the Server Controls concept. These are what we are concentrating on for this book and so let's define what they are.

What Are Server Controls?

Server Controls are bundles of logic that provide a browser-independent user interface component that exposes properties and methods, and raises events on the server each time the page is submitted (we write code to respond to these events). Server Controls can detect the client device type and render themselves in the supported markup language (HTML, XML, and DHTML; with the Microsoft Mobile Internet Toolkit we can also render WML, CHTML, and so on).

Server Controls live their lives as .NET classes derived from `System.Web.UI.Control` or `System.Web.UI.WebControls.WebControl`. The `Control` class provides properties and methods that are common across all Server Controls (such as `ID`, `ViewState`, `Controls` collection – we will start to look at these in detail in the next chapter). When we author our own Server Controls that do not provide any UI functionality, we will derive from this class. If our control **does** provide a UI, we will derive from the `WebControl` class. This class is derived from the `Control` class and goes a step further to provide properties and methods for UI programming (the `Render` and `LoadViewState` methods, `BackColor` property, and so on). We will look more deeply into the classes and interfaces that are used in developing custom server controls later in the book. The focus of this book is to look at server controls that have UI functionality.

To the user, Server Controls that render a UI might appear to be like any other HTML controls. To the developer, things are very different from traditional ASP. Now we can drag a button or label onto a form, set its properties, write code for the events, and let the individual controls deal with the browser's markup and script language support, by detecting the client type and rendering accordingly. Wait, there's more; they maintain their state, and since they're based on an event-driven programming model, they are in a great position to work with the input and actions of a user browsing a web page.

ASP.NET ships with its own set of Server Controls that include data validation controls, UI controls (such as buttons, textboxes, labels, and so on), and Rich Controls (AdRotator, Calendar) that are all extensible (that means we can inherit from them and build our own controls). Let's look at an example of the `<asp:Button>` control's syntax and talk a bit about how it works and then, in the next section, we will talk about the different types of Server Controls. Here is a snippet of code from an ASPX page (this one happens to be a Web Server Control):

```
<asp:Button id="MyButton"
  runat="server"
  Text="GO!"
  BorderStyle="None"
  OnClick = "MyButton_Click"
>
  GO!
</asp:Button>
```

The tag syntax is actually instantiating an instance of the `System.Web.UI.WebControls.Button` class on the server (we can think of it as an `<object>` tag done right). This new object's properties are populated through the attributes in the tag just as we would if we wanted to set the `href` attribute in a vanilla anchor tag. We can see where we have told the runtime that we would like to have a method called `MyButton_Click` handle the click event of our button by populating the `OnClick` attribute with the name of the method.

Here is the corresponding event handler for the `Click` event (the code for this event handler can be in the ASPX page or the code-behind page associated with the ASPX page). We can see that once on the server, we can refer to Server Controls, programmatically, in the same manner that we are accustomed to from programming within environments such as Visual Basic (using the `Object.Member` syntax):

```
private void MyButton_Click(object sender, System.EventArgs e)
{
  //Incredibly useful code here...
  Response.Write(MyButton.Text);
}
```

We chose to name our button `MyButton` and our event handler `MyButton_Click`, these can change (as long as the names line up with an associated control). What can't change is the argument list, `object` and `System.EventArgs`. The `object` contains a reference to the control that raised the event and `System.EventArgs` contains information about the event as well as a few utility methods (we will go deeper into this in Chapter 3).

Wiring the control to the event handler is very similar to designating methods to be called during client-side events in JavaScript. Were this in a page along with a JavaScript method called `myClientSideEvent`, clicking the button would call the JavaScript method and execute the accompanying code:

```
<Input type="button" onclick="myClientSideEvent()" value="Regular HTML Button!">
```

whereas an ASP.NET `Button` having similar syntax would call a method that resides in code on the server. Notice the `asp` tag prefix, control type (`Button`), and the `runat` attribute have been added now that it is a Server Control:

```
<asp:Button id="Button1" OnClick=" Button1_MyServerSideMethod" runat="server"
Text="Web Form Control Button..."></asp:Button>
```

Types of Server Controls

There are six types, or families, of Server Controls, grouped according to the functionality they provide. These controls will be familiar to us from our study and use of ASP.NET, so we will simply list them with a brief description of each type. These controls are:

❑ **ASP.NET Web Form Controls** – This group of controls maps very closely to standard HTML controls, but these have a server-based event-driven programming model and a consistent approach to setting properties across all controls.

❑ **ASP.NET Validation Controls** – These controls make validating form data trivial by packaging common form validation routines and one that we can customize (such as the `RequiredFieldValidator`, `CompareValidator`, and the `CustomValidator`).

❑ **ASP.NET List Controls** – This group consists of controls such as the HTML `<select>` element, `ASP:ListBox`, and `ASP:DataGrid`. These data-bindable controls provide easy-to-use functionality to display data on our pages.

❑ **ASP.NET Rich Controls** – Controls that have a specific task to handle, such as the `AdRotator` and `Calendar`.

❑ **ASP.NET Mobile Controls** – A set of controls geared towards Internet-connected cell phones and PDAs that will detect the client device type and render the appropriate markup code.

❑ **HTML Server Controls** – HTML elements/controls that have their `runat` property set to `server`. These controls provide the same type of event programming model the Web Form Controls do, but without the consistent property model. The properties for these controls are set through the HTML attributes, so familiarity with HTML is necessary (there is a one-to-one relationship between HTML Server Controls and the controls found in raw HTML).

We also have Custom controls that come in two varieties that we can create ourselves: They are:

❑ **User Controls** – A user control is a reusable portion of ASP.NET UI code that has been saved with the extension ASCX (for simple repeated elements within a specific site or application).

❑ **Custom Controls** – these controls can combine the functionality of several other server controls (called **composite controls**), create new controls from the ground up, or add functionality to preexisting controls. They are fully compiled and have no UI code contained in an ASPX page as all rendering is controlled programmatically. They are designed to provide functionality that can be reused across many applications, for example, a metric-to-imperial calculator, or a tree view control for representing file systems or XML file structure.

The New Way in Control Creation

The advantages to these new controls are not just limited to the results they produce in our application; they actually make for a more efficient development tool. Now we can develop our web applications in a more modular fashion, which makes maintenance and upgrades much more organized and targeted (make the change in one place and all of our pages are updated).

In order to achieve this level of functionality previously, we had to resort to ActiveX controls, overly complex DHTML, or Java Applets. None of these were the perfect solution. ActiveX controls had limited browser support and client installation problems; DHTML was not much better in terms of support and the code tended to be hair-triggered, and Java Applets, well, they are just plain slow. All of this was in pursuit of a stateful, event-driven programming model, something that contradicts the nature of Internet applications. Factor in trying to make code reusable or managing state and developers had some serious battles ahead.

To address this situation ASP.NET provides us with a framework from which we can build our own Custom Server Controls replete with the event mechanism, state management, and the same level of performance as the intrinsic controls. With the ability to create these controls comes the freedom we need to be able to develop applications with the type of rich, event-driven, user experience that the user has come to know through Win32 programs (well, almost).

The .NET Framework also provides support for smooth integration of our **Custom Controls** with the Visual Studio. NET toolbox. We can use the familiar drag-and-drop method of putting controls on a form. We can also have our properties accessible from the property sheet in VS .NET. Couple that with the built-in HTML documentation and we have a powerful tool for creating a fully documented reusable control library for in-house development shops, developing 'third-party' controls for commercial distribution, or enforcing coding standards.

The Server Control Model

One of the first few things we should look at when learning to create our own Server Controls is the class hierarchy that they inherit from and ultimately become a part of. All ASP.NET Server Controls derive either directly or indirectly from `System.Web.UI.Control`. This class defines the events, methods, and properties that all Server Controls share (about 55 in all). We will talk about these, as we need them throughout the book.

What we mean when we say that all Server Controls are derived 'directly or indirectly' from this base class, is that they may instead derive from `System.Web.UI.WebControls.WebControl`, which is a child class of `System.Web.UI.Control`. The `System.Web.UI.WebControls.WebControl` class extends the `System.Web.UI.Control` class to add provisions for controls that will provide some sort of UI functionality. This would include the visibility properties (`BackColor`, `ForeColor`, `Font`, etc), and various methods to manage the state and attitude of the control (`Render`, `LoadViewState`, `SaveViewState`).

We can see in the class hierarchy below how our custom controls will be derived from `System.Web.UI.Control` or `System.Web.UI.WebControls.WebControl` (depending on the control's functionality). We can see at the top of the hierarchy we have the .NET parent class (all classes in .NET have this class at their root), `System.Object`, followed by `System.Web.UI.Control`, which begets the `System.Web.UI.WebControls` namespace (which contains the `System.Web.UI.WebControls.WebControl` class):

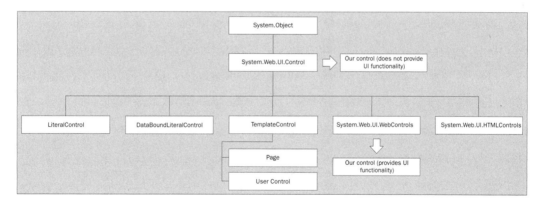

The Life-Cycle of an ASP.NET Server Control

The ability of ASP.NET to give the illusion that its pages and controls are maintaining some sort of state is dependent on the phases the page is put through upon each request from a client device, and how the developer is handling it. Let's look at the phases that an ASP.NET page goes through and then discuss each point:

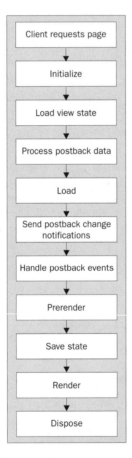

- ❑ **Initialize** – When the client device makes a request to the ASP.NET framework for a page the Init event is raised and can be handled by the developer by overriding the OnInit() method. This is where the control is set to the initial state necessary to set up and create the instance before being added to the control tree ("control tree" is another way to refer to the collection of controls that exist in an ASP.NET page).

- ❑ **Load view state** – at this point in the cycle the controls are checked to see if the control has already had some sort of existence and if there is a need to restore its state (note that the property ViewState is automatically repopulated at the end of this part of the cycle). We will learn in Chapter 4 (*Managing State*) about types that are not storable in ViewState (types other than primitive types, strings, arrays, and hash tables) that will lead to the need to customize this process. To do this we override the LoadViewState() method to add our own steps.

❑ **Process postback data** – If the control implements the `System.Web.UI.IpostBackDataHandler` interface, and is therefore able to access postback data, this is the phase where it will analyze the incoming data and update the appropriate properties. We do this by overriding the `LoadPostData()` method and implementing our own functionality.

❑ **Load** – Actions are performed that are common across multiple requests. This is the point in the cycle that we can first access controls in the control tree, as they are, by now, all created and initialized. Their state has been restored and they should reflect the data from the client. We can control this stage through handling the `Load`.

❑ **Send postback change notifications** – this is the phase in the cycle where all of the controls that raise postback events for the appropriate controls to respond to the change in state. This is another place where the `System.Web.UI.IPostBackDataHandler` interface must be implemented in order for this stage to have any bearing on our control (by overriding the `RaisePostDataChangedEvent()`).

❑ **Handle postback events** – this is the point that the client-side event that caused the postback is handled (override the `RaisePostBackEvent()` method).

❑ **Prerender** – Any updates that need to be made before the output is rendered are done in this stage. Changes made to the state of the control in this phase can be saved (whereas changes made in the rendering phase are lost).

❑ **Save state** – The `ViewState` property in our control will automatically be persisted within a string object at this stage. This is then automatically round-tripped to the client as a hidden form variable. We can override the `SaveViewState()` method to make direct modifications to the `ViewState` property.

❑ **Render** – this is where we will construct the output that we would like our control to return to the client by overriding the `Render()` method.

❑ **Dispose** – This is the stage where final cleanup is performed. Overhead-heavy resource references are release in this stage. We can get our hands into the process by overriding the `Dispose()` method.

Much of what we just covered will be dealt with in detail throughout the book. For the controls that we will build in this chapter we will only break the crust of what is involved in creating custom Server Controls (our controls, being very basic, will deal with `Page_Load` and `Render` only). Let's move on and look at some working examples of a User Control, Server Control, and Composite Control so we can have some sort of feel for the differences between these controls before digging into the core of this book's subject.

> For the benefit of those readers who don't have access to Visual Studio, examples in this section and following sections are designed to be editor-neutral, meaning that all you will need to run these examples is Notepad and a command prompt. If you own a copy of Visual Studio .NET, this code will run fine when plugged into the VS .NET environment. We'll look at Server Control development using Visual Studio .NET in Chapter 8.

When Should We Create Our Own Controls?

When to create and use a Server Control is an important question and there are many things we need to consider in the process of making the decision to use them. Some of the basic questions we should ask ourselves are:

- **Is there some type of functionality that we are finding again and again in our applications?**
  This particular question is not as situation-specific as the next three; it is more 'What can I do right now, that will save me time later?' The first two things that come to mind are user authentication and credit card processing screens. How many times a day across the world are these two coded and recoded? Some other good candidates are:
  - Currency conversion
  - Shipping rates and tax calculation
  - Web-based network diagnostics controls (a ping control, tracert, and so on)
  - Task manager/calendaring
  - Image manipulation controls (maybe detecting and rendering client type and, from a parent graphic, creating an image based on the types supported by the client, automatically generating thumbnails, and similar)
- **Do we need to access properties of a control from code?** Do we need to retrieve the text that the user types into a textbox in our code back on the server? Do we need to update a label's text to reflect a certain action that took place?
- **Do we need to respond to some type of action taken by the user?** Has the selected item in a `<select>` control changed? Did the user click a button?
- **Are we unsatisfied with the performance of an intrinsic Server Control?** Is the `DataGrid` control causing a bottleneck on our high-traffic site and do we need better performance than it has to offer?

User Controls Versus Server Controls

In order to finalize a few ideas about Server Controls, let's contrast them with User Controls; to do this we will create examples of both types later in this chapter. For now, let's discuss some points of each.

User Controls

The simplest definition of a User Control is that it's a reusable portion of ASP.NET UI code that has been saved with the extension ASCX.

User Controls are very easy to create, in that they're essentially portions of ASP.NET pages that are encapsulated into a separate file that can be reused as many times as necessary within an application. They're coded in much the same way as an ASPX page, and we only need a couple of lines in our ASPX page to use them. User Controls can also raise custom events that the control's end-user can use to delegate to their own event handling methods.

However, User Controls are somewhat limited in their scope. They are only available to a single application at a time. If we want to reuse our control in different applications, we have to copy it to the application directory of each successive application. Updating a control that's used in multiple applications would be a long winded process.

If we're using Visual Studio .NET and working with User Controls, once the control is complete and we are ready to use it on an ASPX page, we will find that there is little more than an acknowledgement from Visual Studio .NET that our control is living within the environment and on the .ASPX page. Any properties that we need to set for the control cannot be done through the property sheet, as is the case with, say, a validation control.

User Controls are great for situations where content on our site might need to be pulled from a database for hourly updates and we don't want the control to make the constant round trips to the server to retrieve the same data over and over. For this we use the @OutputCache directive in the control to enable caching. This works in the same way it does in regular .ASPX pages. By enabling caching in our User Control and allowing the host page to remain dynamic, we are doing what is called **fragment caching**.

Custom Controls

These controls are more complex and powerful than User Controls and require more effort and time to design and develop. With Custom Controls it is left up to the developer to programmatically create any rendering code for UI elements and implement the interface requirements of the base class (for handling postback data and events) among other things.

Once the control is complete and we are ready to use it in a host page, it doesn't take much code to use the control. Again, if you have use of Visual Studio .NET, you will find that Visual Studio .NET is very hospitable. .NET provides a set of attributes to enable components to provide metadata to design environments in order for them to be able to expose the object for programming to through things like the Property sheet, as well as the means to create custom designers that allow the developer to modify the design-time look and behavior of the finished controls.

One huge advantage that Custom Controls have over User Controls is in the reusability arena. While User Controls can only be used within one application, Custom Controls can be added to the **Global Assembly Cache** (GAC), which gives all applications on the machine access to them. In the most abstract way, a parallel can be drawn to a COM object's GUID being entered into the Registry, the big difference being that .NET eliminates the problems that go along with this (no more DLL-hell!).

Performance Considerations

Now that we understand how Server Controls rule the earth, let's talk about some of the performance tradeoffs that tend to be a part of the nature of this architecture (if you are curious, run a few performance tests of your own to see the some of the differences). Don't let this statement scare you, early bound Server Controls are about three times faster than the late bound ASP/COM (+)/VBScript objects (while handling style and up-level/down-level support, too!), so we probably won't notice the difference in most situations, .NET handles the lifecycle (create/destroy) of objects very efficiently. Even so, each Server Control adds a slight rendering cost: a bit for the control itself and then a bit more for the style management of the controls on a page.

When designing Server Controls there should be careful consideration put into the rendering and post-back work that we have them do. These are areas that can make or break a Server Control when it comes to performance; we should take special care that we write efficient, well-structured code in these areas. If you find that your control is causing performance degradation, you should look in those methods first.

Creating a User Control

Although the main focus of this book is Creating Custom Server controls, it's worth taking a quick look at how to create a User Control so we can compare and contrast them. One of the great things about User Controls is that you can create them with just a slight change in programming technique from that in creating Web Forms.

> The main differences are that we do not include a `<Form>` element (we leave that up to the containing page), we leave out tags that might conflict with the containing page (`HTML`, `HEAD`, etc.), and we don't include directives that would conflict with the host page (such as the `@Page`), and the file's extension is `.ascx`.

Let's look at a User Control that acts as a drop-down menu that navigates to the selected site when the `DropDownList`'s `SelectedIndexChanged` event is raised. Open your text editor and enter the following code:

```
<%@ Control Language="c#" AutoEventWireup="false" %>
<asp:DropDownList id="lstNavigate"
OnSelectedIndexChanged="lstNavigate_SelectedIndexChanged" AutoPostBack="True"
runat="server" Width="156px" Height="11px">
</asp:DropDownList>

<script runat="server" language="C#">
public void PopulateMenu(ArrayList al){
  Object [] array = al.ToArray();
  for(int i = 0; i <= array.Length-1; i++)
    {
    lstNavigate.Items.Add(new ListItem(array[i].ToString()));
  }
}
private void lstNavigate_SelectedIndexChanged(object sender, System.EventArgs e)
  {
    Response.Redirect (lstNavigate.SelectedItem.ToString());
  }

</script>
```

Save this file as `UserControlExample.ascx` in the root of a folder that's designated as a web application. Now, in a new file enter this code:

```
<%@ Page language="c#" AutoEventWireup="true" Debug="true" %>
<%@ Register TagPrefix="TC" TagName="WUC" Src="UserControlExample.ascx" %>

<%@ Import namespace="System.Reflection"%>
<html>
  <head>
    <Title>Test User Control</Title>
  </head>
  <body>
    <form id="Form1" method="post" runat="server">
      <TC:WUC id="WebUserControl11" runat="server">
      </TC:WUC>
    </form>
  </body>
</html>

<script runat="server" language="C#">
private void Page_Load(object sender, System.EventArgs e)
{
  Control cntrl = Page.FindControl("WebUserControl11");
  Type cntrlType = cntrl.GetType();
  MethodInfo myMethod = cntrlType.GetMethod("PopulateMenu");

Controls method signature
  ParameterInfo [] p = myMethod.GetParameters();

  Object [] parameters = new Object [p.Length];

  ArrayList al = new ArrayList();
  al.Add("");//we want our first entry to be blank
  al.Add("http://www.wrox.com");
  al.Add("http://www.microsoft.com");
  al.Add("http://www.asp.net");

  parameters[0] = al;

  myMethod.Invoke(cntrl,parameters);

}

</script>
```

Save this file as `UserControlTest.aspx` in `wwwroot/Your_Application_Directory/`.

Let's look at what happens when we run this and then we'll talk through how this control is structured and how it works (this will most likely be a refresher course from our ASP.NET studies). Navigate your browser to http://localhost/UserControlTest.aspx. You should see a page with only a drop-down list on it:

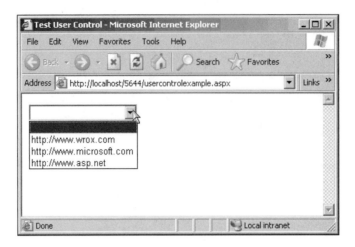

If we choose one of the items from the list we will be sent to the respective default or index page:

Let's look at the code for the control itself. One of the first things we will notice about the control is the @Control directive at the top of the page:

```
<%@ Control Language="C#" AutoEventWireup="false" %>
```

This directive is unique to User Controls. We can think of it as having the same level of importance to an ASCX page that the @Page directive has to an ASPX page; both directives set the attributes that will define how the page/control behaves with regard to events and view state, what it inherits, its class name, etc. We already know the attributes of the @Page directive from our use of ASP.NET so let's look at the @Control directive attributes:

Attribute	Description
AutoEventWireup	This true or false property indicates whether the control's events should be wired-up automatically (false forces us to override the appropriate Page events and true allows us to author event prototypes as needed such as Page_Init). The default is true.
ClassName	This attribute is how you name the class that results from the auto-compilation that occurs when a client requests the host page. Any name that would be valid for a class will be valid here.
CompilerOptions	Any string of compiler options is valid for this property.
Debug	This indicates whether the page should be compiled with debug symbols or not. true indicates that it should be and false if not. Default is false.
Description	This allows the developer to add a text description of the control. Any string is valid here.
EnableViewState	This true/false property indicates whether state for the control should be maintained across page requests.
Explicit	This true/false property tells the compiler if the page should be compiled using the VB .NET Option Explicit mode. The default is false (no). This only has an effect on VB .NET users; C# won't let us declare an un-typed variable.
Inherits	This defines a code-behind file for the User Control to inherit. This can be any class that derives from the System.Web.UI.UserControl class.
Language	This specifies the language for the compiler to target when processing all inline code and server-side script blocks within the page. Any .NET language will be valid here.
Strict	This true/false property indicates whether the page should be compiled using the VB .NET Option Strict mode. It defaults to false.
Src	This specifies the code-behind file to compile when the User Controls containing page is requested (designers such as VS .NET do not use this attribute; rather they use Inherits, which achieves the same result).
WarningLevel	This allows the developer the designate the warning level at which the compiler should abort the compilation of the User Control. Valid values are 0 – 4; these directly correspond to the warnings returned from the compiler when there is trouble.

The next bit of code we see is the tag set for our DropDownList control. Notice we have set it up to run a method called lstNavigate_SelectedIndexChanged when an item is chosen within the control. (we won't go into how this works in the background, please refer back to Professional ASP.NET for a refresher):

```
<asp:DropDownList
  id="lstNavigate"
  OnSelectedIndexChanged="lstNavigate_SelectedIndexChanged"
  AutoPostBack="True"
  runat="server"
  Width="156px"
  Height="11px">
</asp:DropDownList>
```

Next we get to the code that populates the menu with the choices for us to navigate to. This is a method that accepts an ArrayList, which is then cast as an Object[]. Then, within a for loop the values contained by the array is used to populate the lstNavigate control :

```
<script runat="server" language="C#">
lstNavigate control)
public void PopulateMenu(ArrayList al){
  Object [] array = al.ToArray();//create an Object array to hold the items
  for(int i = 0; i <= array.Length-1; i++)//loop to add items to lstNavigate
  {
    lstNavigate.Items.Add(new ListItem(array[i].ToString()));
  }
}
```

The next bit of code we see is the event handler for the SelectedIndexChanged event of the lstNavigate control. This simply redirects the user to the chosen site:

```
private void lstNavigate_SelectedIndexChanged(object sender, System.EventArgs e)
{
  Response.Redirect (lstNavigate.SelectedItem.ToString());
}

</script>
```

That's it for the control itself; now let's look at what it takes to implement it in a host page. We start the page with the directives:

```
<%@ Page language="c#" AutoEventWireup="true" Debug="true" %>
<%@ Register TagPrefix="TC" TagName="WUC" Src="WroxWebUserControl.ascx" %>

<%@ Import namespace="System.Reflection"%>
```

The @Register is doing its job of defining the TagPrefix, TagName, and Src (remember that Src is telling the compiler where to find the actual code for the User Control). We are using the @Import directive to import the System.Reflection namespace so we can late-bind to our User Control's PopulateMenu() method. Following this is our @Page directive doing its usual job. One question that may arise is "why are we late-binding to a control when we all know that late-binding slows performance?" Well, the answer is that there is not a way to early-bind to a User Control. This is due to User Controls not being pre-compiled; the Just-In-Time (JIT) Compiler compiles them.

Further into the page we run across the actual tagset for the implementation of the User Control:

```
<TC:WUC id="WebUserControl11" runat="server">
</TC:WUC>
```

In our `Page_Load()` method is where we get a reference to the control and call the `PopulateMenu()` method using some basic reflection techniques (which we won't be going into in detail here):

```csharp
<script runat="server" language="C#">
private void Page_Load(object sender, System.EventArgs e)
{
  Control cntrl = Page.FindControl("WebUserControl11");
  Type cntrlType = cntrl.GetType();
  MethodInfo myMethod = cntrlType.GetMethod("PopulateMenu");

Controls method signature
  ParameterInfo [] p = myMethod.GetParameters();

  Object [] parameters = new Object [p.Length];

  ArrayList al = new ArrayList();
  al.Add("");//we want our first entry to be blank
  al.Add("http://www.wrox.com");
  al.Add("http://www.microsoft.com");
  al.Add("http://www.asp.net");

  parameters[0] = al;

  myMethod.Invoke(cntrl,parameters);
}

</script>
```

Converting to a User Control

Another way to approach creating a User Control is by taking pre-existing functionality from our site and converting it into a User Control. We might find ourselves doing this after finding that functionality is being duplicated across an application or applications and wanting to consolidate this. This is the same mindset that found developers using include files in traditional ASP. To convert an ASPX page into a valid ASCX file and do this without causing an upset in our application we need to watch out for a few things. They are:

❏ Remove all <html>, <body>, and <form> tags.

❏ If there is an @Page directive, change it to an @Control directive and remove the attributes that the @Control directive does not support, namely:

   ❏ AspCompat

   ❏ Buffer

   ❏ ClientTarget

   ❏ CodePage

- ❑   `Culture`
- ❑   `EnableSessionState`
- ❑   `EnableViewStateMac`
- ❑   `ErrorPage`
- ❑   `LCID`
- ❑   `ResponseEncoding`
- ❑   `Trace`
- ❑   `TraceMode`
- ❑   `Transaction`

❑ Make sure to include a class name in the `@Control` directive; this way we can strongly type the control when it is added to a page or other Server Controls programmatically. Remember, the class name can be any valid name for a class, *any* name.

❑ Change the file extension from `.aspx` to `.ascx` (It is also a good idea to name the file descriptively).

Though User Controls are very easy to create, we cannot use them for everything. They are limited in scope (single application scope) and have limited design-time support. This means that for each application we want to use our User Control in, we have to copy it into our application directory. That means a few things happen that we strive against. One is code redundancy and the other is a maintenance headache. The code redundancy is fairly obvious, but sometimes it's later in the game when we start to think about making updates and then realize that we have to make sure we catch all of the applications that we used the control in. Design-time support in VS .NET is limited to being able to drag the file onto a form and VS .NET creating the necessary headers and tag set for us to use it; there is no visual representation of our control other than a marker letting us know that it is really there. This cuts down on the reusability factor, which is one of the main things that we are striving for when it comes to creating our own controls, whatever the type.

Creating a Custom Server Control

By far the most expansive when it comes to reusability and design time support is the Custom Server Control. With this type of control we have a compiled component that can be designed to integrate with VS .NET to provide the type of drag-and-drop programming that we have with native Server Controls such as the `TextBox`, `DataGrid`, and `DropDownList`. We can design our control to support the setting of properties in the **Property** window, show a custom icon in the toolbox, implement visual editors (for things such as physically locating an image or file to be used within the control), and many other things (we will go into this in Chapter 9 – *Control Designers*).

> *Only classes that directly or indirectly implement* `System.ComponentModel.IComponent` *have design-time support VS .NET.*

Let's look at a basic example of a Server Control in action. This will be less detailed than our other examples in this chapter (this one will be very nearly a "Hello World"); the rest of the book will flesh out the remaining details of authoring these controls.

Enter the following code into a text editor and save the file as OurFirstControl.cs in the root of your application directory:

```csharp
using System;
using System.Web.UI;
using System.ComponentModel;

namespace TestControlNameSpace
{

  [DefaultProperty("Text"),
    ToolboxData("<{0}:TestControl runat=server></{0}:TestControl>")]
  public class TestControl : Control
  {
    private string text;
    private string  message;
    [Bindable(true),
    Category("Appearance"),
    DefaultValue("")]
    public string Text
    {
      get
      {
        return text;
      }

      set
      {
        text = value;
      }
    }
    [Bindable(true), Category("Misc")]
    public string ExMessage
    {
      get
      {
        return message;
      }
      set
      {
        message = value;
      }
    }
    protected override void Render(HtmlTextWriter output)
    {
      output.Write(text + message);
    }
  }
}
```

Before we use this control in a page, let's look at what is happening in the code. Initially, we are importing three namespaces. We mentioned that our Server Controls must inherit from either `System.Web.UI.Control` or `System.Web.UI.WebControls.WebControl`, depending on the control's functionality. In this case, we do not need any of the functionality from the `System.Web.UI.WebControls` namespace, so we inherit directly from `System.Web.UI`, which gives us access to the `Control` class. We also import the `System` namespace, to give us access to the classes it contains. The `System.ComponentModel` namespace that, in this case, will provide support for integration with VS .NET, is also imported. This is followed by our control's namespace declaration:

```
using System;
using System.Web.UI;
using System.ComponentModel;
namespace TestControlNameSpace{...}
```

The next thing we see in the code is the setting of the default class-level property for our control and the `ToolboxData` attribute being used to display the name of the control in the toolbox and provide the default class name for the tag set (this will be covered in detail in Chapter 8). The `{0}` found in the tag set will be replaced by the tag prefix. This is followed by the class declaration indicating that we are deriving our control from the `Control` class. Once in the class itself we have two variables (`text` and `message`) that will be used to store the values for `Text` and `ExMessageProperty`:

```
[DefaultProperty("Text"), ToolboxData("<{0}:TestControl
runat=server></{0}:TestControl>")]
public class TestControl : Control
{
  private string text;
  private string  message;
...
```

Next, we see our declaration of a public property called `Text` with its associated attributes. The `Bindable` attribute is needed for VS .NET to 'hook up' with the property, this enables the IDE to 'see into' the control (again, we will cover this in detail in Chapter 8). Next, we have the `Category` attribute that tells VS .NET where to place the property in the `Property` designer (we chose **Appearance**), and set a default value of an empty string.

For the `Category` property we can choose from (notice that they are directly from the property window in VS .NET) preexisting values or create our own by entering another string of text instead:

- ❏ Appearance
- ❏ Behavior
- ❏ Data
- ❏ Layout
- ❏ Misc

The actual property declaration is straightforward:

```
[Bindable(true),
Category("Appearance"),
DefaultValue("")]
public string Text
{
  get
  {
    return text;
  }
  set
  {
    text = value;
  }
}
```

The setting of the next property is very similar to the way we set the previous one:

```
[Bindable(true), Category("Misc")]
public string ExMessage
{
  get
  {
    return message;
  }
  set
  {
  message = value;
  }
}
```

The final part of our control code is to override the Render() method. Here we take the values that have been set by our properties and return them to the client:

```
protected override void Render(HtmlTextWriter output)
{
  output.Write(text + message);
}
```

The next order of business is to compile the control; to do this, execute the following compile command from the directory where our control code is (make sure that the paths and files names match up correctly). For VS .NET users choose Build from the Build menu.

```
csc /t:library /out:bin\OurFirstControl.dll /r:System.Web.dll OurFirstControl.cs
```

We then take the resulting DLL and place it in the /bin directory of our application that will be using it. We will look at adding it to the GAC (Global Assembly Cache) in Chapter 10 (*Distributing Controls*), which gives greater scope to the control.

Using the Control in a Page

There are a few ways to use our control. One is by coding the page by hand and another is by using a designer such as VS .NET.

By Hand

Using this control in a page is fairly easy. Open a text editor and enter the following code and save it in your web applications directory as `ServerControlTest.aspx`. We can see that we register the tag and set its properties in the same way as we do it with the intrinsic ASP.NET Server Controls:

```
<%@ Page language="c#" AutoEventWireup="True" %>
<%@ Register TagPrefix="TC" Namespace="TestControlNameSpace"
Assembly="OurFirstControl" %>
<html>
<body>
  <form id="Form1" method="post" runat="server">
  <TC:TestControl
    id="TestControl1"
    runat="server"
    EnableViewState="False"
    ExMessage="And so is the ExMessage."
    Text="Text property is working.   ">
  </TC:TestControl>
  </form>
</body>
</html>
```

When we navigate to our page we should see something like this (depending on what we set the property values to):

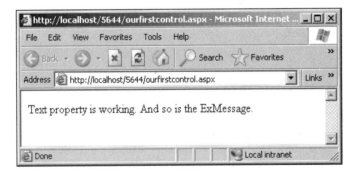

Using Visual Studio .NET

In order to use the control in Visual Studio .NET we need to go through a few steps. We'll look at using Visual Studio .NET to work with server controls in more detail in Chapter 8, but for now we'll look at the main steps involved in getting our control to work.

Step one is to set a reference to it from our toolbox. We do this by right-clicking on the toolbox and choosing Customize ToolBox... from there we find the /bin directory that we put our control in, select the control's .dll and click OK. We should then see something like this (click OK out of this, as well):

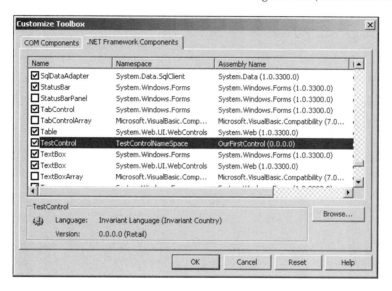

After this step we will find our control in the toolbox. Click and drag it onto the page we would like to use it on and proceed to set the properties in the property window:

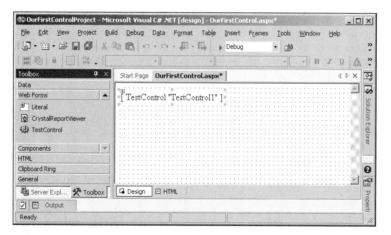

When we navigate to our page we should see the same results as when we coded the page by hand.

This is the basic framework on which the rest of the book will continue to add detail until we have a full understanding of what it takes to build ASP.NET Server Controls for any situation. Now let's move on to Composite Controls and get a feel for how to create them and what they have to offer.

Creating a Composite Control

We can create Composite Controls by combining existing controls using class composition (combining two or more controls within one parent control). The controls used within this new control are now child controls that produce a control that contains the combined functionality of its child controls. This new control renders a user interface that reuses the functionality of existing controls, including the properties and events of these controls. Events raised by the child controls can be handled by the parent control. As with the other types of controls, we can expose custom properties and events as well.

There are a couple of things to consider when authoring a Composite Control. In order to add child controls to its `Controls` collection we must override the protected `CreateChildControls()` method that we inherited from `Control`. Within this method we use the `Controls.Add()` method to add each child control to the control tree.

In order to avoid naming conflicts between child controls and the host page's other controls, we must implement the `INamingContainer` interface. We would use this if our control does any type of data binding, if it is a **templated** control (which we will deal with in Chapter 5 – *Templated Controls and Styles*), or if it needs to route events to its child controls (we talk about this in Chapter 3 – *Events and Event Handling*). `INamingContainer` is an interface that has no methods, and when we implement it the ASP.NET page framework creates a new naming scope under that control. This ensures that the child controls have unique names in the control tree.

> The child controls handle all of the rendering for our control, so we do not need to override the `Render()` method.

Let's look at an example of a Composite Control in action. Our example is a search UI for a mythical medical job site. We have the menus being populated using XML files. This control can be re-factored to cache these files or get the data from another source to make it more efficient.

There are four files involved in creating this example. They are `CompositeControl.cs`, `jobCats.xml`, `state.xml`, and `WebForm1.aspx`. In order to save space we have only include a few states and job categories.

Open your favorite text editor and enter the following code:

```
using System;
using System.Web;
using System.Web.UI;
using System.Web.UI.WebControls;
using System.Xml;
using System.Xml.XPath;

namespace Search
{
  public class Composite : Control, INamingContainer
  {
    protected override void CreateChildControls()
    {

      Controls.Add(new LiteralControl("<p> </p><b>Job
      Search</b><P>Search our large database of current medical
      job postings now!<p><b>Step 1:</b>  (Optional)<br>Choose a
      specialty from the list below.<p>"));

      DropDownList skills = new DropDownList();

      skills.Items.Add("--------------");
      populateList(ref skills,"jobCats.xml","JobCategory");
      Controls.Add(skills);
      Controls.Add(new LiteralControl("<P><b>Step 2:</b>
      (Optional)<br>Narrow your search by choosing a
      location.<P>"));

      DropDownList states = new DropDownList();
      states.Items.Add("--------------");

  populateList(ref states,"state.xml","State");
  Controls.Add(states);

  Controls.Add(new LiteralControl("<P><b>Step 3:</b>
  (Optional)<br>Narrow your search even further by entering a
  Keyword. <P>"));

  TextBox textBox1 = new TextBox();
  textBox1.Width = 150;
  Controls.Add(textBox1);
  Controls.Add(new LiteralControl("<br>"));
```

```
    Controls.Add(new LiteralControl("<br>"));

    Button button1 = new Button();
    button1.Text = "Search";
    Controls.Add(button1);
    button1.Click += new EventHandler(this.Clicked);

    }

    private void Clicked(Object sender, EventArgs e)
    {
      DropDownList ctrl = (DropDownList) Controls[1];
      System.Web.HttpContext.Current.Response.Write("Our Click
      Event Fired! The job category that you chose to search was
      <strong>" + ctrl.SelectedItem + "</strong>");
    }

    private void populateList(ref DropDownList list, string
    xmlFileName, string node){
      string rawCurrentPath =
      System.Web.HttpContext.Current.Request.PhysicalPath;
      int lastPos = rawCurrentPath.LastIndexOf("\\");
      int totalChars = rawCurrentPath.Length;
      int removeTotal = totalChars - lastPos - 1;
      string strXMLPath =
      rawCurrentPath.Remove(lastPos+1,removeTotal)+ xmlFileName;
      XmlDataDocument XMLDataDoc = new XmlDataDocument();
      XMLDataDoc.DataSet.ReadXml(strXMLPath);
      XmlNodeList col = XMLDataDoc.GetElementsByTagName(node);

      foreach(XmlNode oNode in col){
        list.Items.Add(oNode.FirstChild.FirstChild.Value);
      }
    }

    protected override void OnPreRender(EventArgs e){}

    }
}
```

Save this file as CompositeControl.cs, compile it, and save the CompositeControl.dll in your application's /bin directory.

Now enter this code and save it as CompositeControl.aspx in the root directory of your application. Notice that we are implementing the control in the same way as we implement native ASP.NET Server Controls:

```
<%@ Register TagPrefix="Custom" Namespace="Search" Assembly = "CompositeControl"%>
<html>
  <body>
    <br>
    <form runat="server" ID="Form1">
      <Custom:Composite id="Composite" runat="server" />
    </form>
  </body>
</html>
```

Now let's put together the XML files. This file is available in full in the download for this book as jobCats.xml, from www.wrox.com. The code below is a slightly briefer version with less categories. Enter this code and save it as jobCats.XML in the same directory as the ASPX page.

```xml
<?xml version="1.0" standalone="yes" ?>
<Jobs>
  <JobCategory>
    <description>Burn Unit</description>
  </JobCategory>
  <JobCategory>
    <description>CCU</description>
  </JobCategory>
  <JobCategory>
    <description>Transplant</description>
  </JobCategory>
</Jobs>
```

Next we create the state.xml file by entering this code and saving it as state.xml in the same directory (again, the code presented in the book is a slightly cut-down version, and the full version is available for download):

```xml
<?xml version="1.0" standalone="yes" ?>
<StateList>
  <State>
    <Name>Alabama</Name>
  </State>
  <State>
    <Name>Alaska</Name>
  </State>
</StateList>
```

Let's see it work and then talk through the pertinent control code. Navigate to http://localhost/YourApplicationDir/CompositeControl.aspx and you should see this:

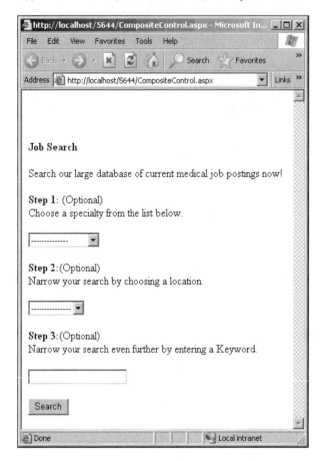

After choosing a specialty and clicking Search you should see something like this (notice that our controls have automatically maintained their state):

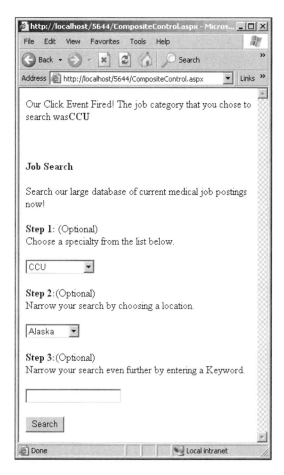

Without going line-by-line through the code we will touch on the points that are significant to our control.

The first thing we do is declare the namespace and class. Notice that our class, Composite, is derived from Control and implements the INamingContainer interface:

```
namespace Search
{
    public class Composite : Control, INamingContainer
    {}
}
```

The next significant piece of code is our overriding of the CreateChildControls() method.

```
protected override void CreateChildControls()
{
```

Within this method we add our text as a `LiteralControl`:

```
Controls.Add(new LiteralControl("<p> </p><b>Job Search</b><P>Search our large
database of current medical job postings now!<p><b>Step 1:</b>
(Optional)<br>Choose a specialty from the list below.<p>"));
```

We add our skills `DropDownList` by instantiating it, adding a dummy entry, then passing it to our `populateList()` method to populate it from the `jobCats.xml` file (the same protocol is followed for the `states` menu). Upon its return it is added to the `Controls` collection using the `Controls.Add()` method:

```
DropDownList skills = new DropDownList();
skills.Items.Add("--------------");
populateList(ref skills,"jobCats.xml","JobCategory"); //get list of skills that we
want in our list from an xml file
  Controls.Add(skills);
```

Further down in the code we add the `Button` control and set the method to handle the `Click` event:

```
Button button1 = new Button();
button1.Text = "Search";
Controls.Add(new LiteralControl("<br>"));
Controls.Add(button1);
button1.Click += new EventHandler(this.Clicked);

}
```

When the `Click` event for the `Button` control is raised our `Clicked()` method handles it (all we do within here is prove that it fired):

```
private void Clicked(Object sender, EventArgs e)
{
  DropDownList ctrl = (DropDownList) Controls[1];
  System.Web.HttpContext.Current.Response.Write("Our Click Event Fired! The job
category that you chose to search was <strong>" + ctrl.SelectedItem +
"</strong>");
}
```

Summary

In this chapter we looked at what Server Controls are, and how they fit into the ASP.NET picture. We've taken a brief refresher on ASP.NET, looked at how Server Controls are handled when a page is loaded, and looked at why and when to use Server Controls and User Controls. We've then looked at how to create the different types of Controls available to us as developers in ASP.NET.

We should now be familiar with:

❑   What Server Controls are, and why we would need to create our own

❑   How they are used

❑   Where our controls fit within the control hierarchy

❑   The execution lifetime of a Server Control

❑   Creating a simple User Control

❑   Creating a simple Server Control

❑   Creating a basic Composite Control

In the next chapter we will get into the dirt of rendering Server Controls when we cover the `HtmlTextWriter`, which we can use whenever we want to create a custom user interface for our control. We'll also look at adaptive Server Controls, and the issues involved in the rendering process.

Professional ASP .NET Server Controls

2

Rendering Server Controls

In the previous chapter, we learned the steps involved in creating a Server Control. We also had a brief look at the classes, interfaces, properties, and methods exposed by the .NET Framework Class Library for control authors to create rich Server Controls. In this chapter, we will expand on our knowledge of Server Controls by taking an in-depth look at their rendering process. Specifically, we will:

❑   Discuss the properties, methods, and features of the `HtmlTextWriter` class that provides the core foundation for creating Server Controls in ASP.NET

❑   Consider how to use `HtmlTextWriter` class to create dynamic, and flexible Server Controls

❑   Take a look at custom Mobile Controls and understand how rendering plays an important role in creating cross-device compatible applications

❑   Finally we will take a look at the built-in validation controls supplied by ASP.NET and discuss their benefits in the context of generating browser-independent output

We will kick off the chapter by understanding the basics of rendering and what steps are involved in rendering a Server Control to an output device (which may be a browser, or any other mobile device such as a PDA, cell phone, and so on).

What is Rendering?

Rendering can be defined as the process of drawing the visual contents of a control into a target output device. The target output device may be a browser, a mobile device, or any other output mechanism. It is important to realize that the actual rendering of the contents, sent down to the client by the server, takes place only on the client-side. However it is the ASP.NET runtime on the server that is responsible for sending down the appropriate contents to the requesting devices depending on their rendering capabilities. For example, if the browser supports JavaScript, the ASP.NET runtime automatically detects this and performs all validations on the client by sending down the appropriate client-side script along with the display HTML. We will see an example of this in action when we look at the `HttpBrowserCapabilities` class later in the chapter, where we will cover the rendering process from the server's point of view and understand how it results in the generation of output tailored to the capabilities of the client.

HtmlTextWriter Class

The `HtmlTextWriter` class not only allows us to write HTML contents, and text, but also provides us with the formatting capabilities including tag management, adding styles to the HTML content and so on, when rendering HTML content to the requesting clients. Before we will take a look at an example application that uses the `HtmlTextWriter` class, let us understand the important methods and properties exposed by `HtmlTextWriter`.

The following list describes some of the important utility methods exposed by the `HtmlTextWriter` class:

Method	Description
AddAttribute	Allows us to add an HTML attribute and its value to an `HtmlTextWriter` output stream
AddStyleAttribute	Allows us to add an HTML style attribute to the `HtmlTextWriter` output stream
WriteAttribute	Allows us to write an HTML attribute to the output stream
RenderBeginTag	Permits us to write the opening tag of an HTML element to the output stream
RenderEndTag	Permits us to write the end tag of an element to the output stream
WriteBeginTag	This method is similar to the `RenderBeginTag` method except for the difference that it does not write the closing > character for the HTML element
WriteEndTag	Allows us to write the closing tag of an HTML element that is already written using the `WriteBeginTag` method

Server Control Creation

One of the most important methods exposed by the base class `System.Web.UI.Control` is the `Render` method that allows us to supply the Server Control contents to an `HtmlTextWriter` object, which can then output the contents on to the client device. When developing Server Controls, we can override this method to generate contents for an ASP.NET page (that acts as the container for the Server Control). There are two different ways of writing HTML contents onto a client:

❑   Invoke the `Write` method and pass in the markup content to be written directly in the form of `string`. This is similar to writing content from an ASP page using `Response.Write` statements.

❑   Use the utility methods of the `HtmlTextWriter` class to write the contents instead of writing the markup content directly.

We will discuss both of these methods in detail and then discuss the advantages of using the utility methods as opposed to using the `Write` method and passing the markup content directly. We will start with the creation of a simple control and then build upon that to include all of the above functionality offered by the `HtmlTextWriter` class.

Writing the Markup Content Directly

Now that we have quickly reviewed the important properties and methods of the `HtmlTextWriter` class, let's consider a simple example to demonstrate the techniques of creating ASP.NET Server Controls. This example will encapsulate the logic for rendering a hyperlink on any type of browser. The following code listing is contained in the file called `RenderExample01.cs`:

```
using System;
using System.Web.UI;
using System.Web.UI.WebControls;

namespace RenderExample01
{
  public class MyLinkControl : Control
  {
    protected override void Render(HtmlTextWriter output)
    {
      output.Write
        ("<a href='http://www.wrox.com'>This is a link to the Wrox site</a>");
    }
  }
}
```

In this short code example, we start by importing all the required namespaces, and creating a namespace for our control. Once we've done this, we then declare the control, and derive it from the base class `Control`.

Once we've done this we can easily override the `Render` method of the `Control` base class by using the following line of code. It is important to realize that the `Render` method is a **virtual method**:

```
protected override void Render(HtmlTextWriter output)
```

Here the `Render` method is passed the `HtmlTextWriter` object as an argument, so we can use the properties and methods of the `HtmlTextWriter` object to write to the output stream directly. In this example, we invoke the `Write` method to write an HTML stream to the output stream:

```
output.Write(
    "<a href='http://www.wrox.com'>This is the link to wrox site</a>");
```

Now that we have created the control, we need to compile it. Make sure your `.cs` file is saved in the root folder of your web application, and then create a new subdirectory called `bin` within this directory. For example, say you had a folder on your C drive called `ServerControlsTest`, referenced as a web application with an alias of `SCTest`. Place your code in the `ServerControlsTest` directory, then create a `bin` directory within this directory. Now, all you need to do to compile your code is either to type in the appropriate command from the command line, or create a `.bat` file. For example, open Notepad, type in the following (changing paths as appropriate) and save the file as `Compile.bat` in the application root directory.

```
set outdir=c:\ServerControlsTest\bin\%1.dll
set assemblies=System.dll,System.Web.dll
csc /t:library /out:%outdir% /r:%assemblies% %1.cs
```

Whenever you need to compile any server control within this directory, all you need to do is open a command prompt, change directory to the application root directory, then type the following statement (the section in bold after the command prompt):

```
c:\ServerControlsTest> compile RenderExample01
```

The C# compiler will then compile the `RenderExample01.cs` file, referencing the required assemblies, and create a `.dll` in the `bin` directory with the same name (`RenderExample01.dll`).

Now that we've compiled our control, we'll move on to consume that control in an ASP.NET page. The following code demonstrates how to do this:

```
<%@ Register TagPrefix="Wrox" Assembly="RenderExample01"
                    Namespace="RenderExample01" %>
<%@ Page language="c#" %>
<HTML>
  <HEAD>
  </HEAD>
  <body>
    <form id="Form1" method="post" runat="server">
      <Wrox:MyLinkControl runat="server" id="MyLinkControl1">
      </Wrox:MyLinkControl>
    </form>
  </body>
</HTML>
```

We start by declaring the name of the assembly as well as the name of the namespace that contains the Server Control using the **Register** directive. We also associate a tag prefix with the namespace of the control by using the TagPrefix attribute:

```
<%@ Register TagPrefix="Wrox" Assembly="RenderExample01"
                    Namespace="RenderExample01" %>
```

Once we've declared the control, the next step is to embed it in our ASP.NET page. This is done using the following statement:

```
<Wrox:MyLinkControl runat="server" id="MyLinkControl1">
</Wrox:MyLinkControl>
```

Building the web application and navigating to the ASP.NET page produces the following output:

Using the Utility Methods of the HtmlTextWriter Class

In the above example, we simply passed the HTML as an argument to the Write method of the HtmlTextWriter class. As we already mentioned, the HtmlTextWriter class also exposes utility methods that allow us to abstractly write HTML to the client browser. This has the following advantages:

❑   Allows us to create less error-prone applications by providing tag management

❑   Renders appropriate content for up-level and down-level browsers depending on the requesting browser

Let's modify the above example to use the utility methods of the HtmlTextWriter class to render similar output. The following lines of code are required to accomplish this:

```
using System;
using System.Web.UI;
using System.Web.UI.WebControls;

namespace RenderExample02
{
```

```
public class MyLinkControl : Control
{
    protected override void Render(HtmlTextWriter output)
    {
        output.AddAttribute(HtmlTextWriterAttribute.Href,
                                        "http://www.wrox.com");
        output.AddStyleAttribute(HtmlTextWriterStyle.FontSize,"20");
        output.AddStyleAttribute(HtmlTextWriterStyle.Color,"Blue");
        output.RenderBeginTag(HtmlTextWriterTag.A);
        output.Write("This is a link to the Wrox web site");
        output.RenderEndTag();
    }
}
```

Let's take a look at the lines of code that are different from our previous example.

The Render method is the one that controls the output of the Server Control:

```
protected override void Render(HtmlTextWriter output)
```

Then, by making a call to the AddAttribute method, we specify that the next element should have an attribute called Href with a specified value:

```
output.AddAttribute(HtmlTextWriterAttribute.Href,
                                        "http://www.wrox.com");
```

The HtmlTextWriterAttribute enumeration exposes all of the HTML tags as part of its enumeration and we can pass one of its values as an argument to the AddAttribute method of the HtmlTextWriter class to represent an HTML element. Some of the HTML elements represented by HtmlTextWriterAttribute include AccessKey, Align, Alt, Background, Color, Height, MaxLength, Target, and Title.

Now that we've added the Href attribute, we can go on to add the attributes related to styling using the AddStyleAttribute method. For this purpose, we will make use of the style related enumeration HtmlTextWriterStyle contained in the System.Web.UI namespace. The HtmlTextWriterStyle enumeration lists all of the HTML styles available. The HtmlTextWriter class can make use of these styles when rendering output. The exposed HTML styles include:

- BackgroundColor
- BackgroundImage
- BorderCollapse
- BorderColor
- BorderStyle
- BorderWidth
- Color

- ❏ FontFamily

- ❏ FontSize

- ❏ FontStyle

- ❏ FontWeight

- ❏ Height

- ❏ TextDecoration

- ❏ Width

In our example, we use the enumeration values FontSize and Color to specify the font size and color for our hyperlink control:

```
output.AddStyleAttribute(HtmlTextWriterStyle.FontSize,"20");
output.AddStyleAttribute(HtmlTextWriterStyle.Color,"Blue");
```

Next, the call to RenderBeginTag tells the HtmlTextWriter to output a start tag for the element <a>. Apart from this, it also outputs any attributes that have previously been added using AddAttribute, or AddStyleAttribute:

```
output.RenderBeginTag(HtmlTextWriterTag.A);
```

By invoking the Write method, we tell the HtmlTextWriter to output the specified content to the HTML stream. As we have already seen, there are various overloads for Write that provide the means for passing in any type. All of these types will be converted to become a string and written to the output stream:

```
output.Write("This is a link to the Wrox web site");
```

Finally, we use the RenderEndTag to tell HtmlTextWriter to output the close tag for the recently opened tag using the RenderBeginTag method:

```
output.RenderEndTag();
```

The above Server Control, when hosted in an ASP.NET page produces the following output:

Exposing Attributes as Properties

Now we have a Server Control that is of specified font size and color that can display links. To make it really reusable, we need to remove the hard-coded values such as font size and color and expose them as properties. Once we do this, the clients of the control can set the values and customize the look of our control based on their requirements. To accomplish this, we need to modify our Hyperlink control to look like the following:

```
using System;
using System.Web.UI;
using System.Web.UI.WebControls;
using System.ComponentModel;
using System.Drawing;

namespace RenderExample03
{

    public class MyLinkControl : Control
    {

      Color color = Color.Blue;
      string hyperLink = "http://www.wrox.com";
      string text = "This is the Wrox site";
      int fontSize = 20;

      public Color LinkColor
      {
        get
        {
          return color;
        }
        set
        {
          color = value;
        }
      }

      public string HyperLink
      {
        get
        {
          return hyperLink;
        }
        set
        {
          if (value.IndexOf("http://") == -1)
          {
            throw new Exception("Specify Http as the protocol");
          }
          hyperLink = value;
        }
      }
    }
```

```
public string Text
{
  get
  {
    return text;
  }
  set
  {
    text = value;
  }

}

public int FontSize
{
  get
  {
    return fontSize;
  }
  set
  {
    fontSize = value;
  }
}

protected override void Render(HtmlTextWriter output)
{
  output.AddAttribute(HtmlTextWriterAttribute.Href,hyperLink);
  output.AddStyleAttribute(
                HtmlTextWriterStyle.FontSize,fontSize.ToString());
  output.AddStyleAttribute(
          HtmlTextWriterStyle.Color,ColorTranslator.ToHtml(color));
  output.RenderBeginTag(HtmlTextWriterTag.A);
  output.Write(text);
  output.RenderEndTag();
}
}
}
```

This code is similar to the previous example, except for the fact that we have replaced the hard-coded values with parameters that are exposed in the form of properties.

We did this by declaring local variables to hold the attributes of our hyperlink control as well as any default values:

```
Color color = Color.Blue;
string hyperLink = "http://www.wrox.com";
string text = "This is the Wrox site";
int fontSize = 20;
```

Once we've done this we can expose them through public properties. The local variable `color` that determines the color of our hyperlink control is exposed through a public property named `LinkColor`:

```
public Color LinkColor
{
  get
  {
    return color;
  }
  set
  {
    color = value;
  }
}
```

The URL in our hyperlink control is exposed through a public property called `HyperLink`. In this property setter, we also perform validation to ensure that the URL of our hyperlink control always starts with `"http://"`. If this `string` is not present, we raise an exception back to the control's client saying that the `Hyperlink` attribute should have the string `"http://"` in it:

```
public string HyperLink
{
  get
  {
    return hyperLink;
  }
  set
  {
    if (value.IndexOf("http://") == -1)
    {
      throw new Exception("Specify http:// as the protocol");
    }
    hyperLink = value;
  }
}
```

The following ASP.NET page will host the Server Control. Again we use the `Register` directive to create an association between the tag prefix and the namespace:

```
<%@ Page language="c#" %>
<%@ Register TagPrefix="Wrox" Assembly="RenderExample03"
                       Namespace="RenderExample03" %>
<html>
  <head>
    <title>Render Example 3</title>
  </head>
  <body>
    <form id="Form1" method="post" runat="server">
    <Wrox:MyLinkControl FontSize="30" Text="This is a link to Wrox site"
                     LinkColor="Red" runat="server" id="MyLinkControl1">
      </Wrox:MyLinkControl>
    </form>
  </body>
</html>
```

In the above code, we pass style-related characteristics, such as `FontSize` and `LinkColor`, as attributes of the HTML element and they are mapped to public properties of the `MyLinkControl` class. If you navigate to the above ASP.NET page in a browser, you will get the following output:

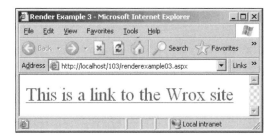

When we defined the property set for the `HyperLink` property, we included validation logic to ensure that the users of the control always set the URL for the `Hyperlink` property to use HTTP.

Using the WebControl Class for Control Creation

By deriving our class from the `WebControl` class, rather than the `Control` class, we can take advantage of the features provided by the `WebControl` class for controlling the appearance and behavior of ASP.NET Server Controls. For example, we can control the background color, foreground color, border width, and border style, among others.

The `WebControl` class also exposes methods to assist in the rendering process. By overriding the `AddAttributesToRender` method, we can specify additional attributes and CSS styles for rendering in conjunction with the HTML tag that is specified in the constructor. To illustrate this, let us consider our previous example and modify it to use the `WebControl` class.

When we derive our control from the `WebControl` class, we can use the `RenderBeginTag` and `RenderEndTag` methods to write the beginning and ending HTML element tags. The `RenderContents` method enables a control to specify the content within the tags. When we write text to the output stream of a Server Control, we should override the `RenderContents` method instead of overriding the `Render` method. This ensures that the rendering functionality implemented by `WebControl` (such as emitting attributes) is preserved. Since the `WebControl` class provides support for style management functionalities such as background color, foreground color, and so on, we can remove the UI-related properties that we defined in our previous code:

```
using System;
using System.Web.UI;
using System.Web.UI.WebControls;
using System.ComponentModel;
using System.Drawing;

namespace RenderExample04
{

  public class MyLinkControl : WebControl
  {

    string hyperLink ;
    string text ;
```

```
    public MyLinkControl() : base (HtmlTextWriterTag.A)
    {

    }

    public string Text
    {
      get
      {
        return text;
      }

      set
      {
        text = value;
      }
    }

    protected override void OnInit(EventArgs e)
    {
      if (hyperLink == null)
      {
        hyperLink = "http://www.wrox.com";
      }

      if (text == null)
      {
        text ="This is a hyperlink to the Wrox site";
      }
    }

    public string HyperLink
    {
      get
      {
        return hyperLink;
      }
      set
      {
        if (value.IndexOf("http://") == -1)
        {
            throw new Exception("Specify Http as the protocol");
        }
        hyperLink = value;
      }
    }

  protected override void AddAttributesToRender(HtmlTextWriter output)
  {
    output.AddAttribute(HtmlTextWriterAttribute.Href,hyperLink);
    base.AddAttributesToRender(output);
    }
```

```
      protected override void RenderContents(HtmlTextWriter output)
      {
        output.Write(text);
        base.RenderContents(output);
      }
    }
  }
```

Unlike the previous examples, this time we derive from the WebControl class:

```
public class MyLinkControl : WebControl
```

In the following lines of code, we declare the local variables that are used to hold the attributes related to the hyperlink control:

```
string hyperLink ;
string text ;
```

In the constructor of the MyLinkControl class, we invoke the constructor of the WebControl base class. To this, we pass the HTML element we want to render as an argument. So, in our example, since we want to render an HTML anchor tag, we pass in the enumeration HtmlTextWriterTag.A:

```
public MyLinkControl() : base (HtmlTextWriterTag.A)
```

As in our previous examples, we then expose the text for our hyperlink control in the form of properties:

```
public string Text
{
  get
  {
    return text;
  }

  set
  {
    text = value;
  }
}
```

But now, instead of initializing the local variables at the time of declaration, we can initialize them using the OnInit method that allows us to perform any initialization steps that are required to create and set up an instance of the Server Control:

```
protected override void OnInit(EventArgs e)
{
  if (hyperLink == null)
  {
    hyperLink = "http://www.wrox.com";
  }
```

```
        if (text == null)
        {
          text ="This is a hyperlink to the Wrox site";
        }
      }
```

By overriding the virtual `AddAttributesToRender` method, we can write our custom attributes to the output stream. In the `AddAttributesToRender` method, we add the attributes related to our hyperlink Server Control to the `HtmlTextWriter` output stream. To add the `Href` attribute, we use the enumeration `HtmlTextWriterAttribute.Href`. Once we have added the `Href` attribute, we can invoke the `AddAttributesToRender` method of the `WebControl` class to ensure that the attributes related to the base `WebControl` class are rendered properly:

```
protected override void AddAttributesToRender(HtmlTextWriter output)
    {
        output.AddAttribute(HtmlTextWriterAttribute.Href,hyperLink);
        base.AddAttributesToRender(output);
    }
```

After the attributes are rendered, we need to render the actual contents of the hyperlink, which is done using the `RenderContents` method. As with the `AddAttributesToRender` method, we make a call to the `RenderContents` method of the base class to ensure that we do not overwrite its contents:

```
    protected override void RenderContents(HtmlTextWriter output)
    {
      output.Write(text);
      base.RenderContents(output);
    }
  }
}
```

Now that we have created the control, let's see what it looks like when hosted in an ASP.NET page:

```
<%@ Page language="c#" %>
<%@ Register TagPrefix="Wrox" Assembly="Example04"
                                      Namespace="Example04" %>
<html>
  <head>
    <title>Render Example 4</title>
  </head>
  <body>
    <form id="Form1" method="post" runat="server">
    <Wrox:MyLinkControl HyperLink=
      "http://www.asptoday.com" Text="This is a link to ASPToday"
                Font-Size="30" ForeColor="Blue" runat="server">
    </Wrox:MyLinkControl>
    </form>
  </body>
</html>
```

As you can see, we specify `HyperLink` and `Text` attributes that will be automatically mapped to the public properties of the Server Control class `MyLinkControl`. We also specify `Font-Size` and `ForeColor` attributes that are mapped to public properties of the base `WebControl` class:

```
<Wrox:MyLinkControl HyperLink=http://www.asptoday.com Text="This is a link to
ASPToday" Font-Size="30" ForeColor="Blue" runat="server">
</Wrox:MyLinkControl>
```

When displayed in a browser, the output from the ASP.NET page looks like this:

Now that we've looked at the steps involved in creating simple custom controls, let's exercise our knowledge of Server Controls by considering a more complicated example.

A Complex Control Creation Example

For this example, we will create an ASP.NET Server Control called `MyDataGridControl` that has the capability to display data from a SQL server database in a grid format. To be able to display the data, it requires the following two important parameters:

❏ Connection string – Allows us to specify the database to connect to

❏ SQL query – Allows to specify the `SELECT` query to be executed

The control also exposes public properties such as `TableBorder`, `TableHeight`, `TableWidth`, `BGColor`, and `HeaderColor`.

> **The complete code listing for this example is quite extensive, and can be downloaded from www.wrox.com. For brevity, we will not present it all here, but will instead consider those points where it differs from our previous examples. Databound controls are covered in more detail in Chapter 6.**

We import the `System.Data`, and `System.Data.SqlClient` namespaces that expose a set of classes that are required for executing SQL queries against the SQL server database:

```
using System.Data;
using System.Data.SqlClient;
```

Then the following code is added to allow us to indicate to the base `WebControl` class that we want to render the HTML table element as part of the Server Control. Once we specify the HTML `Table` element as part of the constructor, we can then add attributes to the `Table` element by overriding the `AddAttributesToRender` method. We will see the code of the `AddAttributesToRender` method in a moment:

```
public MyDataGridControl() : base (HtmlTextWriterTag.Table) {

}
```

As you can see from the above code listing, we expose the following public properties from our control: `ConnectionString`, `SqlQuery`, `TableHeight`, `TableWidth`, `TableBorder`, `BGColor`, and `HeaderColor`. By setting these properties to appropriate values, the clients of our Server Control can control the output generated.

In the `AddAttributesToRender` method, we set the attributes for the `Table` element that was passed to the constructor of our control class:

```
protected override void AddAttributesToRender(HtmlTextWriter output)
{
  output.AddAttribute(HtmlTextWriterAttribute.Border,border.ToString());
  output.AddAttribute(HtmlTextWriterAttribute.Bgcolor,bgColor);
  output.AddAttribute(HtmlTextWriterAttribute.Height,height.ToString());
  output.AddAttribute(HtmlTextWriterAttribute.Width,width.ToString());
  base.AddAttributesToRender(output);
}
```

In the `RenderContents` method, we specify the contents that will be rendered by our Server Control:

```
protected override void RenderContents(HtmlTextWriter output)
{
    string str = null;
```

In this line of code, we instantiate the `SqlConnection` object by passing to it the connection string that is used to establish connection with the database:

```
SqlConnection sqlConn = new SqlConnection(connectionString);
```

Now we open the connection by invoking the `Open` method:

```
sqlConn.Open();
```

We then create an instance of `SqlCommand` object by using this line of code. To the constructor of the `SqlCommand` class, we pass in the query to be executed and the `SqlConnection` object as arguments:

```
SqlCommand sqlComm = new SqlCommand(sqlQuery,sqlConn);
```

Once we have an instance of the `SqlCommand` object, we can then execute a query against the database and return an `SqlDataReader` object by calling the `ExecuteReader` method of the `SqlCommand` object:

```
SqlDataReader sqlReader =
                sqlComm.ExecuteReader(CommandBehavior.CloseConnection);
```

We get the number of columns returned by the `SqlCommand` object in a local variable:

```
int fieldCount = sqlReader.FieldCount;
```

To display the heading (**Wrox Data Display Table Control**) for our control, we create a TR element, and then add a TD element. We also invoke the `AddAttribute` method multiple times to write out the proper attributes required for our Server Control:

```
output.RenderBeginTag(HtmlTextWriterTag.Tr);
output.AddAttribute(HtmlTextWriterAttribute.Colspan,
fieldCount.ToString());
output.AddAttribute(HtmlTextWriterAttribute.Align,"Center");
output.AddAttribute(HtmlTextWriterAttribute.Bgcolor,"Red");
output.RenderBeginTag(HtmlTextWriterTag.Td);
output.RenderBeginTag(HtmlTextWriterTag.B);
output.Write("Wrox Data Display Table Control");
output.RenderEndTag();
output.RenderEndTag();
output.RenderEndTag();
```

Now that we have defined the characteristics of the common header of our control, let's look at the code required for displaying the column names as sub-headings in our control. To display all the column names returned by the execution of the query in a separate row, we loop through all of the columns and then call the `GetName` method of the `SqlDataReader` class:

```
//Specify the BGColor of the column headers
output.AddAttribute(HtmlTextWriterAttribute.Bgcolor,
                                        headerColor);
//Add the column headers
output.RenderBeginTag(HtmlTextWriterTag.Tr);
//Loop thru all the columns and display their title
for (int i=0;i<fieldCount;i++)
{
  output.RenderBeginTag(HtmlTextWriterTag.Td);
  output.Write(sqlReader.GetName(i).ToUpper());
  output.RenderEndTag();
}
output.RenderEndTag();
```

Now that we have completed the rendering of the column names, we can render the actual contents of the code. To display this, we enumerate the `SqlDataReader` object by calling its `Read` method. While enumerating the contents, we also check to see if a column contains a `null` value, and if it does then we assign an **empty string** to the local variable `str`, which is used as an intermediate variable to display the value present in a column:

```
while(sqlReader.Read())
{
  output.RenderBeginTag(HtmlTextWriterTag.Tr);
  for(int i=0;i<fieldCount;i++)
  {
    output.RenderBeginTag(HtmlTextWriterTag.Td);
  if (sqlReader.IsDBNull(i))
  {
    str= "";
  }
  else
  {
```

In this next section, we use a `switch` statement to determine the data type of the column. Once we've done this, we can then use the appropriate Get*XXX* method to retrieve the value:

```
switch (sqlReader.GetFieldType(i).ToString())
{
  case "System.Int16":
    str = sqlReader.GetInt16(i).ToString();
    break;
  case "System.Int32":
    str = sqlReader.GetInt32(i).ToString();
    break;
  case "System.Int64":
    str = sqlReader.GetInt64(i).ToString();
    break;
  case "System.Decimal":
    str = sqlReader.GetDecimal(i).ToString();
    break;
  case "System.DateTime":
```

```
                    str = sqlReader.GetDateTime(i).ToString();
                    break;
                case "System.String":
                    str = sqlReader.GetString(i).ToString();
                    break;
                case "System.Boolean":
                    str = sqlReader.GetBoolean(i).ToString();
                    break;
                case "System.Guid":
                    str = sqlReader.GetGuid(i).ToString();
                    break;
                case "System.Double":
                    str = sqlReader.GetDouble(i).ToString();
                    break;
                case "System.Byte":
                    str = sqlReader.GetByte(i).ToString();
                    break;
            }
        }
```

Now we write the value contained in the local variable `str` to the output by calling the `Write` method. After that we also close the `TD` element tag by making a call to the `RenderEndTag` method:

```
        output.Write(str);
        output.RenderEndTag();
    }
```

The following call to `RenderEndTag` is used to close the `TR` element that we opened previously:

```
        output.RenderEndTag();

    }
    base.RenderContents(output);
        }
        }
    }
```

Now that we have created the control, let's take a look at the code required for hosting our control in an ASP.NET page:

```
<%@ Page language="c#" %>
<%@ Register TagPrefix="Wrox" Namespace="RenderExample05"
Assembly="RenderExample05" %>

<HTML>
  <HEAD>
    <title>WebForm1</title>

  </HEAD>
  <body>
    <form id="Form1" method="post" runat="server">
      <Wrox:MyDataGridControl TableHeight="800" TableWidth="900"
```

59

```
            HeaderColor="Skyblue" SqlQuery="Select * from Titles"
            TableBorder="1"
            ConnectionString="server=localhost;database=pubs;uid=sa;pwd=;"
            BGColor="DeepSkyBlue" runat="server"
            ID="MyDataGridControl1"></Wrox:MyDataGridControl>
      </form>
    </body>
  </HTML>
```

In the above code, it is important to understand that we supply the connection string, and the SQL query to be executed as **attributes** to the MyDataGridControl. The output produced by the above code looks like the following:

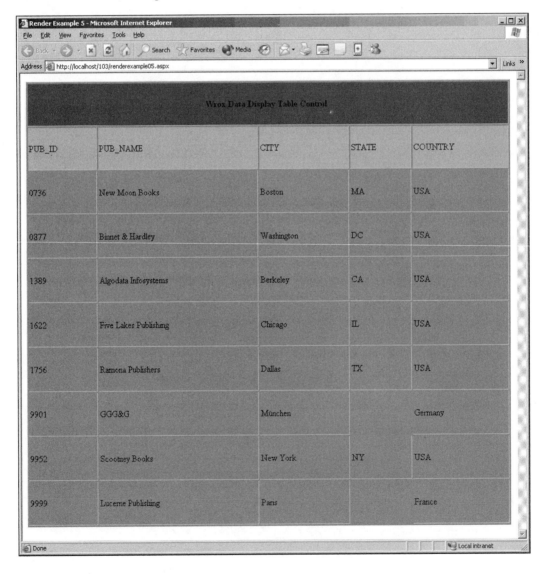

Applications of the HtmlTextWriter Class

Now that we have seen examples of the `HtmlTextWriter` class, let's summarize the benefits of using it for creating Server Controls:

❑ Exposes a number of properties and methods to provide rich formatting capabilities

❑ Allows us to create less error-prone applications by providing tag management

❑ Allows us to create reusable and easy-to-read code by exposing a rich set of properties and methods

❑ Renders appropriate content for up-level and down-level browsers depending on the requesting browser

❑ Simplifies HTML page creation for the designer

❑ Provides style management using the `Style` class

Custom Mobile Controls

Mobile Controls are Microsoft's answer to the problem of creating cross-device compatible mobile web applications. One of the main motivations behind the creation of a separate set of controls is to provide developers with a feature-rich toolset that makes it possible for them to create mobile applications that perform equally well on multiple devices without having to worry about the rendering details on the client devices. Furthermore, it also exposes programmatic interfaces that allow us to create applications using device-independent syntax.

Before we take a look at the rendering process of Mobile Controls, we need to understand the common pitfalls associated with creating traditional mobile applications. Once we understand the issues, we will then see for ourselves how Mobile Controls help alleviate these problems.

One of the important issues causing much concern to web developers at the moment is the rapid growth of the mobile device market. Literally hundreds of different types of device are appearing, none of which really match the physical or display characteristics of the ubiquitous PC-based web browsers. This range of devices is not limited to wireless devices. We also have cellular phones and Pocket PCs, and we are also seeing a huge growth in things like Web TV, games consoles with web access, and so on. Many of these devices do not support HTML as a language, or the range of effects such as colors, screen size and resolution, sound, interactivity, and so on, that PC-based browsers do. So, creating HTML as output from your web pages is not always an ideal solution. Instead, we need to create a range of different output types based on the client that we're responding to.

To provide this kind of feature, Microsoft has introduced a set of **Mobile Controls** along with the Mobile Internet Toolkit that can intelligently vary their output based on the requesting device type. For example, if the requesting device is a cellular phone that expects pages coded in WML, then that's what the Mobile Controls will render. If it's Microsoft Mobile Explorer on a PocketPC that expects HTML, then the control will automatically render that format.

However, the point is that the controls are intelligent enough to be able to create output that offers the same functionality irrespective of the device type or the output language. For example, a <mobile:List> control should create the same list on mobile phone as on a PocketPC or a traditional PC. Even though the way it is actually rendered will depend on the capabilities and display characteristics of the device, the functionality should be identical. Furthermore, programmers should be able to do this without having to concern themselves about what the device is, and how it tackles the specific requirements of the device type.

Device Detection and Customized Rendering

One of the great features of Mobile Controls is their ability to automatically render appropriate content to a variety of devices. However there may be times when we may have to generate content relevant to a specific device. This becomes especially important when we want to take advantage of the capabilities of a specific device.

If you take a look at the web.config file after installing Mobile Internet toolkit, you can see that a number of entries have been added. Most of these are related to determining the capabilities of the connecting device. For example, it can include such entries as whether a device has a color screen, the screen dimensions, type of input, and so on. There are sections for many current devices. At run time, this information is compared with the HTTP_USER_AGENT header to identify the device, and set the capabilities accordingly.

The great thing about this approach is that it provides an extensible system. There are a plenty of devices already on file. However, if we want to add our own device, we can accomplish that simply by adding a new entry to web.config. Once these device capabilities have been added in the web.config file, we can access them from our application code at run time by using either of the following two ways:

❑ Using the MobileCapabilities class

❑ Using device-specific filters

We will start by taking a look at the MobileCapabilities class.

Using the MobileCapabilities Class

It is important to realize that the MobileCapabilities class is built into the standard browser detection capabilities of ASP.NET. When a client makes a request to an ASP.NET mobile web application, the ASP.NET runtime recognizes the device and attaches a MobileCapabilities object to the request. Once this object is filled with information, the application can access it through the Browser property of the HttpRequest object.

The MobileCapabilities class acts as a single source of information for accessing capability-related information about a client device. It also provides the means for executing queries against device capabilities. MobileCapabilities class has a number of properties that relate to device characteristics. For example, it can include properties such as the number of characters that fit in a screen row, whether color is supported, the preferred markup language, and so on.

Using Device-Specific Filters

This method of accessing the device capabilities involves setting up filters and then using them declaratively in our code. To set up filters, we need to add <filter> elements to the <devicefilters> section of the <system.web> section of the web.config filer.

The format of the `<filter>` element is as follows:

```
<filter name="capability"
        compare="capabilityName"
        argument="comparestring"/>
```

In the above declaration, we specify the name for the filter with `capability`, a device capability with `capabilityName`, and a string to compare with the string content of the capability in the `comparestring` arguments.

Once we have defined these filters in the `deviceFilters` section of the `web.config` file, we can then customize the output of the mobile application by specifying the filter for each type of device by using a combination of `DeviceSpecific` and `Choice` elements. The `<DeviceSpecific>` control is simply an outer container for holding a number of choices. Inside the `DeviceSpecific` element, we have `<Choice>` elements that represent the device characteristic/value pair. To add a device-specific content for a control, we need to add a `<DeviceSpecific>` element as a child element of the control.

Let's say, for example, we want to have different types of images rendered based on the type of requesting device. As mentioned already, to produce device-specific content for a control, we need to add a `<DeviceSpecific>` element as a child element of the control. In this case, since we want to customize the type of image rendered by the `mobile:Image` control, we add the `<DeviceSpecific>` element as a child element of the `mobile:Image` control:

```
<mobile:Image runat=server ImageURL="ordinary.gif">
    <DeviceSpecific>
        <Choice Filter="isColor" ImageURL="colorImage.gif"/>
        <Choice Filter="IsWML" ImageURL="wirlessbitmap.wbmp"/>
    </DeviceSpecific>
</mobile:Image>
```

In the above code snippet, the `Filter` property allows us to specify the device filter to evaluate. During the execution, the mobile runtime chooses which `<Choice>` element to use by going through each specified choice in order, and evaluating the filter specified by `Filter` property. If the filter matches the current target device, the choice is picked.

Before we wind up our discussion on the mobile controls, let us identify the advantages as well as the limitations of mobile controls:

Advantages of Mobile Controls

- ❑ Does not require the developer to do browser checks and then deliver appropriate content based on the target device

- ❑ Obviates the need for the developer to be proficient in WML, CHTML, and so on

- ❑ Provides a highly extensible server-side programming model that is easy to use and scalable

- ❑ Allows for drag-and-drop application development with Visual Studio .NET

- ❑ Also provides automatic pagination support based on the device capabilities

Limitations of Mobile Controls

❑ Obviously they bind you to Windows platform and Microsoft.NET-related development

❑ At the time of writing, mobile controls have been fully tested on only the following devices:

    ❑ Pocket PC with Microsoft Pocket Internet Explorer version 4.5

    ❑ Mitsubishi T250 phone

    ❑ Nokia 7110 phone

    ❑ Nokia WAP Toolkit 2.0 Beta simulator for the Nokia 7110

Validation Controls

If you take a look at most of the commercial web sites today, you will notice that they are filled with forms that clearly execute a lot of handwritten code in JavaScript to perform validation. Validation code is not particularly easy to write. Validation of web applications is particularly frustrating for other reasons as well. In this section of the chapter, we will first understand the problems associated with traditional validation techniques and then see for ourselves how validation controls abstract away a lot of the plumbing that is required for creating applications that work seamlessly across the different kinds of browsers.

Limitations of Current Validation Techniques (Client-Side and Server-Side)

As we already mentioned, validation code is not easy to write and maintain due to the amount of JavaScript code needed to accomplish validation. The following list describes the limitations of current validation techniques:

❑ Even though it is possible to create powerful validations using browser script, it can be hard to justify, because scripting support is not present in all browsers.

❑ Client-side scripting support offered by down-level browsers is very limited. For example, HTML 3.2 is so limited in what you can control and what feedback you get from the user that you can't apply the same tricks you can use on a richer client, such as preventing the user from entering certain characters, or making beep sounds.

❑ Relying completely on client-side validations may jeopardize the security of the site as someone can very easily take a page with script and disable or change it. In other words, you should not rely on client-side script to stop bad data getting into to your system. This should only be used to provide more immediate feedback to your users.

❑ While the JScript language is reasonably well standardized, the Document Object Model (DOM) that is used for interacting with HTML documents in browsers does not have a universally accepted standard. As a result, client-side validation cannot be guaranteed to work equally well in all browsers.

❑ Due to the number of listed limitations in performing validations using client-side script, it becomes necessary to perform validations on the server-side as well. But again completely depending on the server-side for validation means that there is a network roundtrip every time we want to perform validation checks.

So we need a sophisticated validation mechanism that uses a combination of client-side and server-side validations depending on the capabilities of the client, but without compromising the security of the site.

Plumbing Provided by the Validation Controls

Having realized the need to provide the plumbing for most of the frequently performed validations, Microsoft has built in a set of validation controls in the form of classes into the ASP.NET object model. The following list describes the built-in validation controls that are part of the ASP.NET:

Validation control	Description
RequiredFieldValidator	This control is used to prevent the user from skipping the entry for an input control
CompareValidator	Allows us to compare the user's input against a constant value, or against a value of another control, using any of the supplied comparison operators
RangeValidator	Allows us to ensure that the user's input is between the specified upper and lower limits
RegularExpressionValidator	Allows us to check the user's entry against a pattern defined by a regular expression
CustomValidator	Allows us to validate the user's input against custom validation logic at run time

The validation controls supplied as part of ASP.NET are quite powerful, and will most likely be able to perform most of the validation checks that developers may have to write while constructing web applications. To be able to take advantage of the features of the validation controls, we need to associate them with the input controls that need to be validated. Once they are attached to input controls, when the user's input is being processed, ASP.NET passes the user's entry to the appropriate validation control. The location (client or server) in which the validation takes place depends on the capabilities of the client. For example, if the client browser supports dynamic HTML (DHTML) such as Internet Explorer 4.0 and above, validation controls emit client-side script that makes it possible for the validation to take place in the client-side. When the validation occurs on the client-side, it is possible to provide immediate feedback of the user's entry, thereby avoiding the extra round trip to the server.

Even though some validation is performed on the client-side, validation still takes place on the server-side as well. Due to this, not only we can carry out advanced validations, but also provide security against malicious users trying to bypass validation. The great thing about validation controls is that we do not have to make any changes to our page or to the validation controls for them to render appropriate contents so that they work equally well on different browsers. They detect automatically if the browser supports DHTML and render accordingly.

Detecting Browser Capabilities

ASP.NET brings with it a number of features and functions that enable us to build web applications suitable for any browser. Many of these new features, such as validation controls and data-bound grid controls, and so on, can be rendered by the ASP.NET runtime as either HTML 3.2, or HTML 4.0 with JavaScript support. The decision on how to render the page is dependent on the browser type and the version of the browser that is making the request. And also there will likely be situations where you will want to evaluate a browser and its capabilities and generate output accordingly. In previous versions of ASP, we used the browser capabilities component to find out information about the requesting browser. The classic ASP version of the browser capabilities component provided attributes for checking such things as browser name, version, support for frames, and so on. In ASP.NET, the functionality of the browser capabilities component has been encapsulated in the HttpBrowserCapabilities class.

Before we take a look at the different ways of detecting browser capabilities, let us briefly look at the different kinds of browsers that we may have to deal with while creating web applications. We can broadly classify browsers and client devices into two different groups: up-level and down-level. This classification is based on the capabilities of the browser or the client device, which determine the presentation, and behavior of a loading page from a web server.

Up-level browsers usually provide support for the following:

❑   ECMAScript version 1.2

❑   HTML version 4.0

❑   The Microsoft Document Object Model (MSDOM)

❑   Cascading style sheets (CSS)

Down-level browsers support only the following:

❑   HTML version 3.2

Let's take a look at the built-in browser detection capabilities supplied by ASP.NET that allow for customization of content according to the capabilities of the browser.

HttpBrowserCapabilities Class

Due to the wide range of variation in the number of features supported by different browsers, it becomes a challenge to create applications that work across all the browsers and still provide the best possible user experience. As a result, often it becomes necessary to detect a certain browser or client device configuration to determine the level of support offered for our page content. To accomplish this, we can invoke the Browser property of the built-in HttpRequest object and get reference to the HttpBrowserCapabilities class. As we already mentioned, the HttpBrowserCapabilities class enables a server to compile information on the capabilities of the browser that is making the request. The HttpBrowserCapabilities class is contained in the System.Web namespace.

The `HttpBrowserCapabilities` class exposes a rich set of properties and methods that allows us to gather information about the capabilities of the client browser that is making the request. When a client makes an HTTP request, the `HttpBrowserCapabilities` object is filled with information about the browser or client device properties. Some of the important information gathered by the `HttpBrowserCapabilities` object includes the kind of browser and its version, scripting support available on the client-side, and so on. Detecting the capabilities of the browser allows for customization of output to provide different behaviors on different browsers thereby making it possible to fully exploit the potential capabilities of the client. For example, we can create an ASP.NET Server Control that performs validation on the client-side to provide rich user experience by taking advantage of the scripting support available on the client-side.

To get a reference to the `HttpBrowserCapabilities` class, we must call the `Browser` property of the `Request` object:

```
HttpBrowserCapabilities browserCap = Request.Browser;
```

Once we have an instance of the `HttpBrowserCapabilities` class, we can use its properties to perform evaluations, and generate appropriate content.

The following table summarizes the important properties of `HttpBrowserCapabilities` class:

Property	Description
ActiveX Controls	Allows us to determine whether the client browser supports ActiveX controls
JavaScript	Indicates whether the client browser supports JavaScript
Frames	Gets a value indicating if the client browser supports frames
ClrVersion	Provides the version number of the .NET Common Language Runtime installed on the client computer
MSDomVersion	Gets the version of MS DOM (Document Object Model) that the client browser supports
Cookies	Allows us to determine if the client browser supports cookies
Crawler	Allows us to determine if the client browser is a web crawler search engine
Browser	Gets the browser string that was sent with the request in the user-agent header

The following code snippet shows how to dynamically redirect page requests based on the capabilities of the requesting browser:

```
<%@ Page language="c#"%>
<html>
  <head>
    <title>WebForm1</title>
    <script runat="server">
    private void Page_Load(object sender, System.EventArgs e)
    {
      // Put user code to initialize the page here
      HttpBrowserCapabilities bc = Request.Browser;
      if (bc.Frames == true)
      {
        Response.Redirect("Frames.aspx");
      }
      else
      {
        Response.Redirect("NoFrames.aspx");
      }
    }
    </script>
  </head>
  <body MS_POSITIONING="GridLayout">
    <form id="Form1" method="post" runat="server">
    </form>
  </body>
</html>
```

In the above code listing, we evaluate the browser's capabilities to check if the browser supports HTML frames. We do this by checking the Frames property of the HttpBrowserCapabilities class. If the user supports frames, we then redirect the user to a page that is frame-enabled. If the browser does not support frames, we then redirect the user to a page that does not use frames.

When using the HttpBrowserCapabilities class to evaluate the browser's functionality, we need to clearly understand that the HttpBrowserCapabilities class is limited to evaluating only the built-in functionality of a browser. It does not evaluate the current state of a browser's functionality. For example, imagine you are evaluating the client-side JavaScript support provided by the browser. If the requesting browser is IE 5.5, this will return true since the browser supports client-side JavaScript support. However, if the user has the scripting capabilities turned off, the JavaScript property still returns true.

Using ClientTarget Property to Affect the Output of a Server Control

So far, we have discussed the means of detecting browser capabilities and generating appropriate content that renders properly depending on the requesting browser. Now let us turn our attention to see how to override the default rendering behavior of the ASP.NET Server Controls by using the ClientTarget property.

Most of the ASP.NET Server Controls will render JavaScript for up-level browsers, including all the validation controls and the data controls that use paging or sorting. In some instances you may want to have more control over how the output is rendered. The Page class allows us to set the ClientTarget property so all requests are rendered for a specified browser type, either UpLevel or DownLevel.

UpLevel is the default and it will not only force validation on the client-side form but also perform validations on the server-side as well. This way no one can copy our web pages and submit garbage to our application. In our Server Control, if we set the ClientTarget attribute to UpLevel, the Server Control automatically emits client-side script without us having to write any client script. As we already discussed, this is valid for browsers that support HTML 4.0 (for example Internet Explorer 4.0 and higher).

By setting the ClientTarget attribute to DownLevel, we can force all browsers to receive HTML 3.2 with no JavaScript even if the browser is an up-level browser.

To understand the impact on the rendering process when we set the ClientTarget attribute to DownLevel, let us consider the following example:

```
<%@ Page language="c#" ClientTarget="DownLevel"%>
<HTML>
  <HEAD>
  </HEAD>
  <body>
    <form id="Form1" method="post" runat="server">
      <asp:TextBox id="txtContents" style="Z-INDEX: 101; LEFT: 229px;
          POSITION: absolute; TOP: 124px" runat="server"></asp:TextBox>
      <asp:Button id="btnValidate" style="Z-INDEX: 102; LEFT: 276px;
          POSITION: absolute; TOP: 160px" runat="server" Height="25px"
          Width="74px" Text="Validate"></asp:Button>
      <asp:RequiredFieldValidator id="RequiredFieldValidator1"
          style="Z-INDEX: 103; LEFT: 390px; POSITION: absolute; TOP: 127px"
          runat="server" ErrorMessage="Enter text"
          ControlToValidate="txtContents"></asp:RequiredFieldValidator>
      <asp:Label id="lblTitle" style="Z-INDEX: 104; LEFT: 85px;
          POSITION: absolute; TOP: 122px" runat="server" Width="114px"
          Height="19px">Enter the Text:</asp:Label>
    </form>
  </body>
</HTML>
```

If you navigate to the above ASP.NET page, you will see an output that is somewhat similar to the following:

As you can see in the above code, we have placed a simple textbox control, a RequiredFieldvalidator control, and a button. The RequiredFieldValidator control is used to ensure that the user does not skip the entry of the textbox control. Since we set the ClientTarget attribute to DownLevel, when the ASP.NET page emits HTML, it does not generate any client-side script, instead it performs all of the validations on the server side.

The above page generates the following HTML:

```html
<html>
  <body>
    <form name="Form1" method="post" action="WebForm1.aspx" id="Form1">
    <input type="hidden" name="__VIEWSTATE" value="dDwtMTUwMDQzMzEyMTs7Pg=="
    />

    <input name="txtContents" type="text" id="txtContents"
           style="Z-INDEX:    101; LEFT: 229px; POSITION: absolute;
           TOP: 124px" />
    <input type="submit" name="btnValidate" value="Validate"
           onclick="if (typeof(Page_ClientValidate) == 'function')
           Page_ClientValidate(); " language="javascript" id="btnValidate"
           style="Z-INDEX: 102; LEFT: 276px; POSITION: absolute; TOP: 160px"
           />
    <span id="lblTitle" style="Z-INDEX: 104; LEFT: 85px;
      POSITION: absolute; TOP: 122px">Enter the Text:</span>
    </form>
  </body>
</html>
```

As you can see, it does not have any client-side script rendered as part of the HTML output. All of the entire validation is done on the server side.

In the previous code listing, if we change the `ClientTarget` attribute to `UpLevel` and make it look like the following:

```
<%@ Page language="c#" ClientTarget="UpLevel"%>
```

We get the following HTML output:

```
<!DOCTYPE HTML PUBLIC "-//W3C//DTD HTML 4.0 Transitional//EN" >
<HTML>
  <HEAD>
    <meta name="GENERATOR" Content="Microsoft Visual Studio 7.0">
    <meta name="CODE_LANGUAGE" Content="C#">
    <meta name="vs_defaultClientScript" content="JavaScript (ECMAScript)">
    <meta name="vs_targetSchema"
                    content="http://schemas.microsoft.com/intellisense/ie5">
  </HEAD>
  <body MS_POSITIONING="GridLayout">
    <form name="Form1" method="post" action="WebForm1.aspx"
          language="javascript" onsubmit="ValidatorOnSubmit();" id="Form1">
     <input type="hidden" name="__VIEWSTATE"
                                      value="dDwtMTUwMDQzMzEyMTs7Pg==" />

    <script language="javascript"
      src="/aspnet_client/system_web/1_0_3215_11/WebUIValidation.js">
    </script>

      
     <input name="txtContents" type="text" id="txtContents"
        style="Z-INDEX: 101; LEFT: 229px; POSITION: absolute;
        TOP: 124px" />
     <input type="submit" name="btnValidate" value="Validate"
        onclick="if (typeof(Page_ClientValidate) == 'function')
        Page_ClientValidate(); " language="javascript" id="btnValidate"
        style="height:25px;width:74px;Z-INDEX: 102; LEFT: 276px; POSITION:
        absolute; TOP: 160px" />
     <span id="RequiredFieldValidator1" controltovalidate="txtContents"
         errormessage="Enter text"
         valuationfunction="RequiredFieldValidatorEvaluateIsValid"
         initialvalue="" style="color:Red;Z-
         INDEX:103;LEFT:390px;POSITION:absolute;TOP:127px;
         visibility:hidden;">Enter text
     </span>
     <span id="lblTitle" style="height:19px;width:114px;
        Z-INDEX: 104; LEFT: 85px; POSITION: absolute; TOP: 122px"
              >Enter the Text:
     </span>

     <script language="javascript">
     <!--  var Page_Validators =  new Array
                          (document.all["RequiredFieldValidator1"]);
      // -->
      </script>
```

```
    <script language="javascript">
    <!--
      var Page_ValidationActive = false;
      if (typeof(clientInformation) != "undefined" &&
                  clientInformation.appName.indexOf("Explorer") != -1) {
        if (typeof(Page_ValidationVer) == "undefined")
          alert("Unable to find script library
          '/aspnet_client/system_web/1_0_3215_11/WebUIValidation.js'.
          Try placing this file manually, or reinstall by running
          'aspnet_regiis -c'.");
        else if (Page_ValidationVer != "125")
          alert("This page uses an incorrect version of WebUIValidation.js.
          The page expects version 125. The script library is
          " + Page_ValidationVer + ".");
        else
          ValidatorOnLoad();
    }

    function ValidatorOnSubmit() {
        if (Page_ValidationActive) {
            ValidatorCommonOnSubmit();
        }
    }
    }
    // -->
    </script>


        </form>
      </body>
    </HTML>
```

The above HTML output (HTML 4.0) is sprinkled with JavaScript functions that enable client-side validation of the form. It is important to realize that all the JavaScript in the above code listing was dynamically created by the ASP.NET runtime.

Even though we can easily customize the HTML output generated by the ASP.NET Server Controls by using the `ClientTarget` attribute, it is important that we exercise caution and understand the implications of doing so. For example, it is not advisable to set the `ClientTarget` property to `UpLevel` unless you are sure that all the browsers using your web application will be able to support the up-level functionality.

However there might be some situations where we might want to ensure that all of our web site visitors have exactly the same experience. In that case, we must build our web site for the lowest common denominator, in other words, for a down-level browser. To accomplish this, we need to tell the ASP.NET runtime to render the pages in our web site as down-level, with HTML 3.2 and no client-side JavaScript support, by setting the `ClientTarget` attribute to `DownLevel`.

Summary

In this chapter we have understood the basics of Server Controls and the processes involved in creating them. Specifically we've covered:

❑ The role of the `HtmlTextWriter` class in Server Control creation

❑ How `HtmlTextWriter` aids in the creation of cross-compatible output to support multiple clients

❑ How to create Server Controls using the utility methods of the `HtmlTextWriter` class

We saw how to emit attributes dynamically during the rendering of a Server Control, and discussed how to add tag management and style management functionality to our controls, before taking a brief look at mobile controls. We've considered the rendering process of validation controls and understood how validation controls provide the plumbing for creating cross-browser compatible applications. Finally we looked at the browser detection capabilities supplied by ASP.NET and also realized the importance of browser detection.

Professional ASP .NET Server Controls

3

Events and Event Handling

So far we have covered creating simple controls and rendering them to the output stream so they can be sent to a client. In order to make our controls interactive, either to the user or to other classes and controls, we need to add some more functionality to them; that is where **events** come in. Events are present in all aspects of the .NET Framework and allow the developer of controls or classes to implement powerful, loosely-coupled designs. One such design that fits perfectly with events is that of an observer. Generally, when using events there will be a class, in this case our control, that raises events and other classes that are interested in knowing when these events occur. Those classes or controls interested in the events that our control will raise will register a handler for that event, which will be called when the event occurs. The control never needs to know about these "observers", it simply raises its events.

In this chapter, we will be discussing how the event model in the .NET Framework operates and then applying that knowledge to building custom Server Controls for ASP.NET. Along the way, we will be discussing how to define and create our own events, including how to define the proper event handler and custom event arguments. We will also discuss important concepts such as how to manage events when working with contained controls including when to "bubble" those events to parent controls and how to expose them as events on our own class. In addition, we will examine the handling of PostBack events and data in the context of managing our control to know when to raise events.

Events in the .NET Framework

Events in the .NET Framework are made up of three key pieces: the class that raises the event; an event handler or method that should be called when the event is raised; and a means to connect the two. We will cover each of these items and how they come together in this section.

Delegates

We will start from what may seem like the end, which is to discuss the mechanism by which events are connected to their handlers: **delegates**. A delegate is a special type in .NET whose primary purpose is to hold a reference to a method. As such, delegates are defined with a signature, much like a method, and can only hold a reference to methods that match this signature. For those developers who have used function pointers in languages such as C and C++, this will be a familiar concept. However, delegates in .NET differ significantly from pointers in two ways. Firstly, they are **object-oriented**, and, secondly, they are **type-safe**. Thus, many of the problems with pointers that have plagued developers are now eliminated.

A delegate is declared by using the special keyword "delegate" and providing the method signature for methods to which it can hold a reference. The example below defines a delegate that can hold references to methods that do not have return values and that take two parameters: an object reference to the sender and arguments of type EventArgs:

```
public delegate void EventHandler(object sender, EventArgs e);
```

A method to match this signature would look like the following:

```
public void Button_Clicked(object sender, EventArgs eArgs)
{...}
```

Delegates, in the scope of working with events, provide the mechanism for indicating to a class the method(s) to be called when an event is raised. By using delegates as pointers to the methods to be called when the event is raised, the class raising the event does not need to know anything about those classes acting as observers. It simply uses the delegate to invoke the methods on the observer.

When we declare a delegate using the syntax above, we get what is called a **Multicast Delegate**. A multicast delegate can hold references to more than one method, meaning that several observers can register for an event and all will be notified when the event is raised. The multicast delegate holds a list of the methods added to it and when invoked goes through this list to call each of the methods in order.

For events that do not provide any extra data there is a predefined delegate: EventHandler. The EventHandler delegate has the following signature:

```
void EventHandler(object sender, EventArgs e);
```

The first parameter is of type object, meaning that it will accept any type in the .NET Framework since all objects ultimately derive from object. The second argument is of type EventArgs; the built-in class to be used when an event does not have any event data. Unless an event that you are defining will be providing event data, you should use this delegate and the EventArgs class to define the signature of event handling methods.

You might be wondering why we need the EventArgs class if it does not provide any data. There are two reasons, the first being that the EventHandler delegate provides a template for other delegates, as we will see in the section on naming conventions. The second reason is that the EventArgs class, while not providing any data for the event, does serve as the base class for all custom event arguments classes.

Defining an Event

Before we can connect event handler methods to an event, we have to define an event that other objects will be interested in. To define an event, we use the `event` keyword and a delegate object that indicates the method signature that any event handlers for this event must follow:

```
public event EventHandler Click;
```

The above example defines an event named "`Click`", which uses a delegate of type `EventHandler`. This means that interested observers can be notified of the event but will not receive any event data. For example, in a click event, it might be useful to know where on the control the user clicked. In our example, that would not be possible. However, we will cover how to provide event data shortly.

We have defined our event and indicated the type of delegate it uses, thus identifying the signature of any method that wishes to listen for events on this object. However, we have yet to actually raise the event. In order to raise the event, we call the event as if it were a method, passing in the arguments that fit the signature of the event's delegate. By convention, the action of raising an event occurs in a method named OnEventName. For example, the `Click` event described above would be raised in a method named OnClick. Using this mechanism provides a clean model for raising events from within the class as well as from derived classes.

The code below provides a sample of raising an event using the method just described:

```
protected void OnClick()
{
 if(Click!=null)
 {
 Click(this, new EventArgs ());
 }
}
```

We first check to make sure there are observers for our event without which it would be `null`. Next we raise the event by calling the event as we would a method, passing in **this** reference to our control or class to indicate it as the sender of the event and a new instance of the `EventArgs` class as the second argument. Because the event is defined as an instance of the `delegate` class, this call matches the signature of the `delegate` and calls the observing methods with the arguments we have specified here.

Consuming an Event

Once an event and its corresponding delegate have been declared, an object that wishes to respond to events from the class must add an event handler for the event. An event handler is a method whose signature matches that of the delegate connected to the event. The event handler is the method called when the event it raised. In order to do this, we use the following syntax:

```
object.EventName += new DelegateType(EventHandlerMethod);
```

For the example given above, we would use the following code to add a handler to the defined click event:

```
button1.Click += new EventHandler(CustomButton_Click);

public void CustomButton_Click(object sender, EventArgs e)
{
 //handle the raised event
}
```

Notice that the method we assign as the handler, CustomButton_Click, has the same signature as the EventHandler delegate. The parameters do not have to have the same name but must have the same type and order as the delegate definition. Keep in mind that one of the strengths of the event handling framework is that the methods assigned as event handlers can be either instance methods or static methods of a class.

> There is no guarantee of the order in which handlers will be called when multiple handlers are assigned to a single event. Therefore you should not count on event handlers firing in a particular order.

Event Sample

The code below shows how all of these ideas come together. We build a simple control that defines an event using the predefined EventHandler delegate and a page that contains this control and registers a handler for the event.

> Note that this sample will not work as expected in its current form, as there is no action to raise the event. However, barring that, the event is ready to be raised and acted upon when there is cause to raise it.

This sample is available for download from the Wrox web site as EventBox.cs:

```
using System;
using System.Collections.Specialized;
using System.Web.UI;
using System.Web.UI.WebControls;
using System.ComponentModel;
using System.Text;

namespace TestEventControl
{
  public class EventBox : System.Web.UI.WebControls.WebControl
{

  //declare event named TextChanged
  public event EventHandler TextChanged;
```

```
    private string text;

    public string Text
    {
    get
    {return text;}

    set
    {text = value;}
    }

    protected override void Render(HtmlTextWriter output)
    {
    //rendering logic here
    }

    //this is the method that is used to raise the event
    public void OnTextChanged(EventArgs e)
    {
    //if we have anyone registered for our event then raise it
    if (TextChanged != null)
     TextChanged(this, e);
    }


    }
}
```

In our control we declare an event that uses the EventHandler delegate called TextChanged. We further define a method, OnTextChanged, which is used to raise the event if there are any registered listeners. What is missing is that there is no code to call the OnTextChanged method to raise the event. We will cover how and when this method should be called shortly.

This sample is available for download as WebForm1.aspx:

```
<%@ Page language="c#" AutoEventWireup="true" %>
<%@ Register TagPrefix="WROX" Namespace="TestEventControl"
Assembly="TestEventControl" %>
<!DOCTYPE HTML PUBLIC "-//W3C//DTD HTML 4.0 Transitional//EN" >
<HTML>
  <HEAD>
  <title>WebForm1</title>
  <script language="C#" runat="server">
  private void Page_Load(object sender, System.EventArgs e)
  {
  // Put user code to initialize the page here
   EventBox1.TextChanged+= new EventHandler(EventBox1_OnTextChanged);
  }

  protected void EventBox1_OnTextChanged(object sender, EventArgs e)
  {
  Message.Text = "Text Changed";
  }
```

```
    </script>
    </HEAD>
    <body>
    <form id="Form1" method="post" runat="server">
    <WROX:EventBox id="EventBox1"
      name="eventbox"
    runat="server">
    </WROX:EventBox><br>
    <asp:Button id="submitter"
      runat="server">
    </asp:Button>
    <br>
    <asp:Label id="Message"
    runat="server"
    enableviewstate="False">
    </asp:Label><br>
    </form>
    </body>
</HTML>
```

In our ASP.NET page we have registered our control namespace and added an event handler for the TextChanged event using a method that matches the assigned delegate, EventHandler in this case. In the event handler method we set the text on our label control to indicate that the event was raised. We ensure that the label updates when the event occurs by not allowing the label to maintain state between requests.

Custom EventArgs and Delegates

To this point, when discussing events, we have been using the predefined EventHandler delegate and EventArgs class. Most of the time, these classes will suffice for our custom events. There are times, however, when it makes sense to define new event arguments and new delegates to meet your needs.

For example the MouseEventArgs class defines properties that allow an event handler to determine the actions taken by the user including which mouse button was clicked and its position. Similarly, you might want to pass event-specific data to those methods acting as event handlers for your method. To do so, we simply create a new class that derives from System.EventArgs and add some properties or methods to it. For example, the code below defines a new set of event arguments for the TextChanged method seen earlier:

```
//represents the arguments passed to event handlers
//for the text changed event
public class TextChangedEventArgs:EventArgs
{
  //member variables to hold values
  protected string _newText;
  protected string _oldText;

  //default constructor
  public TextChangedEventArgs()
  {}
```

```
        //alternate constructor
        public TextChangedEventArgs(string newText, string oldText)
        {
        _newText = newText;
        _oldText = oldText;
        }

        //property accessors for both values
        public string NewText
        {
        get{return _newText;}
        }

        public string OldText
        {
        get{return _oldText;}
        }
    }
```

The TextChangedEventArgs class defines a simple object that has two properties, OldText and NewText, that will provide consumers of our event with the old text and the new text based on the change. Now that we have added this new EventArgument type, we must modify our delegate declaration to use it. We create a new delegate with a new name and the signature that allows for the new EventArgs to be passed:

```
public delegate void EventBoxEventHandler(object sender,
                                    TextChangedEventArgs e);
```

Likewise, we must update any event handler methods to match the new delegate. Because the delegate signature has changed, the event handler methods must also be changed to match this. Adding an event handler to our new delegate is shown below:

```
EventBox1.TextChanged+= new
                    EventBoxEventHandler(this.EventBox1_TextChanged);

public void EventBox1_TextChanged(object sender, TextChangedEventArgs e)
{
  //handle event
}
```

Now that we have new event arguments, we can stuff information into them that might be helpful to listeners and use the data passed on the receiving end. In our example, we pass the old and new text to the listener that can then decide what to do based on the comparison of the data. If the new data is invalid, for instance, the old data is available to use to change the value of the textbox back to its previous state. The updated web page that hosts our control is shown overleaf.

> **Note that now when we handle the event, we update a message on the client to indicate the old and new text for the control.**

This sample is available for download as `WebForm1.aspx`.

```
<%@ Page language="c#" AutoEventWireup="true" %>
<%@ Register TagPrefix="WROX" Namespace="TestEventControl"
Assembly="TestEventControl" %>
<!DOCTYPE HTML PUBLIC "-//W3C//DTD HTML 4.0 Transitional//EN" >
<html>
  <head>
  <title>WebForm1</title>
  <script language="C#" runat="server">
    private void Page_Load(object sender, System.EventArgs e)
    {
    // Put user code to initialize the page here
    EventBox1.TextChanged+= new
    EventBoxEventHandler(EventBox1_OnTextChanged);
  }

  protected void EventBox1_OnTextChanged(object sender,
                                          TextChangedEventArgs e)
  {
    Message.Text = "Text Changed from " + e.OldText + " to " +
                                            e.NewText;
  }
  </script>
  </head>
  <body>
  <form id="Form1" method="post" runat="server">
  <WROX:EventBox id="EventBox1" name="eventbox"
                            runat="server"></WROX:EventBox><br>
  <asp:Button id="submitter" runat="server"></asp:Button>
  <br>
  <asp:Label id="Message" runat="server"
                        enableviewstate="False"></asp:Label><br>
  </form>
  </body>
</html>
```

A Word About Naming

When programming within a framework, one of the helpful practices is naming conventions. Once we understand the way things are done for a particular part of the .NET Framework, for example, it is helpful to be able to use that knowledge when working with other parts of the Framework. That is why you will find that there are consistent naming patterns in many areas of .NET, and events are no different.

In general, we use the event name with a prefix or suffix to indicate the role of the item we are declaring. As an example, the MouseEventArgs mentioned earlier is very descriptive in that it helps us see that we are dealing with a class the represents arguments to an event handler that is interested in mouse events. Even more helpful is the fact that we use the MouseEventHandler along with the MouseEventArgs to handle events of this type. The consistency in naming, both within an event and throughout the Framework in regards to events, helps us in our development efforts. Opposite is a table that outlines some of the basic naming guidelines when working with events. For each, the part of the event structure is identified along with the naming pattern and an example:

Event part	Pattern	Example
Delegate	*EventName*EventHandler	`ClickEventHandler`
Event	*EventName*	`Click`
Event Raising Method	On*EventName*	`OnClick`
Event Handler	*ObjectName_EventName*	`Button1_Click`

In addition to the naming conventions listed here, it is also a convention that the delegate for events follows the pattern we have been using so far. The event handler methods should have an initial parameter of type `object` called "sender" and the secondary parameter should be a type that derives from `EventArgs` and is labeled "e". An example should help clarify:

```
public void Button1_Click(object sender, EventArgs e)
{}
```

Events in ASP.NET Controls

In order to understand when and how we call for the events in our control to be raised, it is important to first understand events in the context of ASP.NET Server Controls. ASP.NET, unlike traditional ASP provides for a rich server-side environment that is an event-driven model of programming. All controls and pages for that matter get processed on the server in the course of processing a client request. As controls are processed, a number of methods are called and events are raised. This series of events covers the entire lifetime of the control from its initialization to its destruction after the request has been processed. This Control Lifecycle was covered in Chapter 1. In terms of working with events, the phases we are most interested in involve the handling of `PostBack` events and data that will be discussed in the next section.

Postback – Responding to Events and Data

In ASP.NET a common practice is for the main server form to post back to itself. This architecture allows for cleaner code, rich state management, and, important for our purposes here, a rich event-driven page processing model that allows for continuity between requests. In order to provide for this continuity, we need a mechanism for comparing the current values with the values that were sent to the client on the previous request.

Form data is posted to the page just as it is in traditional form processing. Name-value pairs of data are sent in the body of the request. In traditional ASP and in ASP.NET we have access to this information through the `Form` object accessed via the `HttpRequest`. This same information is used in handling events on the server. The data in all form fields is passed to the server; this includes the `viewstate` field, a special field that will be discussed in the next chapter. Suffice to say here that this is an integral part of providing the user a seamless experience and used extensively in the processing of pages and controls.

In order to process the data that is posted to the page, controls need to follow certain guidelines. For those controls that need to be able to determine when their state has changed between requests, there is the `IPostBackDataHandler` interface. Controls that need to be able to examine data posted to the page and determine if that data has changed on the client implement this interface. The `IPostBackDataHandler` interface defines two methods with the following signatures:

```
public bool LoadPostData(string postDataKey, NameValueCollection postData);
public void RaisePostDataChangedEvent();
```

The `LoadPostData` method, when implemented on a control, is called to allow for examining the data posted to the page. The second parameter is a collection of values posted to the page, much like the `Form` collection. The first parameter is the key value that identifies the data for the current control. Therefore, to access the control data in the collection, we use the syntax below:

```
string newData = postData[postDataKey];
```

Within this method, we examine the value of the posted data and compare it with data that was sent to the client. If the data has changed, then we return `true`, if not, we return `false`. If the method returns `true`, then the other method defined by this interface, `RaisePostDataChangedEvent`, is called by the Framework so that the control can raise events based on the changes in the data. We also provide an implementation to the `RaisePostDataChangedEvent` method when dealing with `PostBack` so that we can raise the proper events for our control. It is within this method that we would call the `OnEvent` method to raise our events. A basic example of this is shown here:

```
public void RaisePostDataChangedEvent()
{
  OnClick();
}
```

We can now update our example textbox to raise the `OnTextChanged` event by comparing the posted data to the data that we sent to the client. If the two values are different, then we will raise the event.

The example below extends our simple event definition above. By adding support for the `IPostBackDataHandler` interface, we can check to see if the text in our textbox has changed and raise the event we defined.

This sample is available for download as `EventBox.cs`:

```
using System;
using System.Collections.Specialized;
using System.Web.UI;
using System.Web.UI.WebControls;
using System.ComponentModel;
using System.Text;

namespace TestEventControl
{
  public class EventBox : System.Web.UI.WebControls.WebControl,
                                    IPostBackDataHandler
  {
  public event EventHandler TextChanged;
```

```
private string text;

public string Text
{
get{return text;}

set{text = value;}
}

protected override void Render(HtmlTextWriter output)
 {
StringBuilder builder = new StringBuilder(100);
builder.Append("<input type=\"text\" name=\"" + this.UniqueID + "\"
                                    value=\"" + Text + "\">");
output.Write(builder.ToString());
}


//we use these methods to maintain our control text between each request
//see chapter 5 for more information on using and maintaining state
protected override object SaveViewState()
{return (object)Text;}

protected override void LoadViewState(object state)
{Text = (string)state;}

//the method of IPostBackDataHandler that gets called to allow us
//to review the data posted to the page
public bool LoadPostData(string postDataKey, NameValueCollection
postData)
{
//get the value posted and the past value
string PostedValue = postData[postDataKey];
string val = Text;

//if the value changed, then reset the value of the text property
//and return true so the appropriate event can be raised
if(PostedValue==null || val!=PostedValue)
{
Text=PostedValue;
return true;
}

//otherwise, return false to indicate that no change took place and
// no events should be raised
return false;
}

//called by the Framework if the LoadPostData method returns true
public void RaisePostDataChangedEvent()
{
//call the method to raise our event
OnTextChanged(EventArgs.Empty);
}
```

```
//the method which raises the text changed event to any listeners
public void OnTextChanged(EventArgs e)
{
//make sure we have at least one listener and then raise the event
if (TextChanged != null)
 TextChanged(this, e);
}


}
}
```

This control now raises the TextChanged event when the text in it changes. When data is posted back to the page, because we have implemented IPostBackDataHandler, we are given the opportunity to review the data posted and indicate if postback events for the control should be raised by returning true. In this case, we only have one event and one condition that would cause the event to be raised. As we will see in a later example, there are cases when we will have multiple events that may or may not get raised based on the posted data. Likewise, in the case of a control that contains, or renders, multiple child controls, there might be multiple events and multiple pieces of data to be checked.

We will look more closely at containment and event handling later in this chapter, but first it is important to understand a few key facts about the postback data handling mechanism. The postDataKey parameter passed to the LoadPostData method above is actually the Name attribute of the server control as it is rendered on the client. Thus, we can easily examine the other data posted to the page, if we know the value of the name attribute for the control whose data we want to examine. For example, a control that allowed for changing a password might have three textboxes on it, one for the old password, one for the new, and a confirmation box for the new password. On postback, we would examine the value of both the new password textbox and the confirmation textbox, to compare them and make sure they are the same. If not, then we would fire an event indicating that the passwords were not a match. In order to do this, we would access the posted data for both the password and the confirmation using the Name attribute for each.

In the following example, available for download as PasswordChange.cs, we create a simple password change control that renders three textboxes and a button. When the user chooses to change their password and posts the form, we examine the data and raise an event if the new password and the confirmation are not the same:

```
using System;
using System.Collections.Specialized;
using System.Web.UI;
using System.Web.UI.WebControls;
using System.ComponentModel;

namespace TestEventControl
{
  public class PasswordChange :
        System.Web.UI.WebControls.WebControl,IPostBackDataHandler
  {
  //definition of the event to raise when the passwords don't match
  public event EventHandler InvalidPasswordConfirmation;
```

```
//variables to hold the posted values
private string newPassword;
private string confirmPassword;

//called by the Framework if we implement IPostBackDataHandler
//and we have data posted back with a name that matches the uniqueID of
//our control
public bool LoadPostData(string postDataKey, NameValueCollection
                                                 postData)
{
//get the value for both the text boxes using their name attribute
//as the key value to the collection
newPassword = (string)postData[this.UniqueID+":newpwd"];
confirmPassword=(string)postData[this.UniqueID+":confirmpwd"];

//if the values are the same, then there is no need to raise an event
//so we return false so RaisePostDataChangedEvent won't be called
if(newPassword==confirmPassword)
  return false;
else
  return true; //values differ, so raise the event
}

//called if the previous method returns true, this method
//is where we start to raise our event
public void RaisePostDataChangedEvent()
{
OnInvalidPasswordConfirmation();
}

//this is the method that actually raises the event
public void OnInvalidPasswordConfirmation()
{
//if we have an observer, then raise the event
if(InvalidPasswordConfirmation!=null)
 InvalidPasswordConfirmation(this, new System.EventArgs());
}

// Render this control to the output parameter specified.
protected override void Render(HtmlTextWriter output)
{
//render first row including old password
output.RenderBeginTag(HtmlTextWriterTag.Table);
output.RenderBeginTag(HtmlTextWriterTag.Tr);
output.RenderBeginTag(HtmlTextWriterTag.Td);
output.Write("Old password");
output.RenderEndTag(); //end cell
output.RenderBeginTag(HtmlTextWriterTag.Td);
//we use the uniqueid of our control so that postback
//data methods get called
output.Write("<input type=\"password\" name=\"" + this.UniqueID + "\"
                                             width=\"25\">");
output.RenderEndTag(); //end cell
output.RenderEndTag(); //end row
```

```
        //render second row with the new password field
        output.RenderBeginTag(HtmlTextWriterTag.Tr);
        output.RenderBeginTag(HtmlTextWriterTag.Td);
        output.Write("New password");
        output.RenderEndTag(); //end cell
        output.RenderBeginTag(HtmlTextWriterTag.Td);
        //we give this textbox a name, using the unique id of our control,
        //that we can access in the posted data collection later
        output.Write("<input type=\"password\" name=\"" + this.UniqueID +
                                    ":newpwd\" width=\"25\">");
        output.RenderEndTag(); //end cell
        output.RenderEndTag(); //end row

        //render the confrimation box, with a unique name attribute
        //so we can access it in the postback methods
        output.RenderBeginTag(HtmlTextWriterTag.Tr);
        output.RenderBeginTag(HtmlTextWriterTag.Td);
        output.Write("Confirm password");
        output.RenderEndTag(); //end cell
        output.RenderBeginTag(HtmlTextWriterTag.Td);
        output.Write("<input type=\"password\" name=\"" + this.UniqueID +
                                    ":confirmpwd\" width=\"25\">");
        output.RenderEndTag(); //end cell
        output.RenderEndTag(); //end row

        //render a submit button so we can post the form data
        output.RenderBeginTag(HtmlTextWriterTag.Tr);
        output.AddAttribute(HtmlTextWriterAttribute.Colspan,"2");
        output.RenderBeginTag(HtmlTextWriterTag.Td);
        output.AddAttribute(HtmlTextWriterAttribute.Type,"Submit");
        output.AddAttribute(HtmlTextWriterAttribute.Value,"Change Password");
        output.RenderBeginTag(HtmlTextWriterTag.Input);
        output.RenderEndTag(); //end submit
        output.RenderEndTag(); //end cell
        output.RenderEndTag(); //end row

        output.RenderEndTag(); //end table
    }
  }
}
```

We start by defining our control class and then immediately declare our InvalidPasswordConfirmation event using the standard EventHandler delegate. Next we define two string variables to hold the values of the posted data as we work with it. Because we have declared our class as implementing the IPostBackDataHandler interface, we must provide the LoadPostData method to access the data posted by our control.

Note that we use unique names for the controls to access their data in the collection. These names are given to the controls in our render method where we concatenate the overall control name with a unique name for the individual textboxes. We then simply compare the strings to see that the values are the same. If they are not, we return true so that the RaisePostDataChangedEvent method will get called and our event can be raised.

Another way to access the posted data values for multiple contained controls is to set the name attribute for all of the textboxes to be the `UniqueID` of our control. Then, when accessing the data, we use the `postDataKey` parameter to get the data. By the nature of HTML forms, this will give us a comma-separated list of the values in the textboxes, because they share the same name. We can then use the split function on the string class to access the items. The example below shows the code we would use to extract the values of our textboxes from the `postData` collection:

```
public bool LoadPostData(string postDataKey, NameValueCollection postData)
{
  string[] values;
  values=postData[postDataKey].Split(new char[]{','});
  //skip the first one that is the main control
  newPassword=values[1];
  confirmPassword=values[2];

  //if the values are the same, then there is no need to raise an event
  //so we return false so RaisePostDataChangedEvent won't be called
  if(newPassword==confirmPassword)
    return false;
  else
    return true;//values differ, so raise the event}
```

We simply declare an array of strings and then use the split function on the returned string for our control. This provides us with an array of strings, each of which belongs to a control in the collection. The first belongs to the old password textbox so we skip that and only get the new and confirmation values. We then process them just as we did before checking for a mismatch and returning `true` if there is one.

The `IPostBackDataHandler` allows us to work with the data that is posted but there is another important interface related to postback and that is the `IPostBackEventHandler` interface. This interface defines a single method with the following signature:

```
void RaisePostBackEvent(string eventArgument);
```

Generally, when we think of forms being posted, it is due to a submit button being pressed. However, in the ASP.NET Framework, many controls actually cause the form to be posted to the server. Therefore, we need a mechanism by which we can create controls that initiate this postback, and to handle the fact that our control initiated this action. The `RaisePostBackEvent` method is called on a control if it was the control that initiated the postback. Postback is initiated either by supplying a submit button for the form, or by calling the `__doPostBack` client-side script function. This function takes as parameters the `UniqueID` of the control that is initiating the postback as well as an event argument that gets passed to the control on the server. It is this argument that serves as the single parameter to the `RaisePostBackEvent` shown above.

Like the postback data, these events can be initiated through normal HTML methods. Therefore, we can have any control, or subcontrol, initiate postback by calling the client-side script function and passing in valid values for the source and arguments. For example, we can extend our password change example by adding a new button to the output to reset the password and changing our old button to indicate that it will change the password. Each button will have a different argument so that we can differentiate which one initiated the postback.

This example is available for download as `PasswordChange.cs`:

```csharp
using System;
using System.Collections.Specialized;
using System.Web.UI;
using System.Web.UI.WebControls;
using System.ComponentModel;

namespace TestEventControl
{
  public class PasswordChange :
System.Web.UI.WebControls.WebControl,IPostBackDataHandler,
                                          IPostBackEventHandler

  {

    //definition of the event to raise when the passwords don't match
    public event EventHandler InvalidPasswordConfirmation;

    //definition of the event to raise
    //when the user has indicated a reset
    public event EventHandler ResetPassword;

    //variables to hold the posted values
    private string newPassword;
    private string confirmPassword;


    . . .

    {
    //if we have an observer, then raise the event
    if(InvalidPasswordConfirmation!=null)
      InvalidPasswordConfirmation(this, new System.EventArgs());

    }

    //called because we implement IPostBackEventHandler
    //the argument is passed from the client script
    public void RaisePostBackEvent(string eventArgument)
    {
    //if the argument is the reset argument, then
    //raise the event to indicate this.
    if(eventArgument=="Reset")
     OnResetPassword();
    }

    //raise the reset password event
    protected void OnResetPassword()
    {
    if(ResetPassword!=null)
     ResetPassword(this, new EventArgs());
    }
```

```
// Render this control to the output parameter specified.
protected override void Render(HtmlTextWriter output)
{
//render first row including old password
output.RenderBeginTag(HtmlTextWriterTag.Table);
output.RenderBeginTag(HtmlTextWriterTag.Tr);
output.RenderBeginTag(HtmlTextWriterTag.Td);
output.Write("Old password");
output.RenderEndTag(); //end cell
output.RenderBeginTag(HtmlTextWriterTag.Td);

...

//add a client side click handler that calls the postback
//method on the client passing in an argument
//this argument is what gets passed to the RaisePostBackEvent
//method when the form is posted. We use the uniqueID
//of our control so that it has its method called.
output.AddAttribute(HtmlTextWriterAttribute.Onclick,
Page.GetPostBackEventReference(this, "Change"));
output.RenderBeginTag(HtmlTextWriterTag.Button);
output.Write("Change Password");
output.RenderEndTag(); //end button
output.RenderEndTag(); //end cell

//render the button to indicate a reset
//we pass in a different argument this time
//so we can discrimate between the two clicks
output.RenderBeginTag(HtmlTextWriterTag.Td);
output.AddAttribute(HtmlTextWriterAttribute.Onclick,
Page.GetPostBackEventReference(this,"Reset"));
output.RenderBeginTag(HtmlTextWriterTag.Button);
output.Write("Reset Password");
output.RenderEndTag(); //end button
output.RenderEndTag(); //end cell
output.RenderEndTag(); //end row

output.RenderEndTag(); //end table

}
}
}
```

To extend our control we have added a definition for a new event, ResetPassword, and created the OnResetPassword method that raises this event when it is called. We have also implemented the IPostBackEventHandler and provided the implementation for the RaisePostBackEvent method. In this method we do a check of the eventArgument parameter to see if it indicates a reset, and if so, call the OnResetPassword method to raise our event. The eventArgument is set in our render method where we create the reset button and the change password button. For each of the buttons we have defined a client-side OnClick event that calls the _doPostBack client-side function to initiate postback of the form. This client-side method takes as its parameters the source or target of the event and an argument. In our rendering method we define the argument based on the button that we are rendering. In this way, we can discriminate which control initiated the postback and act accordingly. In this case, we only call the OnResetPassword method when the argument is "Reset".

The two different `PostBack` interfaces provide for identifying, and therefore raising, different types of events. The `IPostBackDataHandler` interface provides for working with events related to changed data in the control, while the `IPostBackEventHandler` allows for working with events caused by an action on the control that resulted in the page being posted back. Simple examples would be that a `TextBox` control would use the `IPostBackDataHandler` interface to be able to examine the text property and see if it had changed, while a button control would implement the `IPostBackEventHandler` to react to a user clicking on it. The interface you use will depend on the functionality of the control you are creating. In some cases both of these interfaces may be used in a single control as in our previous example.

One very important fact to keep in mind when designing your control for postback is the mechanism by which the methods of the two interfaces we have discussed get called. When a form is posted to the server, the Framework examines the fields posted and looks for controls whose `UniqueID` matches the name of the field and which implement the `IPostBackDataHandler` interface. Therefore, in order for a control to receive postback data, its name attribute must match its `UniqueID`. For the `IPostBackEventHandler` interface, the `UniqueID` of your control must be specified in the `_eventtarget` form field. This is usually accomplished using the `_doPostback` client side script function.

Inheritance and Containment

As described in earlier chapters, we have a few options when creating Server Controls. We can write a custom control that handles all of its own rendering, derive from an existing control, or use our control as a container for existing controls. Each of these situations involves unique handling of events. When dealing with custom controls we must define our events and determine what causes them to be raised as well as make decisions on whether to use custom delegates and event arguments. When working with controls that derive from an existing control, we have to determine how to handle events that are defined on the base class. And, finally, when working with contained controls, we have to figure out how to handle events that are raised by those contained controls. We have already covered events in a custom, self-rendering control so we will focus on the other two situations in this section.

Handling Events in Base Controls

One of the great new benefits of working with ASP.NET is its object-oriented development capabilities. Even when we don't think much about it, we use the power of inheritance any time we create an ASP.NET page or control. When working with events in inherited controls, we handle the events defined in a base class a bit differently from how we do an event in the derived class or a contained class. Because we are inheriting from a base class, our control has access to any protected members in the base class. For this reason, and in keeping with the design patterns in .NET and object-oriented programming, when we want to handle events that are defined in the base class, we do not do it by hooking up event handlers.

Instead, we override the method that is used to raise the event: the `OnEventName` method. By overriding this method, we are following good practice for object-oriented design and truly taking advantage of the power that comes along with such capabilities. In addition, it makes for a cleaner implementation since we don't know what other listeners will attach to the event and in what order they will be called. By overriding this method, when our class or the base class calls this method to raise events, our base class will have the opportunity to manage this process. Therefore, if we need or want to make changes to our object before the event is raised, we could do so in this method. Similarly, we have the opportunity to do screening on the object. If we do not want to raise the event, based on some condition in our derived class, then we can choose not to call the base classe's implementation of this method.

With all that being said, the most common implementation of this type of situation is to do any work necessary in the derived class and then make a call to the base class implementation of the *OnEventName* method. For example, we might want to ensure that a particular field is not `null` or that our child controls have been created before calling into the base class implementation of the method. This allows us to ready our control not only for the base class and the raising of the event, but also for the actions that may be taken by the various event handlers that are observing our class for this event.

For example, the code below shows a typical implementation of this type of behavior. We first make sure our derived control is completely ready and instantiated before calling for the event to be raised:

```
protected override void OnTextChanged(EventArgs e)
{
   this.EnsureChildControls();
   base.OnTextChanged(e);
}
```

While many of the controls that ship with the .NET Framework do not allow developers to override their events, it is possible to declare our events as virtual and allow them to be overridden just as methods can be. In this way, a base class can override the method entirely and hide the event in the base class. However, as mentioned, many of the base classes do not allow this, so if we want to create a control that has the same event but with a different delegate and `EventArgs` implementation, we have to call it something different and implement it apart from the one defined in the base class.

Events in Contained Controls

In most of our previous examples we have used rendering as opposed to composition for our complex controls. While rendering provides for greater performance than containment, it also takes a good deal more work to get the functionality we need. When dealing with events, containment brings with it some special considerations.

Contained controls often expose events of their own and it is the work of the control developer to determine how, or if, to handle these events. There are two ways to "capture" events from contained controls. The first is to use the methods we learned about earlier in the chapter to create an event handler and connect it to the event using a delegate. The second, that will be covered shortly, is handling bubbled events.

When a control is contained in our custom control, it is fairly straightforward to create an event handler to be called when the event is raised. Once that event is raised and captured, we have several options on how our control will react. We can expose the same event as a top-level event on our control and simply pass the call along to our own *OnEventName* method to raise the event at the top level. Or, we can use this event internal to our control, not raising an event from our control, to alter the state or operation of our control. Finally, we can expose another event on our control, possibly with a custom delegate and event arguments, that gets raised when the internal event is raised. Any combination of these solutions might also be possible. For example, the raising of an internal control's event might cause us to change our state and then raise an event of our own.

Because an internal control is not directly accessible by a consumer of our control, if the events raised by the contained controls are not raised as top-level events on the parent control, then the events on that class are partially hidden. Only partially because the consumer of the control could do some analysis of our control and, via the Controls collection, gain access to the contained control in order to assign event handlers directly. This would not generally be good practice as it breaks encapsulation and if, as the designer of the control, we decide to move to rendering versus composition, for example, the use of our control would break the consumer's application.

In the example below, available for download as PasswordChangeComposite.cs, we have recreated our Password Change control using containment and handling the events of the child control rather than using the IPostBackDataHandler and IPostBackEventHandler interfaces. We use the events on the buttons to raise our own events based on the values of our controls:

```
public event EventHandler InvalidPasswordConfirmation;
public event EventHandler ResetPassword;


//local variables for textboxes we need to compare
protected TextBox oldPwd;
protected TextBox newPwd;
protected TextBox confirmPwd;


//raise invalid password confirmation event
public void OnInvalidPasswordConfirmation()
{
if(InvalidPasswordConfirmation!=null)
  InvalidPasswordConfirmation(this, EventArgs.Empty);
}


//raise password reset event
public void OnResetPassword()
{
if(ResetPassword!=null)
{
  ResetPassword(this, EventArgs.Empty);
}
}
```

```
protected override void CreateChildControls()
  {
//start control table
Controls.Add(new LiteralControl("<table><tr><td>Old
Password</td><td>"));

//add text box for old password
oldPwd = new TextBox();
oldPwd.Width = new Unit(15, UnitType.Em);
oldPwd.TextMode=TextBoxMode.Password;
Controls.Add(oldPwd);
```

```
//add new password textbox
Controls.Add(new LiteralControl("</td></tr><tr><td>New
password</td><td>"));
newPwd = new TextBox();
newPwd.Width = new Unit(15,UnitType.Em);
newPwd.TextMode=TextBoxMode.Password;
Controls.Add(newPwd);

//add cofirm password textbox
Controls.Add(new
LiteralControl("</td></tr><tr><td>Confirm</td><td>"));
confirmPwd = new TextBox();
confirmPwd.Width = new Unit(15, UnitType.Em);
confirmPwd.TextMode = TextBoxMode.Password;
Controls.Add(confirmPwd);

//add submit button
Controls.Add(new LiteralControl("</td></tr><tr><td>"));
Button submit = new Button();
submit.Text = "Change Password";
Controls.Add(submit);

//add event handler for submit button
submit.Click+=new EventHandler(this.submit_Click);

//add reset button
Controls.Add(new LiteralControl("</td><td>"));
Button reset = new Button();
reset.Text="Reset Password";
Controls.Add(reset);

//add event handler for reset button
reset.Click+=new EventHandler(this.reset_Click);

Controls.Add(new LiteralControl("</td></tr></table>"));
}

//event handler for submit button click
protected void submit_Click(object sender, EventArgs e)
{
//if the passwords don't match, then raise the exposed event
if(newPwd.Text!=confirmPwd.Text)
{
  OnInvalidPasswordConfirmation();
}
}

//local event handler for reset button click event
protected void reset_Click(object sender, EventArgs e)
{
//call our exposed event
OnResetPassword();
}
}
}
```

95

The first thing to notice is that our control now implements the INamingContainer interface. This interface acts as a marker interface, meaning that it does not define any specific methods or other members that need to be implemented but is simply used to mark a class for certain actions. In the case of INamingContainer, those actions include the creation of a naming container with our control as the parent. This causes all of the contained controls to have their name attributes modified to include the name of the parent control. This naming structure allows the Framework to correctly identify the controls and their parents in order to create the control hierarchy on the server. Without this interface declaration on our control, the handlers for the events will not be properly initialized and our control will not work as expected.

> The **INamingContainer** interface must be implemented on your control when using containment and listening for events on child controls.

We create class level variables to refer to the textboxes in our control so that we can refer to them in all of our methods. We then override the CreateChildControls method, instead of the Render method used when directly rendering, and create our control structure. We use LiteralControl objects for all of the table tags and add our textbox controls to the Controls collection at the appropriate location. In addition, this is the point at which we attach our event handlers for the click events of the two buttons.

Finally, we define the event handlers for the click events on the buttons and act accordingly when the event is raised. For the Reset button, we raise our ResetPassword event and for the submit button's click event we compare the values of the new and confirm passwords and raise the InvalidPasswordConfirmation event if the two do not match.

This example has shown how we can observe the events of our contained controls and expose those events as different top-level events on our control. We could just as easily have identified a Click event on our control and raised that event when any of the buttons were clicked. Additionally, we could have modified the CommandEventArgs that would be exposed through our top-level event. Likewise, we could have used the event information to change some variables and exposed the new values of the contained controls rather than raising an event from our control.

Bubbling Events

The methodology for handling events on contained controls works fine if you have a few well defined controls, but gets complicated when dealing with complex control scenarios. For example when building data-bound or templated data-bound controls, the number of controls that may raise events can get extremely large. It is neither efficient nor easy to manage all of the events in which we might be interested in this type of situation. That is where event bubbling becomes a very important mechanism to understand.

Event bubbling is the notion of sending an event up the control hierarchy so that parent controls can examine the event and act upon it if they wish. At any time in the chain, a control can handle the event and cancel the bubbling. In order for an event to be bubbled, a control must explicitly bubble the event. We will examine how a control bubbles an event and how to capture and act on these events in this section.

The base control class for web controls, `System.Web.UI.Control`, defines two methods that comprise the mechanics of event bubbling. The two methods and their syntax are described in the following table:

Method	Description	Syntax
RaiseBubbleEvent	Called to send an event up the control hierarchy to its naming container	`protected void RaiseBubbleEvent(object sender, EventArgs e);`
OnBubbleEvent	Overriden to capture events bubbled up from child controls	`protected bool OnBubbleEvent(object sender, EventArgs e);`

When designing a control that should bubble its events up to parent controls, use the `RaiseBubbleEvent` method passing in the source of the event and the event arguments. Keep in mind that because we derive our custom event arguments from the base `EventArgs` class, we can pass any derived class of event arguments to this method. In fact, passing a custom event arguments object is the most useful way to use bubbled events, as there is no other indicator of the actual event that has taken place.

In the control or page that wishes to examine bubbled events we override the `OnBubbleEvent` method to receive notification of bubbled events. In this method, the most common actions are to examine the event arguments to find out what type they are, and thus the event type that raised them, and evaluate the contents of the arguments to determine what actions to take.

The `OnBubbleEvent` method has a `Boolean` return value. The value returned indicates whether the bubbled event was handled. Therefore, a control can handle certain events as they are bubbled and allow other events to continue up the control hierarchy. For example, we might be interested in Command Events fired by the contained controls so we could handle those events and return `true` to indicate that the event has been handled while for other events we would return `false` so that the event will continue to bubble.

Essentially, when calling `RaiseBubbleEvent`, the control's parent is found and the `OnBubbleEvent` method is called on the parent control passing along the arguments that were indicated in the `RaiseBubbleEvent` method.

In the following example we modify our password change control to use event bubbling instead of directly hooking up event handlers to the click events of the buttons:

```
//raise invalid password confirmation event
public void OnInvalidPasswordConfirmation()
{
if(InvalidPasswordConfirmation!=null)
  InvalidPasswordConfirmation(this, EventArgs.Empty);
}

protected override bool OnBubbleEvent(object sender, EventArgs e)
{
//make sure it is a command event
if(e is CommandEventArgs)
{
```

```
    //check the command name to determine if //we should
    //raise event
  if(((CommandEventArgs)e).CommandName=="Change")
    {
    if(newPwd.Text!=confirmPwd.Text)
    {
      OnInvalidPasswordConfirmation();
    }
  }
  else if(((CommandEventArgs)e).CommandName=="Reset")
  {
    OnResetPassword();
  }
  //stop events from children from bubbling up
  return true;
  }
  }

  //raise password reset event
  public void OnResetPassword()
  {
  if(ResetPassword!=null)
  {
    ResetPassword(this, EventArgs.Empty);
  }
  }
. . .
```

By overriding the OnBubbleEvent method we remove the need to provide explicit event handlers for the click events of each of the buttons. In the OnBubbleEvent method we examine the event arguments to see if it is an instance of the CommandEventArgs class. If so, we use the CommandName member of the event arguments to determine whether we should raise an event.

As stated before, the event bubbling mechanism makes it much easier to handle events from child controls when dealing with data-bound controls or other extremely complex controls. As we will see in upcoming chapters, when using templating and data binding it can get difficult or unwieldy to manage the events in the child controls and assign event handlers to them. However, when working with discrete simple controls, the standard event handling framework is sufficient and cleaner to implement.

Shopping Cart Loader

We'll finish off this chapter with a sample control that brings together the concepts we have been talking about. The control is a shopping cart loader that provides two functions. The first is that it can be rendered as a button on a product page to add the item to the shopping cart. Secondly, the control can be rendered on a shopping cart display page to allow for updating the number of items or removing the item from the cart.

We start with namespace declarations for the control including the
`System.Collections.Specialized` namespace where the `NameValueCollection` class resides.
This is necessary for the `LoadPostData` method's `postData` parameter. Next we define an
enumeration that will allow a consumer of our control to identify whether it is located on a product
page and should just show the "**Add to cart**" button, or if it is on a shopping cart page and should show
the textbox and buttons for updating or removing the item. Finally, in this section, we define a delegate
that uses a custom event arguments class that we'll define next.

This sample is available for download as `CartLoader.cs`:

```
using System;
using System.Collections.Specialized; //for name value collection class
using System.Web.UI;
using System.Web.UI.WebControls;
using System.ComponentModel;

namespace TestEventControl
{
  //define an enumeration for the mode or type
  //of our control
  public enum LoaderType{DetailLoader, CartLoader};

  //define a new delegate that uses
  //our custome CartLoaderEventArgs class defined below
  public delegate void CartLoaderEventHandler(object sender,
                                              CartLoaderEventArgs e);
```

The next step is to define our custom event arguments class. We want this class to be able to represent the
important information that a consumer of our class might be interested in when the event fires. In this case,
that information is going to include the product number, for saving to a database or otherwise adding to a
shopping cart, and the number of items. We provide constructors for our class that allow for initializing the
product number alone or the product number and the item count for easier construction of the arguments:

```
//cart loader event arguments class
//which provides access to the product #
//and the number of items
public class CartLoaderEventArgs:EventArgs
{
//instance variables
private int _itemCount;
private string _productNumber;

//default constructor
public CartLoaderEventArgs()
{}

//alternate constructor
public CartLoaderEventArgs(string ProductNumber)
{
```

```
_itemCount = 0;
_productNumber = ProductNumber;
}

//alternate constructor
public CartLoaderEventArgs(string ProductNumber, int NumberOfItems)
{
_itemCount = NumberOfItems;
_productNumber = ProductNumber;


}

//property accessors
public string ProductNumber
{
get{return _productNumber;}
set{_productNumber = value;}
}

public int NumberOfItems
{
get{return _itemCount;}
set{_itemCount=value;}
}
}
```

Now it is time to define the control itself. We start by deriving from `WebControl` and implementing the `IPostBackDataHandler` and `IPostBackEventHandler` interfaces so that we can appropriately deal with postback data and events. We define three events that use the delegate we defined above to alert a consumer when the user chooses to add, remove, or update the product associated with the control. Properties for the product number, item count, and the mode of the control are defined next along with accessors for each. The mode is one of our enumerated values to indicate how we should render the control:

```
//control class which implements the post back
//interfaces
public class CartLoader : System.Web.UI.WebControls.WebControl,
IPostBackEventHandler,
IPostBackDataHandler
{

//event declarations
public event CartLoaderEventHandler ItemAdded;
public event CartLoaderEventHandler ItemUpdated;
public event CartLoaderEventHandler ItemRemoved;

//private member variables
//default to detail loader
private LoaderType _location=LoaderType.DetailLoader;
private string _productID;
private int _itemCount;
```

```
//property accessors
public LoaderType Location
{
get{return _location;}
set{_location=value;}
}

public string ProductID
{
get{return _productID;}
set{_productID = value;}
}

public int ItemCount
{
get{return _itemCount;}
set{_itemCount=value;}
}
```

Once we have the properties and the events defined, we need methods to raise the events so we provide each of the OnEventName methods. In each we make sure the event has observers and then raise the event passing in the product ID to each. For the ItemAdded and ItemUpdated we also pass the item count so the consumer has access to it. However, because when an item is removed there will be no count; we simply pass the product number:

```
//event raising methods
protected void OnItemAdded()
{
if(ItemAdded!=null)
  ItemAdded(this, new CartLoaderEventArgs(_productID, _itemCount));
}

protected void OnItemUpdated()
{
if(ItemUpdated!=null)
  ItemUpdated(this,new CartLoaderEventArgs(_productID, _itemCount));
}

protected void OnItemRemoved()
{
if(ItemRemoved!=null)
  ItemRemoved(this, new CartLoaderEventArgs(_productID));
}
```

Next we implement the methods defined by the postback interfaces. In the LoadPostData method we extract the item count from the textbox posted and check it against the count that was sent with the control to the client. If the two are different, we know that the user has updated the count so we raise the ItemUpdated event and update the item count to match the posted value. Note that this method will only get called when a form element with a name attribute matching the unique ID of our control is posted. Because our control only renders the textbox when in CartLoader mode, this method will only get called when we are in that mode.

We also handle events initiated on the client by our control. As we will see, in the render method we indicate that each button will initiate postback of the form. We check the event argument passed to the method in order to determine which button initiated postback and to act accordingly. If it was the remove button, then we reset the count to zero and raise the `ItemRemoved` event. Likewise, if the add button was clicked, we increment the count by 1 and raise the `ItemAdded` event:

```
//implemented to load the data in the text box
public bool LoadPostData(string postDataKey, NameValueCollection postData)
{
  //get the posted value and compare with the
  //old value. If different, then raise update
  //event and update item count property
  int count = Int32.Parse(postData[postDataKey]);
  if(_itemCount!=count)
  {
    _itemCount=count;
    return true;
  }
  else
    return false;
}


  //called if the data changed and the
  //previous method returned true
  public void RaisePostDataChangedEvent()
  {
    OnItemUpdated ();
  }


  //called if this control initiates postback
  //i.e. one of the buttons is clicked
  public void RaisePostBackEvent(string eventArgument)
  {
  //check event argument and raise the appropriate
  //event for the command
  if(eventArgument=="AddToCart")
  {
    OnItemAdded();
    _itemCount++; //increment count since adding
  }
  else if(eventArgument=="RemoveFromCart")
  {
    OnItemRemoved();
    _itemCount=0; //removed to reset to 0
  }
}
```

Finally, we render the control based on the mode or location of the control. If the control is located on a detail page, we simply render a `DIV` tag with style to make it appear as a button and connect its click event with the postback method on the client. If the control is on a shopping cart list then we render a textbox with the item count as its value and two buttons, a remove and an update, that initiate postback:

```csharp
//render the control to the output
protected override void Render(HtmlTextWriter output)
{
  //if the control is in detail mode, render
  //a single button to add it to the cart
  if(_location==LoaderType.DetailLoader)
  {
    output.AddAttribute(
            HtmlTextWriterAttribute.Onclick,Page.GetPostBackEventReference(
                                              this,"AddToCart"));
    output.AddAttribute(HtmlTextWriterAttribute.Style,
              "Display:inline;BORDER-RIGHT: gray thin outset; BORDER-TOP:
              gray thin outset; BORDER-LEFT: gray thin outset; CURSOR:
              hand; BORDER-BOTTOM: gray thin outset; FONT-FAMILY: 'Comic
              Sans MS'; BACKGROUND-COLOR: lightgrey");
    output.RenderBeginTag(HtmlTextWriterTag.Div);
    output.Write("Add to cart");
    output.RenderEndTag();
  }
  else //we are on a cart detail so display
    //two buttons and text box
  {
    //output textbox with item count in it
    output.AddAttribute(HtmlTextWriterAttribute.Width,"5");
    output.AddAttribute(HtmlTextWriterAttribute.Name,UniqueID);
    output.AddAttribute(
                HtmlTextWriterAttribute.Value, _itemCount.ToString());
    output.RenderBeginTag(HtmlTextWriterTag.Input);
    output.RenderEndTag();

    //render remove button
    output.AddAttribute(HtmlTextWriterAttribute.Style, "Display:inline;
                BORDER-RIGHT: gray thin outset; BORDER-TOP: gray thin
                outset; BORDER-LEFT: gray thin outset; CURSOR: hand;
                BORDER-BOTTOM: gray thin outset; FONT-FAMILY: 'Comic
                Sans MS'; BACKGROUND-COLOR: lightgrey");
    output.AddAttribute(
                HtmlTextWriterAttribute.Onclick,
                Page.GetPostBackEventReference(this,"RemoveFromCart"));
    output.RenderBeginTag(HtmlTextWriterTag.Div);
    output.Write("Remove");
    output.RenderEndTag();

    //render update button
    output.AddAttribute(HtmlTextWriterAttribute.Style, "Display:inline;
                BORDER-RIGHT: gray thin outset; BORDER-TOP: gray thin
                outset; BORDER-LEFT: gray thin outset; CURSOR: hand;
                BORDER-BOTTOM: gray thin outset; FONT-FAMILY: 'Comic
                Sans MS'; BACKGROUND-COLOR: lightgrey");
    output.AddAttribute(HtmlTextWriterAttribute.Onclick,
                            Page.GetPostBackEventReference(this,""));
    output.RenderBeginTag(HtmlTextWriterTag.Div);
    output.Write("Update");
    output.RenderEndTag();
  }
}
```

```
  //these methods are used to maintain the item count
  //property and discussed elsewhere in the book
  protected override object SaveViewState()
  {
    return (object)_itemCount;
  }

  protected override void LoadViewState(object state)
  {
    _itemCount = (int)state;
  }
 }
 }
```

To use the Server Control, we would include it on a `form`, set its mode and product number and, optionally, an initial number of items. We would then connect event handlers to the events we have defined and use the event data to perform a useful action, such as update the shopping cart in a database or other storage location. The page shown below (available for download as `ProductDetail.aspx`) shows the control being used in both modes with the appropriate event handlers connected. In this case we simply update a label rather than providing an implementation to manage the shopping cart:

```
<%@ Register TagPrefix="WROX" Namespace="TestEventControl"
Assembly="TestEventControl" %>
<%@ Page language="c#" Codebehind="ProductDetail.aspx.cs" AutoEventWireup="true"%>
<!DOCTYPE HTML PUBLIC "-//W3C//DTD HTML 4.0 Transitional//EN" >
<HTML>
  <HEAD>
  <title>ProductDetail</title>

  <script language="C#" runat="server">
  public void Page_Load(object sender, EventArgs e)
  {
    loader.ItemAdded+=new CartLoaderEventHandler(loader_ItemAdded);
    loader2.ItemUpdated+=new CartLoaderEventHandler(loader2_ItemUpdated);
    loader2.ItemRemoved+=new CartLoaderEventHandler(loader2_ItemRemoved);
  }

  public void loader_ItemAdded(object sender, CartLoaderEventArgs e)
  {
    Message.Text = "Product " + e.ProductNumber + " added to cart";
  }

  public void loader2_ItemUpdated(object sender, CartLoaderEventArgs e)
  {
    Message.Text = "Product " + e.ProductNumber + " updated to " +
                                          e.NumberOfItems;
  }

  public void loader2_ItemRemoved(object sender, CartLoaderEventArgs e)
  {
    Message.Text = "Product " + e.ProductNumber + " removed from cart";
  }
```

```
    </script>
  </HEAD>

    <body MS_POSITIONING="GridLayout">

    <form id="ProductDetail" method="post" runat="server">
    <WROX:CartLoader id="loader"
      ProductID="WROX01"
      Location="DetailLoader"
      runat="server">

    </WROX:CartLoader><br><br>
    <WROX:CartLoader id="loader2"
      ProductID="WROX02"
      Location="CartLoader"
      runat="server">

    </WROX:CartLoader><br><br>
      <asp:Label id="Message"
      enableviewstate="False"
      runat="server">

    </asp:Label>
    </form>

    </body>
  </HTML>
```

Summary

In this chapter we have learned about the event Framework in .NET and how it applies to Server Controls. Specifically, we have covered the following:

❑   Delegates including how to declare them and their purpose

❑   Events and how to declare and raise them

❑   Event Arguments and how to create our own custom event arguments to be used with our events and custom delegates

❑   Postback events and data in the scope of Server Controls and how we can use these mechanisms to raise our own events

❑   How to work with derived and contained controls to provide the best interface to consumers of our control

Professional ASP .NET Server Controls

4

Managing State

Managing state within a server control is not the same process as managing state within a web form application with familiar state objects such as the `Application` or `Session` object. The application and session state objects provided by ASP.NET allow a web form application to persist data across many page requests. The goal of maintaining state in a server control is to persist a server control's properties across many postback events.

A postback event is fired when a web form posts or sends form data back to itself, hence the term postback. Postback is a technique used by server controls to handle events raised by the form controls it rendered. There is a new tool provided by ASP.NET that takes advantage of postback events to send state data back to a server control on each postback event; the new tool is called ViewState.

In this chapter, we are going to explore two ways that a server control can access state information. First, we will see how to use ViewState to persist state data across postback events. Then we will look at accessing state data held within the web form application it may be running in.

Specifically, the topics we'll look at in this chapter are:

❑ Introduction To ViewState

❑ Mechanics of ViewState

❑ ViewState with Simple Controls

❑ ViewState with Composite Controls

❑ Control Class Properties and Methods Affecting ViewState

❑ ViewState and Performance

❑ ViewState and Security

❑ Accessing Application and Session State Variables

By the end of this chapter you should be able to use ViewState effectively to maintain state within a server control and access the application and session scope variables when applicable.

Introduction to ViewState

The .NET forums are alive with comments such as "What is this ViewState thing showing up in my HTML source?" and "If I disable ViewState will it eat my house plants?" To begin this chapter, we are going to demystify ViewState by explaining what it is and how it works:

A New Spin on an Old Ally

There is nothing groundbreaking about ViewState once you understand what it is doing. ViewState is the persistence of a server control's property values across postback events. ViewState is instance of the `StateBag` class, and stores name-value pairs, which store the values of a server control's properties during a postback, such as `LightIsOn=False`. Server controls can read and write their property values to ViewState during execution. Near the end of a server control's execution lifecycle, which we will see shortly, the information contained in the ViewState `StateBag` is written to the client computer as an HTML hidden form control called __VIEWSTATE.

Upon postback, the information is read from the __VIEWSTATE hidden form control and the server control's properties are populated once again by ViewState name-value pairs.

ViewState takes advantage of an old technique, hidden form fields, and automates a process that web developers have been doing manually for years. The string written to the client machine in the form control, __VIEWSTATE looks like the code example below.

```
<input type="hidden" name="__VIEWSTATE" value="dDw2MDk5MTE2MDk7Oz4=" />
```

This code was generated by ViewState for a form control we will build shortly. While we discuss ViewState within this chapter we will refer to it in three contexts. First, ViewState refers to the conceptual idea of ViewState. Second, the term ViewState refers to the actual `StateBag` object itself. Third, __VIEWSTATE refers to the hidden form field written to client-side HTML code by ViewState. Without further ado, let's begin to explore ViewState and how it works more closely.

Mechanics of ViewState

ViewState is a property of the Control Class. As you have learned, all server controls are derived from either the `Control` or `WebControl` class, making ViewState an inherited property of these two classes, since `WebControl` derives from `Control`. The `ViewState` property is a dictionary object of the `State` class type, allowing it to hold information in name-value pairs. Dictionary data types make retrieving and setting values in ViewState easy to do because you can reference the value by a readable name such as `FirstName = Value`. To use ViewState, you create properties on a server control that reference ViewState values in their `get` and `set` methods, which load ViewState data into the property. There are exceptions to this statement, however, in that you can manually control how ViewState data is loaded by overriding specific methods – we will introduce you to this concept in a moment. Within this chapter, however, all the examples will use properties to `get` and `set` values directly from the ViewState `StateBag`.

There are two processes that make ViewState work: postback and the server control execution lifecycle. Postback as you know, occurs when the form submits data back to itself. The server control's execution lifecycle contains various steps, which examine the data sent by a postback event and load it appropriately for use by the server control. We will look at both processes separately to see how they ultimately work together.

PostBack Data

By now, you should have a firm grasp of what a postback event is, so we will only spend a few moments on this topic. When a server control is executed for the first time, `__VIEWSTATE` contains only default information about the server control and no information necessarily on ViewState persisted properties. Quite frequently, the default values of a server control are empty or `null`, such as in the case of a `TextBox` control without a value in its `Text` property. Upon postback, any values the user entered into the form are stored in ViewState and available to the server control. Upon subsequent postback events, the server control's property state during the previous postback is available in ViewState. This allows a server control to monitor what its previous state was before the postback event it is currently handling occurred. The flow chart below shows an example of how data is handled during postback by ViewState:

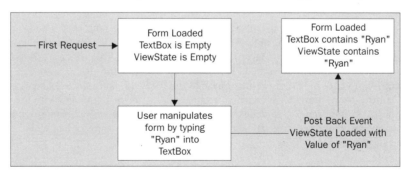

Server Control Execution Lifecycle:

You probably noticed in the flow chart above that the data within the TextBox is loaded into ViewState during the postback process. This is due to the execution cycle of the server control itself. There are two phases during the control's execution lifecycle when the ViewState property is loaded and saved: the **Load ViewState** and **Save ViewState** phases. To understand where these two phases fall into place, we will review the execution lifecycle of a server control briefly. In this section, we will only pay detailed attention to the two phases that affect a server control; for a detailed look at the entire execution lifecycle, see Chapter 1. As a refresher, however, the graphic below illustrates the entire server control execution lifecycle; the two phases we will discuss in detail are titled in bold:

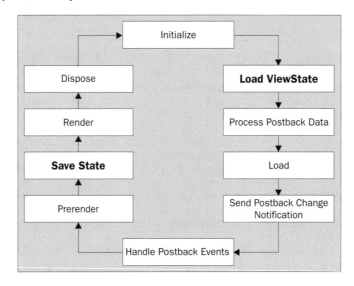

Load ViewState Execution Phase

The Load ViewState phase of a control's lifecycle is marked by the LoadViewState() method of the Control class. This method is responsible for populating the ViewState property bag with the name-value data pairs submitted with the __VIEWSTATE hidden form field. This process is automatic; unless you need to specifically change the way data is read to and written from the ViewState property, nothing is required of your control to fire this phase of the lifecycle. During the LoadViewState() phase, server control properties that get and set from ViewState are populated with the values that match the name index the property specifies. Populating properties from ViewState is automatically done for any property, which receives its data from the ViewState property bag when LoadViewState() is not overridden.

Save State Execution Phase

This phase works with the LoadViewState() method and is marked by the method SaveViewState(). This method is an opportunity to save any changes made in the server control's state during execution prior to writing the __VIEWSTATE hidden form control. This method also gives you an opportunity to write custom data types to __VIEWSTATE if required or simply to control the values saved to ViewState to improve performance.

To summarize, overriding the `LoadViewState()` and `SaveViewState()` methods allows you to customize the way state is created, managed, and saved within a specific server control. You will learn how to override and use `LoadViewState()` and `SaveViewState()` methods in Chapter 6. If you do not override these methods, ViewState will be saved and loaded automatically, loading the proper values in your server control automatically as explained in the Load ViewState Execution Phase section above.

Data Types Supported by ViewState

ViewState stores data on the client in a Base64-encoded format. This means any data written to a ViewState `StateBag` object must be able to serialize to Base64 format. By default, ViewState contains filters to serialize only a handful of data types, which are:

- ❑ `String`
- ❑ `Integer`
- ❑ `Boolean`
- ❑ `Array`
- ❑ `ArrayList`
- ❑ `HashTable`

If you need to store a different type of data object you must write a custom Type Converter to serialize its data.

ViewState in a Clustered Environment

Any developer who has written an application that requires state has dealt with the problem of persisting state in a clustered environment such as a web farm. ViewState writes state information to the `__VIEWSTATE` hidden form field, which in turn is sent back to the server during a postback event. Each server in a web farm should have the same code base, which means the same server control will be on each server. The state data sent back to the web farm by ViewState during postback can be processed the same way regardless of which server handles the request.

ViewState Compared to Other State Tools

As you can see already, ViewState was born to help server controls maintain state across post-back events. But in regards to maintaining state, there are other tools available, which web developers have long used to maintain form control and variable or property state across postbacks as well. In this section we will look at some competitors to ViewState.

ViewState vs. the HTML Hidden Form Control

But didn't we just say that ViewState uses an HTML Hidden Form Control? Yes we did; however, take a moment to appreciate what ViewState is doing by using the hidden form control as its data container. By itself, the HTML hidden form field is simply a form field, which can hold data but not expose itself on the user interface of a form. Its data is submitted back to the server with every postback but that's where its usefulness ends. In order to use a hidden form field, the processing script on the server must know ahead of time what the form field's name is so it can look for it and if the form must be redrawn on postback, the script must manually populate the hidden form control again. During each postback, this process is repeated making the process a mess to maintain state with.

ViewState capitalizes on the hidden form field control by naming it `__VIEWSTATE` and writing dynamic data to that field. ASP.NET automates the process of writing to `__VIEWSTATE`, and reading from it during postback. The server control need not be concerned with what the hidden field `__VIEWSTATE` is doing, rather it only needs to access a nice packaged `StateBag` with the name of `ViewState` and any properties received during postback pre-filled.

ViewState vs. Cookies

The cookie is a useful tool for writing data to a client machine you would like to persist for a user's session or longer. Cookies are small files written to a client machine and sent with the HTTP header. Server controls can access cookies and set them; however, again, the process of reading and writing is manual where ViewState is maintained automatically and the only requirement of a server control is to name properties that populate from ViewState. Cookies can also be disabled by a client computer, which renders them useless. ViewState is a server-side process and writes to a standard HTML form control.

ViewState vs. Application and Session State:

We will talk about this further in the last section of this chapter; however, to put it simply, `Application` and `Session` state variables are not meant to persist state data between postback events. They are designed to maintain state across an entire application or one particular user's session. ViewState is not designed to persist information that should be available to entire application; it's designed to maintain server control state across postbacks making these two state management tools completely separate beasts.

ViewState with Simple Controls

Now that we have looked at the theory, it's time to get our hands dirty by building a simple server control, which clearly demonstrates how ViewState works. The server control is called `ViewStateLightBulb.cs` and its purpose is to turn on and off various light bulb graphics, which it renders, based upon the ViewState of its properties. The finished application is illustrated below with one bulb in its "on" status and the other two in their "off" status.

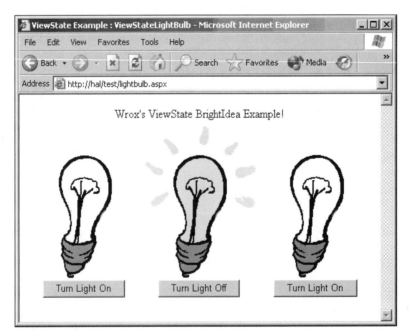

As each server control is executed, ViewState will be used to examine the state of each "light bulb" on the web form prior to a Button click event raising a postback event. With its state information available, the server control will know whether it should render a light on or render it off in response to the button click event. It's a simple control that will override the Render() method to draw out the proper image link. All of the graphic files used in this application, as well as the sourcecode are available for download from the Wrox web site at www.wrox.com.

We will begin by building the server control first. Create a new file in your web application directory called ViewStateLightBulb.cs, enter the code below, and save the file.

```csharp
using System;
using System.Web;
using System.Web.UI;

namespace ProServerCtrls {

public class ViewStateLightBulb: Control, IPostBackEventHandler{

    // Property Declarations

    public String ImgOn {
      get { return (String) ViewState["ImgOn"]; }
      set { ViewState["ImgOn"] = value; }
  }
  public String ImgOff {
    get { return (String) ViewState["ImgOFF"]; }
    set { ViewState["ImgOFF"] = value; }
  }
  public Boolean IsOn {
    get { return (Boolean) ViewState["IsOn"]; }
    set { ViewState["IsOn"] = value; }
  }
  public String ImgPath {
    get { return (String) ViewState["ImgPath"]; }
    set { ViewState["ImgPath"] = value; }
  }

  // Declare Delegate Method to handle Event
  protected void OnSwitchFlip(EventArgs e)
  {
    if(this.IsOn){
      // It's on, turn it off
      this.IsOn = false;
    } else {
      // It's off, turn it on.
      this.IsOn = true;
    }
  }

  // raise postback event
  public void RaisePostBackEvent(string eventArgument){
    OnSwitchFlip(new EventArgs());
  }
```

```
    protected override void Render(HtmlTextWriter writer)
    {
      if(IsOn){
        writer.Write("<img src=\"" +
          this.ImgPath + this.ImgOn + "\"><br>");
        writer.Write("<input type=submit name=" +
          this.UniqueID + " value='Turn Light Off'/>");
      } else {
        writer.Write("<img src=\"" + this.ImgPath +
          this.ImgOff + "\"><br>");
        writer.Write("<input type=submit name=" +
          this.UniqueID + " value='Turn Light On'/>");
      }
    } // End Render
  } // End ViewStateLightBulb
} // End ServerCtrlsChapter5
```

The first block declares the namespaces we will need to use and sets up the proper namespaces and class for this server control. We then implement the properties required of the server control, which is where we encounter our first new item of code:

```
    // Property Declarations

    public String ImgOn {
      get { return (String) ViewState["ImgOn"]; }
      set { ViewState["ImgOn"] = value; }
    }
  public String ImgOff {
    get { return (String) ViewState["ImgOFF"]; }
    set { ViewState["ImgOFF"] = value; }
  }
  public Boolean IsOn {
    get { return (Boolean) ViewState["IsOn"]; }
    set { ViewState["IsOn"] = value; }
  }
  public String ImgPath {
    get { return (String) ViewState["ImgPath"]; }
    set { ViewState["ImgPath"] = value; }
  }
```

These three properties are set up similarly to any normal property with the exception of where their data is populated. If you wish a property to be populated by values of the same name within the ViewState StateBag, you simply use the get{} statement:

```
    return (type) ViewState["ValueName"];}
```

where (type) is the data type to be returned, and "ValueName" is the name of the name-value pair you would like to access. Using the syntax above in public property statements, ASP.NET will populate these properties for you automatically from ViewState or a passed-in value if one is present such as <Wrox:ViewStateLightBulb IsOn="false">.

Before we write an .aspx web form to call this server control, we must compile it. If you need to recap on how we do this, you may want to refer back to Chapter 3, where we created a simple .bat file that could be used to compile our controls.

Now we need an ASP.NET web form to display this server control. We will make multiple ViewStateLightBulb.cs controls to display three lights. Each light will be independent of the others and maintain its own state within the __VIEWSTATE hidden form field. Create a new ASPX file in your application directory called LightBulb.aspx, and save the following code to it:

```
<%@ Page Language="C#" runat="Server" trace="true" debug="true"%>
<%@ Register TagPrefix="Wrox" NameSpace="ProServerCtrls"
Assembly="ViewStateLightBulb"%>
<html>
<head>
  <title>ViewState Example : ViewStateLightBulb</title>
</head>
<body>
<form action="lightbulb.aspx" method="post" runat="server">
<table width="450" cellspacing="0" cellpadding="2">
  <tr>
  <td align="center" colspan="3">
    Wrox's ViewState BrightIdea Example!
  </td>
  </tr>
  <tr>
  <td align="center">
    <Wrox:ViewStateLightBulb id="Bulb1" IsOn="false"
      ImgOn="bulbOn.gif" ImgOff="bulbOff.gif"
      ImgPath="http://127.0.0.1/ProSrvCtrls/"
      runat="server"/>
  </td>
  <td align="center">
    <Wrox:ViewStateLightBulb id="Bulb2" IsOn="false"
      ImgOn="bulbOn.gif" ImgOff="bulbOFF.gif"
      ImgPath="http://127.0.0.1/ProSrvCtrls/"
      runat="server"/>
  </td>
  <td align="center">
    <Wrox:ViewStateLightBulb id="Bulb3" IsOn="false"
      ImgOn="bulbOn.gif" ImgOff="bulbOFF.gif"
      ImgPath="http://127.0.0.1/ProSrvCtrls/"
      runat="server"/>
  </td>
  </tr>
</table>
</form>
</body>
</html>
```

This file is straightforward and doesn't really warrant detailed explanation, since we should be familiar with calling events and server controls by now.

With the `.aspx` form complete we can review our work thus far, run `LightBulb.aspx` from a web browser, and turn some lights on and off. The running program was illustrated in the beginning of this section.

Note that the ViewState value persists from postback to postback, enabling our server control to keep its light on even when not clicking the specified button to initiate a postback event. A closer examination of the `__VIEWSTATE` field reveals a larger data field now that more values are stored in it:

```
<input type="hidden" name="__VIEWSTATE"
value="dDwtMTk4Mjg0ODU2Mjt0PDtsPGk8MT47PjtsPHQ8O2w8aTwzPjtpPDU+O2k8OT47aTwxMT47Pjt
sPHQ8cDxsPEltZ1NvdXJjZTs+O2w8YnVsYk9uLmdpZjs+Pjs7Pjt0PHA8bDxJbWdTb3VyY2U7PjtsPGJ1b
GJPbi5naWY7Pj470z47dDxwPHA8bDxUZXh0O0o47bDxUdXJuIG9mZjs+Pjs+Ozs+O3Q8cDxwPGw8VGV4dDs
+O2w8VHVybiBvZmY7Pj47Pjs+Pjs+" />
```

The only remaining point to make about this server control is the autonomous nature of its design. We will talk more about autonomy later but this control is a decent example of building a control not dependent on the application using it. The user can customize the bulb pictures they wish to use and no page-level code is required other than the `onClick` button and the call to the server control.

With the conclusion of this example, you now see that using ViewState to persist server control property values across multiple postback events is not difficult and we are ready to move on to more complex ViewState topics.

ViewState with Composite Controls

Our first example dealt with a rendered server control. In this example we will look at using ViewState within a composite server control. As we learned in Chapter 1, composite server controls take advantage of ASP.NET intrinsic controls by instantiating child controls, such as `TextBox` controls, within the parent control. The ASP.NET intrinsic controls each implement ViewState as applicable, so managing ViewState data in the parent control requires the control to capture ViewState data in various properties and assign the data back to the proper child control upon postback. This is easy enough to do and the server control we build will encompass various child controls to demonstrate.

There are some structural differences between a composite server control and a rendered server control so you will see in this example we make use of the `CreateChildControl()` method to write our controls to the client rather then building them from scratch using the `Render()` method.

As you may recall from Chapter 1, you can expose the properties of a child control publicly with a property statement similar to the syntax below:

```
public string Text
{
  get
  {
  EnsureChildControls();
  return Button.Text;
  }
  set
  {
  EnsureChildControls();
  Button.Text = value;
  }
}
```

This method works very well for properties that are hard-coded each time the server control is called such as:

```
<Wrox:SlotMachine Text="Spin The Wheel" runat="server"/>
```

Unfortunately, ViewState is a dynamic property and some values may be null until the first postback event happens. Additionally, the point of ViewState is to persist a value across a postback event, and the above example is designed to receive current data from each postback event.

The composite control we build in this chapter runs a virtual slot machine. The diagram below illustrates the structure of the SlotMachine.dll file:

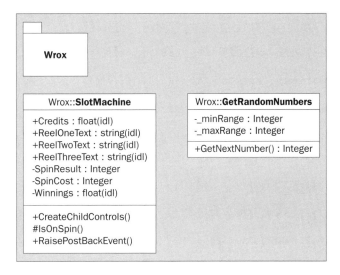

There are two classes within this server control, SlotMachine.cs, which is public, and an internal class called GetRandomNumbers that serves as the slot machine's random number generator. This control uses ViewState to persist the last known value of the player's Credits (their money), and update a label control with that value. Additionally, it will persist the values of each slot window in ViewState, which will provide a seed number for the GetRandomNumbers class.

We should point out that the purpose of the example is not to build an efficient slot machine. As built, this slot machine would take the largest casino's coffers to the poor house. The purpose is to illustrate how ViewState values can be persisted across postback events within a composite control.

We will build the server control first and then step through the code together. First, create a new file in your web application directory named SlotMachine.cs and save the following code to it:

```
using System;
using System.Web;
using System.Web.UI;
using System.Web.UI.WebControls;

namespace ProServerCtrls {
```

```
public class SlotMachine : Control, IPostBackEventHandler {

  // Private data member
  private int SpinResult;
  private int SpinCost = 5;
  private double Winnings = 0.00;

  // Properties

  public double Credits
  {
    get { return (double)ViewState["Credits"]; }
    set { ViewState["Credits"] = value; }
  }
  // Expose three label text properties for the slot
  //machines "Slot Reels".
  public int ReelOneText
  {
    get { if(ViewState["ReelOneText"] == null){
        return 10;
      } else {
        return (int)ViewState["ReelOneText"];
      }
    }
    set { ViewState["ReelOneText"] = value;  }
  }
  public int ReelTwoText
  {
    get { if(ViewState["ReelTwoText"] == null){
        return 10;
      } else {
        return (int)ViewState["ReelTwoText"];
      }
    }
    set { ViewState["ReelTwoText"] = value;  }
  }
  public int ReelThreeText
  {
    get { if(ViewState["ReelThreeText"] == null){
        return 10;
      } else {
        return (int)ViewState["ReelThreeText"];
      }
    }
    set { ViewState["ReelThreeText"] = value;  }
  }


  // Declare Event Handlers

  protected void OnIsSpin(EventArgs e)
  {
    GetRandomNumbers newSpin = new GetRandomNumbers();
    SpinResult = newSpin.GetNextNumber(ReelOneText);
      ReelOneText = SpinResult;
```

```
    SpinResult = newSpin.GetNextNumber(ReelTwoText);
      ReelTwoText = SpinResult;
    SpinResult = newSpin.GetNextNumber(ReelThreeText);
      ReelThreeText = SpinResult;

    //Deduct their credits
    Credits = (Credits - SpinCost);

    // Calculate Winnings

    if(ReelOneText == ReelTwoText)
    {
      // First Two matched
      Winnings = 100.00;

      if(ReelOneText == ReelThreeText)
      {
        // All Three matched
        Winnings = 1000.00;
      }
    }
    else if (ReelTwoText == ReelThreeText){
      //Second Two Matched
      Winnings = 200.00;

    }
    else if  (ReelOneText == ReelThreeText){
      //First & Third Matched
      Winnings = 300.00;
    }

    // Add Winnings
    Credits = (Credits + Winnings);
}

// raise post-back event
public void RaisePostBackEvent(string eventArgument){
  OnIsSpin(new EventArgs());
}
protected override void CreateChildControls()
{

// Render Table Container
Controls.Add(new LiteralControl("<table cellspacing=0 cellpadding=2
                                align=center width=450><tr><td>"));
  Label reelOne = new Label();
  reelOne.Text = this.ReelOneText.ToString();
  reelOne.Width=80;
  reelOne.Height=80;
  reelOne.BorderWidth = 1;
  reelOne.Font.Size = 15;
  Controls.Add(reelOne);
```

```
      Controls.Add(new LiteralControl("</td><td>"));
        Label reelTwo = new Label();
        reelTwo.Text = this.ReelTwoText.ToString();
        reelTwo.Width=80;
        reelTwo.Height=80;
        reelTwo.BorderWidth = 1;
        reelTwo.Font.Size = 15;
        Controls.Add(reelTwo);

    Controls.Add(new LiteralControl("</td><td>"));
        Label reelThree = new Label();
        reelThree.Text = this.ReelThreeText.ToString();
        reelThree.Width=80;
        reelThree.Height=80;
        reelThree.BorderWidth = 1;
        reelThree.Font.Size = 15;
        Controls.Add(reelThree);

    Controls.Add(new LiteralControl("</td></tr><tr><td colspan=3>Credits
                               Remaining:   "));

        Label creditsDisplayed = new Label();
        creditsDisplayed.Text = this.Credits.ToString();
        Controls.Add(creditsDisplayed);

    Controls.Add(new LiteralControl("</td></tr><tr><td colspan=3>"));

    Controls.Add(new LiteralControl("<input type='submit' name='" + this.UniqueID
                               + "' value='Spin The Slot!'>"));
    Controls.Add(new LiteralControl("</td></tr></table>"));
        }
} // End SlotMachine Class

internal class GetRandomNumbers : Random {

  // Private data members
  // Default values for the rand range

  private int _minRange = 0;
  private int _maxRange = 10;

  public int GetNextNumber(int seed)
  {

    if(seed < 9 && seed > 0)
    {
      // load the min range number
      _minRange = seed;
    }
    return Next(_minRange, _maxRange);
  }
}
} // End Wrox namespace
```

Even though the code is a bit longer than that we wrote in the previous example, most of it should be rather familiar to you with a few exceptions. We will step through the code now and explain each part:

First, we set up the proper namespaces to use within a composite control. The first bit of code that works with ViewState is again found in the property statements with the syntax for ReelOneText shown below:

```
public int ReelOneText
    {
      get { if(ViewState["ReelOneText"] == null){
         return 10;
         } else {
           return (int)ViewState["ReelOneText"];
         }
      }
      set { ViewState["ReelOneText"] = value;  }
    }
```

This property is established as our previous ViewState examples were; however, we have added a check to see if the ViewState name-value pair to populate the property with is null. If it is, we set a default value of 10 that will be displayed in the correct label control later in the CreateChildControls() method. This default value of 10 is not arbitrary. You'll see that in the GetRandomNumber class, 10 is an exception seed value for the random number range of 1–10; thus, if 10 is passed as a seed value, the GetRandomNumber class will seed itself from default values. This helps to ensure a wider variety of random numbers.

Once all the server control properties are loaded we define the event handlers required for this control. There is only one, named appropriately IsOnSpin. This event handler goes through the process of obtaining a random integer for each slot label from the GetRandomNumber class in the code shown below:

```
protected void OnIsSpin(EventArgs e)
    {
      GetRandomNumbers newSpin = new GetRandomNumbers();
      SpinResult = newSpin.GetNextNumber(ReelOneText);
        ReelOneText = SpinResult;
      SpinResult = newSpin.GetNextNumber(ReelTwoText);
        ReelTwoText = SpinResult;
      SpinResult = newSpin.GetNextNumber(ReelThreeText);
        ReelThreeText = SpinResult;

   //Deduct their credits
      Credits = (Credits - SpinCost);
```

This code also sets the ViewState properties to the new random number generated by the call to GetNextNumber().

Once the new numbers are generated and the proper ViewState properties are populated, the control will then see if any of the generated numbers matched; if so we add some credits to the winnings and that is all that is required of our post-back event handler.

Within the `CreateChildControls` method, the control renders all the child controls inside an HTML table, making it easy for a page developer to use the control on their web form:

```
protected override void CreateChildControls()
    {

    // Render Table Container
    Controls.Add(new LiteralControl("<table cellspacing=0
        cellpadding=2 align=center width=450><tr><td>"));
     Label reelOne = new Label();
     reelOne.Text = this.ReelOneText.ToString();
     reelOne.Width=80;
     reelOne.Height=80;
     reelOne.BorderWidth = 1;
     reelOne.Font.Size = 15;
     Controls.Add(reelOne);
```

We won't look at the entire code for `CreateChildControls` because it's very similar, but the snippet above illustrates what the control is doing very well. First we add an HTML table tag using the new `LiteralControl` method to begin the client-side code. The first label is created using the new `Label()` method as you have seen before. The only item to take note of in this code is the way the `Text` property is set. We must convert the value in ViewState to a string with the `ToString()` method or the `.Text` property of the label will not be able to handle the data received from ViewState because it is expecting a string value, not an integer:

```
internal class GetRandomNumbers : Random {

  private int _minRange = 0;
  private int _maxRange = 10;

  public int GetNextNumber(int seed)
  {
    if(seed < 9 && seed > 0)
    {
      // load the min range number
      _minRange = seed;
    }
    return Next(_minRange, _maxRange);
  }
}
```

The internal class inherits from the `Random` class and uses the `Next` method to generate a random number within a range of numbers. This ties into the discussion we just had on seeding the random number generator from ViewState values for the label controls. You can see here that if the number is 10, it is treated as out of bounds and the default seed of 0 is used. Compile this server control as `SlotMachine.dll`.

We will now create the client code that will call this server control. Create a new file in your application directory called `SlotMachine.aspx` and save the following code to that file:

```
<%@ Page Language="C#" runat="Server" trace="true" debug="true"%>
<%@ Register TagPrefix="Wrox" NameSpace="ProServerCtrls" Assembly="SlotMachine" %>

<html>
<head>
  <title>ViewState Example : Composite Control Slot Machine
  </title>
</head>
<body>
<form action="SlotMachine.aspx" method="post" runat="server">
<table width="450" cellspacing="0" cellpadding="2" align="center" border=1>
  <tr>
    <td align="center">ViewState Slot Machine!<br>
                (Each Spin Costs 5 Credits)
  </td>
  </tr>
  <tr>
    <td>
      <Wrox:SlotMachine Credits="5000.00" runat="server"/>
    </td>
  </tr>
</table>
</form>
</body>
</html>
```

We register the new server control and then call it. Notice the only attribute required from the caller is the `Credit` attribute. This will start the user off with some money to begin playing with.

The final result should look like the illustration below:

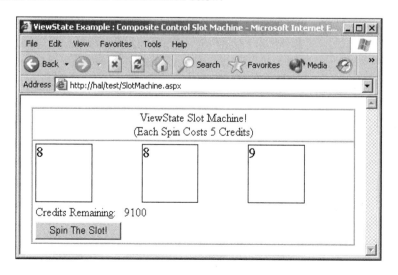

As you can see, I have been playing for a bit and thanks to our "loose" number generator I am not doing that badly either!

Remember that when using ViewState to populate child control values you are not hooking the properties to the child controls directly, rather you can use ViewState to capture the data and then assign it to the child control as you please in the `CreateChildControls()` method.

Control Class Properties and Methods Affecting ViewState

Since ViewState is a property of the `Control` class, there are various methods and properties residing in `Control` that can be used or overridden by you server controls. In the table below we take a look at each method and property and discuss how they can be used within your server control to affect its behavior.

Property or Method Name	Type	Description	Default Value
EnableViewState	Boolean	This property disables or enables the server control's ability to maintain its state information within ViewState. By setting this property to `false`, the control and any child controls it creates will not be able to use the ViewState `StateBag`. Disabling ViewState for controls that do not require state management will increase the performance of your web form application by reducing the amount of data the client is required to download.	true
IsTrackingViewState	Boolean	This property advises whether or not the control is tracking changes made to the values within its ViewState `StateBag`. This property can be used to detect changes in ViewState values when overriding `LoadViewState()` and `SaveViewState()` to determine when changes need to be written to the ViewState `StateBag`.	
ViewStateIgnoresCase	Boolean	This property will advise you if the ViewState `StateBag` object is case-sensitive or not. It will test `true` if the `StateBag` is case-sensitive.	true

Property or Method Name	Type	Description	Default Value
HasChildViewState	Boolean	This property will test `true` if any child controls created by the server control contain any saved ViewState values.	
ClearChildViewState	Protected Method	This method will clear out any values saved in the ViewState `StateBag` for a child control of the parent control.	
LoadViewState	Protected Method	Loads all ViewState values saved on the previous postback operation. Override this method when implementing a custom ViewState schema.	
SaveViewState	Protected Method	Used in partnership with `LoadViewState()`. This method saves the name-values pairs desired to the ViewState `StateBag` to be written to the hidden form field `__VIEWSTATE`.	
TrackViewState	Protected Method	Enables the control to track changes to ViewState values.	

Many of these won't be necessary unless you are implementing a custom view state system by overriding `LoadViewState()` and `SaveViewState()`, which, as we mentioned earlier, you'll learn about in the next chapter. But it is still important to review what is available and introduce you to their purposes now since the topic is ViewState.

ViewState and Performance

I have read many posts within ASP.NET newsgroups from concerned developers who are unsure what the `__VIEWSTATE` that appears in their code is all about and what it does to their server. Up to this point in this chapter we have cleared up what ViewState is and how to use it, but now we should look at what effect it has on performance. As with anything in programming, new features give and take when it comes to application performance and ViewState is certainly not immune, but you will be pleased to know the outlook is not that gloomy.

ViewState performance issues can be summed up in two halves: client performance and server-side performance.

ViewState Server Performance:

There are several things you can do on the server side to enhance the performance of ViewState. We will step you through each one in this section.

Disabling ViewState

ViewState is enabled by default for every server control; even controls that do not render a user interface still contain __VIEWSTATE data for the page itself such as the string below:

```
<input type="hidden" name="__VIEWSTATE"
                    value="dDw2OTcyNzUyNDQ7Oz4=" />
```

When ViewState is not required for a particular server control you should disable it by setting its EnableViewState property to false. To disable ViewState for a server control, simply pass the EnableViewState attribute in its calling tag as shown below:

```
<asp:button id="Switch3" EnableViewState="false"
        Text="Turn On" OnClick="Bulb3_Switch" runat="server"/>
```

This will effectively disable the control from maintaining ViewState data. It will also disable ViewState for any child controls it may create, which may not be a desired effect.

You can disable ViewState in a composite control by explicitly turning on or off ViewState for each control created within the composite control. To do this, you set the EnableViewState property to false on the control when it is created:

```
protected override void CreateChildControls() {
  Label LabelControl = new Label();
  LabelControl.Text = "This control does not keep state";
  LabelControl.EnableViewState = false;
Controls.Add(LabelControl);
  }
}
```

You should disable ViewState globally if the server control does not handle any events and does not contain any dynamic properties. The server controls we built in this chapter have dynamic properties; a server control without dynamic properties either has no properties at all, or the data within those properties is hard-coded every single time the server control is called.

Storing Proper Data in ViewState

The next step you can take within a server control to increase performance has to do with the type of data you store in ViewState. ViewState provides efficient data serialization filters for six basic data types. These filters are very fast and are designed to create the smallest data "footprint" possible within the __VIEWSTATE hidden form field. Ensuring the data written to ViewState uses one of these data types will ensure an efficient serializing operation for each value increasing speed on the server and decreasing the amount of data in __VIEWSTATE transferred on each round trip.

If you must store an object that is not covered by a default data serialization filter, write your own type converter by inheriting from the Type Converter class to help serialize the data to a smaller __VIEWSTATE footprint. Remember, objects such as data sets, multiple dimension arrays, and large enumerations are slow to be written to ViewState. Storing a large number of objects can slow down the read-write performance of ViewState. You'll see this demonstrated in Chapter 7 when we learn how to connect to data sources and store data in ViewState.

Server Resources

Since the data used in ViewState is written to the client machine, ViewState will not take as heavy a toll on server resources (such as memory) as a state variable stored within the session or application state scopes. The data in ViewState is also available across multiple servers so it will scale well in multiple server environments such as a web farm.

Security

We will learn about security in the next section; however, as a general rule, the more security you place on the data within ViewState the slower the read/write process will be. Combining encrypted ViewState data with an SSL connection will always be slower than writing unencrypted data to ViewState and transferring the data via the standard HTTP port 80. We recommend you test your server control under various loads using a stress tool such as Microsoft's Web Application Stress Toolkit to determine how higher levels of encryption and security affect overall read-write performance of a particular server control.

ViewState Client Performance

Since ViewState stores its data in a hidden form field, the primary issue concerning the use of ViewState for client computers is the total byte payload of the ASPX page they are requesting.

The controls built within this chapter do not contain a heavy ViewState burden so their corresponding __VIEWSTATE hidden fields do not grow very large. You will learn in the next chapter, however, that DataSets can be persisted in ViewState as well, which can potentially create very large __VIEWSTATE data fields adding to the overall amount of data a client must download when rendering the web form. In the age of high speed internet connections and corporate LANs, it may not appear that your page suffers from poor download times until you test it on a slower connection such as a 56k modem.

To guard against creating unnecessary data in the __VIEWSTATE field, ensure that you disable ViewState for any controls that do not require state information and test large data sets stored in __VIEWSTATE to ensure they do not create a performance problem for users with a slower connection.

ViewState and Security

When you look at the __VIEWSTATE hidden field with a human eye it appears to be nothing more than a bunch of meaningless characters. We know this to be untrue, however, the values stored in the __VIEWSTATE hidden field are encoded in a Base64 format to ensure the values are not corrupted while making their way through various platforms between the client and the server during a postback operation. Regardless of the encoded state of the data, it is by no means secure. The Base64-encoded format is primarily used in e-mail files; however, it is simply a format of printable characters that allows a binary object to be represented and transferred in files such as ASPX web forms. To illustrate what type of data is stored within a __VIEWSTATE hidden form field we return to our ViewStateLightBulb.cs server control we built earlier.

After turning on the first two light bulbs and leaving the third light bulb off, the __VIEWSTATE hidden form field contains data that appears like the statement below:

```
dDwtMTk4Mjg0ODU2Mjt0PDtsPGk8MT47PjtsPHQ8O2w8aTwxPjtpPDM+O2k8NT47aTw3PjtpPDk+O2k8MT
E+Oz47bDx0PHA8bDxJbWdTb3VyY2U7PjtsPGJ1bGJPbi5naWY7Pj47Oz47dDxwPGw8SW1nU291cmNlOz47
bDxidWxiT24uZ21mOz4+Ozs+O3Q8cDxsPEltZ1NvdXJjZTs+O2w8YnVsYk9uLmdpZjs+Pjs7Pjt0PHA8cD
xsPFRleHQ7PjtsPFR1cm4gb2Zm0z4+Oz47Oz47dDxwPHA8bDxUZXh0h0Oz47bDxUdXJuIG9mZjs+Pjs+Ozs+
O3Q8cDxwPGw8VGV4dDs+O2w8VHVybiBvZmY7Pj47Pjs7Pjs+Pjs+
```

We won't go into the detail of how to decode Base64 data here because it's not relevant to ViewState; however, if you were to apply Base64 decoding to the string above the result is as shown below:

```
t<-1982848562;t<;l<i<1>;>;l<t<;l<i<1>;i<3>;i<5>;i<7>;i<9>;i<11>;>;l<t<p<l<ImgSourc
e;>;l<bulbOn.gif;>>;;>;t<p<l<ImgSource;>;l<bulbOn.gif;>>;;>;t<p<l<ImgSource;>;l<bu
lbOn.gif;>>;;>;t<p<p<l<Text;>;l<Turn off;>>;>;;>;t<p<p<l<Text;>;l<Turn
off;>>;>;;>;t<p<p<l<Text;>;l<Turn off;>>;>;;>;>>;>>;>
```

If you're interested in learning more about the Base64 Encoding Format, visit the Internet Engineering Task Force web site at www.ietf.org. Base64 is defined in RFC 2045.

As you can see, the values of each server control property are easy to find making this data rather insecure. With a little effort, a malicious user could modify the property values in the decoded Base64 string, recode it, and post it back to the server. There are some simple things you can implement to help secure the __VIEWSTATE form field. The first is obvious but we should mention it anyway:

> **Ensure you never place sensitive data about the user such as a password or credit card number into the ViewState StateBag.**

The next two topics will explain some steps you can take to enable a checksum and encryption system on the __VIEWSTATE data string.

Using EnableViewStateMAC Page Class Attribute

This attribute is not inherited by server controls from the Control class, rather is a member of the Page class so using this property means setting it at the page level, which effectively changes the ViewState service for an entire web form rather than a single control. This property will assist your application in identifying __VIEWSTATE data that has been modified when a postback request is made. When EnableViewStateMAC is set to true, ASP.NET will append a hash code to the end of the Base64-encoded string sent to the client. The hash code generated by EnableViewStateMAC is hash type SHA1 generated by the SHA1 class. Detailed information on SHA1 can be found by visiting http://www.w3.org/PICS/DSig/RSA-SHA1_1_0.html. This hash type is a unique value of fixed length which weighs in at a light 160 bits so you do not add a heavy overhead to the ViewState string by using it. The hash is generated, added to ViewState, and then rebuilt when a post-back event happens. When it is rebuilt, it must match the original hash value or the data is rejected; small changes in the data will create very large changes in the hash value that makes this algorithm very efficient for checking the content of the ViewState string.

Server controls waiting to process data that is discarded will revert to their default values and lose any state information available to them on the previous request.

The `EnableViewStateMAC` property can be enabled at the page level or application level. To activate it at the page level, use the `<%@ Page %>` directive as shown in the statement below:

```
<%@ Page Language="C#" EnableViewStateMAC="True" RUNAT="Server" %>
```

Alternatively, it can be enabled at the application level in `Global.asax` as shown below:

```
<script language="C#" runat="server">
  void Application_Start(){
EnableViewStateMAC = true;
  }
</script>
```

Unless you absolutely need every string of ViewState data to be checked, it is best practice to enable this property at the page level only when needed.

Alternatively, you can use the `MD5` class hash algorithm instead of SHA1 by setting the `machineKey` validation attribute to `"MD5"` within the `machine.config` file as shown below:

```
<machineKey validation="MD5" />
```

MD5 is very similar in that small changes in the data will create large unpredictable changes in the hash code value. MD5 provides better performance than SHA1 hash algorithms, however, it is not as secure.

Using 3DES Encryption

Encrypting the data within the `__VIEWSTATE` form control is simple to implement at the page level as well. First, set the `EnableViewStateMAC` property to `true` and then set the `machineKEY` validation attribute to `3DES` as shown in the two example statements below:

```
<%@ Page Language="C#"
                  EnableViewStateMAC="True" RUNAT="Server" %>
```

```
<machineKey validationKey="AutoGenerate"
          decryptionKey="AutoGenerate" validation="3DES"/>
```

*Note: 3DES Encryption allows either a 128 bit or 192 bit key value, this `machine.config` statement shown above **AutoGenerates** a key to be used but you could specify your own key as long as it meets the 128 or 192 bit requirements.*

The process used to encrypt subject data while using 3DES Encryption is to sweep the data three successive times using the algorithm and the specified key value.

Recall how easy it was to display the values within __VIEWSTATE when the data was in Base64 format? When Triple DES (3DES) is used, the contents of __VIEWSTATE are shown below:

```
r/i8UeqRGAaalFJZTNeu3PXlcXquYh5LRdhlgejk2NrTOeTmEgrHs/cvswVpxOgnsI/mh6kM5sUtbCVd1x
JBTBRU3W2StmNzaTIGgncxWwMIghShqlG8s96XnwSn6nwr9s8OEgR7lOQBXL7KzfEM1/yIzOqoMkK8TPzO
5s+mxK5QPHXH6tnAWxsd0ULZT92idogYUK26J0sL/8Uv+Lho2UIvKw7hVFMKEhx5M1t6w3P6i2tcaajdm4
pn5D8llQL2qHYRS1KpI0Dly3ufzhIk+PgQ+UKUEOaz/2vLds2iJjnpc8horH8sD4ZhB1368wV3Pa8puTZ9
+FdVBRPg4EkOBtiEaNrtxPfjlseE2bl6fCpRxF2xf/ZhuWUkLg7VatYswaytzUKJgKOtmqaTl3JzUQ==
```

The first thing noticeable, is the ViewState string is now 408 characters long – 24 characters larger than its non-encrypted version and second, when Base64 decoded, we get the following gibberish:

```
<AF><F8><BC>Q<EA><91><18><06><9A><94>RYL<D7><AE><DC><F5><E5>qz<AE>b<1E>KE<D8>e<81>
<E8><E4><D8><DA><D3>9<E4><E6><12>
<C7><B3><F7>/<B3><05>i<C4><E8>'<B0><8F><E6><87><A9><0C><E6><C5>-
1%]<D7><12>AL<14>T<DD>m<92><B6>csi2<06><82>w1[<03><08><82><14><A1><AA>Q<BC><B3><DE
><97><9F><04><A7><EA>|+<F6><CF><0E><12><04>{<97>D<01>\<BE><CA><CD><F1><0C><D7><FC>
<88><CC><EA><A8>2B<BC>L<FC><CE><E6><CF><A6><C4><AE>P<u<C7><EA><D9><C0>[<1B><1D><D1
>B<D9>O<DD><A2>v<88><18>P<AD><BA>'K<0B><FF><C5>/<F8><B8>h<D9>B/+<0E><E1>TS
<12><1C>y3[z<C3>s<FA><8B>k\i<A8><DD><9B><8A>g<E4>?%<95><02><F6><A8>v<11>KR<A9>#@<E
5><CB>{<9F><CE><12>$<F8><F8><10><F9>B<94><10><E6><B3><FF>k<CB>v<CD><A2>&9<E9>s<C8>
h<AC><7F>,<0F><86>a<07>]<FA><F3><05>w=<AF>)<B9>6}<F8>WU<05><13><E0><E0>I<0E><06><D
8><84>h<DA><ED><C4><F7><E3><96><C7><84><D9><B9>z|*Q<C4>]<B1><7F><F6>a<B9>e$.<0E><D
5>j<D6>,<C1><AC><AD><CD>B<89><80><A3><AD><9A><A6><93><97>rsQ
```

For further security, you can transfer encrypted ViewState data over a Secured Sockets Layer (SSL) protocol. With that, you have two methods of enabling data validation and encryption for ViewState values sent to and from your ASP.NET server controls.

Accessing Application and Session State Variables

Before we close this chapter, there is another section of state management that we should touch on, which is Application and Session state. You have learned in this chapter that state can be maintained between postback events by using ViewState but they are other state variable scopes, which can be accessed within a server control if absolutely necessary.

We say "absolutely necessary" because there are specific reasons why you should not use Application and Session scope variables within a server control. You have learned in most designs, server controls are perfect for carrying out repeated operations that could be encapsulated into one small reusable control such as drawing a form control. Examples of this autonomous design are the ASP.NET intrinsic server controls such as <asp:DropDownMenu/>. These server controls render items that are commonly repeated in many web form applications. Items such as textboxes, buttons, drop-down menus and labels. The ASP.NET intrinsic controls are autonomous to the application in which they reside. They can be plugged in from one Web Form Application to the next, without requiring knowledge of the application they run within (Application state) or the user currently connected to it (Session state).

Our point is that exposing the application and session state to a server control makes the control dependent upon the application it is used within. The result is a less flexible server control that cannot be reused as easily as an autonomous control. Careful thought should be taken prior to building a control that requires the use of Application and Session state variables. Some criteria to apply when deciding include:

❑   Is there a global variable within the application, such as a database connection string that is required by the control?

❑   Is the control required to know who the client is (Session state variables such as a username)?

❑   Would the services of this control be useful to many different web form applications? If so, designing it to be autonomous will be very useful.

❑   Is the control performing a proprietary task that only this application will require?

Run these questions through your server control design before exposing session or application state information and they will help you clear up whether your server control design should be autonomous or not.

The next two examples are nothing fancy, just a tool to illustrate how accessing application and session state variables can be done within a server control.

Exposing Application State Variables to a Server Control

The application state is a tool to maintain an application instance across a number of ASPX web form files located within a single virtual directory tree within IIS. The application instances are instantiated by creating and using the global.asax file. This file should be placed within the root directory of the web form application you wish to create. Application-scope variables will be available to all web forms within the directory tree under a root directory containing a global.asax file and are typically set within the global.asax file. This is a 30,000-foot look at global.asax and Application state. Since this a server control book we will not be covering it in great detail, if you are not familiar with Application state or Web Form Applications, we suggest Wrox's *Professional ASP.NET* book as a study guide.

We discussed earlier that Application variables are typically set in the global.asax file so we will create one now and save it to your application directory.

Save the code below as global.asax:

```
<script language="C#" runat="server">
  void Application_Start(){
    Application["MyName"] = "Ryan";
  }
</script>
```

This code should be familiar to you; we are simply using the Application_Start function to set an Application variable when the application is created by ASP.NET.

Now we will create the page that calls our server control. Save the code below as index.aspx:

```
<%@ Page Language="C#" runat="Server" %>
<%@ Register TagPrefix="TestControl" NameSpace="TestControl"
Assembly="TestControl" %>
<html>
<head>
  <title>Application Variables in a Server Control</title>
</head>
<body>
Hello, my name is:
<form method="post" action="index.aspx" runat="server">
<TestControl:ShowGoodies Runat="Server"/>
</form>
</body>
</html>
```

This code should also be familiar to you by now. As you can tell by the code in index.aspx, our server control will be called TestControl and the class will be called ShowGoodies. Let's build our server control. Save the code below to your application directory as TestControl.cs.

```
using System;
using System.Web;
using System.Web.UI;

namespace TestControl {
  public class ShowGoodies : Control {
    public String MyName {
      get {
        return (String) Context.Application["MyName"];
      }
    }

    protected override void Render(HtmlTextWriter writer){
      writer.Write(MyName);
    }
  }
}
```

The server control simply references the proper system namespaces, and declares a class called ShowGoodies that inherits the Control class from System.Web. Let's examine the code below a little closer:

```
public String MyName {
  get {
    return (String) Context.Application["MyName"];
  }
}
```

Here we are setting a public property on our server control called MyName. The property at this point is read-only because there is only a get method on the property. There is nothing that difficult about getting Application scope variables, just take note here that we are asking to return the variable as a String from the object context that is created for the server control when it is executed within the .NET Framework.

The output of our program will look like the figure below:

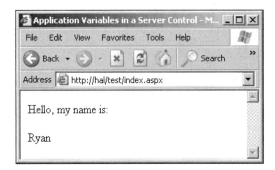

Creating a Read/Write Application Property

It is simple to change our server control and give it the ability to write to the ASP.NET application scope as well. Simply add a `set` statement to the `MyName` property as shown below:

```
namespace TestControl {
  public class ShowGoodies : Control {
    public String MyName {
      get {
        return (String) Context.Application["MyName"];
      }
      set {
        Context.Application["MyName"] = value;
      }
    }

    protected override void Render(HtmlTextWriter writer){
      MyName = "Allen";
      // writer.Write(MyName);
    }
  }
}
```

To prove this works, I have commented out the `writer.Write()` method so this server control does not return any data to the client. It only sets the `MyName` application variable to "Allen" rather than "Ryan". To complete this test, change the code within `index.aspx` to reflect the code below:

```
<%@ Page Language="C#" runat="Server" %>
<%@ Register TagPrefix="TestControl" NameSpace="TestControl"
Assembly="TestControl" %>
<html>
<head>
  <title>Application Variables in a Server Control</title>
</head>

<body>
```

```
Hello, my name is: <br>
<br>
 <form method="post" action="index.aspx" runat="server">
<TestControl:ShowGoodies Runat="Server"/>
</form>
<%=Application["MyName"] %>
</body>
</html>
```

You should have noticed here that I am calling the same server control, but since no output is sent from the server control, we output the `Application` variable using page code, `<%=Application["MyName"] %>`.

The result after compiling the server control again, is shown below:

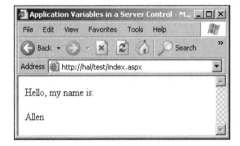

Exposing Session State Variables to a Server Control

We'll now have a quick look at modifying our `TestControl.cs` file to read and write a `Session` variable. Accessing `Session`-scoped variables within a server control is done identically to accessing `Application`-scope variables as shown in the previous section. Modify your `TestControl.cs` with the changes shown here:

```
using System;
using System.Web;
using System.Web.UI;

namespace TestControl {
  public class ShowGoodies : Control {
    public String MyName {
      get {
          return (String) Context.Application["MyName"];
        }
      set {
          Context.Application["MyName"] = value;
        }
    }
    public String MySessionName {
      get {
          return (String) Context.Session["MySessionName"];
        }
```

```
        set {
            Context.Application["MySessionName"] = value;
        }
    }

    protected override void Render(HtmlTextWriter writer){
        MyName = "Allen";
        writer.Write(MyName);
        writer.Write("<br> And My Session Name is: " +MySessionName);
    }
  }
}
```

Now add the following code to instantiate a session within `global.asax`.

```
<script language="C#" runat="server">

  void Application_Start(){
    Application["MyName"] = "Ryan";
  }

  void Session_Start(){
    Session["MySessionName"] = "Christine";
  }
</script>
```

You can see here we added a new session variable when the user's session starts. Lastly, remove from `index.aspx` the line of code that looks like this:

```
<%=Application["MyName"] %>.
```

Compile `TestControl.cs` and you will see the results below while viewing `index.aspx`.

As you can see, setting and getting application and session scoped variables within a server control is not difficult at all.

Again, words of design caution before we close this section. It may be tempting to build a control that can access session information such as a user name or an application-scope database string but we do not recommend it. Creating a server control dependent on `Application` or `Session` state variables is not good design and should be avoided whenever possible to ensure the control can be reused easily in other web form applications.

Summary

In this chapter we took a good long look at a new but elusive tool provided by the .NET Framework. We learned what ViewState is and how it compares to other state management tools within the .NET Framework. We learned where ViewState is handled within a server control's execution lifecycle. We learned how ViewState stores data on the client and how we can access that data within a server control.

Our example applications provided various ways to use ViewState to maintain the state of form controls rendered on the client, and public properties on the server control itself. Once you had an understanding of how ViewState works for rendered and composite controls, we looked at the performance issues associated with using ViewState and how to secure the data placed within the __VIEWSTATE hidden form control.

We also looked at making a server control aware of `Application` and `Session` state information and discussed the pros and cons of writing a server control dependent on the web form application it runs within.

Overall you should have received a well-rounded education on a new tool available within the .NET Framework. In the next chapter, you will receive more valuable information when we expand upon ViewState by implementing a custom ViewState loading and saving process and learn how to access data from within a server control.

Professional ASP .NET Server Controls

Templated Controls and Styles

Up to this point in the book the controls we have been creating have rendered themselves based on the logic and code within the control. The consumers of our controls have not had the ability to directly define the layout and style of the control's content. One of the goals of ASP.NET is to separate presentation from logic. We see this with the code-behind mechanism of ASP.NET pages, which allows us to separate our HTML, or presentation, from the logic, our C# or Visual Basic .NET code. Templated controls and styles allow us to create controls that define operations and implementation without concern for the bulk of the layout, leaving that to a designer or a consumer of our control. In this way, our controls become much more flexible and useful as the implementation is not tied directly to the output.

Templated controls and styles allow the consumer of the control to define the layout and the look and feel of the control. With templates, the consumer provides the definition for one or more sets of HTML tags that define where and what information is displayed by the control when it is rendered to the output. Styles allow the separation of content from the look and feel of that content. More specifically, styles allow for controlling such things as background color, font size, and borders. When creating Server Controls there are several ways to allow the consumer of your control to manage the styles applied to it.

In this chapter we will be covering several topics that allow us to create Server Controls that give the consumer the ability to specify the layout. We will be covering **templates** and how we can allow the consumer to specify the positioning of the control contents as well as examining how to apply **styles** to our controls and expose specific or general style properties to allow the user to further control the presentation.

Specifically, this chapter will cover:

❑ How to create controls that allow a content developer to define templates, or blocks of HTML tags, for the presentation of the control

❑ Working with multiple templates in a single control

❑ Dynamic templates that allow the template to vary based on program logic

❑ Understanding styles and how to expose the style properties of a control

Templated Controls

Before we get started on how to create our own templated controls, we will first look at how we use templated controls to be better prepared to discuss the issues related to these types of controls. ASP.NET comes with several built-in controls that include templates to allow a developer to define the presentation. The DataList and the Repeater controls provide the best examples of templated controls. The Repeater is a control that simply repeats the content found in its templates. This control is bound to a data source that defines how many items are displayed and provides some of the content. Both controls provide template properties for things such as the header, footer, item, and alternating item.

When we use templated controls, we define the various templates by nesting an element in the HTML for our form. Within this element we place the HTML and code that defines the output. The following example should help make this clearer. It provides a snapshot of defining the item template for the DataList control:

```
<asp:DataList id="templatedControl" runat="server">
  <ItemTemplate>
    <b><%# Container.DataItem %></b>
  </ItemTemplate>
</asp:DataList>
```

When the page contents are parsed in order to compile the page on the first access, the ItemTemplate element shown here is bound to a property of the same name on the DataList control. The control then uses the information in this template to render its data. This particular template definition instructs the control that when it renders an item, it should render, in bold, the value of the DataItem property on the template's container. Don't worry if this doesn't make complete sense at this point. As we discuss how to create our own controls we will cover how to expose these properties to consumers of our controls and how all of these pieces fit together.

In the example below we take a look at consuming the repeater control in a Web Form. We will define several templates for the control to mold the layout to fit our needs.

Samples in this chapter consist of Server Controls and Web Forms. In order to get the samples to work, you will need to complete the following steps:

❑ Create an IIS virtual directory on your web server.

❑ Create a bin directory in the folder you virtual directory points to.

❑ Copy any Web Form files (files with an ASPX extension) from the code download into the virtual directory.

❑ Compile the source files for the Server Controls (files with a CS extension) into an assembly named Chapter5.dll and place this assembly in the bin directory. These files can all be compiled into the same assembly or each sample can be compiled one at a time.

In our example, we first define an ArrayList that will serve as the data source for our control. Databinding will be discussed in the next chapter, but for now it is enough to know that we will have one instance of our item, or alternating item templates, for each element in the ArrayList:

UseTemplates.aspx

```
<%@ Page language="c#"  AutoEventWireup="true" %>
<%@ Import Namespace="System.Collections" %>
<!DOCTYPE HTML PUBLIC "-//W3C//DTD HTML 4.0 Transitional//EN" >

<html>
  <head>
    <title>UseTemplates</title>

    <script runat="server" language="C#">
    public void Page_Load(object sender, EventArgs e)
    {
     ArrayList list = new ArrayList(25);

     for(int i = 1; i< 26; i++)
     {
      list.Add(i);
     }

     sample.DataSource = list;
     sample.DataBind();

     list = null;
    }

    </script>
  </head>
  <body >

    <form id="Use" method="post" runat="server">
     <asp:Repeater id="sample" runat="server">

      <HeaderTemplate>
      <h3>Using a repeater control to create a list</h3>
      <ul>
      </HeaderTemplate>
```

141

```
    <ItemTemplate>
     <li>Item: <%#Container.DataItem%> </li>
    </ItemTemplate>

    <AlternatingItemTemplate>
     <li>Alternating Item<%#Container.DataItem%> </li>
    </AlternatingItemTemplate>

    <FooterTemplate>
    </ul>This custom list has been brought to you by
                       the <b>repeater</b> control.
    </FooterTemplate>

    </asp:Repeater>
    </form>

  </body>
</html>
```

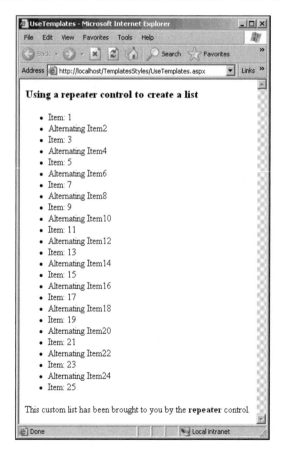

In this example we use the repeater control to create an HTML unordered list. In the header we provide text and HTML tags that we wish to appear before all other content:

```
<HeaderTemplate>
<h3>Using a repeater control to create a list</h3>
<ul>
</HeaderTemplate>
```

Because the header appears only once and before the item and alternating item templates, we can do things such as adding opening tags for HTML elements as we have done here with the `<UL>` element. We follow the header template with simple templates for items and for alternating items that provide the layout for the items in the data source of the control. Each of these items is wrapped in a list item element (`<li>`) so that each appears as an element of the unordered list:

```
<ItemTemplate>
 <li>Item: <%#Container.DataItem%> </li>
</ItemTemplate>

<AlternatingItemTemplate>
 <li>Alternating Item<%#Container.DataItem%> </li>
</AlternatingItemTemplate>
```

Finally, in our footer we close the list tag and provide closing remarks:

```
<FooterTemplate>
</ul>This custom list has been brought to you by
                    the <b>repeater</b> control.
</FooterTemplate>
```

The repeater control is a very simple templated control. It takes the content of the template and renders it to the display exactly as we have defined it. However, you can see how even a basic control such as this can make developing complex web pages easier. Despite, or perhaps because of, the simple nature of this control, it makes a perfect example for understanding how to create templated controls. There are several important things to notice about the use of the repeater control and to keep in mind when developing your own controls.

First, the names of the templates are straightforward and provide insight into how the information in those templates will be used. This allows the consumer of the control to quickly gain an understanding of how to use the templates exposed by your controls. When naming your templates make sure the names give the consumer an idea of where on the control they can expect to see the layout they define, as well as the intended use of the template. As a developer, 'Header' tells me that this template will most likely be at the top of the control when it is rendered and that I should put content in the template that will appear once at the beginning of the control.

Next, if you look at the source rendered by the repeater control you will notice, as mentioned above, that the control simply renders the content defined. This is not mandatory for templated controls. The DataList control, for example, would render the same way in our browser given the templates we defined above. However, the DataList would render the content using an HTML table. It is up to you, as the control designer, to decide the best way to render your control. Templates are meant to give the consumer some, but not necessarily total authority over the layout of your control.

143

In the sections that follow we will be examining how to create templated controls and the issues that need to be addressed to be successful in doing so. Specifically we will be covering:

❑   Templated control basics – the essential information you need to know about templated controls

❑   Creating a simple templated control – we will create a straightforward control with a single template

❑   Creating an advanced templated control – we will create a daily specials templated control for a web site

❑   Defining a custom template – how to define a custom template class to use for template properties of templated controls

❑   Loading templates from files at run time

Creating Templated Controls

A templated control is actually made up of two objects: the control itself and a container for the template items it exposes. In the repeater example above, we referred to the container object when we displayed the numbers from the array list using the following syntax:

```
<%# Container.DataItem %>
```

The container variable serves as a reference to the control that acts as the container for our template. The container for the control does not have to be another class. A templated control can act as its own container whenever that makes sense. However, it is common practice to create a container for the templates named *ControlName*Item. The DataList uses the DataListItem while the Repeater uses the RepeaterItem to act as containers for their templates.

We will cover containers in more detail shortly. First, it is important to understand the role of the **ITemplate** interface in creating templated controls. This interface is the datatype we use for any template properties we wish to expose on our control.

A simple definition of a template property on a control looks like the following:

```
//private member variable
private ITemplate _itemTemplate;

//public property accessor
public ITemplate ItemTemplate
{
  get{return _itemTemplate;}
  set{_itemTemplate = value;}
}
```

This exposes our template as a property of the class allowing consumers to specify a template through code or declaratively in a Web Form. Once we have a template defined, we need a way to add the content of that template into the control hierarchy. The ITemplate interface defines a single method, InstantiateIn, which allows a template to be created within another control:

```
public void InstantiateIn(Control container);
```

We use this method to take an instance of a template, provided by our property above, and add it to the controls collection of another control. Because the content provided in a template property is usually provided declaratively in a Web Form, this function provides an easy way to add the content as a child control, hiding much of the complexity of taking the content provided by the user and building it into a control that can be manipulated.

The control you pass to the `InstantiateIn` method will be the container for your template. As mentioned before, it is common practice to have this as a separate class but it is not necessary. You can pass any control to the `InstantiateIn` method, but you will most often pass a control that implements `INamingContainer`. This interface will be discussed shortly.

Essentially, when the `InstantiateIn` method is called, the ASP.NET Runtime parses the template contents and creates controls based on the tags and code in the template. These controls are then added to the container passed into the method. For example, if a template contained a single `Label` tag, then that tag would be parsed into a `Label` control and added to the controls collection of the container.

We have mentioned containers several times now and the concept is fairly straightforward: A container is the control that the defined template(s) get added to. One thing that might not be as clear is how we tell the ASP.NET Framework what the container for our template is. While we have said that a template can technically be instantiated in any control, in order for the consumer of our control to be able to do anything useful with the control, we need to identify the type of the control that will act as the container. We do this by using the **TemplateContainerAttribute**. This attribute precedes each template property that we expose, as each template needs to have a container defined in order to let the Framework know the type of the control we are referring to when we use the container syntax shown in previous examples. If a type is not provided, via this attribute, then ASP.NET will treat references to the container of a template as references to an instance of the `Control` class. This does not provide the consumer access to the properties and data available from the container.

Different templates within or across controls can share a container, or have different classes act as containers. For example, if we define an `ItemTemplate` and an `AlternatingItemTemplate`, then we would most likely use the same container for them since they will be exposing similar data and information, just with a different layout.

The code below shows the same template property on a control as above but this time with the appropriate attribute applied:

```
//private member variable
private ITemplate _itemTemplate;


//public property accessor
[TemplateContainerAttribute(typeof(myTemplateContainerClass))]
public ITemplate ItemTemplate
{
  get{return _itemTemplate;}
  set{_itemTemplate = value;}
}
```

The `TemplateContainerAttribute` constructor takes as an argument the type of the class that will act as the container for our template property. This attribute is scoped to allow it to be applied to properties only. In our example, we have applied this attribute to the `ItemTemplate` property of our control indicating to the runtime that when this template is processed, the container for the template will be an instance of the `myTemplateContainerClass` class.

The class that this attribute points to should implement the **INamingContainer** interface. This interface does not define any methods or properties that need to be implemented by inheriting classes. Instead it is known as a **marker interface**. It simply marks the class that implements it so that other classes can act on the implementer in specific ways.

In the case of the `INamingContainer` interface the Framework uses this interface to mark the start of a new naming scope. What this means is that the unique ID of any control contained within this control will have its unique ID modified to include the class implementing this interface. In other words, if a control has a unique ID of 'myctrl' this would be its ID. However, if that same control were housed inside a control that implemented the `INamingContainer` interface, with an ID of 'myNewContainer' then the unique ID of the contained control would become 'myNewContainer:myctrl'. This containment is akin to the namespace hierarchy used to organize the Base Class Library and allows the Framework to correctly identify top-level elements and their children for things such as event bubbling (discussed in Chapter 3).

We saw at the beginning of this chapter that to consume a templated control we simply define elements within the HTML and then provide the layout for our content. In order for our control to consume this inner HTML and treat it as properties we have to use the **ParseChildren Attribute**. This attribute, when applied to a control, indicates how the page parser should treat inner HTML elements. These inner elements can be treated as either properties of the control in which they appear or as child controls of that parent control. In the case of templates we need them to be treated as properties as we will see. In other instances, the controls you create will house other controls and should allow these elements to be parsed and added to the controls collection of the Server Control.

In order to have the elements we define treated as children we mark our class with this attribute passing `true` to indicate that children should be parsed as properties. The example syntax below illustrates this point:

```
[ParseChildren(true)]
public class MyControl:WebControl
{}
```

The `WebControl` class already has this attribute applied and set to `true`. It is therefore unnecessary to apply this attribute to your control if you derive from `WebControl` and want this behavior. However, it is good practice to explicitly apply this attribute so that others reviewing your code will know your intentions. Likewise, if you, or another developer, decided at a later time to change the control to derive from the `Control` class, your control would stop functioning as expected.

The items covered so far are the basic items necessary to create a complete templated Server Controls. As a quick recap the steps are:

❑ Mark your control class with the `ParseChildren` attribute to allow for your template properties to be set declaratively in the HTML of a Web Form

❑ Expose public properties of the type `ITemplate` for each template you wish to define

❑ Decorate your template properties with the `TemplateContainer` attribute to inform the runtime of the control type that will house your template

❑ Use the `InstantiateIn` method to create an instance of your template within the template container class and add the container to the controls collection of your Server Control

❑ Define the container class you will use with your templates

In the next section we will see each of these concepts in action as we create a very basic templated Server Control.

Basic Templated Controls

Now that we have covered the concepts of creating a templated control, it should be helpful to see all of them applied to creating a very basic control. The first control we will create is a very basic control that does nothing more than output the user's template the number of times they indicate. We provide a `RepeatCount` property that lets the user specify the number of times the template should be output and an `ItemTemplate` property that lets the user define the template they wish to instantiate:

SuperSimpleRepeater.cs

```csharp
using System;
using System.Web.UI;
using System.Web.UI.WebControls;
using System.ComponentModel;

namespace WROX.ProASPNetServerControls.Chapter5.TemplateControls
{

    //define our class as deriving from WebControl and
    //implement INamingContainer
    [ParseChildren(true)]
    public class SuperSimpleRepeater :
        System.Web.UI.WebControls.WebControl,
            INamingContainer
    {

        //define a variable to hold the number of times
        //to instantiate the template and the template
        //itself
        private int _repeatCount;
        private ITemplate _itemTemplate;

        //public property accessors for the repeat count
        public int RepeatCount
        {
            get{return _repeatCount;}
            set{_repeatCount = value;}
        }
```

```csharp
//our property for the template specifying
//that this class will act as the container
[TemplateContainer(typeof(SuperSimpleRepeater))]
public ITemplate ItemTemplate
{
  get{return _itemTemplate;}
  set{_itemTemplate=value;}
}


//override the control creation and instantiate
//the template the number of times specified
protected override void CreateChildControls ()
{
  //clear out the control colletion if there
  //are any children we want to wipe them out
  //before starting
  Controls.Clear();

  //as long as we are repeating at least once
  //and the template is defined, then loop and
  //instantiate the template in a panel
  if ((RepeatCount > 0)&&(_itemTemplate!=null))
  {
    for(int i = 0; i<RepeatCount;i++)
    {
      Panel container = new Panel();
      _itemTemplate.InstantiateIn(container);
      Controls.Add(container);

    }
  }
  else    //otherwise we output a message
  {
    Controls.Add(new LiteralControl("Specify the record
      count and an item template"));
  }
}
}


}
}
```

We start by defining our control class and deriving from WebControl. We also implement the INamingContainer interface since, for this simple example, we will be acting as our own container. We also decorate our class with the ParseChildren attribute to allow our template to be specified in the HTML. Next we define two properties, the RepeatCount and ItemTemplate properties, to allow the user to specify the template and the number of times it should be instantiated. We expose the ItemTemplate property as an ITemplate, which will allow us to call the InstantiateIn method on it.

In order to create the control hierarchy, we override the `CreateChildControls` method of the `Control` class and put our own logic in for creating the controls. We check to make sure that both the template and the repeat count have been specified. If one or the other has not been provided by the consumer, then we create a `LiteralControl` object putting out a message. In production we would not output a message such as this; instead, we would likely do nothing or raise an exception so the control developer knew they were improperly defining the control. If we have a count and a template, then we simply execute a `for` loop creating a new instance of the `Panel` class and instantiating our control in it. We then add the panel to the controls collection so that it will be rendered to the client. The `Panel` is a simple control that gets rendered as a `DIV` tag and provides a lightweight control to act as our container.

To use the control in a page we first make sure to register the tag in a directive so the parsing engine knows where to find our control. Next we add our control specifying the `RepeatCount` as an attribute and providing a template to be repeated:

SimpleRepeaterHost.aspx

```
<%@ Page language="c#"%>

<%@ Register TagPrefix="WROX"
Namespace="WROX.ProASPNetServerControls.Chapter5.TemplateControls"
Assembly="Chapter5" %>

<!DOCTYPE HTML PUBLIC "-//W3C//DTD HTML 4.0 Transitional//EN" >

<html>
  <head>
    <title>SimpleRepeaterHost</title>
  </head>
  <body>

    <form id="SimpleRepeaterHost" method="post" runat="server">
    <WROX:SuperSimpleRepeater id="sample" runat="server" RepeatCount="10">
     <ItemTemplate>
     <div align="center">
      <hr>
       Creating templated controls is <b>easy</b> and <i>fun</i>.<br>
       <hr>
       </div>
     </ItemTemplate>
    </WROX:SuperSimpleRepeater>

    </form>

  </body>
</html>
```

In our control we request that our template be repeated ten times by setting the `RepeatCount` attribute. We then define a simple template using a `DIV` tag to center the content, two horizontal rule elements (`<hr>`) and some text with formatting elements applied. The output is rendered as follows:

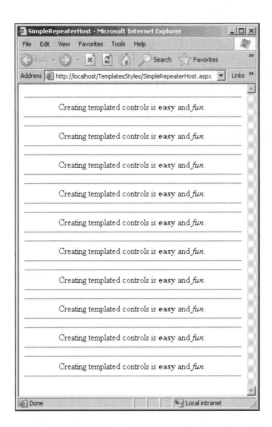

As you can see, creating a basic templated control does not have to be difficult and does not take a great deal of code. However, while someone might find some use for this control, as it stands it is not very useful. Let's expand it to use a separate container and expose properties on the container to allow access to data in the control. We will expand our control to provide an item number representing the index of the template in the series as well as the total count. In addition, rather than a single item template, we will provide header and footer templates and an alternating item template. With these four templates our user will have much more control over the layout of the content.

We start by defining our container class, `SimpleRepeaterItem`. It is a very simple class made up of a constructor and two read-only properties. In the `CreateChildControls` method we will create instances of the container by passing in the current index and the total count for all of our templates. This allows the consumer of our class to access this data in their templates. It is common practice when creating data-bound templated controls to create a `DataItem` property on the container class. When a data item is read from the data source, the item is passed to the container, which then exposes it. In this way the control becomes ultimately flexible, as it does not have to know anything about the data. The consumer of the control provides the data and consumes it in the control and so is most knowledgeable about the source of the data:

SuperSimpleRepeater2.cs

```
using System;
using System.Web.UI;
using System.Web.UI.WebControls;
using System.ComponentModel;

namespace WROX.ProASPNetServerControls.Chapter5.TemplateControls
{
  //this is the class that acts as the container for our templates
  public class SimpleRepeaterItem:WebControl, INamingContainer
  {

    //two simple field variables
    int _index;
    int _total;

    //a constructor that allows for setting the index and total count
    public SimpleRepeaterItem(int itemIndex, int totalCount)
    {
      _index = itemIndex;
      _total = totalCount;
    }


    //public property accessors for the current index of the
    //item and the total number of item we will be showing
    public int Index
    {
      get{return _index;}
    }

    public int Total
    {
      get{return _total;}
    }

  }
}
```

Next we begin our control class by declaring private variables and public properties for the three new templates we wish to expose. In addition, we decorate each of these new templates, and our existing `ItemTemplate` with the `TemplateContainer` attribute indicating the `SimpleRepeaterItem` class:

```
//define our class as deriving from WebControl and
//implement INamingContainer
[ParseChildren(true)]
public class SuperSimpleRepeater2 :
  System.Web.UI.WebControls.WebControl,
  INamingContainer
{
```

```csharp
//define a variable to hold the number of times
//to instantiate the template and the templates
//we are going to expose
private int _repeatCount;
private ITemplate _itemTemplate;
private ITemplate _headerTemplate;
private ITemplate _footerTemplate;
private ITemplate _alternatingItemTemplate;
//public property accessors for the repeat count
public int RepeatCount
{
   get{return _repeatCount;}
   set{_repeatCount = value;}
}

//our property for the template specifying
//that this class will act as the container
[TemplateContainer(typeof(SimpleRepeaterItem))]
public ITemplate ItemTemplate
{
   get{return _itemTemplate;}
   set{_itemTemplate=value;}
}

//our property for the template specifying
//that this class will act as the container
[TemplateContainer(typeof(SimpleRepeaterItem))]
public ITemplate AlternatingItemTemplate
{
   get{return _alternatingItemTemplate;}
   set{_alternatingItemTemplate=value;}
}

//our property for the template specifying
//that this class will act as the container
[TemplateContainer(typeof(SimpleRepeaterItem))]
public ITemplate HeaderTemplate
{
   get{return _headerTemplate;}
   set{_headerTemplate=value;}
}

//our property for the template specifying
//that this class will act as the container
[TemplateContainer(typeof(SimpleRepeaterItem))]
public ITemplate FooterTemplate
{
   get{return _footerTemplate;}
   set{_footerTemplate=value;}
}
```

Next we modify the CreateChildControls method to instantiate our templates inside the container. For each template we always check to make sure the template is not null. If a user does not specify a template, our control should not throw an error. If your control requires that a particular template be provided, first check for that template before processing and throw an exception if it has not been provided.

The header template gets rendered first if it is present. We instantiate an instance of the container class and then call `InstantiateIn` on the header template passing in the container class. Next, we call `databind` on the container to ensure that consumers of our control can access the properties of the container with the data-binding syntax. And finally, we add the container to the controls collection of our control.

For the item and alternating item template we follow the same procedure, with the exception that we alternate between the two if both are provided. If no alternating item template is provided then the item template is used for each item. When all of the items have finished, we check to see if we have a footer template and add that to the controls as well:

```
//override the control creation and instantiate
//the template the number of times specified
protected override void CreateChildControls()
{
  //clear out the control colletion if there
  //are any children we want to wipe them out
  //before starting
  Controls.Clear();

  //as long as we are repeating at least once
  //and the template is defined, then loop and
  //instantiate the templates in the container class
  if ((RepeatCount > 0)&&(_itemTemplate!=null))
  {
    //start by outputing the header template if one
    //was supplied
    if(_headerTemplate!=null)
    {
      SimpleRepeaterItem headerContainer = new
        SimpleRepeaterItem(0,_repeatCount);
      _headerTemplate.InstantiateIn(headerContainer);
      headerContainer.DataBind();
      Controls.Add(headerContainer);
    }

    //output the content the specified number of times
    //use the alternating template if specified
    for(int i = 0; i<RepeatCount;i++)
    {
      SimpleRepeaterItem container = new
        SimpleRepeaterItem(i+1,RepeatCount);

      //is this an alternating item and do we have
      //a template?
      if((i%2==0)&&(_alternatingItemTemplate!=null))
      {
_alternatingItemTemplate.InstantiateIn(container);
      }
      else    // then use the item template
      {
        _itemTemplate.InstantiateIn(container);
```

```
            }
            container.DataBind();
            Controls.Add(container);
        }


        //once all of the items have been put out
        //we add the footer template if one was given
        if(_footerTemplate!=null)
        {
            SimpleRepeaterItem footerContainer = new
SimpleRepeaterItem(_repeatCount, _repeatCount);
            _footerTemplate.InstantiateIn(footerContainer);
            footerContainer.DataBind();
            Controls.Add(footerContainer);

        }
    }
    else    //if no repeat count or item template we output a message
    {
      Controls.Add(new LiteralControl("Specify the record
      count and an item template"));
    }
  }


}
```

To use this control in a page we register the tag information and then create our control as shown in the Web Form below. We still provide the RepeatCount but we now also supply header, footer, item, and alternating item templates to specify the layout:

SimpleRepeater2Host.aspx

```
<%@ Page language="c#"%>
<%@ Register TagPrefix="WROX"
Namespace="WROX.ProASPNetServerControls.Chapter5.TemplateControls" Assembly="
Chapter5" %>
<!DOCTYPE HTML PUBLIC "-//W3C//DTD HTML 4.0 Transitional//EN" >

<html>
  <head>
    <title>SimpleRepeater2Host</title>
  </head>
  <body">

    <form id="SimpleRepeater2Host" method="post" runat="server">

<WROX:SuperSimpleRepeater2 id="sample" runat="server" RepeatCount="10">
 <HeaderTemplate>
  <h2 style="Color:Red">Super Simple Repeater Strikes Again!</h2>
  Now showing <%# Container.Total %> Items for your viewing pleasure.
 </HeaderTemplate>
```

```
<ItemTemplate>
<div align="center">
<hr>
 Item <%# Container.Index %> of <%# Container.Total%><br>
 <hr>
 </div>
</ItemTemplate>

<AlternatingItemTemplate>
<div align="center" style="border-right: fuchsia double; border-top: fuchsia
double; border-left: fuchsia double; border-bottom: fuchsia double">
 Item <%# Container.Index %> of <%# Container.Total%>
 </div>
</AlternatingItemTemplate>

<FooterTemplate>
 <i>This presentation of the Simple Repeater Control brought
                     to you by the letter <b>W</b></i>
 </FooterTemplate>

</WROX:SuperSimpleRepeater2>

    </form>

  </body>
</html>
```

We define each of our templates with the HTML and text we want them to contain. In this case we have made the alternating and item templates very different for the purposes of demonstration. In the header and each of the item templates we have also used the simple binding syntax to indicate that we want to output the value of the Index and Total properties on the container of our template. Notice that the names of the properties match those defined in our container class. Without the TemplateContainerAttribute on the template properties we defined, the ASP.NET page compiler would complain that the properties did not exist on the class Control. When a container class is not specified, the Control class is assumed. This works fine if you don't plan on binding any of the container's properties in the display. It is only when you attempt to access the container or any of its properties that this causes a problem.

The next figure shows the outcome of using our new control in this way. Notice that the alternating template with the border defined appears for each odd numbered item while the item template appears for each even item:

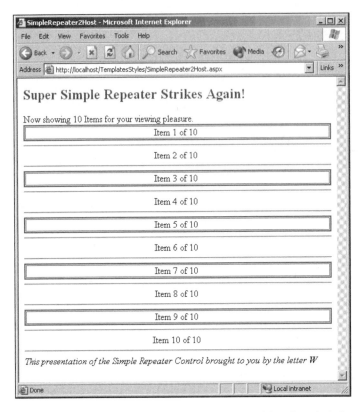

The controls we have created so far would only be minimally useful but they do help to understand the basics of making a template control. In the next section we will see how to make a more complex control.

Advanced Templated Control

The previous examples were intentionally simple in order to make it easier to see the concepts of templated controls in action. In this section we will take a look at creating a more complex control that takes full advantage of templates. We will be building a Daily Special control that will read the special of the day from an XML file and expose the information about the special in a templated control. The control will have five templates: a header and a footer template to allow the consumer to frame the contents of the control as well as left, item, and right templates, each of which appears in between the header and footer. We will use the table web controls to build the structure around our templates and provide a simple grid as shown in the following diagram:

Header Template		
Left Template	Item Template	Right Template
Footer Template		

An example of the XML file that contains our data is shown below. Each item is a **special** element with a `date` attribute that indicates the date this special is in effect. In this example we have only included one item in the file, but any number of items will work with the code. The data for this example comes from the `GrocerToGo` sample supplied and used in the .NET Quickstarts samples. The images used are also found in the web site installed by the Quickstarts setup:

DailySpecials.xml

```xml
<?xml version="1.0" encoding="utf-8" ?>
<SPECIALS>
 <SPECIAL date="12/2/2001">
  <ProductID>1001</ProductID>
  <CategoryID>1</CategoryID>
  <ProductName>Chocolate City Milk</ProductName>
  <ProductDescription>Chocolate City Milk Description</ProductDescription>
  <UnitPrice>2.25</UnitPrice>
  <SalePrice>1.75</SalePrice>
  <ImagePath>./images/milk5.gif</ImagePath>
 </SPECIAL>
</SPECIALS>
```

`DailySpecials.cs` contains the class definition for our control as well as the container class `DailySpecialsItem`.

We start by adding the namespace `using` statement for `System.Xml` as well as adding a reference to the `System.Xml.dll` assembly. In VisualStudio .NET this is accomplished by using the **Add Reference** wizard and choosing the `System.Xml.dll` file. With the command-line compilers, the a `/r` switch is used to specify the `System.Xml.dll` assembly. Next we declare the variables for our control including the string that will hold the path to the XML file and the variables for our five templates and provide public property accessors for each. Notice that we have decorated each of the template properties with the `TemplateContainer` attribute indicating the container for the template. In this example we will be writing a class called `DailySpecialsItem` that will serve as the container for our templates and expose the data in the XML file:

DailySpecials.cs

```csharp
using System;
using System.Globalization;
using System.Xml;
using System.Xml.XPath;
using System.Web;
using System.Web.UI;
using System.Web.UI.HtmlControls;
using System.Web.UI.WebControls;
using System.ComponentModel;

namespace WROX.ProASPNetServerControls.Chapter5.TemplateControls
{
  public class DailySpecials : System.Web.UI.WebControls.WebControl
  {
```

```csharp
//member variables for our templates
//and the filename where we will retrieve
//our data
private string _specialsFile;
private ITemplate _headerTemplate;
private ITemplate _itemTemplate;
private ITemplate _footerTemplate;
private ITemplate _rightTemplate;
private ITemplate _leftTemplate;

//define the property for the path to the source file
public string SpecialsFile
{
  get
  {return _specialsFile;}
  set{_specialsFile = value;}
}

//define template properties
[TemplateContainer(typeof(DailySpecialsItem))]
public ITemplate HeaderTemplate
{
  get{return _headerTemplate;}
  set{_headerTemplate=value;}
}

[TemplateContainer(typeof(DailySpecialsItem))]
public ITemplate FooterTemplate
{
  get{return _footerTemplate;}
  set{_footerTemplate=value;}
}

[TemplateContainer(typeof(DailySpecialsItem))]
public ITemplate ItemTemplate
{
  get{return _itemTemplate;}
  set{_itemTemplate=value;}
}

[TemplateContainer(typeof(DailySpecialsItem))]
public ITemplate LeftTemplate
{
  get{return _leftTemplate;}
  set{_leftTemplate=value;}
}

[TemplateContainer(typeof(DailySpecialsItem))]
public ITemplate RightTemplate
{
  get{return _rightTemplate;}
  set{_rightTemplate=value;}
}
```

Now that we have the properties defined, we do the real work in the control, which is to override the `CreateChildControls` method and build our control hierarchy. We build the hierarchy by creating table controls such as `Table`, `TableRow`, and `TableCell`, instantiating our templates within their container and adding the container to the table cell. For the header and footer we determine how many columns there are, based on the number of templates defined, and set the column span appropriately. Before creating any of this, however, we take the important step of making sure that we have a path to the XML file that contains our data:

```
//this is where we do most of the work in creating
//the control hierarchy based on the templates
//which have been defined.
protected override void CreateChildControls()
{
  //get the number of columns in the second row
  int numberOfColumns=GetColumnCount();

  //clear our control state before beginning
  Controls.Clear();

  //make sure we have a file to work with and throw
  //an exception if we do not
  if((_specialsFile!=null)&&(_specialsFile!=String.Empty))
  {

    //create a new table object which we will use to
    //hold our template content when we render
    HtmlTable t = new HtmlTable();

    //if the header template is defined, create a
    //table row and cell to put it in, instantiate
    //it in the container class and then add it to the
    //table cell.
    if(_headerTemplate!=null)
    {
      HtmlTableRow r = new HtmlTableRow();
      HtmlTableCell c = new HtmlTableCell();

      //set the column span based on how many
      //columns there are in the middle row

      c.ColSpan=numberOfColumns;

      DailySpecialsItem headerContainer = new
        DailySpecialsItem();

      //call createitem to get the data for the control
      CreateItem(ref headerContainer);
      _headerTemplate.InstantiateIn(headerContainer);
      headerContainer.DataBind();

      //add the header to the table cell,
      //then put that in the row, and add
      //the row to the table
      c.Controls.Add(headerContainer);
      r.Controls.Add(c);
      t.Controls.Add(r);
    }
```

```
//new row for the left, item and right templates
HtmlTableRow row = new HtmlTableRow();

//add each of the other items in the same way
//as we did the header
if(_leftTemplate!=null)
{
  HtmlTableCell c = new HtmlTableCell();

  DailySpecialsItem container = new
    DailySpecialsItem();

  CreateItem(ref container);

  _leftTemplate.InstantiateIn(container);
  container.DataBind();

  c.Controls.Add(container);
  row.Controls.Add(c);

}

//item, or center template
if(_itemTemplate!=null)
{
  HtmlTableCell c = new HtmlTableCell();

  DailySpecialsItem container = new
    DailySpecialsItem();

  CreateItem(ref container);

  _itemTemplate.InstantiateIn(container);
  container.DataBind();

  c.Controls.Add(container);
  row.Controls.Add(c);

}

//right template
if(_rightTemplate!=null)
{
  HtmlTableCell c = new HtmlTableCell();

  DailySpecialsItem container = new
    DailySpecialsItem();

  CreateItem(ref container);

  _rightTemplate.InstantiateIn(container);
  container.DataBind();
```

```
          c.Controls.Add(container);
          row.Controls.Add(c);

        }

        //add the row containing these three templates
        t.Controls.Add(row);


        //create the footer just as we did the header
        if(_footerTemplate!=null)
        {
          HtmlTableRow r = new HtmlTableRow();
          HtmlTableCell c = new HtmlTableCell();
          c.ColSpan = numberOfColumns;

          DailySpecialsItem footerContainer = new
            DailySpecialsItem();
          CreateItem(ref footerContainer);
          _footerTemplate.InstantiateIn(footerContainer);
          footerContainer.DataBind();
          c.Controls.Add(footerContainer);
          r.Controls.Add(c);
          t.Controls.Add(r);
        }

        //add the table to the controls collection
        Controls.Add(t);

        //indicate that we have created the child controls
        ChildControlsCreated=true;
      }
      else
      {
        throw new ApplicationException
                            ("A valid source file must be specified.");

      }
    }
  }
```

Once we have added all of the defined templates to the table, we add the table to the Controls collection for our control. When our control is rendered, the table will render itself and all of our templates within its various cells. For each of the template containers we called the CreateItem method to extract the data from the XML file and set the properties on the container before instantiating our template in the container and adding it to the table. In this method we use the HttpRequest object for this request to map a path to the XML file provided by the SpecialsFile property. We then open this file with an XmlTextReader and XmlDocument and use the SelectSingleNode method of the XmlDocument and XmlNode objects to extract the values from the file. If the node we are interested in is not found, we set the product description to a message. In a real scenario, business rules for the application would dictate the desired outcome if there were no specials for the day:

```
//loads the data from the XML file and
private void CreateItem(ref DailySpecialsItem item)
{
  XmlNode node;
  XmlTextReader rdr;
  XmlDocument doc;

    //map the path to the specials XML file
    string path =
      HttpContext.Current.Request.MapPath(_specialsFile);

    //create an XML document and load the file
    doc = new XmlDocument();
    rdr = new XmlTextReader(path);

  try
  {
    doc.Load(rdr);

    //get the node for today's specials
    node = doc.SelectSingleNode(@"SPECIALS/SPECIAL[@date='" +
      DateTime.Today.ToShortDateString() + "']");

    //make sure we got a node and then set the properties
    //on the DailySpecialsItem object from the XML
    if(node!=null)
    {
      item.SpecialsFile = _specialsFile;
      item.ImgUrl =
        node.SelectSingleNode("//ImagePath").InnerText;
      item.NormalPrice =
      float.Parse(node.SelectSingleNode("UnitPrice").InnerText,NumberStyles.
      Currency,new CultureInfo("en-US"));
      item.SalePrice = float.Parse(node.SelectSingleNode("SalePrice")
      InnerText,System.Globalization.NumberStyles.Currency);
      item.ProductDescription =
      node.SelectSingleNode("ProductDescription").InnerText;
      item.ProductName =
        node.SelectSingleNode("ProductName").InnerText;
    }
    else  //set some plain values
    {
      item.ImgUrl = "";
      item.NormalPrice = 0.0f;
      item.SalePrice = 0.0f;
      item.ProductDescription = "";
      item.ProductName = "No product, make sure you have set the
        dates properly in the dailyspecials.xml file";
    }

  }
  catch(Exception e)
  {
    HttpContext.Current.Response.Write(e.Message.ToString());
  }
```

```
      finally  //clean up regardless of the outcome
      {
        rdr.Close();
        node = null;
        doc=null;
        rdr=null;
      }
   }
```

We also need a method that provides the number of templates that have been specified for the middle row. To do so we simply check each of the templates for `null` and increase the counter if the template has been specified. This method was called in the `CreateChildControls` method to set the `ColumnSpan` property for the table cells used to house the header and footer templates:

```
      //based on the number of templates in the second
      //row of the table, gets the number of columns
      //so we can properly fit our header and footer
      private int GetColumnCount()
      {
        int count=0;
        if(_leftTemplate!=null)
          count++;
        if(_itemTemplate!=null)
          count++;
        if(_rightTemplate!=null)
          count++;

        return count;
      }
   }
```

Finally, we need to define the container class for our templates. This is a simple class with six properties that provide access to the information about the daily special. In the `CreateItem` method we set these properties with the information from the XML file that defines our specials:

> Notice that we implement **INamingContainer** to provide a new naming context for each of our templates and the controls they may contain.

```
  //the dailyspecialsitem class acts as our container
    //exposing properties that will allow the consumer of
    //our control to get the data they need to display the
    //control properly
    public class DailySpecialsItem:WebControl, INamingContainer
    {
      private string _productName;
      private string _productDescription;
      private float _normalPrice;
      private float _salePrice;
      private string _imgUrl;
      private string _specialsFile;
```

```
    public DailySpecialsItem()
    {}

    //properties for each of the items
    public string ProductName
    {
      get{return _productName;}
      set{_productName=value;}
    }

    public string ProductDescription
    {
      get{return _productDescription;}
      set{_productDescription=value;}
    }

    public float NormalPrice
    {
      get{return _normalPrice;}
      set{_normalPrice=value;}
    }

    public float SalePrice
    {
      get{return _salePrice;}
      set{_salePrice=value;}
    }

    public string ImgUrl
    {
      get{return _imgUrl;}
      set{_imgUrl = value;}
    }

    public string SpecialsFile
    {
      get{return _specialsFile;}
      set{_specialsFile=value;}
    }

  }
}
```

Now that we have the control, it is time to use it in a Web Form. The `DailySpecials.aspx` file contains two instances of our control with varying layouts. We can easily move around the prices as well as the product information and image, with control over the layout:

DailySpecials.aspx

```
<%@ Page language="c#"%>
<%@ Register TagPrefix="WROX"
Namespace="WROX.ProASPNetServerControls.Chapter5.TemplateControls" Assembly="
Chapter5" %>
<!DOCTYPE HTML PUBLIC "-//W3C//DTD HTML 4.0 Transitional//EN" >
<HTML>
 <HEAD>
  <title>DailySpecials</title>
 </HEAD>
 <body ms_positioning="GridLayout">
  <form id="DailySpecials" method="post" runat="server">

    <WROX:DailySpecials id="sample" runat="server"
                          specialsfile="DailySpecials.xml">
     <HeaderTemplate>
      <h4>Today's Special:
       <%# Container.ProductName %>
      </h4>
     </HeaderTemplate>
     <LeftTemplate>
      <img align="middle" src='<%# Container.ImgUrl %>'>
     </LeftTemplate>
     <ItemTemplate>
      <%# Container.ProductDescription %>
     </ItemTemplate>
     <FooterTemplate>
              Normally <i>
       <%# String.Format("{0:c}",Container.NormalPrice)%>
      </i> today only <b>
       <%# String.Format("{0:c}",Container.SalePrice) %>
      </b>
     </FooterTemplate>
    </WROX:DailySpecials>
    <br>
    <hr>
    <br>

    <WROX:DailySpecials id="Dailyspecials1" runat="server"
                        specialsfile="DailySpecials.xml">
     <HeaderTemplate>
      <h4>Today's Special</h4>
     </HeaderTemplate>
     <ItemTemplate>
      <img align="middle" src='<%# Container.ImgUrl %>'>
     </ItemTemplate>
     <LeftTemplate>
       Daily Price <i>
       <%# String.Format("{0:c}",Container.NormalPrice) %>
      </i><br>
       Today only <b>
       <%# String.Format("{0:c}",Container.SalePrice) %>
      </b>
```

```
        </LeftTemplate>
      <FooterTemplate>
      <h3><%# Container.ProductName %></h3>
      <%# Container.ProductDescription %>
      </FooterTemplate>
    </WROX:DailySpecials>
  </form>
 </body>
</HTML>
```

This control shows that without much code we can make a very flexible control that provides the consumer with a great deal of flexibility in the layout of the control content. Templates are a very powerful way to increase the usefulness of the controls you create by allowing them to be used in multiple situations or sites. A Daily Specials control like this one, with a bit more work, could be used on many different sites. In addition, the control could be made more general by allowing it to be bound to any XML file and simply returning the node with the current date as an attribute.

In the next section we will see how we can make our control even more dynamic by creating classes we can use to programmatically supply templates for our control rather than supplying them declaratively in a Web Form. This becomes important when we need both the flexibility of defining the layout separate from the implementation and the power of dynamic content.

Dynamic Templates

The concepts we have covered so far give us a great deal of control over the layout of our control and to some extent the content. If we do not want a piece of data on the control, we do not have to put it in. But what if we want the content in our template to be more dynamic? For example, what if we want the content of our control to vary based on the user or the role a user is in?

When the need arises to have a dynamic template, there are two choices: implement ITemplate or load templates from a file. The first of these choices involves creating a class that implements ITemplate and providing an implementation for the InstantiateIn method. The second consists of creating a template definition in a separate file and then loading that template at run time. We will examine both in this section.

Implementing ITemplate

Remember that the template properties on our Server Control are of the type ITemplate. This means that in order to set this property we need only to pass a class that implements ITemplate. Therefore, we can create, in code, our own template and assign it to the template property of the control. In this way we have total control over the creation of the control hierarchy within the template. This mechanism is more powerful than the declarative approach we have been using up to this point. However, this power comes with some costs. Designing a template class can take more time than using declarative syntax and requires a developer rather than a web designer.

As a short example we will create a class that acts as a template for the header in our DailySpecials control. This header will output heading text for all users. If the user logged into the site and is in the administrators group on the machine, we will also add a link that allows the user to view the XML source file. This is a simple example of the power of creating templates programmatically but there are many uses for this type of functionality.

We start by defining a class that implements the ITemplate interface. Note that this class does not have to derive from Control or WebControl, as all we are interested in is the implementation of the InstantiateIn method. In our control, we use this method to create the control hierarchy, rather than allowing ASP.NET to do it for us based on the template provided in the HTML:

DynamicTemplate.cs

```
using System;
using System.Web;
using System.Web.UI;
using System.Web.UI.HtmlControls;
using System.Web.UI.WebControls;

namespace WROX.ProASPNetServerControls.Chapter5.TemplateControls
{
  //custom class that can act as a template when used
  //in code. Used rather than declarative template
  //to provide custom content. Must implement ITemplate
  public class DynamicTemplate:ITemplate
  {
    public DynamicTemplate()
    {}
```

```
//implement the only method defined in ITemplate
public void InstantiateIn(Control container)
{
  //create a generic control for the heading
  //and add it to the container passed in
  HtmlGenericControl hdr = new HtmlGenericControl("span");
  hdr.Attributes.Add("style", "font-weight:bolder");
  hdr.InnerText="Today's Special  ";

  container.Controls.Add(hdr);

  //check the user role and if they are an administrator
  //then give them the view source link which will link to
  //the XML source file
  if(HttpContext.Current.User.IsInRole("BUILTIN\\Administrators"))
  {
    //create a new HTML anchor tag and set its text
    HtmlAnchor viewSource = new HtmlAnchor();
    viewSource.InnerText="View Source";

    //connect an event handler to the databinding event
    //of the anchor so we can set its content when the
    //DailySpecialsItem container is bound
    viewSource.DataBinding+=new EventHandler(this.ViewSource_Bind);

    //add the control to the container passed in
    container.Controls.Add(viewSource);
  }

}

//the method that handles the databinding event for our
//html anchor.
protected void ViewSource_Bind(object sender, EventArgs e)
{
  //cast the sender to an anchor
  //and then get its naming container
  //which will be a DailySpecialsItem
  HtmlAnchor a = (HtmlAnchor)sender;
  DailySpecialsItem container =
    (DailySpecialsItem)a.NamingContainer;

  //set the HREF property of the anchor with the path to the
  //XML source file.
  a.Href = container.SpecialsFile;
}
}
}
```

In the `InstatiateIn` method we create a span element and add it to the controls collection of the container control passed in. Next, we check to see if the user is in the built-in administrators role and use this to determine if we will output an HTML link. If the user is in the administrator's role, we create an HTML anchor element and set the text property. We also add an event handler that will handle the data binding event of the anchor. This event handler is necessary because we wish to access a property on the container when those properties are bound to the control. If we did not need to access this information, the addition of the event handler would be unnecessary. See Chapter 6 for more details.

In the `ViewSource_Bind` method, our event handler for the `DataBinding` event of the control, we get a reference to the anchor control we created in our `InstantiateIn` method and use its `NamingContainer` property to get a reference to the `DailySpecialsItem` control that acts as the container for the template. Using the `SpecialsFile` property we set the `href` for the anchor control.

When we use our `DailySpecials` control in a Web Form, we can now specify the header template in the HTML or specify it in code. To do it in code, we define an instance of the `DynamicTemplate` class and pass it to the `HeaderTemplate` property of the control as shown in the example below:

DynamicTemplateHost.aspx

```
<%@ Page language="c#"  AutoEventWireup="true" %>
<%@ Register TagPrefix="WROX"
Namespace="WROX.ProASPNetServerControls.Chapter5.TemplateControls" Assembly="
Chapter5" %>
<%@ Import Namespace="WROX.ProASPNetServerControls.Chapter5.TemplateControls" %>
<!DOCTYPE HTML PUBLIC "-//W3C//DTD HTML 4.0 Transitional//EN" >
<HTML>
 <HEAD>
  <title>DynamicTemplate</title>

  <script language="C#" runat="server">

  private void Page_Load(object sender, EventArgs e)
  {
   DynamicTemplate header = new DynamicTemplate();
   DailySpecials1.HeaderTemplate = header;


  }
  </script>


 </HEAD>
 <body ms_positioning="GridLayout">
  <form id="DynamicTemplate" method="post" runat="server">
   <WROX:DailySpecials id="DailySpecials1" runat="server"
                       specialsfile="DailySpecials.xml">
    <ItemTemplate>
     <img align="middle" src='<%# Container.ImgUrl %>'>
    </ItemTemplate>
    <LeftTemplate>
      Daily Price <i>
      <%# String.Format("{0:c}",Container.NormalPrice) %>
     </i><br>
```

```
      Today only <b>
      <%# String.Format("{0:c}",Container.SalePrice) %>
      </b>
      </LeftTemplate>
    <FooterTemplate>
    <h3><%# Container.ProductName %></h3>
    <%# Container.ProductDescription %>
    </FooterTemplate>
    </WROX:DailySpecials>
  </form>
 </body>
</HTML>
```

> In order to get this example to work, we need to modify the `web.config` file for our web application to use Windows authentication so that we can log in as a Windows user.

By setting the authentication mode to Windows and allowing access to anonymous users we allow the site to continue as it has been. However, we add a location tag to specify that access to our host file does not allow anonymous access. The relevant sections of the `web.config` file are shown below:

web.config

```
<?xml version="1.0" encoding="utf-8" ?>
<configuration>

  <system.web>

  . . .

    <authentication mode="Windows" />
    <authorization>
     <allow users="?"></allow>
    </authorization>

  . . .

  </system.web>

<location path="DynamicTemplateHost.aspx">
 <system.web>
  <authorization>
   <deny users="?"></deny>
  </authorization>
 </system.web>

</location>
</configuration>
```

Now that the configuration is set, we can browse to the page and access it with a user account that does not belong to the administrators group. Then, after closing the browser and reopening it, we can log in with an administrator account. When logged in as an administrator the link will appear, but when logged in as a normal user, there will be no link. The following figure shows the control as rendered when an administrator is logged in:

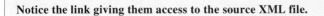

Notice the link giving them access to the source XML file.

This type of dynamic content can be very useful not only in situations where the content should vary based on the user, but when the content should differ based on the environment, such as time of day, or previous shopping patterns.

Loading Templates

A happy medium between the somewhat static declarative approach we started with and the dynamic but technical ITemplate implementation is to load templates from a file at run time. This provides the ease of design that comes with the declarative approach for authoring the templates, but provides flexibility in that our code behind provides the logic to determine which template to load.

Templates that are to be used in this way are defined in the same way as user controls in a file with an ASCX extension. To load the template, we use the `LoadTemplate` method of the `TemplateControl` class. This class is the base class for the `Page` class so we can easily access this method in the code for our page.

We'll modify our previous dynamic template example by adding another `DailySpecials` control to the page and loading its template from a file. We can still do a security check and load the appropriate template based on the user. The following examples show the two templates that we will create:

DailySpecialHeaderTemplate.ascx

```
<b>Today's Special</b>
```

DailySpecialAdminHeader.ascx

```
<b>Today's Special</b>  <a href="dailyspecials.xml">View Source</a>
```

These templates are intentionally simple. Templates loaded from a file can have other ASP.NET Server Controls in them as well as data binding syntax so that they can be truly dynamic. The code below shows our updated `DynamicTemplateHost` file with the second control added and the code to dynamically load the template we want from a file:

DynamicTemplateHost.aspx

```
<%@ Import Namespace=
        "WROX.ProASPNetServerControls.Chapter5.TemplateControls" %>
<%@ Page language="c#"  AutoEventWireup="true" %>
<%@ Register TagPrefix="WROX" Namespace=
        "WROX.ProASPNetServerControls.Chapter5.TemplateControls"
        Assembly="Chapter5" %>
<!DOCTYPE HTML PUBLIC "-//W3C//DTD HTML 4.0 Transitional//EN" >
<HTML>
 <HEAD>
  <title>DynamicTemplate</title>
  <script language="C#" runat="server">

  private void Page_Load(object sender, EventArgs e)
  {
   DynamicTemplate header = new DynamicTemplate();
   DailySpecials1.HeaderTemplate = header;

    //check whether to load the admin template
    if(Context.User.IsInRole("Builtin\\Administrators"))
    {
     DailySpecials2.HeaderTemplate =
     LoadTemplate("DailySpecialAdminHeader.ascx");
    }
    else
    {
      DailySpecials2.HeaderTemplate =
     LoadTemplate("DailySpecialHeaderTemplate.ascx");
    }
  }
```

```
    </script>
  </HEAD>
<body ms_positioning="GridLayout">
  <form id="DynamicTemplate" method="post" runat="server">
   <WROX:DailySpecials id="DailySpecials1" runat="server"
                        specialsfile="DailySpecials.xml">
    <ItemTemplate>
     <img align="middle" src='<%# Container.ImgUrl %>'>
    </ItemTemplate>
    <LeftTemplate>
      Daily Price <i>
      <%# String.Format("{0:c}",Container.NormalPrice) %>
    </i><br>
      Today only <b>
      <%# String.Format("{0:c}",Container.SalePrice) %>
    </b>
      </LeftTemplate>
    <FooterTemplate>
     <h3><%# Container.ProductName %></h3>
     <%# Container.ProductDescription %>
    </FooterTemplate>
   </WROX:DailySpecials>
   <br>
   <hr>
   <br>
    <WROX:DailySpecials id="DailySpecials2" runat="server"
                         specialsfile="DailySpecials.xml">
    <ItemTemplate>
     <img align="middle" src='<%# Container.ImgUrl %>'>
    </ItemTemplate>
    <LeftTemplate>
      Daily Price <i>
      <%# String.Format("{0:c}",Container.NormalPrice) %>
    </i><br>
      Today only <b>
      <%# String.Format("{0:c}",Container.SalePrice) %>
    </b>
      </LeftTemplate>
    <FooterTemplate>
     <h3><%# Container.ProductName %></h3>
     <%# Container.ProductDescription %>
    </FooterTemplate>
   </WROX:DailySpecials>
  </form>
 </body>
</HTML>
```

As can be seen from the code, the noticeable differences between this approach and implementing `ITemplate` are that we put the logic for template decisions in the page and we are still able to define our template declaratively. Because this template is in a file with the ASCX extension, a user cannot request it directly as the ASP.NET runtime will prohibit the file from being downloaded. However, there are some performance considerations in using the `LoadTemplate` method. Because these templates are loaded at run time, when the page is first accessed and thus compiled, the actual template is not compiled in. Therefore, this template needs to be loaded from disk each time it is accessed. Obviously in a web site with a lot of volume, this performance difference will be noticeable. However, creating dynamic templates in this way can work fine for smaller sites and does allow for easier definition and editing of content by non-technical staff.

173

Event Bubbling and More

This section is here to cover the minutiae that often plague developers when working with a new or unfamiliar technology. It is intended to provide a short list of things to keep in mind and watch out for when working with or developing templated controls.

Event Bubbling – handling events that arise from the controls defined in your template is often a hard thing for people to get started on. Because the number of templates can vary and the names of the controls are largely out of your hands, identifying all the items that need an event listener and hooking up the events is problematic. Be sure to read the information in Chapter 3 regarding event bubbling. This mechanism is useful in templated controls and allows you as the author to capture events as they are raised from contained controls and expose them to consumers of your control.

Template rendering – when templates are rendered, their content is often rendered within an HTML tag such as a SPAN or DIV and any styles applied are applied to that tag. Because this tag surrounds the content of template, styles and other rendering issues are usually not a problem. However, it is important to be aware of this in cases when you are troubleshooting a rendering problem when dealing with templates.

Styles

Another technology that allows separating content from layout is **style sheets**. Cascading style sheets came about to allow easy separation of HTML content from detailed information about how the content should be rendered. This separation makes it very easy to update a style sheet and have the web site take on an entirely different look.

When dealing with Server Controls that derive from WebControl, the style of the control is exposed in two different properties. The ControlStyle property provides access to an object of type System.Web.UI.WebControls.Style while the Style property accesses a collection of name-value pairs of style attributes that contains any style attributes added declaratively to the control at design time. The latter can have items easily added to it in the code-behind page to dynamically modify the style attributes of a control.

However, for the purposes of writing Server Controls, we will be most interested in the ControlStyle property and the Style class. Because this property exists on the WebControl base class, if we derive from this class we automatically have the ability to support styles in our control. However, in creating our control we must be careful not to remove this ability or interfere unknowingly with the styles that exist.

In this section we will see how to improve the usability of our control by ensuring that the consumer is able to specify the styles that will allow them to control such display features as text size, colors, borders, and any other style that makes sense for our control.

In this section we will be covering the following:

- ❑ Manipulating styles – how to apply and merge style attributes on controls
- ❑ The Style class – working with the ControlStyle property on the WebControl class and exposing additional style properties
- ❑ Exposing specific style elements as properties

Working with Styles

When working with styles in ASP.NET, the traditional methods of applying styles to elements in our Web Form are still present. However, we also have many capabilities that did not exist in previous versions of ASP that allow us more control over the styles applied to our controls. We will cover the various mechanisms that we now have at our disposal for working with styles.

The controls in the `HtmlControls` and `WebControls` namespaces still allow for a style attribute that will get rendered to the client. In fact, any attribute in a control's opening tag that does not map directly to a property on the control gets added to the attributes collection of the control. Most browsers will ignore an attribute if they do not recognize it so this does not cause a problem on the client if an errant attribute gets applied.

Another .NET-specific behavior that impacts on the application of styles and style properties is the mechanism by which properties of a Server Control are accessed. Those properties that map to a basic data type are accessed by using the property name and supplying a value either as an attribute, or, if the control supports it, an inner element. For example, in our `DailySpecials` and `Repeater` examples, we supplied values for the `SpecialsFile` and `RepeatCount` properties by adding attributes to our tag. With properties that have a complex data type, objects in other words, not only can the object itself be set, but we can access the properties of that object as well. We do this by supplying the full path to the property, using hyphens to separate the object itself from its property.

For example, when working with a control that derives from `WebControl`, we can access the styles in the `ControlStyle` property declaratively in our Web Form. The example below shows a button control with the `backcolor` style set to red using this technique:

```
<asp:Button id="mybutton" text="MyButton" ControlStyle-backcolor="red"
runat="server">
```

Because the `ControlStyle` property on the `WebControl` class is an object property, we access the inner properties using the hyphen. The power of this will become apparent as we begin exposing styles on the controls we have been developing up to this point in the chapter. By exposing a single property that is an object type, we give the consumer of our control access to all of the public properties of that control as well. The syntax for accessing the inner properties is common in HTML, such as when accessing styles in Cascading Style Sheets (CSS). It is used in ASP.NET to maintain consistency with this convention, which is already familiar to HTML developers.

We have seen how to apply styles declaratively, but what about programmatically applying styles? If you have a need to dynamically apply styles or if you need more control over combining styles, chances are you will want to do your style manipulation in code. To achieve the same effect as the sample above, that is set the background color to red, we would use the following code:

```
Style s = new Style();    //create the style
s.BackColor = Color.Red;  //set the backcolor property to red
mybutton.ApplyStyle(s);   //apply the style to the control
```

While the latter example is more code and takes more time, this method becomes more powerful when you want to copy, merge, or dynamically create your style at run time. The `Style` class provides two methods that come in handy when manipulating styles: `CopyFrom` and `MergeWith`. The `CopyFrom` method copies the styles from one style object to the calling style object, overwriting current values if they exist. The `MergeWith` method, on the other hand, combines the two styles such that if a value exists for the style attribute in the first style, this will not be overwritten by the style value from the second style object.

The table below should help clarify this point. The first two columns show the values for several style properties on two instances of the style class. The third column shows the updated values for the first style after calling `CopyFrom` and passing in the second style. The last column shows the same values in `Style1` after calling `MergeWith` and passing `Style2` as a parameter.

> Note that **Style2** does not get changed by either of these operations.

	Style1 before	Style2 before	Style1 after CopyFrom	Style1 after MergeWith
BackColor	Black	White	White	Black
ForeColor	White	Black	Black	White
Height	25	Not Set	25	25
Width	Not set	25	25	25

> Notice that in both cases the height and width are the same.

The `Height` does not get changed in either case because it is not set in the second style and is set in the first. So, when `CopyFrom` is called, the new value in `Style2` is not applied because it is missing, and the original value is applied. However, all other items that are set in the second style overwrite those in the first. When we use `MergeWith`, we get the same values for the height and width because the height does not get overwritten by a value in the second because it is already defined. The width on the other hand, is not set to a value so the value from the second style is applied. The `BackColor` and `ForeColor` maintain their original values and are not overwritten by the values from the second style.

Similarly, the `WebControl` class defines two methods, `ApplyStyle` and `MergeStyle`, which act in a like manner when setting the style of the control. The `ApplyStyle` method copies any set style values from the style object to the control, overwriting existing values. The `MergeStyle` property, as you have probably guessed by now, only copies set items that are not already set on the control.

Using these methods, we can create, manipulate, and combine styles on the server and then apply them to a given control. A user of our control, however, also needs the means to add style information to our control that might be outside the realm of the `Style` class. One way this is accomplished is by using the `Style` property on the `WebControl` class. This property, unlike the `ControlStyle` property, which is of type `Style`, is a `CssStyleCollection` class that allows the simple addition of named style attributes. It is used by providing a name for the key and a value as shown here:

```
myWebControl.Style["height"] = "25px";
```

This adds the specified name-value pair to the style attribute on the controls HTML tag when rendered. For consumers of a control, this provides the power they may want by allowing them to add any style to the control. However, this method is not intended to be used by control developers. When developing a custom control, it may make sense to define style properties that make sense to your control. For an example, the Calendar control included in the ASP.NET Framework provides several style properties for things such as `DayStyle`. This provides a better interface to your control and can allow a user, as in this example, to set the style for only particular parts or subcomponents of your control.

In the next two sections, we will be discussing how to expose strongly typed style properties on your control and how to apply those styles when the control is rendered to the client.

Exposing Styles as Properties

Earlier in the chapter we created a simple repeater control that allowed for creating a template or templates a given number of times. However, it was up to the user to supply HTML elements and attributes to style the templates the way they wanted to have them appear. We will update the control to add style properties for each of the four templates we defined. In this way we will allow the consumer of our control to not only set the layout of the content with templates, but to control the styling of the control with the addition of another HTML element.

The sample below started as an exact copy of the `SuperSimpleRepeater2.cs` file we used to build our second incarnation of the repeater control earlier. The entire code will not be shown to simplify things. Instead relevant sections that need to be added to the control will be provided. We have added four internal variables of type `Style` to hold the values for any styles specified and four matching property accessors for those styles. In addition, in the `CreateChildControls` function, we now apply those styles when appropriate:

StyledSimpleRepeater.cs

```
...
    //added four style objects to hold supplied styles
    private Style _itemStyle;
    private Style _alternatingItemStyle;
    private Style _headerStyle;
    private Style _footerStyle;
...
    //style properties that allow the user to customize
    //the style of the control templates
    public Style ItemStyle
    {
      get{
        if(_itemStyle!=null)
          return _itemStyle;
        else
          return new Style();
      }
      set{_itemStyle = value;}
    }
```

```csharp
    public Style AlternatingItemStyle
    {
      get{
        if(_alternatingItemStyle!=null)
          return _alternatingItemStyle;
        else
          return new Style();
      }
      set{_alternatingItemStyle = value;}
    }

    public Style HeaderStyle
    {
      get{
        if(_headerStyle!=null)
          return _headerStyle;
        else
          return new Style();
      }
      set{_headerStyle = value;}
    }

    public Style FooterStyle
    {
      get
      {
        if(_footerStyle!=null)
          return _footerStyle;
        else
          return new Style();
      }
      set{_footerStyle = value;}
    }
...
  //override the control creation and instantiate
    //the template the number of times specified
    protected override void CreateChildControls()
    {
      //clear out the control colletion if there
      //are any children we want to wipe them out
      //before starting
      Controls.Clear();

      //as long as we are repeating at least once
      //and the template is defined, then loop and
      //instantiate the templates in the container class
      if ((RepeatCount > 0)&&(_itemTemplate!=null))
      {
        //start by outputing the header template if one
        //was supplied
        if(_headerTemplate!=null)
        {
          SimpleRepeaterItem headerContainer = new
                   SimpleRepeaterItem(0,_repeatCount);
          _headerTemplate.InstantiateIn(headerContainer);
```

```
  //apply style if one was supplied
  if(_headerStyle!=null)
  {
    headerContainer.ApplyStyle(_headerStyle);
  }

  headerContainer.DataBind();
  Controls.Add(headerContainer);
}


//output the content the specified number of times
//use the alternating template if specified
for(int i = 0; i<RepeatCount;i++)
{
  SimpleRepeaterItem container = new SimpleRepeaterItem(i+1,RepeatCount);
  Style altStyle = new Style();
  altStyle.MergeWith(ItemStyle);
  altStyle.CopyFrom(AlternatingItemStyle);

  //is this an alternating item and do we have
  //a template?
  if((i%2==0)&&(_alternatingItemTemplate!=null))
  {
    _alternatingItemTemplate.InstantiateIn(container);
    container.ApplyStyle(altStyle);
  }
  else    // not then use the item template
  {
    _itemTemplate.InstantiateIn(container);
    container.ApplyStyle(ItemStyle);

  }
  container.DataBind();
  Controls.Add(container);
}

//once all of the items have been put out
//we add the footer template if one was given
if(_footerTemplate!=null)
{
  SimpleRepeaterItem footerContainer = new
          SimpleRepeaterItem(_repeatCount, _repeatCount);
  _footerTemplate.InstantiateIn(footerContainer);

  if(_footerStyle!=null)
  {
    footerContainer.ApplyStyle(_footerStyle);
  }
  footerContainer.DataBind();
  Controls.Add(footerContainer);
```

```
        }
      }
      else    //if no repeat count or item template we output a message
      {
        Controls.Add(new LiteralControl("Specify the record count and an item
                                    template"));
      }
   }
```

The next figure shows our new styled repeater as it appears in the browser. You can see that the styles we have defined for each of the template have been applied to the elements:

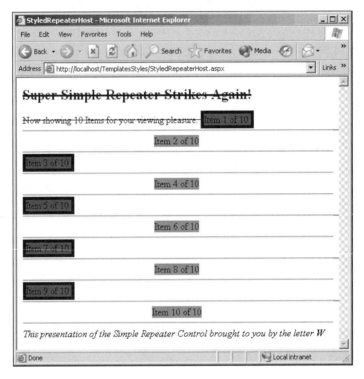

As you can see, it's fairly simple to expose and apply styles of this kind. After adding the properties and the requisite variables to hold the style values, we apply those styles that have been provided to the appropriate container. One thing to notice is that for the alternating item, we have chosen to apply the item style plus any styles that are redefined in the alternating item style. In this way the user can define an item style that they want applied to all of the items and an alternating item style with just those items that they want to be applied to alternating item style, without having to redefine the styles from the item style again.

The following lines of code accomplished this in our example:

```
Style altStyle = new Style();
altStyle.MergeWith(ItemStyle);
altStyle.CopyFrom(AlternatingItemStyle);
```

We create a new style and then merge any items that are defined in the `ItemStyle` to get any defined style attributes from the item. We then do a `CopyFrom` with the alternating item style as an argument allowing us to apply any defined styles in the alternating style, despite what may already be defined. This type of behavior should be documented for your control so that users of the control can know what to expect when supplying several different styles.

Exposing Style Elements as Top Level Properties

While providing access to the `Style` object to set some of the display attributes is helpful, at times you may wish to be more explicit with the styles you expose. For example, it might make sense for your control to explicitly define a border property that allows a user to directly set the size of the border rather than going through the `ControlStyle` property. Or, perhaps your control should expose styles that are not present in the set of styles available on the `Style` object.

There are two ways to go about exposing your styles in a more 'custom' manner. The first is to expose simple properties on your control and use those values to set properties on the style of a particular control, or your entire control. The other, slightly more complicated way, is to subclass the `Style` class and create your own style with properties that map to style attributes on your control. Good examples of this in the ASP.NET controls are the `TableStyle` and `TableItemStyle` classes. The `TableStyle` class exposes table-specific style properties such as `cellpadding` and `cellspacing` to provide easier access to these attributes.

As an example, we will extend the Daily Specials example that we provided earlier to expose style properties in two ways. First, we will create some top-level style properties that we will apply to the control as we render it. Second, we will create a custom style class and create a property on our control with a type of this new style. These two mechanisms will allow consumers of our control to specify strongly typed style information at design or run time and should provide good examples of how you can extend your own controls' style properties.

In this case, we will be adding the simple table styles of `CellPadding`, `CellSpacing`, and `Border` to our `DailySpecials` control. To begin, just copy the sourcecode for the `DailySpecials` control and rename the class to `StyledDailySpecials`. We will first add the styles as top-level properties and then we will create a custom style class that derives from `Style` and expose a property on our control of that type.

> Note that for example purposes and in order to keep the code and writing concise, we have exposed the same style attributes on our control in two different ways. In general this would not be done and you would choose one or the other. The exception would be if you were creating a style for a contained control and wanted to duplicate some of the style properties that already existed on the containing control or the base **WebControl** class.

Again, for the sake of clarity, only modified code is shown. The full source for the control is included in the download for this chapter. To begin, we need to update the Daily Specials control with three new variables and corresponding properties for the three style elements.

StyledDailySpecials.cs (excerpts)

```
...
    //top level style property fields
    //initialized to safe values
    int _cellPadding = 0;
    int _cellSpacing = 0;
    int _border = 0;
...
    //define style properties similar to those exposed by the
    //table style class
    public int CellPadding
    {
      get{return _cellPadding;}
      set{_cellPadding = value;}
    }

    public int CellSpacing
    {
      get{return _cellSpacing;}
      set{_cellSpacing=value;}
    }

    public int Border
    {
      get{return _border;}
      set{_border=value;}
    }
...
```

Now that we have successfully allowed a user to specify these properties, we need to apply them to our control. We do this by modifying the attributes collection of the control we wish to apply the changes to. In this case, we will update the attributes for our table control in the `CreateChildControls` method.

```
//this is where we do most of the work in creating
//the control hierarchy based on the templates
//which have been defined.
protected override void CreateChildControls()
{
  //get the number of columns in the second row
  int numberOfColumns=GetColumnCount();

  //clear our control state before beginning
  Controls.Clear();

  //make sure we have a file to work with and throw
  //an exception if we do not
  if((_specialsFile!=null)&&(_specialsFile!=String.Empty))
  {
```

```
        //create a new table object which we will use to
        //hold our template content when we render
        Table t = new Table();

        //add our strongly typed style attributes to the
        //table control where they belong

        t.Attributes.Add("CellPadding",_cellPadding.ToString());

        t.Attributes.Add("CellSpacing",_cellSpacing.ToString());
        t.Attributes.Add("Border", _border.ToString());
    ...
```

To set these properties on the control, the user now simply sets these properties by supplying attributes on the tag in their Web Form. The code below shows our control being used in a web page.

StyledDailySpecials.aspx

```
<%@ Page language="c#" Codebehind="DailySpecials.aspx.cs" AutoEventWireup="false"
Inherits="Chapter5.StyledDailySpecials" %>
<%@ Register TagPrefix="WROX"
Namespace="WROX.ProASPNetServerControls.Chapter5.TemplateControls"
Assembly="Chapter5" %>
<!DOCTYPE html public "-//w3c//dtd html 4.0 transitional//en" >
<HTML>
 <HEAD>
  <title>DailySpecials</title>
 </HEAD>
 <body ms_positioning="GridLayout">
  <form id="DailySpecials" method="post" runat="server">

   <WROX:StyledDailySpecials id="Dailyspecials1"
   runat="server"
   specialsfile="DailySpecials.xml"
   CellPadding="15"
   CellSpacing="5"
   Border="3">
   <HeaderTemplate>
    <h4>Today's Special</h4>
   </HeaderTemplate>
   <ItemTemplate>
    <img align="middle" src='<%# Container.ImgUrl %>'>
   </ItemTemplate>
   <LeftTemplate>
     Daily Price <i>
     <%# String.Format("{0:c}",Container.NormalPrice) %>
    </i><br>
     Today only <b>
     <%# String.Format("{0:c}",Container.SalePrice) %>
    </b>
     </LeftTemplate>
   <FooterTemplate>
    <h3><%# Container.ProductName %></h3>
    <%# Container.ProductDescription %>
   </FooterTemplate>
   </WROX:StyledDailySpecials>
  </form>
 </body>
</HTML>
```

The highlighted text indicates the changes made to our previous declarations of the DailySpecials control. Just the addition of these properties now allows our control to display the styles defined. You can see how explicitly defining these strongly typed styles makes working with the control much easier for page designers as they are able to continue to work in a manner that is familiar to them. A screen image of this sample appears in the next section when we build a custom style class.

Creating a Custom Style Class

As mentioned before, it may at times be the case that simply exposing top-level properties for styles or using existing style classes will not meet your needs. For example, a complex Server Control may require that the user be able to specify different values for the same style attribute because they need to be able to style different parts of the control. They may need to specify different fonts for varying parts of the control. In order to expose this type of functionality, we can create our own style class that will derive from the Style class.

In this example, we provide similar functionality to the previous sample, but we do it through a custom style class. This class, DailySpecialStyle, derives from the Style class and provides the same three properties we defined on our previous control: Border, CellPadding, CellSpacing. In addition, we provide an override for a single method that allows us to control the rendering of our style attributes to the control on which they are applied.

The code sample below shows the DailySpecialStyle class in its entirety:

StyledDailySpecials.cs (DailySpecialStyle class)

```csharp
//this class acts as a custom style class which can
//be exposed as a property and have attributes set
public class DailySpecialStyle:Style
{
  int _cellPadding=0;
  int _cellSpacing=0;
  int _border=0;

  public DailySpecialStyle(){}

  public int CellSpacing
  {
    get{return _cellSpacing;}
    set{_cellSpacing=value;}
  }

  public int CellPadding
  {
    get{return _cellPadding;}
    set{_cellPadding=value;}
  }

  public int Border
  {
    get{return _border;}
    set{_border=value;}
  }
```

```
    //we override this method so that we can add
    //the necessary attributes to the output stream when called
    //from the render method of a control
    public override void AddAttributesToRender(HtmlTextWriter writer,
    WebControl parent)
    {
      writer.AddAttribute(HtmlTextWriterAttribute.Border,
        _border.ToString());
      writer.AddAttribute
      (HtmlTextWriterAttribute.Cellpadding,_cellPadding.ToString());
      writer.AddAttribute
      (HtmlTextWriterAttribute.Cellspacing,_cellSpacing.ToString());


    }
  }
```

The `AddAttributesToRender` method is defined on the `WebControl` class and allows us, as control developers, to apply styles and general attributes to our control at rendering time. We override it here to specify that we wish to add the three items as attributes when the control is rendered to the output stream. We then call this method from the render method of our control. The code below is all the code we need to add to our `StyledDailySpecials` code.

StyledDailySpecials.cs (excerpts)

```
  . . .
        //holds a reference to an instance of our
        //custom style class
        DailySpecialStyle _specialStyle;
  . . .
        //expose the custom style we create below
        //as a property called DailySpecialStyle
        public DailySpecialStyle SpecialStyle
        {
          get{return _specialStyle;}
          set{_specialStyle=value;}
        }
  . . .
      protected override void Render(HtmlTextWriter writer)
      {
        // Apply styles to the control hierarchy
        // and then render it out.

        // Apply styles during render phase, so the user can change styles
        // after calling DataBind without the property changes ending
        // up in view state.
        if(_specialStyle!=null)
        {
          _specialStyle.AddAttributesToRender(writer, (WebControl)Controls[0]);
        }

        RenderContents(writer);
      }
```

To use our style, we add a property and corresponding variable for an instance of our custom style class. We then override the `render` method and add a conditional class to call the `AddAttributesToRender` method on our style, thus adding the attributes we specified in our definition of this method. We finish by instructing the rest of the controls to render by calling `RenderContent`.

The code excerpt below shows the new syntax we use to define these control properties in a Web Form. Notice that we now define a new element for the style and provide attributes on that style element. Remember that these attributes are parsed and matched up to their corresponding properties on the style class.

StyledDailySpecials.aspx (excerpt)

```
<WROX:StyledDailySpecials id="sample"
runat="server"
specialsfile="DailySpecials.xml">

<SpecialStyle Cellpadding = "15"
CellSpacing="15"
Border="15"/>

 <HeaderTemplate>
  <h4>Today's Special:
   <%# Container.ProductName %>
  </h4>
 </HeaderTemplate>
 <LeftTemplate>
  <img align="middle" src='<%# Container.ImgUrl %>'>
 </LeftTemplate>
 <ItemTemplate>
  <%# Container.ProductDescription %>
 </ItemTemplate>
 <FooterTemplate>
        Normally <i>
   <%# String.Format("{0:c}",Container.NormalPrice)%>
  </i> today only <b>
   <%# String.Format("{0:c}",Container.SalePrice) %>
  </b>
  </FooterTemplate>
</WROX:StyledDailySpecials>
```

The following figure shows two controls rendered using the two methods described. Both provide a clear and easy way for defining the styles that should be applied to our control. The `simple property` method works if there are a few styles that apply to the control as a whole or only apply to one sub-control. The `custom` class works well when there are multiple contained controls that need to be styled, or you if your control lends itself to a particular set of styles.

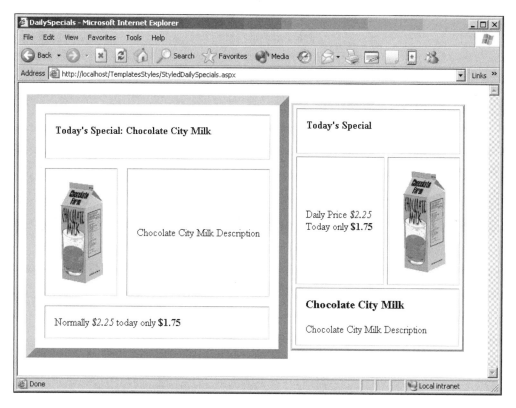

Styles provide for great flexibility in the look and feel of your control and go a long way in making your control more useful to others.

Bits and Pieces

Some details about styles that do not warrant much discussion, but can cause large headaches if you are not aware of them, are presented here for your benefit.

Overwriting – because the WebControl class also defines a ControlStyle property and allows the user to define styles, it is possible that a user will define styles on your control through this mechanism. Therefore, it is important that when applying styles to your control you keep this in mind. One way to handle this is to use the CopyFrom or MergeWith methods of the style class to combine the base class style with your own as shown here.

```
Style s = new Style();
s.CopyFrom(base.ControlStyle);
s.CopyFrom(_itemStyle);
```

Rendering – keep in mind that your control may be viewed in different browsers that offer varying support for styles. In order to provide the best rendering of your control on a given client, you should tailor the mechanism for applying the attributes to an element to the device. Use the browser property of the HttpRequest class to get information about the browser used to view your control and adapt accordingly.

Summary

In this chapter we have covered the use of two features of the ASP.NET framework to give users of our control more flexibility and power in determining the look and feel of the control. Templates and styles are each powerful tools to give the user this control and together they can make your controls ultimately configurable and therefore more valuable for your users. Combined with the other techniques in this chapter, these two technologies influence the usability of your control to the greatest extent.

Specifically, in this chapter, we covered:

❑ Using Templated Controls

❑ Templated control basics including the core ideas of INamingContainer, ITemplate, ParseChildrenAttribute, and TemplateContainerAttribute

❑ Creating basic templated controls and exposing templates as properties

❑ Exposing and managing multiple templates for a given control

❑ Creating and consuming dynamic templates that can change based on their environment

❑ Using styles with Server Controls

❑ Exposing styles as properties

❑ Exposing strongly typed style properties

❑ Creating a custom style class

In the next chapter we will be looking at how to create controls that work with data.

Professional ASP .NET Server Controls

6

Controls that Work with Data

Dynamic data access has become an integral part of most web applications. Whether it comes from a database server, XML, or some other source, in order for applications to be dynamic, they need data. Being able to extract data from a data source and display it for viewing or editing is a common practice in web development, but until now, ASP developers have had a very limited toolset for working with data. In fact, the only tools available were not web tools at all, but merely data tools used in a web environment. ASP.NET changes that with the introduction of `DataBinding` and `DataBound` Server Controls.

ASP.NET provides a very rich environment for working with data and comes with several built-in controls that solve many data display and editing issues. The `DataGrid` and `DataList` are two of the more powerful controls in the ASP.NET runtime and make many common tasks, which used to take many lines of code, quick and easy to implement. However, there will be times when your application calls for functionality that is not provided by the built in controls, and you will need to create a control that can be bound to data.

It is no surprise then that one of the ways we can make custom Server Controls more powerful is to allow them to be databound. This means that a developer can assign a datasource to your control and the control will take care of building its structure based on the data provided.

In this chapter we will be covering how to create Server Controls that use data. Specifically, we will be covering the following topics:

❑ Using Databound Controls – covering how to consume controls that use or expose data

❑ Databinding Essentials – understanding the internals of databinding and how to make more advanced and dynamic controls

❑ Creating a Templated Databound Control – how to create a basic control that renders templates for each item in the data source

❑ Creating a Simple Databound Control – essential steps to creating a simple control that uses data to build its structure and layout

❑ Advanced Databound Control – creation of a templated databound control which covers advanced topics of databound control creation

> **This chapter is not a discussion of ADO.NET. For more information on ADO.NET see** *Professional ADO.NET Programming* **published by Wrox Press.**

Using Databound Controls

DataBound controls come in two major flavors: **simple** and **templated**. A simple databound control is one that consumes the data provided to render itself. Examples of simple controls include the DataGrid and DropDownList controls. The DropDownList, for example, uses the datasource it is provided with to populate the option items of an HTML SELECT tag. Templated controls such as the Repeater and DataList controls use the datasource to determine how many instances of a given template or templates to create and add to the control hierarchy. The control hierarchy is essentially the content and structure of all of the controls contained within the Server Control. They then expose a single data item from the datasource through a property, or properties, on the template's container. The data item might be a row from a DataView or an item in an array. This allows a user of the control to use databinding syntax, such as that shown below, in their template to access the data in the datasource:

```
<%# Container.DataItem["ProductName"] %>
```

We will briefly examine the use of two controls that provide examples of a simple and templated control. By seeing how these controls work, we will get a baseline understanding needed to create custom controls that act similarly in regards to consuming data. The first control we will look at is the **DropDownList** control included in the ASP.NET Framework. The following figure shows the control as it will be rendered when we are finished:

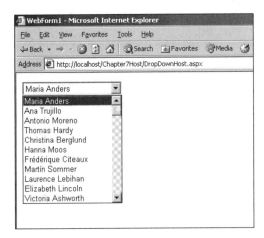

The dropdownlist control exposes several properties that are important to databinding, namely:

- ❑ `DataSource`
- ❑ `DataMember`
- ❑ `DataTextField`
- ❑ `DataValueField`

`DataSource` is a common property on controls that work with data. This property usually has a type of `IEnumerable`, `IList`, or another collection interface. By using an interface for the `DataSource` property, the control can be more flexible by allowing for a larger variety of objects that can act as a datasource. Each of these interfaces has its strengths for common use as well as specific to Server Controls that bind to data. For example, the `IList` interface provides indexed access to items in a collection while the `IEnumerable` interface enables enumerating over the objects in the collection. `ICollection` provides everything in `IEnumerable` plus members to provide synchronized access and a count property. Many collection classes implement multiple interfaces to provide richer support for the typical actions that developers expect from collections. In selecting the interface for your controls, the needs of your control will most likely dictate the interface type you use for the data source. For example, if your control design dictates that indexed access to the data source is a necessity, then the `DataSource` property for your control will most likely be `IList` or another interface that supports this type of access.

> **It is not a requirement that the data source for a Server Control inherit a collection interface. The primary requirement is that as the control developer, you must be able to get at each item in the datasource. The collection interfaces make this much more manageable and provide for a more flexible design.**

The `DataMember` property allows for identifying a specific member within the `DataSource` that will provide the data for the control. For example, if the `DataSource` were a `DataSet`, then the `DataMember` might be the name of a `DataTable` within that `DataSet`. The `DataTextField` and `DataValueField` properties signify the names of the fields in the datasource that supply the values for the `Text` and `Value` of the control. In our example of the drop-down control, each `Option` element in the `Select` control has a `value` and a `text` representation. The `DataTextField` will be used to get values for the `text` representation while the `DataValueField` will be used to populate the `Value` attribute of the `option` element. A brief example should help make this clearer.

The HTML below shows an HTML `Select` element with a single option. Note the placement of the `DataValueField` and the `DataTextField`. For each item in the data source, an option element will be created and the value attribute will be populated with the value from the `DataValueField` of the datasource while the text of the option will be populated from the `DataTextField`:

```
<select>
  <option value="DataValueField">DataTextField</option>
</select>
```

A Word About Setup

Before we begin looking at some examples, a word about the setup required to get the examples working on your computer:

The examples in this chapter consist of two distinct projects that are compiled into two different assemblies. The **Web Forms** (files ending with an ASPX extension) are part of the `Chapter6Host` project while the controls that we create are in the `Chapter6` project. How you work with these files depends on how your building the projects:

❑ If you are working with Visual Studio .NET, create a new **Web Control Library** project called **Chapter6** and add each of the control files to this project. Then, create a new ASP.NET **web application** called **Chapter6Host** and add a reference to the **Chapter6** project.

❑ If you are using the command-line compilers, compile the controls into a library called `Chapter6.dll` making sure to reference the `System.Web.dll` assembly. Create a virtual directory in IIS called **Chapter6Host**, add a `bin` directory to the new virtual directory and copy the `Chapter6.dll` assembly into the `bin` directory.

For simplicity the projects, including the Visual Studio .NET project files, are included in their respective folders in the code download for this chapter from wrox.com

Now, we'll look at an example of using the `DropDownList` control in a Web Form. The code below is a simple Web Form that uses data from the `Customers` table in the `Northwind` database to populate a `DropDownList` control. We include the appropriate namespaces and then create a `SqlDataReader` by executing a command against the local SQL Server:

DropDownHost.aspx

```
<%@ Page language="c#" AutoEventWireup="true" %>
<%@ Import Namespace="System.Data.SqlClient" %>
<%@ Import Namespace="System.Data" %>
<!DOCTYPE html public "-//w3c//dtd html 4.0 transitional//en" >
<html>
 <head>
  <title>WebForm1</title>
   </head>
 <script runat="server" language="C#">
 public void Page_Load(object sender, EventArgs e)
 {

 //if this is request is not a post back, then get the data
   if(!IsPostBack)
   {
 //open a connection and execute a select statement
   SqlConnection cnn = new
   SqlConnection("server=(local);database=northwind;uid=sa;pwd=;");
     SqlCommand cmd = new SqlCommand("Select CustomerID, ContactName from
   customers",cnn);
   SqlDataReader rdr;

     cnn.Open();
     rdr=cmd.ExecuteReader(CommandBehavior.CloseConnection);
```

```
//set the data properties of the dropdownlist control
    dropdownSample.DataSource=rdr;
    dropdownSample.DataTextField = "ContactName";
    dropdownSample.DataValueField="CustomerID";

//call DataBind on the page causing all controls to bind to their data
    DataBind();

//clean up data access objects
    rdr.Close();
    cnn.Dispose();
    cmd.Dispose();
    }
}

</script>
<body>

  <form id="DropDownHost" method="post" runat="server">
    <asp:DropDownList id="dropdownSample" runat="server"></asp:DropDownList>
  </form>

</body>
</html>
```

Once we have a data reader, we then set this object as the datasource for the drop-down control. Next, we set the `DataTextField` to "ContactName", which indicates that the text item for each of the `Option` tags will be drawn from the "ContactName" field in the data reader. We also set the `DataValueField` to indicate which field will be used to populate the `Value` attribute of each `Option` tag. In this case we will be using the "customerid" field.

Lastly, we call the `DataBind` method to bind the data to our control. This method is defined on the `Control` class and, as we will see, is often overridden in custom controls that support `DataBinding`. When the `DataBind` method of a control, or the `Page` in this case, is called, the call cascades to each of the contained controls. Thus, when we call `DataBind` on the page, the `DataBind` method is called on each of the controls that exist on the page. Likewise, if we call `DataBind` on a control that contains other controls, the `DataBind` method of all the child controls should be called.

The following figure shows the `WebForm` as it renders in a browser. You will notice that the `select` list is populated with the customer names, as we desired:

Another thing to notice is that we only supply data to the control when the page request is an original request and not the result of a **postback**. We do this by checking the `IsPostBack` property of the `Page`. The following short piece of code accomplishes this for us:

```
if(!IsPostBack)
{ //execute actions for the initial request
}
```

There are several benefits to only loading the data on the initial request of the page. Perhaps the largest benefit is that the load on the data source is reduced because it is not accessed every time the page is loaded. In addition, several of the more powerful features of ASP.NET and Server Controls rely on a control maintaining its state between calls. For example, postback events, discussed in Chapter 3, *Events and Event Handling*, rely on using the previous state of a control and comparing it to posted values.

When the data is not supplied directly to the control, on a postback for example, the control must manage its own data state and does so using `ViewState`. If the view state for a control is disabled, then the data will need to be loaded each time the page is processed. The tradeoff is that without view state you send less data to the client each time but put more load on the data source – while using view state can have the opposite effect. For more information about View State see Chapter 4, *Managing State,* and Chapter 3, *Events and Event Handling,* contains more information about postback events.

This distinction about where the data is coming from will become more important, and apparent, as we begin to develop our own controls. Regardless of the source of the data, the control will usually render itself in a similar fashion.

The `DropDownList` control provides a great example of a simple databound control and also shows some of the extensions we can use such as the `DataTextField` and `DataValueField` properties used to specify which data field to use for populating the specific parts of the control.

The `DataList` control is an example of a databound templated control. This type of control allows the user to define templates to produce their layout. See Chapter 5, *Templated Controls and Styles*, for more information on templated controls. In this type of control, the particular data item from the datasource is usually exposed as part of the control interface allowing the user to access the data in the templates.

In the next example, we use the `DataList` control to expose the same data as previously. However, you will notice that the mechanism by which we create the output and access the data differs from before:

DataListHost.aspx

```
<%@ Page language="c#" AutoEventWireup="true"%>
<%@ Import Namespace="System.Data"%>
<%@ Import Namespace="System.Data.SqlClient" %>
<%@ Import Namespace="System.Data.Common" %>
<!DOCTYPE HTML PUBLIC "-//W3C//DTD HTML 4.0 Transitional//EN" >

<html>
  <head>
    <title>DataListHost</title>
    </head>
```

```
<script runat="server" language="C#">
public void Page_Load(object sender, EventArgs e)
{

//if this is not a postback of the page
  if(!IsPostBack)
  {
//connect to sql server and run select statement
    SqlConnection cnn = new
    SqlConnection("server=(local);database=northwind;uid=sa;pwd=;");
    SqlCommand cmd = new SqlCommand("Select customerid, contactname from
  customers",cnn);
    SqlDataReader rdr;

    cnn.Open();
    rdr=cmd.ExecuteReader(CommandBehavior.CloseConnection);

 //set the datasource of the control
    listsample.DataSource=rdr;

//bind all controls
    DataBind();

//clean up the data objects
    rdr.Close();
    cnn.Dispose();
    cmd.Dispose();
  }
}

</script>
<body>

  <form id="DataListHost" method="post" runat="server">
   <asp:DataList id="listsample" runat="server">

   <ItemTemplate>
     <%# ((DbDataRecord)Container.DataItem)["CustomerID"] %>--
     <%# ((DbDataRecord)Container.DataItem)["ContactName"] %>
   </ItemTemplate>

   </asp:DataList>
   </form>

</body>
</html>
```

In using the DataList control, we define an ItemTemplate, one of several templates available on the DataList, which provides the layout for each item in the datasource. Therefore, since there are ninety-one customers in the Northwind database and our SQL statement selected all of them, we get ninety-one instance of our template. We use the simple DataBinding syntax available in ASP.NET to output values from the datasource. The container for the ItemTemplate in the DataList control is the DataListItem. This class exposes a DataItem property that provides access to the data item that corresponds to that instance of the template. Because the datasource is a DataReader in this case, we need to cast the DataItem property to a DbDataRecord to be able to access the data properly. The following syntax allows us to access a specific field in the data record bound to the template:

```
<%# ((DbDataRecord)Container.DataItem)["CustomerID"] %>
```

We cast the DataItem to a DbDataRecord and then access the indexed field using the field name. The following figure shows the DataList rendered with the templates we have specified:

> Note that with databound templated controls it is common practice to expose the data item using a single property called **DataItem.**

These two control usage examples act as a good starting point because they exhibit several common behaviors that will be important as we create our own databound controls. Specifically, these important factors are:

❑ Exposing a datasource property to allow a user to supply the data for our control

❑ Exposing control-specific properties that supplement the data source such as the DataTextField and DataValueField properties

❑ Exposing items from the datasource in a templated control

Databinding Essentials

There are several essential things to understand about working with databound controls. Each of these can make authoring databound controls an easier experience. They include knowing how to handle **DataBind commands,** managing **child control creation,** and being able to handle **varying data sources.**

Before we discuss these topics, it might be helpful to get familiar with the relevant methods and processes of databound controls. The table below lists the methods we will be talking about here and where they can be found in the Framework where appropriate. There are also several methods listed that are not in the Framework, but are recommended methods that a developer should implement when making a databound control:

Method	Description	Used For
System.Web.UI. Control.DataBind()	Signals that a given control should bind data to its controls	Can be overridden to provide custom functionality in the process and is called on controls added to a databound control's child controls.
System.Web.UI.Control. CreateChildControls()	Signals that a control should create its child control hierarchy in preparation for processing postback information or rendering	Overridden when creating composite or templated controls to create the control structure. In the case of data bound controls, it is used to create the control hierarchy from viewstate.
System.Web.UI.Control. OnDataBinding (EventArgs e)	Method that raises databinding events	Overridden in databound controls to determine when to build the child control hierarchy using the supplied datasource
CreateControlHierarchy (bool useDataSource)	Provides a single method to call in order to create the child control hierarchy in a databound control	**This is not a method provided by the Framework.** Rather, this is a recommended approach to creating the control structure whether the data is coming from the data source, or from viewstate.
System.Web.UI. DataBinder. GetPropertyValue (object container, string propertyName)	Extracts the value of a given property on the object passed in	Used to get data values when given a property name such as when provided with a DataValueField property.
System.ComponentModel. TypeDescriptor. GetProperties (object component)	Returns a PropertyDescriptorCollection containing a PropertyDescriptor item for each property on the object passed	Used by the DataBinder. GetPropertyValue method and can be used directly to get property names and values from a given object.

Each of these methods will be discussed in detail in this section as they pertain to creating databound controls. To provide some context for each, the list that follows shows a series of events that occurs when a databound control is used on a page:

Note that there are many steps left out of the process that do not directly apply to databinding.

❑   Data is created or retrieved from a datasource

❑   DataSource and other relevant properties are set on the control

❑   The DataBind method is called on the page

    ❑   The page calls the DataBind method on all of its contained controls

    ❑   The OnDataBinding method is called on each control from its DataBind method

❑   CreateControlHierarchy is called from OnDataBinding passing true to indicate that the control hierarchy should be built using the datasource

    ❑   TypeDescriptor.GetProperties and DataBinder.GetPropertyValue may be used to get information about the datasource or extract data

    ❑   Control hierarchy is created and the ChildControlsCreated property is set to true

❑   CreateChildControls is not called because ChildControlsCreated is true

❑   User interacts with the page and initiates a postback

❑   **No** data source is accessed and data bind is **not** called on the page

❑   CreateChildControls is called by the Framework

❑   CreateControlHierarchy is called from within CreateChildControls passing false indicating that the control should build the hierarchy from view state

❑   A Dummy or Generic data source is used to create the hierarchy using uninitialized controls which will then be populated by the ViewState data

As you can see, there are two different ways that the control hierarchy can be built. The first is that on the initial request for the page, the databind method is called and the control hierarchy is built from the datasource. Upon postback, the CreateChildControls method is called and an empty control hierarchy is built so that the view state can be restored for each of the child controls. In each case, the structure of this hierarchy should be the same. Because of this, the CreateControlHierarchy method comes in extremely handy. Now that we know the high-level processes and information, it is time to get to the details.

The first issue we have to address in a databound control is handling the DataBind command. In order to do this, we override the OnDataBinding method. Within this method we do a number of things to both prepare for the control creation and clean up after the controls are created. Because we do not override the DataBind method, the implementation provided by the Control class will be called. If for some reason your project requires that the child controls not have their DataBind method called, then you could override the DataBind method to keep the Control class from performing this operation. As part of the Control class implementation of the DataBind method, the OnDataBinding method is called. By overriding the OnDataBinding method we provide the control-specific implementation for how our control handles the DataBind call while allowing the base control to continue to handle parts of the implementation. A typical implementation of the OnDataBinding method is shown next:

```csharp
protected override void OnDataBinding(EventArgs e)
{
   //make sure the base control can handle the event too
   base.OnDataBinding(e);

   //clear out any existing controls from the collection
   Controls.Clear();

   //call our helper method to create the controls using
   //the data source
   CreateControlHierarchy(true);

   //Clear out any remaining viewstate of the children
   if(HasChildViewState)
   {
        ClearChildViewState();
   }

   //indicate that the controls are created
   ChildControlsCreated=true;

   //indicate that view state should be tracked for this control
   if(!IsTrackingViewState)
   {
     TrackViewState();
   }

}
```

We start by forwarding the method call to the base control to ensure that it can handle the call as well if it needs to. Next, because we are building our control hierarchy from the data source, we empty out the Controls collection and, if it exists, the ChildViewState. Clearing the child view state ensures that there is no data for contained controls left over from previous instances of the control. We then call our helper method, which we will examine shortly, to create the controls hierarchy, passing true to indicate that we wish to use the datasource to do so. We indicate that the child controls have been created by setting the ChildControlsCreated property to true. This indicates to the ASP.NET runtime that the child controls have already been created, which means other methods of creating the control hierarchy do not need to be invoked. Finally, we track the view state for the control.

This series of steps is used when the DataBind method is called to handle building the control hierarchy, or the collection and structure of child controls, but we need another mechanism to create our control hierarchy when building it without the datasource. For composite or templated controls, the CreateChildControls method is called to create the control hierarchy. We can override this method in order to build our child controls when we are not databinding. Remember that when databinding we set the ChildControlsCreated property to true. In doing so, we indicated that the CreateChildControls method did not need to be called by the ASP.NET runtime because the controls are already created. Our implementation of the CreateChildControls method typically would look like the following:

```csharp
protected override void CreateChildControls()
{
   Controls.Clear();
   CreateControlHierarchy(false);

}
```

Like in the first method, we clear the control collection before we create the control hierarchy. We then simply call our `helper` method, `CreateControlHierarchy`, to create the hierarchy without using the datasource. Now, the `helper` method we have been talking about is where all of the action happens so it is about time we took a look at it.

The goal behind the `CreateControlHierarchy` method is to have one method that creates the same control structure regardless of whether we are binding to the data directly or using `ViewState` to populate our control. Let's take a look at this method and then we will discuss how it works:

```
protected void CreateControlHierarchy(bool useDataSource)
{
  IEnumerator items;

  //set the enumerator to the data source
  //or a substitute collection
  if(useDataSource)
  {
    items = _dataSource.GetEnumerator();
  }
  else
  {
    //get datasource from view state
    items=new DummyDataSource();
  }

  while(items.MoveNext())
  {
    if(useDataSource)
    {
      //create item and call data bind on it
    }
    else
    {
      //create dummy item or item from view state
      //DO NOT call databind because data comes from view state
    }

    //always add the item to the controls collection
    Controls.Add(item);
  }
}
```

This is a fairly straightforward concept in that we set a local variable to be either the datasource or a substitute collection of some sort and then loop through creating an item and, if it is databound, calling the `DataBind` method on the item. We then add whatever item we have created to our control collection. When data is bound to a control (usually when the page is first accessed) the control hierarchy needs to be built based on the datasource so we call this method passing `true`. However, upon postback, the control hierarchy should be built from the `ViewState`, not from the datasource so we can call this method passing in `false` indicating that the datasource should not be used.

Notice that we do not call the `DataBind` method on the items we create when we are retrieving the data from view state. The reason for this is that calling `DataBind` will actually overwrite the values from view state, and defeat the purpose of using it.

Remember that developers will most likely only bind data on the initial request of the page and want to use view state for postbacks so it is important that the data from view state not be destroyed by calling DataBind.

When creating a templated control, the above information may be all you need to successfully author your control. However, when dealing with a simple control you will most likely have a need to access a specific value or the entire set of bindable values on a datasource. For example, if we were to create a drop-down control such as the one we examined earlier, we would need a way to take the name of the DataTextField and DataValueField properties and use them to extract the appropriate value from the datasource. This can be a tricky process but fortunately, there are some utility methods we can use to make the job easier.

The DataBinder class, found in the System.Web.UI namespace, provides a method, GetPropertyValue, that takes an object and the name of a property and returns the value of that property. For example, if we passed a DataRowView or DbDataRecord along with a field name from the query that generated them, then we would get back the value of the data in that field, or an empty string if that field was null. The method signature is shown below:

```
public static object GetPropertyValue(object container, string propName);
```

A sample usage of this might look like the following:

```
string Text;
Text=DataBinder.GetPropertyValue(MyEnumerator.Current, this.DataTextField);
```

This passes the current item in our datasource along with the identified name of the field for which we want the value. The value in the Text variable will either be the value in that field or an empty string.

> Note that if a property does not exist with the name we specify, an exception will be thrown.

This works if someone has given us the name of the property we should use. But what if we need to discover the bindable properties that exist on an object? For example, if we were to create an object such as the DataGrid that builds the columns of an HTML table dynamically from the datasource, we would need to be able to determine the properties on the control that could be used to populate those columns. We can use the same mechanisms that the DataBinder class uses internally to retrieve information about the properties on the datasource; namely using the TypeDescriptor and PropertyDescriptor classes found in the ComponentModel namespace.

The TypeDescriptor class defines several methods that allow a developer to extract information about a particular object including the properties it exposes. The PropertyDescriptor class represents an individual property and can be used to extract the name and value of that property on an instance of an object. To show how these objects work, we will demonstrate using them on a simple class. The class is defined overleaf:

MyControl.cs

```
using System;

namespace WROX.ProASPNetServerControls.Chapter6
{
  public class MyControl
  {
    private string _text;
    private int _itemCount;

    public string Text
    {
      get{return _text;}
      set{_text=value;}
    }

    public int ItemCount
    {
      get{return _itemCount;}
      set{_itemCount=value;}
    }

    private string DateCreated
    {
      get{return DateTime.Now.ToShortDateString();}
    }
  }

}
```

This is a simple class with two public properties, Text and ItemCount and one private property, DateCreated. We can use the TypeDescriptor and PropertyDescriptor classes to get the value of the public properties at run time. The code below creates an instance of the MyControl class in a Web Form and loops through each of the properties for the object, writing out the name and value of each:

PropTest.aspx

```
<%@ Page language="c#" AutoEventWireup="false"%>
<%@ Import Namespace="WROX.ProASPNetServerControls.Chapter6" %>
<%@ Import Namespace="System.ComponentModel" %>
<!DOCTYPE HTML PUBLIC "-//W3C//DTD HTML 4.0 Transitional//EN" >

<html>
  <head>
    <title>PropTest</title>
  </head>
  <script language="C#" runat="server">
  public void GetOutput()
{
  MyControl ctrl = new MyControl();
  ctrl.Text = "My sample text";
  ctrl.ItemCount = 25;
```

```
PropertyDescriptorCollection props = TypeDescriptor.GetProperties(ctrl);

foreach(PropertyDescriptor prop in props)
{
   Response.Write(prop.Name + ":" + prop.GetValue(ctrl));
   Response.Write("<br>");
}
}
</script>
<body>

   <form id="PropTest" method="post" runat="server">
<% GetOutput(); %>
   </form>

</body>
</html>
```

We create an instance of the control and set the two public properties. Then we get all of the properties for the object using the static `GetProperties` method of the `TypeDescriptor` class. This returns a `PropertyDescriptorCollection` object that is a simple wrapper class around `PropertyDescriptor` objects. We can iterate over this collection and for each `PropertyDescriptor` in the collection we write out the name of the property, and then we get the value of the property for our particular instance of the class.

The following shows the simple output from this test. You should note that the private member is not included in the output, which is exactly what we would want – if private members were included then many pieces of information not meant to be consumed outside the class would become publicly visible:

> Notice that the **Text** and **ItemCount** properties don't necessarily come out in the order in which they are defined on the class.

There are many other methods on the `TypeDescriptor` class that can be used as shortcuts or helpers to this process. We will be using these reflection methods described here when we build a databound list control later in the chapter.

Note that both the explicit use of **TypeDescriptor** and the implicit use via **DataBinder.GetPropertyValue** use reflection that can negatively impact on performance. If there is another way to accomplish your task without the use of reflection then it would be best to use it. However, in many situations, such as those described here, reflection is the appropriate mechanism. When using these methods, write your code in a manner that will reduce the number of times they need to be called.

It is important in production that you check the type of the property, as well, to make sure it is a bindable type, that is, a type that you can and want to represent as a string for rendering. For example, a property may expose a collection rather than a simple property type such as a primitive type, string, date, or numeric. Checking the property for one of these types will save exceptions further down the line. The `System.Web.UI.WebControls.BaseDataList` class has a static method called `IsBindableType` that takes as a parameter the type you want to check and returns a `Boolean` value. This method essentially checks whether the type is a primitive, string, Date, Time, or decimal.

Creating a Simple Templated Databound Control

The first control we will create to examine the items we have been discussing is a simple templated control that can be bound to data. We will first create a simple control that binds to a datasource and has item and alternating item templates. This control will be the basis for a shopping cart control that we will complete later in the chapter by adding events and interaction:

ShoppingCart.cs

```csharp
using System;
using System.Collections;
using System.Web.UI;
using System.Web.UI.WebControls;
using System.ComponentModel;

namespace WROX.ProASPNetServerControls.Chapter6
{
  //the class which acts as a container for our templates
  public class ShoppingCartItem:System.Web.UI.WebControls.WebControl,
            INamingContainer
  {
    object _dataItem;

    public ShoppingCartItem(object dataItem)
    {
      _dataItem = dataItem;
    }

    public object DataItem
    {
      get{return _dataItem;}
      set{_dataItem = value;}
    }
  }
}
```

We start by defining the container for our templates, the `ShoppingCartItem` class. This is the class that we will instantiate our templates in and that we will add to the controls collection. The `ShoppingCartItem` class is extremely simple, having one piece of state: the `DataItem`. We pass this item in the constructor and then provide access to it via a property. This will allow users of our control to use the syntax below to get at the item in the datasource that this instance of the template is related to:

```
<%# Container.DataItem %>
```

That is how easy it is to expose a data item on a template container, and, as was mentioned in the *Templated Controls and Styles* chapter (Chapter 5), using the name "DataItem" for the property is conventional and therefore generally good practice as it will be familiar to users of your control. Using this methodology, because the developer provides the datasource for the control, they know the type of the datasource and the items within it, and will be able to cast the `DataItem` object to the appropriate class. In this way, our control never has to know about the type of object or any of its interface definitions, making our control all the more flexible. For example, if a developer using your control is binding a `DataView` from a `DataSet` to the control, then they would know that each item in the data source is a `DataRowView` and could cast the item appropriately in order to access the data within the item.

Next we create a class that will act as a dummy datasource when our control is created on postback. Because we are not using the actual datasource to create our control hierarchy, we need another collection to loop through as we would the datasource in order to create the right number of items. The `DummyDataSource` class acts as an object that supports the `IEnumerable` interface. (Note that this is the same type we have defined for our `DataSource` property.) When creating a control that supports another type of `DataSource`, the `DummyDataSource` should be of the same type so that the two can be used interchangeably.

The `DummyDataSource` class is one that could be created and reused in any of your databound controls. The benefit of using this method, as opposed to say using a `for` loop and an `integer` counter, is that in creating an object that can be treated in the same manner as our data source, we are able to interchange the two in common code situations, making the rest of our code easier to manage:

```
//The DummyDataSource class provides the ability to
//create the control hierarchy on postback.
internal sealed class DummyDataSource : IEnumerable
{
  private int dataItemCount;

  public DummyDataSource(int dataItemCount)
  {
    this.dataItemCount = dataItemCount;
  }

  public IEnumerator GetEnumerator()
  {
    return new DummyDataSourceEnumerator(dataItemCount);
  }

  //the enumerator for our dummy data source which
  private class DummyDataSourceEnumerator : IEnumerator
  {
```

```
      private int count;
      private int index;

      public DummyDataSourceEnumerator(int count)
      {
        this.count = count;
        this.index = -1;
      }

      public object Current
      {
        get{return null;}
      }

      public bool MoveNext()
      {
        index++;
        return index < count;
      }

      public void Reset()
      {
        this.index = -1;
      }
    }
  }
```

The `DummyDataSource` takes an integer as a parameter to its constructor that identifies how many items it should mimic. Within the `DummyDataSource` we have also defined a `DummyDataSourceEnumerator` class. The `DummyDataSource` actually only has one method and purpose, which is to provide access to the enumerator so that the collection can be looped over. Notice that in the `Enumerator` implementation we return `null` for the `Current` property. Because our collection is empty, it is not meant to provide any data, only a mechanism to loop the proper number of times.

Now we need to begin defining our control and we start by laying out variables and properties for the two templates and a `DataSource`. We define the `DataSource` as being of type `IEnumerable` but could have used any suitable collection interface such as `IList` or `ICollection`. The `IEnumerable` interface makes working with a collection very easy in this situation because it makes enumerating the items in the datasource simpler. We can use the `MoveNext` method in a `while` loop or use a `for...each` loop to access each of the items and act on them. The `ICollection` interface derives from the `IEnumerable` interface and adds a count and synchronization properties so it gives a bit more functionality. The `IList` interface provides indexed access but no enumeration mechanism and would therefore usually only make sense in special circumstances where you needed to access a specific item in the datasource:

```
public class ShoppingCart : System.Web.UI.WebControls.WebControl
{
  //private variables for the datasource and templates
  ITemplate _itemTemplate;
  ITemplate _alternatingItemTemplate;
  IEnumerable _dataSource;
```

```
//public properties for the templates
[TemplateContainer(typeof(ShoppingCartItem))]
public ITemplate ItemTemplate
{
  get{return _itemTemplate;}
  set{_itemTemplate=value;}
}

[TemplateContainer(typeof(ShoppingCartItem))]
public ITemplate AlternatingItemTemplate
{
  get{return _alternatingItemTemplate;}
  set{_alternatingItemTemplate = value;}
}
```

```
//property for access to the datasource
public IEnumerable DataSource
{
  get{return _dataSource;}
  set{_dataSource=value;}
}
```

Once the properties are defined, we need to provide the mechanisms for creating our control hierarchy. We start by defining the CreateChildControls method discussed in the previous section:

```
//creates the child controls when not binding to data
protected override void CreateChildControls()
{
  //clear the current controls if there are any
  Controls.Clear();

  //check to see that we have been databound before
  if(ViewState["_ItemCount"]!=null)
  {
    CreateControlHierarchy(false);
  }
}
```

We do a safety check to make sure that the control has been bound before and therefore the actual data exists in the control's view state and can be used to rebuild the control hierarchy. If we leave this out, it is possible that this method would get called before the DataBind method is called. For example, when the EnsureChildControls method is called on the control, this method will be called in response to build the control hierarchy. Since we cannot build a control tree without the data, it would not make sense to call the CreateControlHierarchy method and would likely cause exceptions.

Next we override the OnDataBinding method to handle the initial loading of our control with data. As was discussed earlier, this is where we clear out the Controls collection and child ViewState and create the control hierarchy using the datasource. We then indicate that the controls have been created and indicate that our control should track its view state:

```
protected override void OnDataBinding(EventArgs e)
{
  //allow the base class to react
  base.OnDataBinding(e);

  //clear our child controls and view state
  Controls.Clear();

  if(HasChildViewState)
    ClearChildViewState();

  //create the control hierarchy using the datasource
  CreateControlHierarchy(true);

  //indicate that we have created the controls
  ChildControlsCreated=true;

  //track view state
  if(IsTrackingViewState)
    TrackViewState();
}
```

Note that we check to make sure our control has child view state and that the view state should be tracked before we make the appropriate method calls. There is no need to clear the child view state if it doesn't exist and we should not be tracking view state if view state is not enabled. Next, we define the method that actually creates our control hierarchy. Here we use the data source, or a dummy datasource, and loop through to the appropriate one, creating a ShoppingCartItem object for each one and instantiating a template in it:

```
protected void CreateControlHierarchy(bool useDataSource)
{
  IEnumerable data;
  IEnumerator dataItems;
  int itemCount;
  int itemCounter=0;

  //if we are not using the datasource
  //then create a new dummy data source in order
  //to recreate the control hierarchy
  if(!useDataSource)
  {
    itemCount = (int)ViewState["_ItemCount"];
    data=new DummyDataSource(itemCount);
  }
  else
  {
    data=DataSource;
  }

  //loop through the datasource creating
  //new items for each data item
  dataItems = data.GetEnumerator();
  while(dataItems.MoveNext())
  {
    ShoppingCartItem item = new
      ShoppingCartItem(dataItems.Current);
```

```
      //if we are using the datasource, then we must call
      //databind on the container control, otherwise we don't
      if(useDataSource)
        item.DataBind();

      //if it is an even numbered item, use the alternating
      //template if it is provided,
      //else use the item template
      if(itemCounter%2==0)
      {
        ItemTemplate.InstantiateIn(item);
      }
      else
      {
        if(AlternatingItemTemplate!=null)
        {
          AlternatingItemTemplate.InstantiateIn(item);
        }
        else
        {
          ItemTemplate.InstantiateIn(item);
        }
      }

      //add the item to the controls collection and
      //increment the counter so we can save the number
      //of items
      Controls.Add(item);
      itemCounter++;
    }

    //if we are using the datasource, then we
    //need to set a viewstate item so that
    //we can create the hierarchy on postback
    if(useDataSource)
      ViewState["_ItemCount"]=itemCounter;
  }
}

}
```

We start by checking to see if we should use the DataSource. If so, then we set our local variable to the datasource object, otherwise we set it to a new instance of the DummyDataSource class. Notice that we pass an item count to the DummyDataSource constructor to indicate how many items it should mimic. This number gets set at the end of the method if we are databinding. Since we checked for the presence of this view state property in the CreateChildControls method, we know that it exists. Next, we simply loop through the IEnumerable object and for each item the enumerator; we create a new ShoppingCartItem passing the current enumerator item to the constructor. This becomes the DataItem property for the ShoppingCartItem class.

If we are using the DataSource, we also need to call the DataBind method on the ShoppingCartItem so that users of the control can use the DataBinding Syntax in a Web Form to access the DataItem property. When we are not using the DataSource, we do not want to call the DataBind method, as it will overwrite the value that was previously bound to the control. Instead, we will let the view state manage the updating of the actual value. We instantiate the appropriate template in the control and then add the control to the controls collection. Finally, if we are databinding, then we need to store a value so that when we recreate this control we know how many items to create; that is, what value to pass to our DummyDataSource when we create it.

That's it! We now have a templated control that can be bound to a datasource and will maintain its state between calls to the server. To use the control in a web page we need to acquire some data, bind it to our control, and then define our templates. The code below is a web form that contains an instance of our control. We use a SqlDataReader to provide the data and define two templates that simply output a value from the reader:

ShoppingCartHost.aspx

```
<%@ Page language="c#" AutoEventWireup="true"%>
<%@ Register TagPrefix="WROX" Namespace="WROX.ProASPNetServerControls.Chapter6"
Assembly="Chapter6" %>
<%@ Import Namespace="System.Data" %>
<%@ Import Namespace="System.Data.SqlClient" %>
<%@ Import Namespace="System.Data.Common" %>

<!DOCTYPE HTML PUBLIC "-//W3C//DTD HTML 4.0 Transitional//EN" >

<html>
  <head>
    <title>ShoppingCartHost</title>
  </head>

  <script language="C#" runat="server">
   public void Page_Load(object sender, EventArgs e)
   {
    if(!IsPostBack)
    {
     SqlConnection cnn = new
          SqlConnection("server=(local);database=northwind;uid=sa;pwd=;");
     SqlCommand cmd = new SqlCommand("Select * from customers",cnn);
     SqlDataReader rdr;

     cnn.Open();
     rdr=cmd.ExecuteReader(CommandBehavior.CloseConnection);

     Cart.DataSource=rdr;

     DataBind();

     rdr.Close();
     cnn.Dispose();
     cmd.Dispose();
    }
   }
  </script>
```

```
<body>

    <form id="ShoppingCartHost" method="post" runat="server">
      <WROX:ShoppingCart id="Cart" runat="Server">
       <ItemTemplate>
         <b><%# ((DbDataRecord)Container.DataItem)["ContactName"]%></b><br>
       </ItemTemplate>

       <AlternatingItemTemplate>
         <i><%# ((DbDataRecord)Container.DataItem)["ContactName"]%></i><br>
       </AlternatingItemTemplate>

      </WROX:ShoppingCart>
      <asp:Button id="submit" runat="server" text="submit"></asp:Button>

    </form>

  </body>
</html>>
```

We register our control on the page to hook up the tags using the appropriate assembly and namespace and, because we will be using several of the Data namespaces, we add import statements for them. We define the Page_Load method to connect to the local SQL Server and get a SqlDataReader, which we then set as the DataSource for our control. Note that we only do this if the page is not a postback. If the page request is the result of a postback, then the data will come from ViewState. When we define our control on the page we provide two templates, the ItemTemplate, which bolds the ContactName item of the record and the AlternatingItemTemplate that italicizes the value. We cast the DataItem property of the Container object to a DbDataRecord because we know that a particular row of the SqlDataReader is of this type and it allows us easy access to the properties of that class. We add a submit button so that we can see the effects of posting back and show that the control holds the data. The following figure shows the control as it appears in the browser:

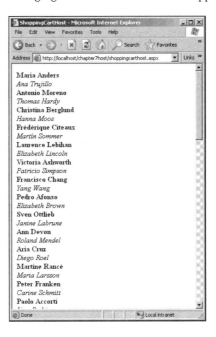

Creating a Simple Data Bound Control

Templated databound controls are often easier to create than simple bound controls as they do not usually require dealing with the data items directly. Rather, those items are just passed through so the user has access to them. In this section, we will build a databound drop-down list that will allow us to see some of the other databinding essentials in action. This list will act much like the web control we used in the earlier sample.

We start by creating a class to represent each item in our list: DbListItem. This class is a simple control that has Text, Value, and Selected properties that correspond to the items in an option tag of a select list:

DbDropDown.cs

```
using System;
using System.Collections;
using System.Collections.Specialized;
using System.Web.UI;
using System.Web.UI.WebControls;
using System.Web.UI.HtmlControls;
using System.ComponentModel;

namespace WROX.ProASPNetServerControls.Chapter6
{

//the control that acts as our Option element
public class DbListItem:System.Web.UI.WebControls.WebControl
{
  string _text;
  string _value;
  bool _selected;

  //empty default constructor
  public DbListItem(){}

  //full constructor to set all values
  public DbListItem(string itemValue, string text, bool isSelected)
  {
    Text=text;
    Value=itemValue;
    Selected=isSelected;
  }

  //properties for text,value and selected
  public string Text
  {
    get{return _text;}
    set{_text=value;}
  }
```

```csharp
    public string Value
    {
      get{return _value;}
      set{_value=value;}
    }

    public bool Selected
    {
      get{return _selected;}
      set{_selected=value;}
    }

    //render the option tag using the properties
    //of the control
    protected override void Render(HtmlTextWriter output)
    {
      //add the value attribute
      output.AddAttribute(HtmlTextWriterAttribute.Value,Value);

      //if this item is selected then add that attribute
      if(Selected)
      {
        output.AddAttribute(HtmlTextWriterAttribute.Selected,"true");
      }

      //render the option tag with the text in it
      output.RenderBeginTag(HtmlTextWriterTag.Option);
      output.Write(Text);
      output.RenderEndTag();
    }

    //internal method to let the list indicate
    //that this object should track its view state
    internal new void TrackViewState()
    {
      base.TrackViewState();
    }

    //load the view state into the object
    protected override void LoadViewState(object state)
    {
      //get the three properties out of
      //the triplet object that is the state
      Triplet tri = (Triplet)state;
      Text=(string)tri.First;
      Value=(string)tri.Second;
      Selected=(bool)tri.Third;
    }

    //save the state of the object
    protected override object SaveViewState()
    {
      //create a new triplet with the three properties
      Triplet tri = new Triplet(Text,Value,Selected);
      return tri;
    }

}
```

Notice that when the control renders itself, it outputs an `Option` tag with the appropriate `Value` and `Selected` attributes and the `Text` property. We will use this simple control within our drop-down list control to represent each of the items in the list. This control also manages its own view state by saving the three properties into a `Triplet` and retrieving them when it loads its view state. We have added an internal method that will allow our list to indicate that this object should track its view state.

Next we begin to define our drop-down control. We start by declaring variables to hold the `DataTextField` and `DataValueField` strings. In addition, we provide a variable to hold the datasource. This variable is of type `IEnumerable`. By using an interface for the member variable and the public property, we make our control more flexible as any class that implements the `IEnumerable` interface can act as the datasource for our control:

```
public class DBDropDown : System.Web.UI.WebControls.WebControl,
IPostBackDataHandler
  {
    private string _dataText;
    private string _dataValue;
    private int _selectedIndex;
    private int _itemCount=-1;
    private IEnumerable _dataSource;

    //properties for datasource and data fields
    public IEnumerable DataSource
    {
      get{return _dataSource;}
      set{_dataSource=value;}
    }

    public string DataTextField
    {
      get{return _dataText;}
      set{_dataText=value;}
    }

    public string DataValueField
    {
      get{return _dataValue;}
      set{_dataValue=value;}
    }

    //selected index property to allow a user
    //to examine from code
    public int SelectedIndex
    {
      get{return _selectedIndex;}
    }
```

We also want to add an event to our control that will signal a change in the selected item. This will be a straightforward event with no custom data so we define it with the `EventHandler` delegate:

```
//event definition for changed index
public event EventHandler SelectedIndexChanged;

//method to raise the index changed event
protected void OnSelectedIndexChanged()
{
  if(SelectedIndexChanged!=null)
  {
    SelectedIndexChanged(this,EventArgs.Empty);
  }
}
```

We need a way to raise the event if the index has changed, so we implement the `LoadPostData` and `RaisePostDataChangedEvent` methods of the `IPostBackDataHandler` interface. For each item in the controls collection that is one of our list items, we check to see if the value matches that posted and mark the item as selected if it does. For all others we mark them as not selected. We only return `true` from this method if the index has changed so that our event can be raised. See Chapter 3, *Events and Event Handling*, for more information on events and using the `IPostBackDataHandler` interface:

```
//load post data allows us to examine the posted value
//to see if the index has changed
public bool LoadPostData(string postDataKey, NameValueCollection postData)
{
  string _selectedValue;
  int currentIndex=0;
  bool hasIndexChanged=false;

  //get the posted value
  _selectedValue = postData[postDataKey];

  //make sure the controls are created
  EnsureChildControls();

  //loop through the controls selecting the appropriate one
  //and deselecting all others
  foreach(Control ctrl in Controls)
  {
    if(ctrl as DbListItem !=null)
    {
      if(String.Compare(((DbListItem)ctrl).Value,
        _selectedValue,true)==0)
      {
        ((DbListItem)ctrl).Selected = true;

        //if the index has changed, flip our flag to
        //true so our event will be raised
        if(_selectedIndex!=currentIndex)
        {
          _selectedIndex=currentIndex;
          hasIndexChanged=true;
```

```
            }
        }
        else
        {
            ((DbListItem)ctrl).Selected=false;
        }
        currentIndex++;
      }
    }
    return hasIndexChanged;
}

//called if LoadPostData returns true
public void RaisePostDataChangedEvent()
{
    OnSelectedIndexChanged();
}
```

Once we have our properties defined we need to create the control structure based on the datasource. We use the pattern discussed earlier and create the CreateChildControls, OnDataBinding, and CreateControlHierarchy methods:

```
//create the child controls using view state
protected override void CreateChildControls()
{
    Controls.Clear();
    //if items were created with data,
    //then create the hierarchy
    if(_itemCount>0)
        CreateControlHierarchy(false);
}
```

In the CreateChildControls method we clear all controls and then check to see if we have been bound to data before by making sure the _itemCount property is greater than zero. If not, then we do not need to create any controls. For the OnDataBinding method, we clear the controls and the child view state and then create the control hierarchy using the datasource. Once that is completed we indicate that the controls have been created and track the view state if necessary. We check the IsTrackingViewState property to determine if we should track the view state. A developer can indicate that a control should not track its view state by setting the EnableViewState property to false, we might want to do this to cut down on the amount of data sent to the client. If this property has been set to false, then we do not want our control to track its view state. As we mentioned earlier, for more information on View State, see Chapter 4, *Managing State*:

```
//data binding is occuring, create controls from data
protected override void OnDataBinding(EventArgs e)
{
    base.OnDataBinding(e);

    //clear child controls and view state
    Controls.Clear();
    if(HasChildViewState)
    {
```

```
      ClearChildViewState();
   }

   //create controls from data
   CreateControlHierarchy(true);

   //indicate that controls are created
   ChildControlsCreated=true;

   //track view state if appropriate
   if(IsTrackingViewState)
   {
     TrackViewState();
   }


}
```

To create our control hierarchy we either use the datasource enumerator or create an instance of our `DummyDataSource` class that we created for our templated control. Using the enumerator of one of these items, we loop through the collection and create the appropriate object. If we are using the datasource we create a new `DbListItem` with all the property values, and if we are not then we simply create an empty `DbListItem`. We finish by adding the item to the controls collection and incrementing a counter so we know how many controls we have created from the datasource. If we used the datasource, we update the `_itemCount` variable so that we will know on postback that we have been bound to data before and how many items were in the datasource:

```
protected void CreateControlHierarchy(bool useDataSource)
{
   int count=0;
   IEnumerator items;
   DbListItem item;

   //set the enumerator to the data source or our
   //item array
   if(useDataSource)
   {
     items = _dataSource.GetEnumerator();
   }
   else
   {
     items = new DummyDataSource(_itemCount).GetEnumerator();
   }

   while(items.MoveNext())
   {
     if(useDataSource)
     {
       string itemText=
         (string)DataBinder.GetPropertyValue(items.Current,
                  DataTextField);
       string itemValue=
```

```
                (string)DataBinder.GetPropertyValue(items.Current,
                    DataValueField);

        //create  new item with the supplied values
        item = new DbListItem(itemValue, itemText,false);
        item.TrackViewState();
      }
      else
      {
        //create new empty item
        item= new DbListItem();
      }

      //always add the item to the controls collection
      Controls.Add(item);
      count++;
    }

    if(useDataSource)
    {
      _itemCount=count;
    }
}
```

When we create new items based on the datasource, we use the `DataBinder.GetPropertyValue` method to extract the proper value for `Text` and `Value` properties. We use the `DataTextField` and `DataValueField` properties of our control as the names of the property to find. In a real-world scenario, always be sure to check that these values are provided by users of your control; otherwise you will get an exception when you try to get the property value.

Finally, we render the control by rendering the opening of a `Select` tag followed by the rendering of all of the child controls, and finish with the closing of the `Select` tag. The `RenderContents` method takes each control in the `Controls` collection and calls the `render` method. Thus, when we call this, all of our items will be rendered:

```
protected override void Render(HtmlTextWriter output)
{
  output.AddAttribute(HtmlTextWriterAttribute.Id,UniqueID);
  output.AddAttribute(HtmlTextWriterAttribute.Name, UniqueID);
  output.RenderBeginTag(HtmlTextWriterTag.Select);
  RenderContents(output);
  output.RenderEndTag();
}
```

In order for the control to work with the `PostBack` mechanism, we have to properly store the state of our list; the child controls already take care of this for themselves. To do so we override the `SaveViewState` and `LoadViewState` methods in order to store the selected index and item count:

```
//restore the view state of the control
protected override void LoadViewState(object state)
{
  //cast the state object to a triplet
  Triplet oldState = (Triplet)state;

  //load the state for the base contrl
  base.LoadViewState(oldState.First);

  //get the selected index out of the state
  _selectedIndex=(int)oldState.Second;

  //get the item count from state
  _itemCount=(int)oldState.Third;
}

//create the view state for this control
protected override object SaveViewState()
{
  //create a new pair with the base state and
  //the selected index of the list
  Triplet state = new Triplet(base.SaveViewState(),_selectedIndex,
                  _itemCount);
  return state;
}
}  //end of class DbDropDown
```

As you can see, the only major differences between a templated control and a simple control are how the data is used to create an item. For the templated control we can simply instantiate the template within the container and pass the date item through. For the simple control, however, we need to do more work to create our controls collection using the information we can glean from the datasource or ask of the user.

We host our control in a Web Form just as we do any other control. The code below shows the control hosted in a Web Form. After selecting data from the SQL Server and setting the SqlDataReader as the datasource of our control, we identify the DataTextField and DataValueField properties for our control. Once the data is bound, we hook up an event handler for the SelectedIndexChanged event and update a label control when the event is raised:

DbDropDownHost.aspx

```
<%@ Page language="c#" AutoEventWireup="true" %>
<%@ Register TagPrefix="WROX" Namespace="WROX.ProASPNetServerControls.Chapter6"
Assembly="Chapter6" %>
<%@ Import Namespace="System.Data.SqlClient" %>
<%@ Import Namespace="System.Data" %>
<!DOCTYPE html public "-//w3c//dtd html 4.0 transitional//en" >

<html>
  <head>
    <title>DbDropDownHost</title>
  </head>
```

```csharp
<script runat="server" language="C#">
public void Page_Load(object sender, EventArgs e)
{
  if(!IsPostBack)
  {
  SqlConnection cnn = new
  SqlConnection("server=(local);database=northwind;uid=sa;pwd=;");
  SqlCommand cmd = new SqlCommand("Select customerid, contactname from
                                   customers",cnn);
  SqlDataReader rdr;

  cnn.Open();
  rdr=cmd.ExecuteReader(CommandBehavior.CloseConnection);

  dropdownSample.DataSource=rdr;
  dropdownSample.DataTextField = "contactname";
  dropdownSample.DataValueField="customerid";

  DataBind();
  rdr.Close();
  cnn.Dispose();
  cmd.Dispose();
  }

  dropdownSample.SelectedIndexChanged+= new
  EventHandler(dropdownSample_SelectedIndexChanged);
}

 public void dropdownSample_SelectedIndexChanged(object sender, EventArgs e)
 {
   Message.Text = "Index Changed";
 }


</script>
<body>
  <form id="Form1" method="post" runat="server">
   <WROX:DBDropdown id="dropdownSample" runat="server">

   </WROX:DBDropdown>
   <br>
   <asp:Button id="submit" runat="server" text="Submit"></asp:Button>
   <br>
   <asp:Label id="Message"
  runat="server"
  enableviewstate="False">
</asp:Label>
  </form>

</body>
</html>
```

The following figure shows our newly created control right after a postback. Notice that an item is already selected, which is the same item that was selected when the user clicked the Submit button and that there is a message indicating that the index has changed. Our control is used just as any other Server Control that binds to data:

Creating An Advanced Templated Databound Control

To complete this chapter we will extend the ShoppingCart templated control we created earlier to include support for varying events. One of the complexities that trouble many developers when they are first working with databound controls is understanding how to manage them once they are created. In any other control, the control hierarchy – while it can be dynamic – usually follows some basic pattern based on the control's state. As the developer of a databound control, we have to create our control not knowing how many items there will be or exactly what the data will look like.

Handling events and gaining access to controls to manipulate them during the creation or binding processes can be difficult. The sample control we will build provides access to the items we are adding to the controls as they are created and when they are databound. This gives the user of our control the ability to manipulate these items when they are being processed. An example of when this might be useful is when working with the DataGrid control; it is often useful to know when an item is databound so that we can access the child controls and manipulate them, perhaps to change the text to a hyperlink.

In addition, because of the fact that we have multiple controls created, the names of the controls are not always what the developer using our control expects. Using the INamingContainer interface, described in Chapter 5, *Templated Controls and Styles* we provide a unique naming context for our items. This comes in extremely handy when we need to do things like bubble events up the control hierarchy as we will see. However, it can also be confusing to figure out how to access the controls we wish to manipulate.

The goal of this sample is to provide insight into how to build controls that expose their items as they are created and manipulated as well as to show a working example of event bubbling in a databound control. A shopping cart control can solve the very real need of componentizing the work involved in adding, removing, viewing, and updating items in a shopping cart. The particular control we will build here is a starting point but by no means a production control. The code shown here will, however, provide a great starting point for a fully functional shopping cart control that you can use over and over.

We will start by defining two new delegates, `ShoppingCartItemEventhandler` and
`ShoppingCartCommandEventHandler`, as well as the accompanying custom `EventArgs` classes
`ShoppingCartItemEventArgs` and `ShoppingCartCommandEventArgs`. The 'Item' delegate,
`ShoppingCartItemEventHandler`, and event arguments, `ShoppingCartItemEventArgs`, will be
used when we expose events that reference an activity occurring on a particular item. For our example
this will be when the item is created and when it is databound. The "Command" delegate,
`ShoppingCartCommandEventHandler`, and event arguments, `ShoppingCartCommandEventArgs`,
will be used when a command bubbles up from within one of our items. In the case of our control, this
command will be bubbling up from the `CartLoader` control that we created in Chapter 3, *Events and
Event Handling*. The code for the `CartLoader` control is included in the download for this chapter but is
not included in the text for clarity. A full discussion of this control can be found in Chapter 3.

ShoppingCart2.cs

```csharp
using System;
using System.Collections;
using System.Web.UI;
using System.Web.UI.WebControls;
using System.ComponentModel;

namespace WROX.ProASPNetServerControls.Chapter6
{
    //the delegate to be used with the shopping cart
    //item events
    public delegate void ShoppingCartItemEventHandler (object sender,
            ShoppingCartItemEventArgs e);

    //custom event arguments class to expose the item
    //referenced by the event
    public class ShoppingCartItemEventArgs:System.EventArgs
    {
        ShoppingCartItem2 _item;

        public ShoppingCartItemEventArgs(ShoppingCartItem2 item)
        {
            _item = item;
        }

        public ShoppingCartItem2 Item
        {
            get{return _item;}
        }
    }

    //delegate to be used for bubbled command events
    public delegate void ShoppingCartCommandEventHandler(object sender,
ShoppingCartCommandEventArgs e);

    //event arguments class for bubbled commands
    public class ShoppingCartCommandEventArgs:System.EventArgs
    {
        CartLoaderEventArgs innerArgs;
        ShoppingCartItem2 _item;
```

```
//create a new instance with the specified
//ShoppingCartItem2 and the event arguments
//from the bubbled event
public ShoppingCartCommandEventArgs(ShoppingCartItem2 item,
                                    CartLoaderEventArgs e)
{
  _item=item;
  innerArgs=e;
}

//provide access to the original event arguments
public CartLoaderEventArgs InnerArgs
{
  get{return innerArgs;}
}

//provide access to the item that raised the event
public ShoppingCartItem2 Item
{
  get {return _item;}
}
}
```

For the Command event arguments we have created a class that exposes the ShoppingCartItem2 that the event took place in as well as an "InnerArgs" property that allows the user to gain access to the CartLoadEventArgs object that was initially raised. The Item event arguments are even simpler providing access only to the ShoppingCartItem2 control that the event concerns. Each of the delegates defines a signature that takes an object defining the sender and the appropriate EventArgs derivative.

Next we need to update the ShoppingCartItem2 class to make it easier to work with for adding custom items and for users of our control responding to events. Just as using tables in HTML makes formatting easier, so too using their equivalent in a Server Control can make the layout of our child controls much easier to manage. Therefore, we have updated our control so that is now derives from the TableRow class. In addition, the constructor for this class now takes as a parameter the name of the data field that represents a product ID. Since this control will be acting as shopping cart control, it needs to know what product the user is acting on.

Within the constructor, we create two table cells and add them to the collection of cells for this row. We will instantiate our templates in the first cell and we use the second cell to add the CartLoader control. Notice that if the dataItem parameter is null, meaning that we are recreating the control hierarchy from view state, we do not set the _dataItem value on the ShoppingCartItem2 control or the ProductID value on the CartLoader control:

```
//the class which acts as a container for our templates
public class ShoppingCartItem2:System.Web.UI.WebControls.TableRow,
                                              INamingContainer
{

  object _dataItem;

  public ShoppingCartItem2(object dataItem, string dataProductField)
  {
    Cells.Add(new TableCell());
    Cells.Add(new TableCell());
```

```
        CartLoader loader = new CartLoader();
        if(dataItem!=null)
        {
          _dataItem = dataItem;
          string itemid =
           DataBinder.GetPropertyValue(dataItem,dataProductField).ToString();
          loader.ProductID = itemid;
        }

        loader.Location = LoaderType.CartLoader;
        Cells[1].Controls.Add(loader);
      }

      public object DataItem
      {
        get{return _dataItem;}
        set{_dataItem = value;}
      }

      //catch any bubbled events and if they are from
      //the cart loader control, then wrap the arguments
      //in a ShoppingCartCommandEventArgs class and bubble the
      //event up
      protected override bool OnBubbleEvent(object sender, EventArgs e)
      {
        if(e as CartLoaderEventArgs!=null)
        {
          ShoppingCartCommandEventArgs args = new
                  ShoppingCartCommandEventArgs(this,(CartLoaderEventArgs)e);
          RaiseBubbleEvent(sender, (ShoppingCartCommandEventArgs)args);
          return true;
        }

        return false;
      }
    }
```

We have also implemented the `OnBubbleEvent` method shown above to capture any raised events. If the events are initiating from our `CartLoader` object, then we wrap the arguments in a new `EventArgs` derivative that fits our delegates and raise a new bubble event. In addition, we signal that the original event has been handled so that it will not get passed up the control hierarchy. In order for this to work properly, we also need to make sure our class implements the `INamingContainer` interface or the events will not properly bubble to our control.

Notice that we check to see if the event arguments passed in are an instance of `CartLoaderEventArgs` to determine the source. Using the type of the event arguments in this way is a common way to determine the type of control that bubbled the event. The following code allows us to check to see if the event arguments are of a particular type, in this case, `CartLoaderEventArgs`:

```
if(e as CartLoaderEventArgs!=null)
{
   //do something with e as a CartLoaderEventArgs
}
```

If e is not an instance of `CartLoaderEventArgs` then the `AS` operator will return `null` and our `if` clause will return `false`. Any number of these `if` statements can be used to perform logic based on the **type** of event arguments.

Event Bubbling was discussed in Chapter 3, *Events and Event Handling*. However, it is shown here because event bubbling really becomes necessary, and helpful, when dealing with controls that build their child control collection based on a datasource. Because these types of controls could have an unknown number of child controls with varying types, it is much easier to define one handler for any events that might be raised rather than trying to hook up event handlers for each and every control in the child controls.

The updated `ShoppingCart2` class adds support for several events including the `ItemCreated` event, which indicates that a new item has been created, the `ItemDataBound` event, which indicates that an item has had its data item bound to it, and the `ItemCommand` event, which indicates that the `CartLoader` control within an item has raised an event. Each of these three events and the corresponding methods to raise them are defined at the beginning of the `ShoppingCart2` class:

```csharp
public class ShoppingCart2 : System.Web.UI.WebControls.WebControl,
INamingContainer
{
  //events
  public event ShoppingCartItemEventHandler ItemCreated;
  public event ShoppingCartItemEventHandler ItemDataBound;
  public event ShoppingCartCommandEventHandler ItemCommand;

  protected void OnItemCreated(ShoppingCartItemEventArgs e)
  {
    if(ItemCreated!=null)
      ItemCreated(this,e);
  }

  protected void OnItemDataBound(ShoppingCartItemEventArgs e)
  {
    if(ItemDataBound!=null)
      ItemDataBound(this, e);
  }

  protected void OnItemCommand(ShoppingCartCommandEventArgs e)
  {
    if(ItemCommand!=null)
      ItemCommand(this,e);
  }

  //catch any bubbled events, and raise the item command
  //if they have args of type ShoppingCartCommandEventArgs
  protected override bool OnBubbleEvent(object sender, EventArgs e)
  {
    if(e as ShoppingCartCommandEventArgs!=null)
    {
      OnItemCommand((ShoppingCartCommandEventArgs)e);
      return true;
    }
    return false;
  }
```

We also implement the `OnBubbleEvent` in this control that will be called if any events are raised from the contained `ShoppingCartItem2` controls or any other controls within the child control hierarchy. We are only interested in those events that are raised from the `ShoppingCartItem2` controls so we filter those out and use them to raise an `ItemCommand` event. For any other `EventArgs` subclasses, we return `false` from the method so the event will continue to bubble up the control hierarchy.

Because we want to be able to provide a product ID to the cart loader control, we expose a `DataProductField` property that allows the user to specify the property to use for the product ID. The same functionality could be achieved in many different ways and this will often not be the best way to do this, but it helps in an example setting to show how to use this field to propagate information to child controls and bind data to them. To be more flexible, neither the cart loader nor the shopping cart control would require the product ID, and simply let the user obtain that information from the `DataItem` property on the `ShoppingCartItem2` control:

```
//private variables for the datasource and templates
ITemplate _itemTemplate;
ITemplate _alternatingItemTemplate;
IEnumerable _dataSource;

//the name of the field to bind to the CartLoader control
string _dataProductField;

public string DataProductField
{
  get{return _dataProductField;}
  set{_dataProductField=value;}
}


//public properties for the templates
[TemplateContainer(typeof(ShoppingCartItem2))]
public ITemplate ItemTemplate
{
  get{return _itemTemplate;}
  set{_itemTemplate=value;}
}


[TemplateContainer(typeof(ShoppingCartItem2))]
public ITemplate AlternatingItemTemplate
{
  get{return _alternatingItemTemplate;}
  set{_alternatingItemTemplate = value;}
}

//property for access to the datasource
public IEnumerable DataSource
{
  get{return _dataSource;}
  set{_dataSource=value;}
}
```

```
//creates the child controls when not binding to data
protected override void CreateChildControls()
{
  //clear the current controls if there are any
  Controls.Clear();

  //check to see that we have been databound before
  if(ViewState["_ItemCount"]!=null)
  {
    CreateControlHierarchy(false);
  }
}

protected override void OnDataBinding(EventArgs e)
{
  //allow the base class to react
  base.OnDataBinding(e);

  //clear our child controls and view state
  Controls.Clear();

  if(HasChildViewState)
    ClearChildViewState();

  //create the control hierarchy using the datasource
  CreateControlHierarchy(true);

  //indicate that we have created the controls
  ChildControlsCreated=true;

  //track view state
  if(IsTrackingViewState)
    TrackViewState();
}
```

There are no changes to the `CreateChildControls` or `OnDataBinding` methods since both of these simply wrap calls to the `CreateControlHierarchy` method. This method does need to be updated to incorporate the change to using a `Table` to hold and render our controls as well as raising the appropriate events. We have to add a declaration for a new `Table` control to start. Then, for each item in the datasource, whether it is the actual source or our dummy datasource, we create a new `ShoppingCartItem2` control passing in the current data item as well as the string value identifying the field to use to retrieve the product ID.

After creating this item, we call the `OnItemCreated` method passing in a new instance of the `ShoppingCartItemEventArgs` initialized for this item. If we are using the datasource, we then call `DataBind` on the item and follow a similar pattern to raise the `ItemDataBound` event by calling the `OnItemDataBound` method. Once we have created the item and, optionally, bound, we add it to the table. And lastly, we add the table to our `Controls` collection so that it and all of its contents can be rendered to the output:

Remember that our `ShoppingCartItem2` *class now derives from* `TableRow` *so we can directly add it to the* `Table` *object's row collection.*

229

```
protected void CreateControlHierarchy(bool useDataSource)
{
  IEnumerable data;
  IEnumerator dataItems;
  int itemCount;
  int itemCounter=0;

  Table tbl = new Table();

  //if we are not using the datasource
  //then create a new dummy data source in order
  //to recreate the control hierarchy
  if(!useDataSource)
  {
    itemCount = (int)ViewState["_ItemCount"];
    data=new DummyDataSource(itemCount);
  }
  else
  {
    data=DataSource;
  }

  //loop through the datasource creating
  //new items for each data item
  dataItems = data.GetEnumerator();
  while(dataItems.MoveNext())
  {
    ShoppingCartItem2 item = new
      ShoppingCartItem2(dataItems.Current,
              _dataProductField);

    OnItemCreated(new ShoppingCartItemEventArgs(item));

    //if we are using the datasourc, then we must call
    //databind on the container control, otherwise we don't
    if(useDataSource)
    {
      item.DataBind();
      OnItemDataBound(new ShoppingCartItemEventArgs(item));
    }

    //if it is an even numbered item, use the alternating
    //template if it exists, else use the item template
    if(itemCounter%2==0)
    {
      ItemTemplate.InstantiateIn(item.Cells[0]);
    }
    else
    {
      if(AlternatingItemTemplate!=null)
      {
        AlternatingItemTemplate.InstantiateIn(item.Cells[0]);
      }
```

```
        else
        {
          ItemTemplate.InstantiateIn(item.Cells[0]);
        }
      }

      //indicate that the item should track its view
      //state
      item.TrackViewState();

      //add the item(as a row) to the table
      tbl.Rows.Add(item);

      itemCounter++;
    }

    //if we are using the datasource, then we
    //need to set a viewstate item so that
    //we can create the hierarchy on postback
    if(useDataSource)
      ViewState["_ItemCount"]=itemCounter;

    //add the table to the controls
    Controls.Add(tbl);
    }
  }
}
```

We are using the `TrackViewState` method exposed earlier on the `ShoppingCartItem2` control to indicate that each item should manage its view state. Thus, when we rebuild the control hierarchy and create, essentially, empty versions of this control, its state will be recreated from `ViewState`, including that of the child `CartLoader` controls.

We use this control in our page just as we did the original `ShoppingCart` control with the exception that we can now use the events to gain access to the controls as they are created and databound. Likewise, on postback we can gain access to controls that have had the `CartLoader` control clicked. The code below shows a Web Form that uses our new control. In the `Page_Load` method we hook up three event handlers for our events that just update the text of an ASP.NET `Label` control. This type of string concatenation is not recommended but allows us to show a visual cue that the event handlers are working:

ShoppingCart2Host.aspx

```
<%@ Page language="c#" AutoEventWireup="true"%>
<%@ Register TagPrefix="WROX"
  Namespace="WROX.ProASPNetServerControls.Chapter6" Assembly="Chapter6" %>
<%@ Import Namespace="System.Data" %>
<%@ Import Namespace="System.Data.SqlClient" %>
<%@ Import Namespace="System.Data.Common" %>

<!DOCTYPE html public "-//w3c//dtd html 4.0 transitional//en" >
```

```
<html>
  <head>
    <title>ShoppingCartHost</title>
  </head>

  <script language="C#" runat="server">
   public void Page_Load(object sender, EventArgs e)
   {

     Cart.ItemCreated+=new ShoppingCartItemEventHandler(Cart_ItemCreated);
     Cart.ItemDataBound+=new
     ShoppingCartItemEventHandler(Cart_ItemDataBound);
     Cart.ItemCommand+= new
     ShoppingCartCommandEventHandler(Cart_ItemCommand);

     if(!IsPostBack)
     {
      SqlConnection cnn = new
     SqlConnection("server=(local);database=northwind;uid=sa;pwd=;");
      SqlCommand cmd = new SqlCommand("Select productid, productname from
     products",cnn);
      SqlDataReader rdr;

      cnn.Open();
      rdr=cmd.ExecuteReader(CommandBehavior.CloseConnection);

      Cart.DataSource=rdr;

      DataBind();

      rdr.Close();
      cnn.Dispose();
      cmd.Dispose();
     }
    }

    public void Cart_ItemCreated(object sender, ShoppingCartItemEventArgs e)
    {
     CreatedMessage.Text+=((DbDataRecord)e.Item.DataItem)["productname"] + "
      created<br>";
    }

    public void Cart_ItemDataBound(object sender, ShoppingCartItemEventArgs
                   e)
    {
     BoundMessage.Text+=((DbDataRecord)e.Item.DataItem)["productname"] + "
      bound<br>";
    }

    public void Cart_ItemCommand(object sender,ShoppingCartCommandEventArgs
     e)
    {
      StatusMessage.Text="Item Updated: " + e.InnerArgs.ProductNumber +
    "<br>" + "Current Amount:" + e.InnerArgs.NumberOfItems;
    }
```

```
    </script>
    <body>

        <form id="ShoppingCart2Host" method="post" runat="server">
        <asp:Label id="StatusMessage" runat="server"></asp:Label>
        <table>
         <tr>
          <td valign="top">
        <asp:Label id="CreatedMessage" runat="server"></asp:Label>
        </td>
          <td valign="top">
        <asp:Label id="BoundMessage" runat="server"></asp:Label>
        </td>
          <td valign="top">

            <WROX:ShoppingCart2 id="Cart"
             DataProductField="ProductID"
             runat="Server">
            <ItemTemplate>
              <b><%# ((DbDataRecord)Container.DataItem)["ProductName"]%></b>
            </ItemTemplate>

            <AlternatingItemTemplate>
              <i><%# ((DbDataRecord)Container.DataItem)["ProductName"]%></i>
            </AlternatingItemTemplate>

            </WROX:ShoppingCart2>
          </td>
          </tr>
        </table>
         </form>

    </body>
</html>
```

The output consists of a table with the `ItemCreated` and `ItemBound` updates appearing in the left two cells. In the right-hand cell we have an instance of our templates for each item in the datasource, plus the `CartLoader` control that we added. Clicking on the update or remove buttons causes the `ItemCommand` event to be raised from our control, which will update the status label at the top of the screen. The following figure shows the control after clicking one of the update buttons:

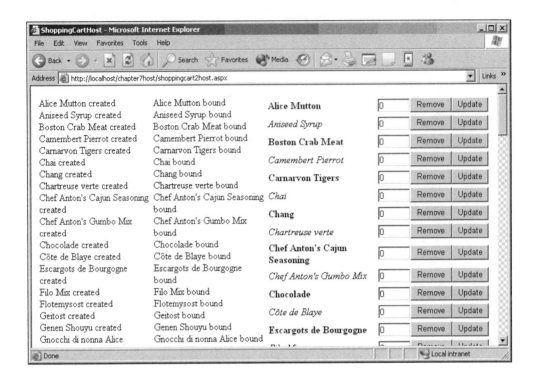

Summary

In this chapter, we have explored several of the key components involved in creating databound controls. In addition, several of the issues that control developers deal with when creating this type of control were explained and shown. Specifically, this chapter has covered:

- ❑ Common patterns and techniques to use when building databound controls
- ❑ Creating a control that builds its control hierarchy based on a datasource
- ❑ Creating a templated databound control and exposing the data items to users of the control
- ❑ Using the classes in the ComponentModel namespace to identify and retrieve property values
- ❑ Working with events and control identification in a databound control

Professional ASP .NET Server Controls

7

Custom Control Builders

This chapter discusses the ins and outs of dictating how a custom control is parsed by the page parser. By this stage in the text it should be recognized that the page parser is what parses an ASP.NET page. When this parser encounters a tag, it determines if the tag has a runat attribute and whether or not the value of the runat attribute is set to server. When the tag is specified as runat=server, then the page parser instantiates an instance of the object specified by the tag. This object is added to the page's server-side component hierarchy. The topic of this chapter is not this component hierarchy, but how the page parser parsers the page's text between the component's start and end tags. With respect to customizing how this parsing takes place, you might use the phrase, "how a control is built". This is rather apropriate terminology, since the name of the class that facilitates this parsing customization is the ControlBuilder class. Each control on a web page is associated with an instance of the ControlBuilder class or a descendant of this class.

By accessing and potentially overriding the ControlBuilder class, the interaction between the page parser and a control can be precisely defined. The granularity of this definition can be categorized as follows:

❑ Modify how the page parser behaves, including how it handles whitespace and how it treats encoded HTML text

❑ Modify the child controls of the parent control being parsed and the attributes of the child controls

❑ Modify the attributes associated with the custom control being parsed

❑ Disable certain functionality of the ControlBuilder so it cannot be used externally

❑ Dictate what data is provided to the ControlBuilder instance by the page parser

❑ Modify the literal HTML contained within the custom control

The approach used to demonstrate the `ControlBuilder` class will be to first show a simple example. This example will modify how the page parser parses a control. As part of this first example, we will also look at how a custom attribute is used to associate a custom control builder with a control. The term attribute in this context refers to a .NET custom attribute, and not the type of attribute associated with an HTML tag. Entire book chapters are dedicated to custom attributes, since it's quite a broad topic (from threading models using `STAThreadAttribute` to aiding XML serialization using `XMLElementAttribute`). In the context of custom control builders, using a custom attribute allows one type of custom control builder to be associated with one or more controls. The page parser behavior dictated by the custom control builder (such as "always leave the HTML on a page encoded") can therefore be associated with multiple controls. Each control is associated with the custom control builder courtesy of a custom attribute.

With a simple example under our belt, precisely how a custom control builder interacts with the page parser can be explored. Reviewing this process will involve a discussion of each method of the `ControlBuilder` class that interacts with the page parser. These methods can ultimately be overridden in order to fine-tune the behavior of each customized version of the control builder class.

A side effect of the parser/`ControlBuilder` overview will be the presentation of how to override each method of the `ControlBuilder` class, thus creating a custom control builder. Actually a custom control builder is a class derived from `ControlBuilder` with one or more methods overridden. Although the example presented overrides every method of the `ControlBuilder` class, this zealous attention to detail is not necessary for a customization. The parser/`ControlBuilder` overview will address further detail in that it also presents and discusses every property exposed by the `ControlBuilder` class.

A variety of controls within .NET already utilize a custom control builder (`HyperLinkControlBuilder`, `TextBoxControlBuilder`, `UserControlControlBuilder`, and so on). A subset of these classes, each derived from the `ControlBuilder` base class, will be reviewed. Particular attention will be paid to the methods each custom control builder overrides with respect to the `ControlBuilder` base class. Explaining why .NET controls override certain methods, more clearly demonstrates why user-developed custom control builders should also override such methods of the `ControlBuilder` class. The rationale for the .NET custom control builders overriding certain methods includes a means to modify parser behavior and to ensure that functionality of the `ControlBuilder` class can also be used externally.

More complex and practical examples of overriding the methods of the `ControlBuilder` will also be presented. These methods will show how additional page data can be requested by the custom control builder and subsequently passed by the page parser. These more complicated examples include choosing child controls at run time rather than relying on those specified within the control being parsed. Another more detailed example discusses localization while others present custom control builders as means by which to filter the literal HTML contained between a custom control's start and end tag. The example that chooses which child controls to use is both practical and powerful. This example serves to demonstrate how a custom control builder can dictate the subordinate controls associated with the parent control being parsed. The localization example serves to demonstrate how the attributes of a child control and the control being parsed can be modified by a custom control builder. The examples that perform filtering show how the literal contents of the page can be altered by the custom control builder.

The most important concept presented by this chapter is that the custom control builder typically does not need to parse the text associated with a control (start tag, inner text, and end tag). The page parser breaks this text down (a.k.a. parses it) and provides it in an efficiently formatted manner to the methods of the `ControlBuilder` class or a descendant of this class.

ControlBuilder Overview

When the page parser encounters a control on a page, it looks for a little help with respect to the parsing of the control. Henceforth, this control will be referred to as the parent control. To demonstrate how the page parser processes a particular parent control, consider the following excerpt from the ASP.NET source file, `WXOverviewControlBuilder.aspx`, where the custom control to be parsed is of type `WXShowOffControlBuilderFeatures`:

```
<CBuilderDemo:WXShowOffControlBuilderFeatures ID="ShowItOff1"
                                         runat="server">
<P><B>WXDemoWXControlBuilderOverview uses WXDemoWXControlBuilderOverview
                                        ControlBuilder</B></P>
Literal text 1 --
<asp:Label ID="Label00" runat="server" Text="A Label 1 -- "></asp:Label>
Literal text 2 --
<asp:Label ID="Label01" runat="server" Text="A Label 2 -- "></asp:Label>
Literal text 3
</CBuilderDemo: WXShowOffControlBuilderFeatures>
```

Within the `WXShowOffControlBuilderFeatures` parent (within the tags of this custom control) reside two child controls of type, `asp:Label`. Residing between the parent control and child controls is literal text. The parsing help requested by the page parser with respect to a parent control is delivered by the `System.Web.UI` namespace's `ControlBuilder` class. The functionality provided to the page parser by the `ControlBuilder` class consists of help building up a collection of child controls for the parent control being parsed. Based on the previous snippet of ASP.NET source, the parent control collection of child controls will include two entries of type `Label` added with the help of the `ControlBuilder` class associated with the custom control, `WXShowOffControlBuilderFeatures`.

The `ControlBuilder` also supports the creation of a literal control (a `LiteralControl` from the `System.Web.UI` namespace) for each region of literal text found within the parent control. The purpose of the `LiteralControl` class is to encapsulate text that does not require server-side processing. The data encapsulated includes HTML elements and plain text. These literal controls are treated as child controls of the parent control and are henceforth added to the parent's collection of child controls. Within the previous excerpt three separate ranges of literal text can be found:

1. Between the `CBuilderDemo:WXShowOffControlBuilderFeatures` start tag and the first `asp:Label`

2. Between the two `asp:Label` controls

3. Between the second `asp:Label` control and the `CBuilderDemo:WXShowOffControlBuilderFeatures` end tag

Clearly there is a hierarchal relationship between controls on a page. A control can contain zero or more children and subsequently the child controls can contain children of their own (grandchildren to original parent control). Similarly there is a hierarchal relationship between `ControlBuilder` instances within the hierarchy. The `ControlBuilder` associated with a parent control has knowledge of each `ControlBuilder` associated with the child controls of the parent. This hierarchy of `ControlBuilder` knowledge extends to each level of descendent `ControlBuilder` instances associated with each level of descendent controls.

A custom control builder (class derived from `ControlBuilder`) is associated with a custom control and hence more precise control can be exercised over the building of controls. If no derivative of the `ControlBuilder` class is specified for a control, then the default control builder (`ControlBuilder`) is accessed by the page parser when a custom control is encountered. The association between control and control builder is specified using the `ControlBuilderAttribute` custom attribute. Before delving into the usage of this custom attribute and the methods of `ControlBuilder` that can be overridden, a simple example will be presented. Hopefully this example will demonstrate just a smidgeon of the flexibility afforded by deriving from the `ControlBuilder` class and overriding a specific method or methods.

A Simple Example using AllowWhitespaceLiterals

The first example demonstrates how the `ControlBuilder` class influences the parsing associated with a custom control. More specifically, this first example will present how the `AllowWhitespaceLiterals` method of a custom control builder can be used to allow or disallow white spaces within a control. This rather modest beginning is designed to simply familiarize the reader with how a custom control is associated with a control builder (either default or custom). Furthermore, this example will demonstrate the basics of how to customize a control builder.

In order to understand how the default control builder is associated with a custom control, consider the following excerpt from the `WXControlBuildDemo` project's `WXControl.cs` source file (you can download the whole file along with the rest of the code for this book at **www.wrox.com**):

```
using System;
using System.Web.UI;

namespace WXControlBuilderDemo
{
  // No ControlBuilderAttribute specified so the default
  // control builder class (ControlBuilder) is used
  public class WXUseDefaultControlBulder : Control
  {
  }
}
```

As the documentation in the previous code snippet states, the `WXUseDefaultControlBuilder` custom control is associated with the default control builder, the `ControlBuilder` class. This is because no specific control builder class was specified using the `ControlBuilderAttribute` custom attribute. Before the `WXUseDefaultControlBuilder` class and its regal elegance is demonstrated on an ASP.NET page, we need to explore a subset of the parsing behavior mandated by the `ControlBuilder` class. In order to understand this behavior, consider the `ControlBuilder` class's `AllowWhitespaceLiterals` method. The aforementioned method is defined as follows:

```
Overridable Public Function AllowWhitespaceLiterals() As Boolean ' VB.NET
public virtual bool AllowWhitespaceLiterals(); // C#
```

When the `ControlBuilder`'s `AllowWhitespaceLiterals` method returns `true`, it indicates that whitespace literals in the control will be processed. If this method returns `false` then whitespace literals in the control will be ignored. Demonstrating this ignoring of whitespace literals is the following snippet from the `WXShowDemoControls.aspx` source file that creates a control of type `WXUseDefaultControlBuilder`:

```
<%@ Register TagPrefix="CBuilderDemo" Namespace="WXControlBuilderDemo"
            Assembly="WXControlBuilderDemo"%>
<HTML>
  <body>
    <pre>
      <CBuilderDemo:WXUseDefaultControlBulder
        ID=AllowWhitespaceLiteralsTrue runat=server>
<B>WXUseDefaultControlBulder uses default ControlBuilder
    (AllowWhitespaceLiterals=true):</B>
<asp:Label ID=Label00 runat="server"
  Text="Three carriage returns to follow.">
</asp:Label>



<asp:Label ID=Label01 runat="server"
  Text="Three carriage returns above.">
</asp:Label>
      </CBuilderDemo:WXUseDefaultControlBulder>
    </pre>
  </body>
</HTML>
```

The previous snippet of HTML contains three carriage returns (the empty lines in the middle of the document). These carriage returns were placed inside the WXUseDefaultControlBuilder control deliberately in order to help demonstrate the ControlBuilder class's AllowWhitespaceLiterals method. The <pre> element was used on the previous page because text within this element is rendered as fixed width. Additionally the <pre> element preserves carriage returns and spaces. By preserving carriage returns, this element allows the ControlBuilder class's AllowWhitespaceLiterals method to be demonstrated, since the default behavior for this method is "allow whitespace literals".

On the previous page an instance of WXUseDefaultControlBuilder is specified (ID=AllowWhiteSpaceLiteralsTrue). This instance contains two Label controls (ID=Label01 and ID=Label01) and between these labels the previously discussed three carriage returns (preserved due to <pre>). When the previous page is displayed, it appears as follows complete with carriage returns:

```
WXUseDefaultControlBulder uses default ControlBuilder
    (AllowWhitespaceLiterals=true):
Three carriage returns to follow.



Three carriage returns above.
```

Clearly the page parsing behavior would have been different if ControlBuilder was super classed and the derived class overrode the AllowWhitespaceLiterals method to return false. The following excerpt from the WXControlBuildDemo project's WXControl.cs source file contains just such a derived class, WXNoWhitespaceLiterals:

```
public class WXNoWhitespaceLiterals : ControlBuilder
{
    public override bool AllowWhitespaceLiterals()
    {
        return false;
    }
}
```

Now that we have an alternative to the ControlBuilder class (WXNoWhitespaceLiterals) we need to associate this alternative with a custom control. This association is performed using the ControlBuilderAttribute attribute and is specifically demonstrated as follows (excerpt from WXControl.cs):

```
[ControlBuilderAttribute(typeof(WXNoWhitespaceLiterals))]
public class WXUseWXNoWhitespaceLiterals : Control
{
}
```

The WXUseWXNoWhitespaceLiterals control in the previous code snippet is associated with the WXNoWhitespaceLiterals ControlBuilder implementation courtesy of the previously mentioned ControlBuilderAttribute custom attribute. This custom attribute should not be viewed as black magic known only to the High Priestess of Custom Attribute Voodoo. Basically, the ControlBuilderAttribute attribute declaration is contained in square brackets, and what follows (in our previous code snippet) can be viewed as follows:

```
[attributeName(constructor parameters)]
```

For our example, the attributeName was ControlBuilderAttribute and the parameter to the constructor was typeof(WXNoWhitespaceLiterals). This custom attribute is implemented by an appropriately-named class, ControlBuilderAttribute, and the lone constructor to this class exposes the following prototype:

```
Public Sub New(ByVal builderType As Type) ' VB.NET
public ControlBuilderAttribute(Type builderType); // C#
```

The builderType parameter in the previous constructor prototype corresponds to calling the C# typeof or VB.NET GetType operator an instance of a ControlBuilder class. By saying "instance of" this includes instances of classes derived from a ControlBuilder class such as WXNoWhitespaceLiterals. The ControlBuilderAttribute class does expose elements in addition to the lone constructor (fields, properties, and methods), but these elements do not add functionality in respect to customizing the parsing of a page and can be readily reviewed by readers by consulting MSDN.

Comfortable in our knowledge of how to associate a ControlBuild instance with a control using the ControlBuilderAttribute class, we can extend the WXShowDemoControls.aspx source file to include a demonstration of our WXUseWXNoWhitespaceLiterals control in action. The following excerpt from WXShowDemoControls.aspx is contained between the <pre> start tag and </pre> end tag in order to take advantage of this tag's fixed-width, carriage-return/space-retaining nature:

```
<CBuilderDemo:WXUseWXNoWhitespaceLiterals
    ID=AllowWhitespaceLiteralsFalse runat=server>
<B>WXUseDefaultControlBuilder uses WXNoWhitespaceLiterals ControlBuilder<br>
(AllowWhitespaceLiterals=false):</B>
<asp:Label ID=Label02 runat="server"
  Text="Three carriage returns to follow.">
</asp:Label>



<asp:Label ID=Label03 runat="server"
  Text="Three carriage returns above.">
</asp:Label>
```

Remember that the WXUseWXNoWhitespaceLiterals instance in the previous code excerpt (ID=AllowWhitespaceLiteralsFalse) is associated with a ControlBuilder instance that ignores white spaces. The output associated with the previous code snippet is as follows and it clearly demonstrates how the whitespace literals (carriage returns) were ignored as part of parsing the page subordinate to the control:

```
WXUseDefaultControlBulder uses WXNoWhitespaceLiterals ControlBuilder
    (AllowWhitespaceLiterals=false):
Three carriage returns to follow.Three carriage returns above.
```

The point of the exercise thus far has been to allude to the capabilities associated with deriving classes from ControlBuilder. Another capability of the ControlBuilder and its descendants is also hinted at, namely filtering. In this rather simple example, white spaces were filtered. The ControlBuilder can actually filter literal text, control's attributes, child controls and child controls' attributes. For example, all "inappropriate words" could be removed from within a control by the control's custom control builder.

The remainder of this chapter will explore the more intricate details of the ControlBuilder class and its derivatives. This breakdown of capabilities includes a variety of different approaches to filtering and a presentation of the various methods that can be overridden in order to customize the parsing behavior associated with a control.

ControlBuilder and Page Parser Interaction

The previous example was rather mundane in nature but it does allude to the tremendous potential that can be exploited by developing a custom control builder. Before delving into the intricacies of which methods of the ControlBuilder can be overridden, we'll take a more detailed look as to how the page parser utilizes a ControlBuilder instance. When the page parser encounters a custom control, an instance of the appropriate control builder (the default control builder, ControlBuilder, or a class derived from ControlBuilder) is created. The page parser as it traverses the page calls a sequence of methods exposed by the ControlBuilder instance. These interactions between page parser and this ControlBuilder are as follows:

1. Page parser initializes `ControlBuilder` using the `Init` method.

2. Page parser queries if the custom control has both an opening tag and a closing tag (`<tag> </tag>` form versus `<tag />` form). This is achieved using the `ControlBuilder` class's `HasBody` method. This method returns `true` if there are a start and corresponding end tag specified for the control. If the control does not have a body then the page parser does not bother to call `HasBody`.

3. For each tag in the parent control, the page parser calls the `ControlBuilder`'s `GetChildControlType` method. This method determines if the tag is associated with a specific control type (a return value of type `Type`). If the tag corresponds to a child control, the child control is processed by the page parser (see description that follows).

4. Page parser provides any remaining literal text to the `ControlBuilder`. This literal text would reside between the last child control and the parent control's end tag. The `AppendLiteralString` string method is called in order to provide the `ControlBuilder` with this literal text.

5. Page parser determines if the custom control needs to process the text that resides between the control's start tag and end tag (the inner text). If the `ControlBuilder`'s `NeedsTagInnerText` method returns `true` then the inner text will be needed by the control builder. The `NeedsTagInnerText` method returns `false` if the page parser does not need to pass the inner text to the control builder.

6. If the `NeedsTagInnerText` method previously returned `true`, then the page parser calls the control builder's `SetTagInnerText` method. The data passed to `SetTagInnerText` by the page parser is the text between the control's start and end tags. If the `NeedsTagInnerText` method returns `false` then the page parser does not call `SetTagInnerText`.

7. Page parser informs `ControlBuilder` that it has been added to the collection of `ControlBuilders` maintained by the parent `ControlBuilder` instance. The `OnAppendToParentBuilder` method of the `ControlBuilder` class is called by the page parser to convey this information.

8. Page parser cleans up the `ControlBuilder` using the `CloseControl` method.

As was mentioned above, certain actions are taken for each child control contained within the parent control. These actions can be detailed as follows:

1. Page parser informs the parent control of any literal text that resided before the child control. This literal text is passed from the page parser to the `ControlBuilder` instance using the `AppendLiteralString` method.

2. Page parser queries the `ControlBuilder` to determine if whitespace literals are permitted. This was the precise subject of the `WXShowDemoControls.aspx` `ControlBuilder` example prevously demonstrated. Determining if whitespace literals are permitted is a matter of the page parser querying the `ControlBuiler's` `AllowWhiteSpaceLiterals` method. For the `ControlBuilder` class itself, this method returns `true` indicating whitespace literals are allowed.

3. Page parser queries the `ControlBuilder` to determine if any HTML residing in the literal should be decoded. The mechanism for determing if any HTML that is encoded should be decoded is provided by the `ControlBuilder` though its method, `HtmlDecodeLiterals`. For the `ControlBuilder` class itself, this method returns `false`, which means (by default) the HTML remains encoded.

4. Page parser appends the child control's `ControlBuilder` instance to the collection maintained by the parent `ControlBuilder`. This is achieved by calling the parent `ControlBuilder's` `AppendSubBuilder` method.

The final step reviewed above (appending the child `ControlBuilder` to its parent's collection of `ControlBuilder` instances) does affect the child `ControlBuilder`. Recall that the `OnAppendToParentBuilder` method for a `ControlBuilder` instance is called when the `ControlBuilder` is added to its parent's collection of control builders.

The previous decomposition of the interaction between page parser and `ControlBuilder` was certainly more intricate than is traditionally found in MSDN. Actually, this behavioral knowledge was acquired by developing a custom control builder that overrides every method of the `ControlBuilder` class that is marked as `virtual` (`Overridable` in VB.NET terms). This class, derived from `ControlBuilder`, is found in the `WXControlBuilderOverview.cs` source file and is aptly named, `WXControlBuilderOverview`. An abbreviate portion of this class's implementation is as follows, where the abbreviation noted is that only the prototypes are provided for the bulk of the methods overridden. Methods shown only as prototypes are so denoted by "..." but it should be recognized that in the `WXControlBuilderOverview.cs` source file, these methods are fully implemented:

```
public class WXControlBuilderOverview : ControlBuilder
{
    public override bool AllowWhitespaceLiterals() ...

    public override void AppendLiteralString(string s) ...

    public override void AppendSubBuilder(ControlBuilder subBuilder) ...

    public override void CloseControl() ...

    public override Type
        GetChildControlType(string tagName, IDictionary attribs) ...
```

```
    public override bool HasBody() ...

    public override bool HtmlDecodeLiterals() ...

    // Helper method used to display contents exposed by IDictionary
    private static void WXShowAttributes(IDictionary attribs)
    {
        foreach(DictionaryEntry entry in attribs)
        {
            Trace.WriteLine(String.Format("Attrib {0}:{1}",
                                    entry.Key, entry.Value));
        }
    }

    public override void Init(TemplateParser parser,
        ControlBuilder parentBuilder, Type type, string tagName,
        string id, IDictionary attribs)
    {
        Trace.WriteLine("***Init (TemplateParser: " + parser.ToString());
        Trace.WriteLine("Parent Control Builder: " +
                    parentBuilder.ToString());
        Trace.WriteLine("Type: " + type);
        Trace.WriteLine(String.Format("Tag: {0}, ID: {1}", tagName, id));
        WXShowAttributes(attribs);
        base.Init(parser, parentBuilder, type, tagName, id, attribs);
    }

    public override bool NeedsTagInnerText()...

    public override void
        OnAppendToParentBuilder(ControlBuilder parentBuilder) ...

    public override void SetTagInnerText(string innerText) ...
}
```

The only virtual method of the `ControlBuilder` class shown in its entirety is the `Init` method. The prototype for this method is as follows:

```
Overridable Public Sub Init(ByVal parser As TemplateParser, _
    ByVal parentBuilder As ControlBuilder, ByVal type As Type, _
    ByVal tagName As String, ByVal id As String, _
    ByVal attribs As IDictionary) ' VB.NET

public virtual void Init(TemplateParser parser,
    ControlBuilder parentBuilder, Type type, string tagName,
    string id, IDictionary attribs); // C#
```

The `Init` method uses the `Trace` class's `WriteLine` method in order to display the parameters passed to the `Init` method. The `Trace` class can be found in the `System.Diagnostics` namespace and the output produced by this class is by default sent to Visual Studio .NET's Output window. This output destination is of course provided you are actually debugging the application that utilizes the `WXControlBuilderOverview` class.

The parameters passed to the Init method include:

- ❏ TemplateParser parser – with regards to how the TemplateParser is used by developers, MSDN provides a rather abrupt description, "This type [TemplateParser] supports the .NET Framework infrastructure and is not intended to be used directly from your code."

- ❏ ControlBuilder parentBuilder – the parent of the ControlBuilder class for the control being parsed. If the control being parsed is at the top level of the hierarchy, the ControlBuilder's parent instance is of type RootBuilder where RootBuilder is found in the System.Web.UI namespace.

- ❏ Type type – the type of control being parsed.

- ❏ string tagName – the tag associated with the control whose ControlBuilder class is being exercised by the page parser.

- ❏ string id – the ID associated with the specific instance of the control whose ControlBuilder class is being exercised by the page parser.

- ❏ IDictionary attribs – the list of attributes (besides ID) of the control being parsed.

The attributes associated with the control (IDictionary attribs) to be built are displayed using the WXShowAttributes method shown previously. The aforementioned method simply uses C#'s foreach construct to iterate over the key-value pairs contained in the collection exposing the IDictionary interface. The WXShowAttributes method is also used by the GetChildControlType method that is another overridden method of the ControlBuilder class. The rationale for this is because the GetChildControlType method utilizes a parameter that represents a collection of attributes associated with a child control (a parameter also referred to as IDictionary attribs):

The most import line of code within the overridden Init method is:

```
base.Init(parser, parentBuilder, type, tagName, id, attribs);
```

If base.Init had not been called then the underlying ControlBuilder class would not have been initialized properly and page parsing could behave erratically (controls not displayed, or displayed improperly). To fully understand the importance of calling the base class's Init method (the Init method associated with the ControlBuilder base class) we need to further categorize the methods of the ControlBuilder class that can be overridden. One category of methods act as de facto properties by simply returning a result and thus not changing the state of the overridden ControlBuilder object. Methods in this category include: HasBody, NeedsTagInnerText, HtmlDecodeLiterals, and AllowWhitespaceLiterals. Each of these methods simply returns true or false to the page parser thus dictating a specific behavior of the page parser with respect to the control being parsed. Another method of this ilk is GetChildControlType, which returns a Type value based on evaluating the current tag being parsed.

The other category of methods actually modify the state of the ControlBuilder instance or provide information that could be crucial to the execution of this instance. Methods so categorized include: AppendLiteralString, OnAppendToParentBuilder, AppendSubBuilder, and SetTagInnerText. For each of the aforementioned methods, it is prudent to call the base class's version of the same method in order to ensure that the ControlBuilder base class is properly configured. For example if base.AppendSubBuilder is not called when AppendSubBuilder is overridden, the ControlBuilder base class will not properly maintain its collection of child control builder instances. To be completely candid it is not always necessary to call the same method in the base class as was overridden. However, doing so avoids a variety of cases where the control does not display correctly.

AppendLiteralString and More Parsing Detail

The `AppendLiteralString` method passes each literal string from the page parser to the `ControlBuilder` instance. If the instance is the `ControlBuilder` itself then the text is displayed within the control precisely as it is passed in from the page parser. If the instance is a class derived from the `ControlBuilder` then the derived class can potentially modify the literal string. When this modified literal string is passed to the `ControlBuilder` base class's `AppendLiteralString` method, the modified literal string will be displayed within the control.

The `WXOverviewControlBuilder.aspx` previously discussed provides an excellent platform with which to demonstrate `AppendLiteralString`:

```
<CBuilderDemo:WXShowOffControlBuilderFeatures ID="ShowItOff1"
                                              runat="server">
  <P><B>WXDemoWXControlBuilderOverview uses WXDemoWXControlBuilderOverview
ControlBuilder</B></P>
   Literal text 1 --
   <asp:Label ID="Label00" runat="server" Text="A Label 1 -- "></asp:Label>
   Literal text 2 --
   <asp:Label ID="Label01" runat="server" Text="A Label 2 -- "></asp:Label>
   Literal text 3
</CBuilderDemo: WXShowOffControlBuilderFeatures>
```

Given that the `AppendLiteralString` method provides literal strings from the page parser to the `ControlBuilder` it is not surprising that this method's prototype takes a single parameter of type string:

```
Overridable Public Sub AppendLiteralString(ByVal s As String) ' VB.NET
public virtual void AppendLiteralString(string s); // C#
```

The parsing of the parent control residing on the `WXOverviewControlBuilder.aspx` page can be broken down as follows and doing so clarifies what is passed as a parameter to the method, `AppendLiteralString`:

❑ Start tag information is provided by page parser to the `ControlBuilder` though the `Init` method. The portion of the page parsed at this stage is as follows:

```
<CBuilderDemo:WXShowOffControlBuilderFeatures ID="ShowItOff1"
                                              runat="server">
```

❑ Parse first control and have page parser call `GetChildControlType` to determine exact nature of the control. The portion of the page parsed at this stage is as follows:

```
<asp:Label ID="Label00" runat="server" Text="A Label 1"></asp:Label>
```

❑ As part of parsing the first control, the page parser calls `AppendLiteralString` in order to specify the literal text that resided before the child control. The portion of the page parsed at this stage is as follows, which just so happens also to correspond to the value of the `string s` parameter passed to `AppendLiteralString`:

```
    <P><B>WXDemoWXControlBuilderOverview uses WXDemoWXControlBuilderOverview
ControlBuilder</B></P>
    <P>Literal text 1</P>
```

❑ Parse second control and have page parser call `GetChildControlType` to determine the exact nature of the control. The portion of the page parsed at this stage is as follows:

```
<asp:Label ID="Label01" runat="server" Text="A Label 2"></asp:Label>
```

❑ As part of parsing the second control, the page parser calls `AppendLiteralString` to specify the literal text that resided before the child control. The portion of the page parsed at this stage is as follows, which is also the value of the `string s` parameter passed to `AppendLiteralString`:

```
<P>Literal text 2</P>
```

❑ Complete parsing body of control and have page parser call `AppendLiteralString` to specify the literal text that resides after the last child control but before the parent control's end tag. The portion of the page parsed at this stage is as follows, which is also the value of the `string s` parameter passed to `AppendLiteralString`:

```
<P>Literal text 3</P>
```

❑ Finalize parsing when the end tag is detected. This finalization is achieved by calling `NeedsTagInnerText`, `SetTagInnerText`, `OnAppendToParentBuilder`, and `CloseControl`. The portion of the page parsed at this stage is the control's end tag, which is as follows:

```
</CBuilderDemo: WXShowOffControlBuilderFeatures>
```

The benefit afforded by the `AppendLiteralString` method is that gives the control builder access to the string literals, which may or may not be parsed programmatically. This is completely up to the discretion of the `ControlBuilder` implementation. A practical example as to why the text passed from page parser to `ControlBuilder` using `AppendLiteralString` should be parsed is as follows.

AppendLiteralString and Filtering

The previous section showed the nuts and bolts of the `AppendLiteralString` method. What the previous section failed to reveal is that when the nuts and bolts are all put together, a Porsche is created. The Porsche in this case (overriding the `AppendLiteralString` method) can be used to implement a filter that modifies the contents of the literal string in order to remove undesirable words. This undesirable word filter for this example will remove the word "NaughtyWord" and replace it with the more acceptable phrase, "PureWord." The `WXTryFilter.cs` file contains the `WXFilterControlBuilder` class that implements this filter. In order to implement such a filter the `WXFilterControlBuilder` class is derived from the `ControlBuilder` base class and this derived class overrides the `AppendLiteralString` method. The implementation of this custom control builder that provides a filter is as follows:

```
using System;
using System.Diagnostics;
using System.Web.UI;

namespace WXControlBuilderDemo
{
    public class WXFilterControlBuilder : ControlBuilder
    {
        public override void AppendLiteralString(string s)
        {
            string filteredPhrase = s.Replace("NaughtyWord",
                                              "PureWord");
            base.AppendLiteralString(filteredPhrase);
        }
    }
}
```

The `string` class's `Replace` method performs the actual filtering by replacing "NaughtyWord" with "PureWord". This sanitized string is then passed to the `ControlBuilder` base class. Passing the filtered string to the base class using `base.AppendLiteralString(filteredPhrase);` ensures that the control will contain the sanitized rather than inappropriate string.

The `WXFilter.cs` source file contains a control whose literal text is to be filtered. This control is the `WXFilter` class and the `WXFilterControlBuilder` custom control builder class provides the filtering:

```
[ControlBuilder(typeof(WXFilterControlBuilder))]
public class WXFilter : Control
{
}
```

The `WXShowFilters.aspx` file contains an instance of the `WXFilter` control. This ASPX file is implemented as follows and as expected the control contains the phrase to be filtered, "NaughyWord":

```
<%@ Register TagPrefix="CBuilderDemo"
             Namespace="WXControlBuilderDemo"
             Assembly="WXControlBuilderDemo"%>
<HTML>
  <body>
    <CBuilderDemo:WXFilter id="WXTryFilter1" runat="server">
      Befuddled, he uttered a NaughtyWord.
    </CBuilderDemo:WXFilter>
  </body>
</HTML>
```

The `WXFilterControlBuilder` custom control builder will swap each instance of "NaughtyWord" found the `WXShowFilters.aspx` file and replace it with "PureWord." The results of this filtering are revealed in the following HTML displayed using `WXShowFilters.aspx` file":

Befuddled, he uttered a PureWord.

The idea of filtering could be further extended. The WXFilterControlBuilder custom control builder class could be associated with multiple controls thus offering a universal way to fine-tune the literal string displayed with a control. The string class's Replace method is not the best way to parse and edit literal strings found within a control. An HTML parser could have been used to actually dissect the literal string.

Parsing the literal string is fraught with possibilities. Consider the case where the method, AppendLiteralString, detects HTML format tags in the literal text that are not displayed correctly using the browser installed in the accounting department. The AppendLiteralString method could swap formatting tags to something that is appropriately displayed in all browsers used by a corporation. Besides the idea of tweaking HTML formatting is ever so much more palatable than implementing a "universal way to censor HTML and undermine free speech".

HasBody

The prototype for the HasBody method is as follows:

```
Overridable Public Function HasBody() As Boolean ' VB.NET
public virtual bool HasBody(); // C#
```

To demonstrate the HasBody method, consider the following page, WebShowHasBody.aspx:

```
<%@ Register TagPrefix="CBuilderDemo" Namespace="WXControlBuilderDemo"
            Assembly="WXControlBuilderDemo"%>
<HTML>
    <body>
        <CBuilderDemo:WXShowOffControlBuilderFeatures ID="ShowHasBodyTrue"
                                                      runat="server">
        </CBuilderDemo:WXShowOffControlBuilderFeatures>

        <CBuilderDemo:WXShowOffControlBuilderFeatures ID="ShowHasBodyFalse"
                                                      runat="server" />
    </body>
</HTML>
```

The WXShowOffControlBuilderFeatures custom control with ID=ShowHasBodyTrue has a start and end tag and hence has a body. For this reason HasBody returns true when queried.

The WXShowOffControlBuilderFeatures custom control with ID=ShowHasBodyFalse does not have matching start and end tag and hence does not have a body. For this reason HasBody returns false when queried. Both the has-body and non-has-body forms are valid. When a control has a start and end tag (has a body) then it can potentially contain child controls and literal text. When a control does not have a body then it can contain no child controls and literal text. With no child controls and literal text, parsing is vastly simplified.

Before searching for more adventurous methods to review, consider the implementation of the HasBody associated with the WXShowOffControlBuilderFeatures class's custom control builder. The WXControlBuilderOverview class is the aforementioned custom control builder and it overrides HasBody as follows:

```
public override bool HasBody()
{
    Trace.WriteLine("***HasBody: " + base.HasBody().ToString());
    return base.HasBody();
}
```

The `Trace` output of the `HasBody` is displayed in Visual Studio .NET for the case of the custom control with `ID=ShowHasBodyTrue`, but is not displayed for the case of the custom control with `ID=ShowHasBodyFalse`. What this means is that where there is a body associated with a control, the page parser has to query the `ControlBuilder` in order to determine if there is a body. If there is no body, then the page parser does not need to query the `ControlBuilder` to determine that there is no body. When documenting how the page parser interacts with the `ControlBuilder` this was a clear inconsistency. This simply reflects the exact way in which the page parser interacts with a `ControlBuilder` implementation and should not be construed as an inaccuracy with respect to how the page parser was previously documented.

CloseControl Method and ControlBuilder Properties

The implementation of each individual method of the `WXControlBuilderOverview` class was not presented in the previous write up on this class (for reasons of brevity). Among the methods not presented in full was the `CloseControl` method, whose prototype is as follows:

```
Overridable Public Sub CloseControl() ' VB.NET
public virtual void CloseControl(); // C#
```

For the case of the `WXControlBuilderOverview` class, the `CloseControl` method is used as a way to display the properties associated with the `ControlBuilder` base class. These properties are available to the descendants of the `ControlBuilder` class. This implementation of the `CloseControl` method should in no way be construed as what a viable, real-world custom control builder might implement. This example override of the `CloseControl` method is simply to demonstrate the properties available to the writers of custom control builders. Within the `CloseControl` method the aforementioned properties are displayed as follows:

```
public override void CloseControl()
{
    Trace.WriteLine("***CloseControl() -- properties -- ");
    Trace.WriteLine("ControlType: " + ControlType.ToString());
    Trace.WriteLine("FChildrenAsProperties: " +
        FChildrenAsProperties.ToString());
    Trace.WriteLine("FIsNonParserAccessor: " +
        FIsNonParserAccessor.ToString());
    Trace.WriteLine("HasAspCode: " + HasAspCode.ToString());
    Trace.WriteLine("ID: " + ID.ToString());
    Trace.WriteLine("InDesigner: " + InDesigner.ToString());
    Trace.WriteLine("NamingContainerType: " +
                    NamingContainerType.ToString());
    Trace.WriteLine("Parser: " + Parser.ToString());
    Trace.WriteLine("TagName: " + TagName.ToString());
    base.CloseControl();
}
```

Notice in the previous implementation of CloseControl that base.CloseControl() is called. This line of code is to ensure that the ControlBuilder base class performs the cleanup tasks performed when CloseControl is executed.

The properties of ControlBuilder displayed within the CloseControl method include:

- ❑ ControlType – this public property returns the type (Type class) of control associated with the ControlBuilder.

- ❑ FChildrenAsProperties – this protected property returns true if the control has a ParseChildrenAttribute attribute and this attribute's ChildrenAsProperties property is set to true. By default the ChildrenAsProperties property is set to true. When this property is true the attributes of the parent control are treated as properties by the parser. If the FChildrenAsProperties property returned false then the page parser treats the parent control's attributes as child controls.

- ❑ FIsNonParserAccessor – this protected property returns true if the control implements the IParserAccessor interface. A control implements this interface so it can be informed when an HTML or XML element is parsed by the page parser with the text associated with the control. This element is then passed to the control through the IParserAccessor interface's AddParsedSubObject method.

- ❑ HasAspCode – this public property returns true if the control contains any ASP code (blocks of code) and false if it does not contain ASP code.

- ❑ ID – this public property accesses the ID property associated with the control to be built.

- ❑ InDesigner – this public property returns true if the custom control is running in Visual Studio .NET's designer. In order to understand this property, consider a custom control that performs some type of expensive task in its custom control builder and that this task is unrelated to the display of the control. For example the control builder could write detailed statistics to SQL Server describing the type of elements within the control be parsed. This non-display-oriented task can be disabled while the custom control builder is running within Visual Studio .NET's designer but can be re-enabled when the control is being built for an actual web page.

- ❑ NamingContainerType – this public property is clearly documented by MSDN, "not intended to be used directly from your code."

- ❑ Parser – this protected property is clearly documented by MSDN, "not intended to be used directly from your code."

- ❑ TagName – this public property accesses the tag name associated with the control to be built.

From a real-world standpoint the reason for overridding the CloseControl method should be clear. If a construct was initialized for a custom control builder then the CloseControl method makes a dandy place to ensure that the construct is cleaned up.

Classes Derived from ControlBuilder

A variety of classes found within .NET are derived from the `ControlBuilder` base class. These derived classes selectively override the methods of `ControlBuilder` in order to customize the parsing behavior associated with a given control. The `System.Web.UI.WebControls` namespace contains a variety of classes derived from `ControlBuilder`, including some that like our first example (source file, `WXShowDemoControls.aspx`) only override the method, `AllowWhitespaceLiterals`. Derived classes in this category include: `HyperLinkControlBuilder`, `LabelControlBuilder`, `LinkButtonControlBuilder`, `PlaceHolderControlBuilder`, and `TableCellControlBuilder`.

The name of the class derived from `ControlBuilder` reflects the name of the control with which this customized control builder is associated. For example, `HyperLinkControlBuilder` is the custom control builder for the `HyperLink` control. `LinkButtonControlBuilder` is the custom control builder for the `LinkButton` control. Demonstrating how these controls and the `Label` control override the `AllowWhitespaceLiterals` method is the source file, `WXDerivedFromCBuilder.aspx`. The implementation of this source file is similar in construction to the implementation of `WXShowDemoControls.aspx`. For example, both `*.aspx` files contain a `<pre>` region surrounding controls that override the `AllowWhitespaceLiterals` method. In the case of both files, the carriage returns (whitespace literals) between controls are not displayed because the overridden `AllowWhitespaceLiterals` method returns `false`. The contents of `WXDerivedFromCBuilder.aspx` are as follows:

```
<%@ Register TagPrefix="CBuilderDemo"
             Namespace="WXControlBuilderDemo"
             Assembly="WXControlBuilderDemo"%>
<HTML>
    <body>
        <pre>
<form runat="server" ID="RequiredForLinkButton">
  <asp:LinkButton id=LinkButton1 runat="server"><B>LinkButton</B>
    <asp:Label ID="Label04" runat="server"
      Text="Three carriage returns to follow.">
    </asp:Label>



    <asp:Label ID="Label05" runat="server"
        Text="Three carriage returns above.">
    </asp:Label>
  </asp:LinkButton>
</form>


<asp:HyperLink id=HyperLink1 runat="server"><B>HyperLink</B>
  <asp:Label ID=Label00 runat="server"
    Text="Three carriage returns to follow.">
  </asp:Label>
```

```
      <asp:Label ID=Label01 runat="server"
        Text="Three carriage returns above.">
      </asp:Label>
  </asp:HyperLink>

  <asp:Label id=Label1 runat="server" ><B>Label</B>
      <asp:Label ID="Label02" runat="server"
        Text="Three carriage returns to follow.">
      </asp:Label>



      <asp:Label ID="Label03" runat="server"
        Text="Three carriage returns above.">
      </asp:Label>
  </asp:Label>
          </pre>
         </body>
  </HTML>
```

The controls (each of whose builder overrides the `AllowWhitespaceLiterals` method and hence this method returns `false`) are highlighted in the previous ASP snippet. Notice in that `LinkButton` is actually the child control of a `Form`. The reason for this is that a `LinkButton` can only be instantiated within a `Form`. If a `LinkButton` is not placed inside a form, a gentle reminder is provided by an exception being thrown and the following text displayed to the browser by default:

Control 'YourButtonIDHere' of type 'LinkButton' must be placed inside a form tag with runat=server

The output from the `WXDerivedFromCBuilder.aspx` source file displays as follows in Internet Explorer (complete with lack of carriage returns):

```
LinkButton
Three carriage returns to follow.Three carriage returns above.

HyperLink
Three carriage returns to follow.Three carriage returns above.

Label
Three carriage returns to follow.Three carriage returns above.
```

Classes Overriding HtmlDecodeLiterals

The `System.Web.UI.WebControls` namespace also contains the `TextBoxControlBuilder` and `ListItemControlBuilder` classes. These classes override the `AllowWhiteSpaceLiterals` method causing it to return `false`. Additionally these classes override the `ControlBuilder` class's `HtmlDecodeLiterals` method so that it returns `true`. The prototype for the `HtmlDecodeLiterals` method is as follows (both VB .NET and C# prototypes):

```
Overridable Public Function HtmlDecodeLiterals() As Boolean ' VB.NET
public virtual bool HtmlDecodeLiterals(); // C#
```

For the `ControlBuilder` base class, `HtmlDecodeLiterals` specifies not to decode the HTML (return value of `false`). To understand HTML decoding and encoding remember that every character in HTML can be represented as its character value (decoded value) such as `'<'`, `'a'` `'&'` or as an encoded variant such as `&gt;`, `&#97;`, and `&amp;`. The letter `'a'` is represented in encoded form as its numeric value (`&#97;`) within the Latin 1 character set. The `'<'` and `'&'` characters can be represented in encoded form either by their numeric value within the character set (`&#62;` and `&#38;` respectively) or by the abbreviations just shown (`&gt;` and `&amp;` respectively). Similar non-numeric abbreviations exist for characters such as the double quote, less than, and non-breaking space.

In support of HTML encoding and decoding the `System.Web.HttpUtility` class exposes the `HtmlDecode` and `HtmlEncode` methods. The functionality provided by these methods is self-documenting (the former decodes HTML text while the latter encodes HTML text). Tables defining the encoded form of HTML are quite prevalent in the world of web documentation. One particularly useful example can be found within MSDN under the topic entitled, "ISO Latin-1 Character Set," which can be found under the URL:

ms-help://MS.VSCC/MS.MSDNVS/DHTML/workshop/author/dhtml/reference/charsets/charset1.htm

The `ms-help` prefix in the URL above is associated with MSDN (the help installed as part of Visual Studio .NET). Do not try this URL on a machine that does not contain MSDN as it will not be recognized.

Thus far an example has been presented where the `ControlBuilder` class was derived from directly and subsequently its methods were overridden. A slightly different approach is to create a custom control builder by deriving a class from a descendant of the `ControlBuilder` class. The descendant to derive from is the `TextBoxControlBuilder` class. By deriving from this class, it will be possible to create a `TextBox` that behaves in a different manner from the off-the-shelf `TextBox` provided by the `System.Web.UI.WebControls` namespace.

To understand what this will accomplish, let's fast-forward in time to the end result:

The screenshot above contains standard `TextBox` (the top textbox in the screenshot) and a special textbox (the bottom textbox in the screenshot). This special textbox (the `WXSpecialTextBox` class found in `WXSpecialTextBox.cs`) is associated with a custom control builder, the `WXSpecialTextBoxControlBuilder` class. The text displayed by both flavors of textbox is identical. The text associated with the upper textbox (**Decode Me! &><**) is decoded while the text associated with the lower textbox (**Deco** etc.) is encoded. The page used to generate the previous screenshot is as follows:

```
<%@ Register TagPrefix="CBuilderDemo" Namespace="WXControlBuilderDemo"
            Assembly="WXControlBuilderDemo"%>
<HTML>
    <body>
        <form runat="server" ID="RequiredForTextBox">
            <P>With HtmlDecodeLiterals=true:</P>
            <asp:TextBox id="TextBox1" runat="server" Width="550px">
&#68;&#101;&#99;&#111;&#100;&#101; &#77;&#101;&#33; &amp;&gt;&lt;&quot;
</asp:TextBox>
            <P></P>
            <P>With HtmlDecodeLiterals=false:</P>
            <CBuilderDemo:WXSpecialTextBox id="TextBox2" runat="server"
Width="551px">
&#68;&#101;&#99;&#111;&#100;&#101; &#77;&#1o1;&#33; &amp;&gt;&lt;&quot;
</CBuilderDemo:WXSpecialTextBox>
        </form>
    </body>
</HTML>
```

It should be clear from the previous page that the form displays a standard TextBox (tag, asp:TextBox) and our special textbox (tag, CBuilderDemo:WXSpecialTextBox). The source file, WXSpecialTextBox.cs, containing the implementation of this special textbox is as follows:

```
using System;
using System.Web.UI; // ControlBuilderAttribute
using System.Web.UI.WebControls; // TextBox, TextBoxControlBuilder

namespace WXControlBuilderDemo
{
    public class WXSpecialTextBoxControlBuilder : TextBoxControlBuilder
    {
        // for every other method rely on the implementation
        // provided by TextBoxControlBuilder
        public override bool HtmlDecodeLiterals()
        {
            return false;
        }
    }

    [ControlBuilderAttribute(typeof(WXSpecialTextBoxControlBuilder))]
    public class WXSpecialTextBox : TextBox
    {
    }
}
```

The implementation of the WXSpecialTextBox is quite simple. This class is derived from the TextBox class. Instead of relying on the control builder provided by the TextBox class, the WXSpecialTextBox class uses its own control builder, WXSpecialTextBoxControlBuilder. This custom control builder is derived from the TextBoxControlBuilder class (the custom control builder for the TextBox class). The lone method overridden was discussed previously, namely HtmlDecodeLiterals, which returns false for the WXSpecialTextBoxControlBuilder class.

From a practical standpoint, it is more likely that a custom control builder will override the ControlBuilder's implementation of the HtmlDecodeLiterals method in order to have this method return true. Remember that by default this method returns false thus displaying a cacophony of characters not readily suited for human consumption. By overriding the HtmlDecodeLiterals method to return true in the same manner in the TextBoxControlBuilder class, human-readable HTML (decoded HTML) will be generated for a class. The practicality of having text be readable to humans is apparent to most web developers.

Classes Overriding AppendSubBuilder

The Literal class is associated with a custom control builder, the LiteralControlBuilder class. The LiteralControlBuilder custom control builder causes the AllowWhitespaceLiterals method to return false – all courtesy of the magic of inheritance and method overriding. This custom control builder also overrides the AppendSubBuilder method. The prototype for this method is defined as follows:

```
Overridable Public _
    Sub AppendSubBuilder(ByVal subBuilder As ControlBuilder) ' VB.NET
public virtual void AppendSubBuilder(ControlBuilder subBuilder); // C#
```

The premise used by the LiteralControlBuilder class in overriding AppendSubBuilder is unique. Rather than extending the functionality exposed by the ControlBuilder through its method, AppendSubBuilder, the LiteralControlBuilder class's override of this method generates an exception of type System.Web.HttpException. This exception is a rather blatant hint to "Please do not call this method every under any circumstances."

The purpose of the AppendSubBuilder method is to append the ContolBuilder classes of the child controls to the collection maintained by the control builder of the parent control. The purpose of the Literal control is to provide "literal" text to the client. This text contains no controls. The AppendSubBuilder method of the LiteralControlBuilder class represents a back-door that could be used by a developer to add a child ControlBuilder (sub-builder). This addition would be made (if permitted) to a custom control builder associated with a control that does not allow child controls. Having the LiteralControlBuilder class's AppendSubBuilder method throw an exception effectively shuts this backdoor.

The WXExerciseLiteral.cs source file's WXExerciseLiteralControlBuilder class is a custom control builder that attempts to exploit this backdoor. This source file is for "demonstration purposes only" since the effort should expressly fail when the LiteralControlBuilder class's AppendSubBuilder method raises an exception. The basic premise of this demo is that a custom control builder is associated with the WXExerciseLiteral custom control. The AppendSubBuilder method of the WXExerciseLiteralControlBuilder custom control builder is called for each control that is a child of a WXExerciseLiteral instance. If this child control of type Literal then its associated ControlBuilder is of type LiteralControlBuilder. Under this precise circumstance the WXExerciseLiteralControlBuilder's override of the AppendSubBuilder method attempts to add a control builder to the LiteralControlBuilder instance. The following excerpt from the WXExerciseLiteral.cs source file demonstrates this:

```
public class WXExerciseLiteralControlBuilder : ControlBuilder
{
    public override void AppendSubBuilder(ControlBuilder subBuilder)
    {
        base.AppendSubBuilder(subBuilder);
        if (typeof(LiteralControlBuilder) == subBuilder.GetType())
        {
            try
            {
                subBuilder.AppendSubBuilder(new ControlBuilder());
            }
            catch(HttpException ex)
            {
                Trace.WriteLine("LiteralControlBuilder.AppendSubBuilder " +
                            "threw exception: " + ex.ToString());
            }
        }
    }
}
```

Since the claim has been made that the WXExerciseLiteralControlBuilder custom control builder is associated with the WXExerciseLiteral control, it behooves us to also show the WXExerciseLiteral.cs source file's WXExerciseLiteral class:

```
[ControlBuilderAttribute(typeof(WXExerciseLiteralControlBuilder))]
public class WXExerciseLiteral : Control
{
}
```

The WXShowExerciseLiteral.aspx file is provided to create a WXExerciseLiteral control instance. This in turn causes a WXExerciseLiteralControlBuilder to be constructed. The end result of the custom control builder's creation is the generation of an exception. This exception is raised when an attempt is made to append a subordinate builder using a LiteralControlBuilder instance.

Inside the WXExerciseLiteralControlBuilder class's implementation of the AppendSubBuilder method, a method is called that generates an exception. The exception is generated when a child control of type Literal has its custom control builder's AppendSubBuilder method called. The WXExerciseLiteralControlBuilder class's implementation of the AppendSubBuilder method catches the exception of type HttpException and displays it to a destination exposed by the Trace class.

Actually the WXExerciseLiteralControlBuilder class's implementation of the AppendSubBuilder method is a bit contrived. It does not make practical sense to randomly append a subordinate control builder to a ControlBuilder instance. Still because the LiteralControlBuilder class overrode the AppendSubBuilder method a potential programmer error was avoided.

It is important to note that the AppendSubBuilder method cannot be used to substitute an alternative ControlBuilder for the one provided. To understand this, consider the case of the TextBox. Recall that the HtmlDecodeLiterals method for the TextBoxControl builder returns true. By creating a new control derived from TextBox and a new custom control builder derived from TextBoxControlBuilder it was demonstrated that HtmlDecodeLiterals could be overridden to return false. An alternative approach to having this method return false can be seen in the following snippet from the WXAppendSubBuilderDemo.aspx source file:

259

```
Text above form
<form runat="server" ID="RequiredForTextBox">
  <asp:TextBox id="TextBox1" runat="server">
&#68;&#101;&#99;&#111;&#100;&#101; &#77;&#101;&#33;
  </asp:TextBox>
  <P>Text between text boxes</P>
  <CBuilderDemo:WXLeaveHTMLLiteralsEncoded id="WXLeaveHTMLLiteralsEncoded1"
                                     runat="server">
    <asp:TextBox id="TextBox2" runat="server">
&#68;&#101;&#99;&#111;&#100;&#101; &#77;&#101;&#33;
    </asp:TextBox>
  </CBuilderDemo:WXLeaveHTMLLiteralsEncoded>
</form>
Text below form
```

The ASPX snippet above contains a form with two textboxes. The top textbox (ID=TextBox1) contains a potpourri of encoded HTML that will be decoded for reasons already discussed. The bottom textbox (ID=TextBox2) also contains a slew of encoded HTML but will this be decoded? This second textbox is contained in a parent control whose name, WXLeaveHTMLLiteralEncoded, casts doubt as to whether the HTML for the TextBox will be decoded. The source file WXLeaveHMTLLiteralEncoded.cs contains the implementation for the WXLeaveHTMLLiteralEncoded class and its custom control builder, WXLeaveHTMLLiteralEncodedControlBuilder. This control builder has overridden its AppendSubBuilder method. The rational for this override is to change on the fly the control builder associated with a TextBox. Rather than having AppendSubBuilder specifying TextBoxControlBuilder, the standard ControlBuilder will be substituted. The reason is because ControlBuilder's HtmlDecodeLiterals method returns false. The classes that implement this strategy are found in the WXLeaveHMTLLiteralEncoded.cs source file:

```
public class WXLeaveHTMLLiteralsEncodedControlBuilder : ControlBuilder
{
    public override void AppendSubBuilder(ControlBuilder subBuilder)
    {
        if (typeof(TextBoxControlBuilder) == subBuilder.GetType())
        {
            subBuilder.AppendSubBuilder(new ControlBuilder());
        }

        else
        {
            base.AppendSubBuilder(subBuilder);
        }
    }
}
    [ControlBuilderAttribute(typeof(WXLeaveHTMLLiteralsEncodedControlBuilder))]
public class WXLeaveHTMLLiteralsEncoded : Control
{
}
```

This altering of control builders for the TextBox child control should (in theory), cause the HTML text not to be decoded. Actually, the HTML literals associated with the TextBox are not decoded because this TextBox is not displayed. Demonstrating this is the screenshot opposite:

Text above form

Decode Me! &><"

Text between text boxes

Text below form

This screenshot displays the first `TextBox` (whose custom control builder was left alone). The second `TextBox` is not displayed and the likely culprit is that this `TextBox`'s custom control builder was changed on the fly. This failed endeavor with the `AppendSubBuilder` method means that the only successful overriding of this method was by the `LiteralControlBuilder` class. This particular custom control builder's override threw an exception that is not much of an override. In its present form the `AppendSubBuilder` method offers few practical reasons to be overridden. Hopefully once the .NET Framework is more mature, it will be possible to assign custom control builders on-the-fly and have the control be displayed.

NeedsTagInnerText and SetTagInnerText

The `ControlBuilder`'s implementation of `NeedsTagInnerText` returns `false`. Given the Boolean nature of this method's return value, the prototype for this method is no surprise:

```
Overridable Public Function NeedsTagInnerText() As Boolean ' VB.NET
public virtual bool NeedsTagInnerText(); // C#
```

When the `NeedsTagInnerText` method returns `true` then the `ControlBuilder`'s `SetTagInnerText` method is called by the page parser. The prototype for the `SetTagInnerText` method is as follows:

```
Overrides Public Sub SetTagInnerText(ByVal innerText As String) ' VB.NET
public override void SetTagInnerText(string innerText); // C#
```

What precisely is passed to the `SetTagInnerText` method is a string containing all the text from the control's start tag to its end tag. If this text is modified and passed to the `ControlBuilder` base class (`base.SetTagInnerText(innerText);` then the modified version of the inner text string is **not** displayed. This last sentence is correct, "The modified version of the inner text string is **NOT** displayed." `SetTagInnerText` cannot be used to filter the inner text in the same manner `AppendLiteralString` was used to filter literal text. Remember that `AppendLiteralString` is passed the literal text between controls and `GetChildControlType` is passed the tag name and attributes of a child control. This pair of methods provides enough functionality to modify the inner text. The text returned by the `SetTagInnerText` method is for information purposes only. It should be noted that this inner text does contain the unparsed version of each child control as opposed to the `GetChildControlType` method that receives the parsed version of each child control (tag name and attributes).

In order to demonstrate that the `SetTagInnerText` method cannot be used as a filter (because it does not modify the inner text), an example will be demonstrated that modifies (filters) the inner text and passes this modified text to the to the `ControlBuilder` base class (`base.SetTagInnerText(innerText);`. The point of this exercise is to show that filtering will not work if implemented in this manner. A more important and practical lesson to be demonstrated by this example is how the custom control being parsed by the page parser can be used to dictate the behavior of the custom control builder. The ASP.NET page associated with the custom control to be filtered unsuccessfully is `WXShowFilters.aspx` and the pertinent portion of this file is as follows:

```
<CBuilderDemo:WXAttemptFilter id="WxAttemptFilter1" UseFilter="true"
                              runat="server">
    The naughty child said a BadWord.
</CBuilderDemo:WXAttemptFilter>
<br>
<CBuilderDemo:WXAttemptFilter id="WxAttemptFilter2" UseFilter="false"
                              runat="server">
    The naughty child said a BadWord.
</CBuilderDemo:WXAttemptFilter>
```

The ASP.NET snippet above contains the literal text "`BadWord.`" The filtering will attempt to change this offensive phrase to "`GoodWord`" (provided the `WXAttemptFilter` custom control does not disable filtering). In the previous ASP.NET snippet there are two custom controls both of type `WXAttemptFilter`:

❑   `id="WxAttemptFilter1"` – this instance of the `WXAttemptFilter` class has its `UseFilter` property set to `true`

❑   `id="WxAttemptFilter2"` – this instance of the `WXAttemptFilter` class has its `UseFilter` property set to `false`

The `WXAttemptFilter` custom control is associated with the appropriately named custom control builder, `WXAttemptFilterControlBuilder` class. When this control builder's `Init` method is called, it looks at the attributes associated with the `WXAttemptFilter` control. If the `UseFilter` attribute is set to `true`, then the control builder sets its `_filteringEnabled` data member to `true`, otherwise it sets this data member to `false`. The sourcecode associated with the `WXAttemptFilter` class and its control builder is found in the `WXFilter.cs` file. The `WXAttemptFilter` class is implemented as follows:

```
[ControlBuilder(typeof(WXAttemptFilterControlBuilder))]
public class WXAttemptFilter : Control
{
    private bool _useFilter = false;

    public bool UseFilter
    {
        get
        {
            return _useFilter;
        }

        set
        {
            _useFilter = value;
        }
    }
}
```

It should be clear from the previous code snippet that the `WXAttemptFilter` custom control is derived from the `Control` base class and exposes a public property, `UseFilter`. The aforementioned property allows the `UseFilter` attribute to be specified when declaring the `WXAttemptFilter` custom control in an ASP.NET file. In the previous code snippet it is also demonstrated that the `ControlBuilder` custom attribute is used to associate the `WXAttempFilter` instance with the `WXAttemptFilterControlBuilder` custom control builder.

The `WXAttemptFilterControlBuilder` custom control builder is implemented in the source file, `WXFilter.cs`, with the following technical assets:

❑ `bool _filteringEnabled` data member – this data member is initially set to `false` indicating that filter is disabled.

❑ `Init` method – this method is an overriden version of the `ControlBuilder` base class's `Init` method. The overriden flavor of the `Init` method looks for the `UseFilter` attribute (`if (attribs.Contains("UseFilter"))`). The value of this attribute (`true` or `false`) is assigned to the `filteringEnabled` data member. If no `UseFilter` attribute is specified, no worries, because the `filteringEnabled` data member was initally set to `false`.

❑ `NeedsTagInnerText` method – this method is an override of the same method exposed by the `ControlBuilder` base class. The `NeedsTagInnerText` method simply returns the value of the `_filteringEnabled` data member where `true` indicates that the inner text is needed because filtering is enabled and `false` indicates that the inner text is not needed because no attempt will be made to filter the inner text.

❑ `SetTagInnerText` method – this method is an override of the `SetTagInnerText` method implemented by the `ControlBuilder` base class. This overriden variant checks the `_filteringEnabled` data member. If this data member is `false`, then no filtering is performed and if this data member is `true`, then the simplistic filtering algorithm is used to change each instance of the offensive pharse, "`BadWord`," to the prim and proper phrase, "`GoodWord`".

The mechanism used by the `SetTagInnerText` method does not explicitly parse the in inner text using a legitimate HTML parser. Instead the `SetTagInnerText` method uses the `String` class's `Replace` method to perform brute-force filtering:

```
string censoredPhrase = innerText.Replace("BadWord", "GoodWord");
```

The downside to this brute-force filtering occurs if the inner text contains an HTML tag or attribute called, "`BadWord`"; this tag or attribute would be changed to "`GoodWord`".

The specific implementation of the `WXAttemptFilterControlBuilder` custom control builder is as follows:

```
public class WXAttemptFilterControlBuilder : ControlBuilder
{
    bool _filteringEnabled = false;

    public override void Init(TemplateParser parser,
                              ControlBuilder parentBuilder,
                              Type type,
                              string tagName,
```

```
                              string id,
                              IDictionary attribs)
    {
        if (attribs.Contains("UseFilter"))
        {
            if (0 == String.Compare(Boolean.TrueString,
                                    (string)attribs["UseFilter"],
                                    true))
            {
                _filteringEnabled = true;
            }

        }

        base.Init(parser, parentBuilder, type, tagName, id, attribs);
    }

    public override bool NeedsTagInnerText()
    {
        // Only need tag inner text if filtering is enabled
        return _filteringEnabled;
    }

    public override void SetTagInnerText(string innerText)
    {
        string censoredPhrase = innerText.Replace("BadWord", "GoodWord");
        base.SetTagInnerText(censoredPhrase);
    }
}
}
```

Recall that the original ASP.NET file contained two instances of the WXAttemptFilter custom control. For one instance of this control filtering was enabled (UseFilter=true) and for the other instance it was disabled (UseFilter=false). If filtering works for the SetTagInnerText class then the term "BadWord" should be swapped with the term "GoodWord" for the custom control instance that enables filtering. The output from the WXShowFilters.aspx file is as follows:

> The naughty child said a BadWord.
> The naughty child said a BadWord.

This screenshot clearly demonstrates that the SetTagInnerText method cannot act as a filter and only provides the inner text for informational purposes. Given this, what was the purpose of presenting such an elaborate example? The idea of having the custom control builder's behavior modified based on an attribute associate with the custom control is a reasonable, real-world premise. If the custom control builder, WXAttemptFilterControlBuilder, had performed the filtering in its AppendLiteralText method then the WXAttemptFilter class's UseFilter property would have legitimately enabled and disabled filtering. Because the SetTagInnerText method cannot implement filtering, the UseFilter property was wishful thinking rather than a property with a practical use.

GetChildControlType

A practical reason to override the `ControlBuilder`'s `GetChildControlType` method would be to change at run time the child controls contained within a parent control. For example a web site could be designed to use either `Button` or `LinkButton` controls under certain circumstances. This choice would represent a configurable, consistent way to handle button-style controls. At run time a configuration file or the Windows registry could be queried in order to determine whether the `Button` or `LinkButton` control should be used. A custom control builder would handle this configuration querying and also handle specifying the type of button-style control to use.

The `WXBetterForm.cs` source file contains a control builder that overrides the `GetChildControlType` method and a control that utilizes this control builder. The control builder is the `WXButtonChooserControlBuilder` class and the control that utilizes it is the `WButtonChooser` class.

When an instance of the `WXButtonChooserControlBuilder` class is created it queries to determine if `Buttons` or `LinkButtons` should be used. This choice is made in the constructor for the `WXButtonChooserControlBuilder` class. The choice is made using a random number where 1 indicates using `Button` and 0 indicates using `LinkButton`. Although a configuration file or the registry could be used to provide consistent configuration the `random` number generator is more real-world since most web sites are only randomly consistent. The `Random` class's `Next` method is used to generate this heads or tails random number. The `_useStandardButton` data member is set to `true` if `Button` is the standard style of button to be used and set to `false` if `LinkButton` is the standard style of button to be used.

The prototype for the `GetChildControlType` method is as follows (both VB.NET and C#):

```
Overridable Public Function GetChildControlType(ByVal tagName As String, _
                            ByVal attribs As IDictionary) As Type ' VB.NET


public virtual Type
    GetChildControlType(string tagName, IDictionary attribs); // C#
```

The `WXButtonChooserControlBuilder` class's override of the `GetChildControlType` method looks for a value of `"MyCustomButton"` with respect to the `tagName` parameter. The tag, `MyCustomButton`, indicates that a standardized button style should be returned: `LinkButton` or `Button`. The snippet below shows how `GetChildControlType` uses the data member `_useStandardButton` to choose between `LinkButton` and `Button`:

```
if (_useStandardButton)
{
    return typeof(Button);
}
else
{
    return typeof(LinkButton);
}
```

The WXButtonChooserControlBuilder class in its entirety is as follows:

```
public class WXButtonChooserControlBuilder : ControlBuilder
{
    private bool _useStandardButton;

    public WXButtonChooserControlBuilder()
    {
        Random picker = new Random();

        if (picker.Next(2) == 1)
        {
            _useStandardButton = true;
        }

        else
        {
            _useStandardButton = false;
        }
    }

    public override Type
        GetChildControlType(string tagName, IDictionary attribs)
    {
        if (string.Compare(tagName, "MyCustomButton", true) == 0)
        {
            if (_useStandardButton)
            {
                return typeof(Button);
            }
            else
            {
                return typeof(LinkButton);
            }
        }

        else
        {
            return base.GetChildControlType(tagName, attribs);
        }
    }
}
```

Notice that the base.GetChildControlType is called in the GetChildControlType method for every tag save the MyCustomButton standard-button-specifying tag. Using the ControlBuilder class's implementation of GetChildControlType ensures that other tag names are resolved correctly.

The WXBetterForm.cs source file also contains the WButtonChooser class, which is derived from Control. This custom control is associated with the WXButtonChooserControlBuilder custom control builder using the ever handy ControlBuilderAttribute attribute. The implementation of the WButtonChooser is demonstrated opposite:

```
[ControlBuilderAttribute(typeof(WXButtonChooserControlBuilder))]
public class WButtonChooser : Control
{
}
```

It should be clear from the WButtonChooser class's Spartan implementation that the sole purpose of this class is to serve as way to let WXButtonChooserControlBuilder standardize the button style used for a page.

The WXDemoCustomChildControls.aspx source file demonstrates the WButtonChooser class being instantiated and the subsequent custom control building being handled by overriding the GetChildControlType method in the WXButtonChooserControlBuilder class. The contents of WXDemoCustomChildControls.aspx are as follows:

```
<%@ Register TagPrefix="CBuilderDemo" Namespace="WXControlBuilderDemo"
        Assembly="WXControlBuilderDemo"%>
<HTML>
    <body>
        <form runat="server" ID="RequiredForLinkButton">
            <CBuilderDemo:WButtonChooser runat="server" ID="WButChooser1">
                <P><MyCustomButton id="MyButton1" runat="server"
                                name="AButton1" Text="Button 1" /></P>
                <P><MyCustomButton id="MyButton2" runat="server"
                                name="AButton2" Text="Button 2" />
                <P><MyCustomButton id="MyButton3" runat="server"
                                name="AButton3" Text="Button 3" />
            </CBuilderDemo:WButtonChooser>
        </form>
    </body>
</HTML>
```

It should be readily apparent from the previous snippet of code that the page contains three buttons as indicated by the MyCustomButton tag. This is the tag that causes the custom control builder's override of the GetChildControlType to choose between Button and LinkButton.

The output generated by the previous ASP.NET page depends on the button standard selected. If the standard style of button is the Button class then the page is displayed as follows:

If the standard style of button is the LinkButton class then the following page is displayed:

Button and LinkButton are excellent candidates for the one-to-one exchange of controls just demonstrated. The reason for this is that both of these controls are derived from a common root, the System.Web.UI.WebControls namespace's WebControl class. This means they inherit a set of common properties. Furthermore both of these controls expose exactly the same properties (CausesValidation, CommandArgument, Text, and CommandName). This means that there is no chance that the GetChildControlType method's IDictionary attribs parameter will contain properties that are valid in Button but not valid in LinkButton or vice-versa.

Using other controls, there will be cases where a developer will have to modify the contents of the IDictionary attribs collection. Elements might have to be removed if they are invalid for the type of control returned or the contents of the elements might have to be modified. For example, on-the-fly localization could be performed by modifying a button's Text attribute. Consider the case of a control localized for English but for the specific locality of "Southern California Surfer Beach". Clearly every button's text attribute would have to localized/modified with the surfer mantra, "Dude like". An example of this localization enhancement where attribs["text"] is modified is as follows:

```
public override Type
    GetChildControlType(string tagName, IDictionary attribs)
{
    if (string.Compare(tagName, "MyCustomButton", true) == 0)
    {
        if (attribs.Contains("text"))
        {
            string localized = "Dude like, " + attribs["text"];
            attribs.Remove("text");
            attribs.Add("text", localized);
        }
        // *** remainder of method identical to previous implementation ***
```

This localization strategy is displayed to the end-user as follows:

Dude like, Button 1

It would be possible for an individual control to localize itself on-the-fly. By using a custom control builder, it would be possible for multiple controls to be localized using the same control builder.

OnAppendToParentBuilder

The OnAppendToParentBuilder method is called when a ControlBuilder is added to the collection of subordinates maintained by its parent control builder. This method is defined as follows:

```
Overridable Public Sub OnAppendToParentBuilder( _
    ByVal parentBuilder As ControlBuilder) ' VB.NET

public virtual void OnAppendToParentBuilder(
    ControlBuilder parentBuilder); // C#
```

The OnAppendToParentBuilder method serves to unify the hierarchy of control builders. For a given control builder, the AppendSubBuilder method previously discussed provides a control with the control builder instance of each subordinate. Going up the control builder instance hierarchy, the OnAppendToParentBuilder method provides a control with the control builder instance of its superior (parent) control builder. This allows a control builder to query the properties of its parent control builder because these properties could affect how the control being parsed is ultimately displayed.

CreateBuilderFromType

The one method not reviewed yet in this chapter is CreateBuilderFromType. Unlike the previous methods discussed the CreateBuidlerFromType method cannot be overridden. This makes sense since the CreateBuidlerFromType method is static (Shared in VB.NET terms) and cannot be declared as virtual (Overridable in VB.NET terms). The prototype for this method is as follows:

```
Public Shared Function CreateBuilderFromType( _
    ByVal parser As TemplateParser, _
    ByVal parentBuilder As ControlBuilder, _
    ByVal type As Type, _
    ByVal tagName As String, _
    ByVal id As String, _
    ByVal attribs As IDictionary, _
    ByVal line As Integer, _
    ByVal sourceFileName As String _
) As ControlBuilder ' VB.NET

public static ControlBuilder CreateBuilderFromType(
    TemplateParser parser,
    ControlBuilder parentBuilder,
    Type type,
    string tagName,
    string id,
    IDictionary attribs,
    int line,
    string sourceFileName); // C#
```

Without decomposing every parameter to the CreateBuilderFromType method, suffice it to say that this method is to create the appropriate control builder for a specific tag (the string tagName parameter) residing on a page. This method is how the page parser initially creates the ControlBuilder that helps to parse the page.

Summary

The chapter reviewed the mechanism provided by .NET in order to fine-tune the processing of a custom control. This mechanism is the ControlBuilder class and this class's relationship to the page parser was broken down in great detail. As part of this break down, each method and property of the ControlBuilder class was discussed. The properties serve to provide additional information about the control being parsed while the methods serve as a means with which to fine-tune the parser process. This fine tuning is achieved by overriding methods.

Certain methods altered how the parser worked by simply returning a Boolean value. The `HasBody` method provided the parser with a way to determine if the parent control was bounded by a start and end tag (the `HasBody` returns `true` case). The `AllowWhitespaceLiterals` method for example configured how white spaces such as carriage returns were handled by the parser. In a similar manner the `HtmlDecodeLiterals` method configured how the parser handled HTML characters that had been previously encoded.

The `NeedsTagInnerText` method changed the parser behavior but only in so much as it represented a request for information from the `ControlBuilder` to the page parser. This information, the text between a control's start and end tag, was provided by the page parser when it called the `ControlBuilder`'s `SetTagInnerText` method. The inner text specified by the `SetTagInnerText` method could not be altered.

A more detailed breakdown of the inner text was provided by the page parser when it called `GetChildControlType`, `AppendSubBuilder`, and `AppendLiteralString`. The `GetChildControlType` method allowed the type of control associated with a subordinate tag to be changed on-the-fly. This method also allowed the attributes associated with a subordinate tag to be read and potentially modified. The `GetChildControlType` method proved to be a most versatile mechanism for fine tuning how a control is laid out on a page as did the `AppendLiteralString` method. This later method, `AppendLiteralString`, allowed the literal HTML contained between a control's start and end tags to be modified. The `AppendSubBuilder` method informed the control builder as to the control builder used by the subordinate class. Without rehashing previous observations, the usefulness in overriding the `AppendSubBuilder` method is limited, which will hopefully be remedied in a future release of the .NET Framework.

Setting up of the control builder and cleaning up the control builder were handled by the `Init` and `CloseControl` methods respectively. The `Init` method allowed the attributes associated with the parent control to be read and potentially modified. Also falling into the setup/cleanup genre is the `OnAppendToParentBuilder` method, which is called when a control builder instance is provided to its parent in the control builder hierarchy so that the parent can maintain a copy of its subordinate control builder in its collection of subordinate control builders.

Examples were provided demonstrating how each overridable method could be overridden in order to more precisely build a custom control. Also demonstrated were a suite of .NET classes that were derived from `ControlBuilder`. These custom control builders included `HyperLinkControlBuilder`, `LabelControlBuilder`, `LinkButtonControlBuilder`, `TextBoxControlBuilder`, and `ListItemControlBuilder`. The value-added of these custom control builders was that they overrode various methods of the `ControlBuilder` base class. By examining these overrides, the practicality of such method overloading was demonstrated in a practical context.

Clearly the relationship between the page parser and `ControlBuilder` is one of mega-minutia. For developers so inclined, the building of a custom control can be broken down, dissected and configured at the sub-atomic level. OK to be more realistic, configured at the molecular level.

Professional ASP .NET Server Controls

8

Building Controls Using Visual Studio .NET

Developing with a new language can be a daunting process. Not only do you have to get used to the syntax of the language itself, you may also have to get used to a brand new user interface to enable you to produce the code.

However, in many respects all commercial and academic languages share some common and simple requirements with each other; all languages need the ability to:

❑   Edit human-readable code

❑   Debug their applications or components

❑   Compile human-readable code into machine code

Therefore it seems, in retrospect, like a sensible approach to actually produce a single and common interface for all languages. Microsoft's solution to this problem of different interfaces for every compiler is to separate the compiler from the Integrated Development Environment (IDE) and develop the IDE as non-language-specific. Another term for this IDE is Visual Studio .NET (VS .NET). This is not a new phenomenon, in fact many other manufacturers such as Borland and Forte offer IDEs, however during this chapter you will see that the new VS .NET interface certainly raises the standard to a new level.

To those who are used to the previous version of the Visual Studio IDE, it will seem an obvious choice to use the new VS .NET IDE, after all it offers all the benefits of the previous version but with significant advancements in operability, syntax, and integration with other languages. For those who have not tried Visual Studio before, the reason to use VS .NET is not so clear.

During this chapter I hope to show you why the VS .NET IDE should not be seen solely as a Microsoft product for Microsoft languages, but as the preferred method of creating code for Server Controls. It should be seen as a critical step in producing code for many supported operating systems and many languages. In addition to an intuitive interface VS .NET can also offer you the following advantages:

❑ Faster development timescales

❑ Intuitive coding style

❑ Ability to create reusable components (Server Controls, User Controls etc.)

❑ Less manually produced code

❑ Multi-language development (over 20 commercial and academic languages proposed)

❑ Multi-language debugging

As developers we often concentrate our skills and experience around a single language such as VB, C++, or Java. This is because it is a huge leap of faith for a VB developer to code in Java without any previous knowledge of the language. There are three considerations when contemplating such a move.

❑ Learning the Interface (IDE)

❑ Benefits and features obtained after the move

❑ Learning the language syntax

VS .NET gives the developer benefits in allowing us to code in our language or languages of choice but using the same interface (IDE) at all times. This common interface allows the developer to concentrate on the syntax of the code rather than learning the peculiarities of a new IDE. An example of this is the ability to create a Server Control in C# and use that same control in C++, VB .NET, or even Perl and JScript. You even have the ability to mix and match components from different languages to create enhanced composite controls.

This chapter will use a series of examples to show you some of the more important features of using VS .NET, the things that make VS .NET and the .NET Framework unique within the development industry and potentially essential as your coding IDE of choice.

What is the VS .NET IDE?

An IDE is a tool that assists a developer in writing code, creating resources, debugging modules, and managing complex projects with multiple dependencies. IDEs are a relatively new incarnation and the term IDE (although probably unheard of 10 years ago) is pretty much taken for granted by today's developers who expect/demand the type of features offered by VS .NET. Although some developers will only use the bare bones features of an IDE, others will push it to the max and utilize all of the very advanced features the software will allow. Such is the nature of the diverse audience and the demands of satisfying both hobbyist developers, enterprise application developers, commercial software driver authors, and everyone in-between.

> **An IDE can be defined as "A user interface that allows a developer to produce code in human-readable form with the ability to offer additional features that aid in the quick development of robust development projects."**

A language has two high-level areas of functionality:

- ❑ The IDE, which allows a developer to create the human readable code
- ❑ The Compiler, which creates the machine-readable code

This separation of compiler and IDE has been best practice for compiler development for some time now and is certainly not ground breaking technology. However .NET has performed two further tasks that make this new .NET technology so astonishing:

- ❑ The .NET IDE (VS .NET) is not language specific
- ❑ The .NET compiler is capable of producing code to run on any operating system (as long as there is a supported Just-In-Time (JIT) compiler; more about JIT later in this chapter)

These two strategic changes of direction for compilers allow the .NET Framework to take on new emphasis as becoming the code editor and compiler of choice. Because the compiler is separate, you can even use a simple editor such as Notepad (as previously done within this book) to create your C#, VB, or C++ code. Then once you're ready for creating your machine-readable code, simply run them through the .NET compilation process.

I hope you spotted the obvious mistake in the previous sentence, those who have spent all day trying to create code in simple Text Editors or IDE's such as Notepad or FrontPage will understand the complexities of coding blind, with little or no help in providing syntax or basic format checking. In reality, coding in Notepad is not seen as part of the RAD development way; it promotes errors and gives no helpful feedback to the developer.

What's the alternative to developing in a simple text editor? This is where VS .NET comes into its own. VS .NET offers an intuitive, friendly front end to manage your code. It's structured in such a way that it contains the ability to allow third-party companies to integrate their own language compilers within the VS .NET IDE.

Features of the VS .NET IDE

While using Visual Studio. NET you should consider that it is only a front end to edit the human-readable code. You could in fact also use Notepad to perform the same task but without any of the special features that VS. NET offers.

These special features greatly expand the ability of developers to produce fast and tight code. VS .NET is meant to increase productivity by alleviating and aiding certain basic tasks such as debugging, syntax checking, and project management to name a few.

These features within VS .NET are broken into two main areas

- ❑ Non-language-centric (feature that is not dependent on code being available)
- ❑ Language-centric (feature that is performed around or to code and changes with each language)

Non-language-centric covers features that are often not related to the specifications or requirements of the language being used. A list of non-language centric features is shown below:

Feature Name	Description
Solution Explorer	List files available within this project and solution. Also enhanced for working with several projects (even languages) simultaneously, which includes access to project management code storage software such as Source Safe.
Toolbox	Contains built-in Server Controls, third-party custom controls, and controls you have built yourself. These can be written in any language and be used within any language.
Dynamic Help & Search	Search for any help and advice within documents or help files. Suggest a change to some code that should solve a problem within the code syntax or while building the project.
Server Explorer	Allows access to databases and storage devices such as SQL Server and Oracle.
Task List	Keep notes within your code; this task list highlights all your notes in one central area. You can also use it to quickly move to a specific task/note situated somewhere within your code. It also stores information on things TODO and keeps track of errors that occur during building your project.
Document Window	Edit the code document files you have within your Solution Explorer. Also create forms and windows controls. Used to edit any document within your project or solution.

Language-centric features are dependent on the individual requirements of the language. However all languages that adhere to Common Language Specification (CLS) will be able to use the features listed below. All these features occur within the Document Window. Language-centric features include:

Feature Name	Description
IntelliSense	Gives the developer dynamic help information related to the active object/class being typed within the VS .NET editor to assist in producing valid code.
Syntax Checking	Checks the syntax of what you are typing as you type it and displays errors in construction or formatting in real time as they occur.
Debugging	Step through code, put in break points, trace etc.
Watching	Watch a value change in real time while debugging your code
Error Trapping	Trap errors and react to them or retrieve information about what error has occurred.
Dynamic Help	Help appears dependent on what you're looking at or during coding depending on what command you're using.
Resource Checking	View code and environment resources during the debugging stage.

Shared Development Environment

VS .NET allows the developer to use its interface for all languages that have a compiler that adheres fully to the Common Language Specification (CLS). This specification lays down some rules that control the general functionality of the compiler allowing it to be embedded within the .NET Framework. In some cases some functionality will be omitted from certain languages, depending on how/if they support particular features.

The current list of compilers that adhere to the CLS is as follows:

- C#
- C++
- VB .NET (includes VBScript)
- J#
- JScript
- Fortran
- Perl
- Cobol
- Smalltalk
- RPG
- Eiffel

There are also an additional ten more commercial and academic languages being proposed and showing support for the .NET infrastructure. To have so many languages supporting or proposing support for the VS .NET IDE and .NET Framework certainly indicates that it has something special to offer.

Look and Feel

One concern with adopting a new IDE such as Visual Studio .NET is that many will be coming across from familiar interfaces such as VB6 and C++ to what may be unfamiliar territory. This however has been alleviated a little by allowing the developer to choose their own look-and-feel or skin for VS .NET; therefore if you're a VB6 developer you can select a template (the first time you run VS .NET, or by using My Profile from the start menu), which makes VS .NET similar to (not exactly the same as) the interface that you're used to.

These skins will allow a developer to feel more comfortable with the movement between development platforms. Below is a list of the currently supported skins:

- Visual Studio Developer
- Visual Basic Developer
- Visual C++ Developer
- Visual InterDev Developer
- VS Macro Developer
- Student Developer
- C# Developer

Customizing the VS .NET IDE Using Template Policy

When you create a project for the first time you will always (unless you choose blank solution) be supplied with a project that has predefined files already created and is used as the template for further development.

Below is the list of template projects that are available when developing in VB .NET:

- ❑ Windows Application
- ❑ Class Library
- ❑ Windows Control Library
- ❑ ASP.NET Web Application
- ❑ ASP.NET Web Service
- ❑ Web Control Library
- ❑ Console Application
- ❑ Windows Service

On selecting one of these template projects the IDE changes its toolbars, menus, task lists help, and even solution explorer according to the relevance to the language and the project template you selected.

You can however set up your own templates using **Enterprise Template Policy**. Template policy allows software architects and teams to give a common look-and-feel to each of their projects when they are first created in the form of default files, menus, toolbars, and so on. Therefore, if your team have any error classes or common components they use on every project, then these can be set up within a specialist template and everyone within the team can use that template.

As with the inbuilt templates already assigned (shown above), your development team can actually have a very complex series of options that are structured/tailored specifically to your own unique and corporate requirements. This type of customization introduces an essential controlling factor when it comes to large team development and control. If, for instance, you don't want developers to be able to create icons, then that ability can be excluded. You can even include or exclude menu options from the main VS .NET IDE infrastructure.

Policy Templates also control how and what is displayed within areas such as the toolbar, therefore if the team does not use the datagrid control, then it can be excluded from the toolbar completely.

It's also important to note that these policies are language-dependent; therefore you can have a different policy for C# from the one you have for VB, C++, or even COBOL development.

Another advantage of using Policy Templates is that currently the .NET technology is still a relatively new product and certainly over the next few years many companies will see how they can take their teams of developers and move them quickly from their existing platform to VS .NET and the .NET framework. As and when new features become available they can be introduced by enforcing new Policy Templates.

As well as Policy Templates controlling the look and feel of new projects, the rules mechanism is actually contained within a specialist XML file, which can be copied onto any existing computers at any time, therefore making sure that rules can be enforced.

Let's now go through an example of how to control the policy of VS .NET and therefore control what's included within the interface. Search your installation directory and sub-directories for files with a TDL extension, and you will find the following two:

❑   DAP.TDL – Default template policy

❑   VSIDE.TDL – Contains all the possible policy items available

Both files by default should reside in the following directory:

```
C:\Program Files\Microsoft Visual Studio .NET\EnterpriseFrameworks\Policy
```

For this example what we are going to do is create a new policy document and disable one of the menu options by copying the default document DAP.TDL and renaming it to MYPOLICY.TDL. Now load it using notepad. You will see that it's simply an XML formatted file; this file, however, controls the menu and interface definitions for VS .NET. Let's see it in action; search within this file for the following element:

```
<ID>projVBProject</ID>
```

Once you have found it then type immediately below it the following lines:

```
<ID>projCSharpProject</ID>
<CONSTRAINTS>
      <MENUCONSTRAINTS>
          <MENUCONSTRAINT>
              <ID>menuProject.NewFolder</ID>
              <ENABLED>0</ENABLED>
          </MENUCONSTRAINT>
      </MENUCONSTRAINTS>
</CONSTRAINTS>
```

What we've effectively done by using the <MENUCONSTRAINTS> element at the right position within the policy template is stopped a developer from creating a new folder from within a C# project only. The reason it's only limited within a C# Project is that we have placed it within the policy template within the section starting with the ID projCSharpProject, which is the critical keyword for C# projects.

You'll also notice the ID for the menu is referring to menuProject.NewFolder; this is not just a keyword that means that particular menu, rather it refers to the following element section later within this same policy template, search for it now and you will see this text:

```
<MENU>
   <ID>menuProject.NewFolder</ID>
   <CMDID>245</CMDID>
   <GUID>{5EFC7975-14BC-11CF-9B2B-00AA00573819}</GUID>
</MENU>
```

The GUID is interesting – it's actually the GUID held in the registry that indicates exactly what component we are referring to when we say we want to disable it.

OK, now we've changed the policy template, let's see it working. Load VS .NET and create a simple C# project (any type), then right-click your mouse on the project name and select Add; you will see the following menu:

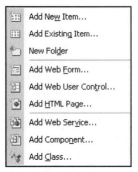

By default VS .NET used the DAP.TDL template, which still allows the New Folder menu item to be enabled. Now click on the project name again and select View then Properties Window.

You can now use the Policy attribute of this properties window to select the newly copied policy template you have created.

When you enter a new policy document you will be asked to reload the solution, which must be done to allow you to see the changes it has made to your interface.

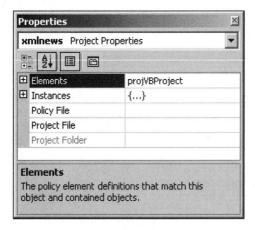

Now to see what this has accomplished simply click on the project name again and right-click your mouse button to see that the menu option for New Folder has now in fact be disabled and cannot be used.

On reflection, it's obvious that repercussions of using the template policy control are not going to be welcomed by all developers, but in a large team project it does allow a considerable reduction in misuse and non-essential use of certain functions.

Multi-Language Debugging

Now that's terminology that, as a developer, I never thought I'd hear! Up until now, integrating multi-language systems has often become a nightmare; if something can go wrong, then it often does. Being previously involved in a team of 50 developing a Visual Basic client with COBOL database access a few years ago it seemed almost an endless task.

With VS .NET you can attach multiple projects into the same solution (solution is another name for a file with an SLN suffix that holds together projects and project files). These projects need not use the same language. But more fascinating is the fact that once you've set up a breakpoint (point where during debugging the code can momentarily pause), you can actually step between any .NET-compliant languages such as C# and VB .NET or even FORTRAN to allow step-by-step debugging on your code to continue.

This versatility will certainly give teams who solely use .NET technology the edge when it comes down to releasing code in a timely and as much of a bug free condition as possible. We'll look at how debugging is used within VS .NET later in this chapter.

Project Management

As you will see further on in this chapter, some of the actual abilities of VS .NET are tailored towards allowing large development teams to manage code production:

- ❏ Template Policy can constrict the VS .NET IDE ability to only what you want developers to use, say if a standard component is not being used, or the team is not allowed to use it, then you can omit it from the toolbox, help, menus, and so on.

- ❏ Revision Control technology is built into VS .NET and allows teams of developers to share projects, files, or solutions easily.

- ❏ Server Components can be developed and used throughout the team, therefore reducing the amount of repetitive work that most teams do. This also reduces the amount of code having to be produced and subsequently the amount of debugging time.

- ❏ Multiple projects can be debugged at the same time.

- ❏ The Task List can be used to keep developer notes or even TODO notes, therefore allowing developing tasks to be moved between colleagues.

Non-Language-Centric Features

> Please remember while reading this section that these features are available to ALL languages, even though we will be coding around the C# and VB .NET languages. Therefore languages such as C++ and JavaScript all have IntelliSense, Syntax Checking, Debugging, and so on.

During the remainder of this chapter, we will cover some of the non-language-centric features that are included within ASP.NET. The aim is to look at how each feature individually can benefit your coding practice and speed.

Below we have shown each of the non-language-centric features as they appear within the VS .NET IDE:

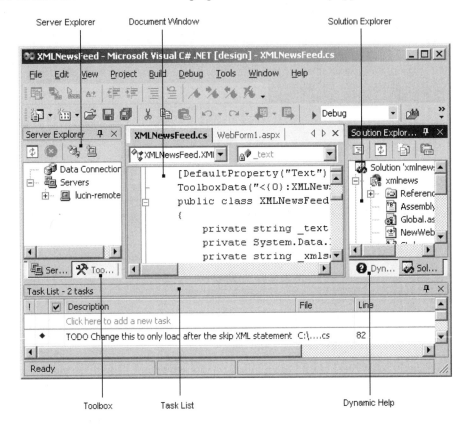

Solution Explorer

The solution explorer in its basic form is simply a visual filing system; it allows files to be grouped into folders and also uses specialist icons to signify the file type actually displayed.

Below is an example of the Solution Explorer window:

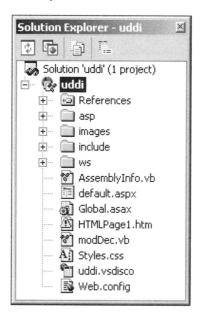

The current project language knows the file type of each file within this window and by right-clicking your mouse on any one a shortcut menu of supported options is displayed for the developer to select from. These menu options range from the simple Copy and Paste options to Build (building project) and View Code.

This hierarchical display also allows for multiple projects to be loaded at the same time to enable easier debugging and also better project management.

By default some of the files and directories within your project will be hidden; to display all files (including code-behind files) click on the following icon:

On closer inspection of the files you will now be able to see hidden files and links to associated code-behind files:

There are two types of containers displayed within the Solution Explorer:

- ❏ Solution – Can contain multiple projects, allowing the development/debugging of separate applications, which may or may not even be in separate languages (.SLN suffix)

- ❏ Project – A suite of files and resources that together form a distinct application or library

A solution file (.SLN) is created even though you may in fact have only one project within it. Another interesting fact about solution files is that they also do not need to have a project; you can create a solution and simply edit any type of miscellaneous file, for example XML files, bitmaps, and icons.

On creation of a solution file, two files are actually produced:

❏   .SLN suffix – Contains the list of projects attached to this solution file. Build configurations that you assigned to a solution.

❏   .SUO suffix – Customization that's been performed on the IDE. (Such as toolbars.)

The solution explorer also controls and checks for project management events such as file changing outside of the project, and read-only and hidden files. If an event occurs the Solution Explorer can either automatically reload newer files or notifies the developer who can make a decision to replace or refresh individual files.

The illustration opposite shows two projects, BuildControls and XMLNewsFeed; we'll be using these projects later on in this chapter. However, in addition to these projects there is also a special folder called Solution Items. This folder is created when you add an item when right-clicking your mouse on the Solution name within the Explorer window.

Solution items are for items that are not directly related to a project but are related to the group of projects; this could be for example a list of developers working on the Solution or even an Excel spreadsheet that allows developers to record the time worked on a solution. Also style sheets, which are relevant to every project, are another good use of Solution Items.

Project management is further enhanced by the Solution Explorer's ability to check in and check out files from an independent central storage revision control system, such as Microsoft's Source Safe. It uses this technique to share either single files or even entire projects between team members.

Similar to Solution Items, you can also have files that are listed within your solution but are not part of the solution; these are called Miscellaneous Files.

To create a miscellaneous file within your solution or project select File, Open, then File from the main menu, then browse and select the file you want added into the Miscellaneous section.

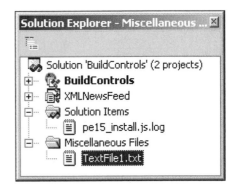

Document Window

The document window is the portion of VS .NET that allows the developer to edit (or view) any type of file for which it has an inbuilt editor (or viewer). Below I have listed the inbuilt editors currently available within VS .NET:

- ❑ Source Code (Text) Editor
- ❑ Source Code (Text) Editor with Encoding
- ❑ HTML/XML Editor
- ❑ HTML/XML Editor with Encoding
- ❑ XML Schema Editor
- ❑ IEXPLORE.EXE
- ❑ Binary Editor
- ❑ Resource Editor
- ❑ Microsoft Visual Basic Editor
- ❑ Microsoft Visual Basic Code Page Editor

Each file type has a default editor. To find out a file's default editor simply click on that file in the Solution Explorer and right-click your mouse button then select **Open With...** from the pop-up menu. The default editor will have the word **Default** along side.

The document window is also the area where all the Language-Critical features tend to take part such as Debugging and IntelliSense. These features will be covered in the next section.

Toolbox

The toolbox is a series of helpful tabs that can be used to store templates, HTML, applications, COM controls, code snippets, files, text, and pretty much everything you see in the Solution Explorer. The tabs on the toolbox can be used to drag and drop items into your Document Window such as Server Controls or COM controls. These items are then used to extend the functionality of your development.

The basic Toolbox is shown below:

Each tab on the toolbox displays items depending on the file type and language you are currently working on. In addition, the Enterprise Policy Template (which is an XML formatted file) uses a filtering mechanism to filter out items that have been excluded deliberately from any of the tabs. An example of this would be when a team developing was not allowed to use the inbuilt datagrid but had to use the repeater control instead, the datagrid control can actually be omitted from the toolbox completely.

Also shown in the illustration opposite are two of the default tabs, General and Clipboard Ring.

The Clipboard Ring is a specialist inbuilt tab that shows you any items you have cut or copied from the Document Window that contain text, such as programming code and HTML.

In the example shown above we have actually renamed one of the clipboard entries to something more meaningful, by right-clicking our mouse button over the toolbar item and selecting 'Rename Item'. Because of the intrinsic, here today and gone tomorrow qualities of the clipboard, one good use of this ability is to simply drag and drop any clipboard entry to the General tab (shown immediately below it), this allows you to create some code snippets which can be reused whenever you want.

You can create your own custom toolbox tabs and assign your own set of items to them using the customize toolbar option. In this way you can add custom Server Controls that you've created into your own toolbox tab and reuse them in other projects. To add a Server Control simply develop your Web Control Library or Windows Control Library project using VS .NET or Notepad and use the customize toolbar option (right-click your mouse on any part of the toolbar you want to add it to) to add the DLL you've created and see it appear in your toolbar.

One other interesting technique is to create your own composite controls. For example you can drag and drop multiple components onto an ASPX page, two from the Web Forms tab and one from the HTML tab, then simply highlight them all and drag them onto your General tab. The illustration below shows the General tab, which contains the Login Details composite control; all the controls in the WebForm2.aspx document have actually been dragged onto that document from the General tab.

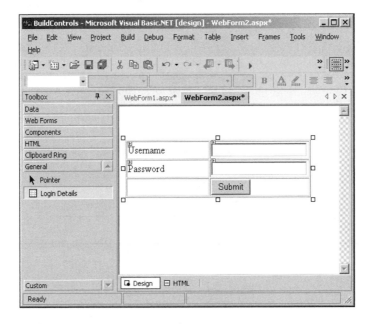

Dynamic Help and Search

In its simplest form, Dynamic Help uses a combination of language and keywords to make sure that the help information that is displayed is always pertinent to the area you are working with. However, in addition, it has some remarkable abilities allowing you to customize the help information and add your own help pages directly into the standard help for whatever language you are working with this has some great advantages for:

IT Training – Ability to add context sensitive information to give a developer extra additional information about a specific command or syntax.

Server and Add-In Vendors – After creating your Server Control you can now create some associated help, which is only displayed when your control is being used.

IT Team Project Management – While working in a specific project or on a specific file you can embed information pertaining to project support or team standards.

Opposite is an example of the dynamic help page:

Let's now see this dynamic help work in context by creating our own dynamic help within VS .NET. To do this first of all we need to create an XML file and put it in the following directory:

```
<$VS .NET INSTALLATION DIR$>\Common7\IDE\HTML\XMLLinks\1033
```

Here's the XML file we need to create:

```
<?xml version="1.0" encoding="utf-8" ?>
<!-- This is an example of an XML file that adds links to the Dynamic Help window
in Visual Studio .NET. -->
<!-- The following is a link to the Dynamic Help schema. -->
<DynamicHelp xmlns="http://msdn.microsoft.com/vsdata/xsd/vsdh.xsd"
xmlns:xsi="http://www.w3.org/2000/10/XMLSchema-instance"
xsi:schemaLocation="http://msdn.microsoft.com/vsdata/xsd/vsdh.xsd">
  <Context>
    <Keywords>
      <!-- Each KItem contains a keyword you want to use for this topic. This must
be a keyword that already exists in Visual Studio. For instance, the following
keyword is used to target Solution Explorer. -->
      <KItem Name="VS.SolutionExplorer"/>
```

```
    </Keywords>
    <Links>
        <!-- Each LItem contains a link to display when the keyword is in the active
context. Use the "LinkGroup" attribute to specify the link group in which to
display your topic link. You can reference any of the five default link groups
specified in context.xml as well as any new link groups that you define.-->
        <LItem URL="http://www.wrox.com" LinkGroup="Help">WROX</LItem>
        <LItem URL="http://www.salcentral.com" LinkGroup="Help">SALCENTRAL - Web
Services Brokerage</LItem>
    </Links>
  </Context>
</DynamicHelp>
```

To display the above help simply reload the VS .NET application and then click on the solution explorer. If the dynamic window is not available press *CTRL+F1*; you should now see in addition to the standard Help links you now have two additional links, one to Wrox and the other to SalCentral. Even though during this example we chose to point towards an internet location you can in fact also point towards a local internet page.

This file contains XML that defines the items we need to display and also the Keywords that they are relevant to. Every item within VS .NET emits a keyword when you click on it, which signals to the VS .NET framework what the name of the item is, for example the solution explorer emits the keyword VS.SolutionExplorer, other items are TextBox, Label, Toolbar or even command keywords within the Document Window. This is how context-sensitive help is displayed to a developer.

> **To see your changes reflected you will need to exit Visual Studio and then start it up again.**

Task List

Like the dynamic help, the task list has some neat functionality as well. The foremost of this is a simple technique that works surprisingly well. It goes like this...
Anywhere in your code place a comment tag, // for C++ and C#, or ' for VB followed by the word TODO which is commonly referred to as a token tag. Now type in any text, for an example:

```
Private Sub Page_Load(ByVal sender As System.Object, _
        ByVal e As System.EventArgs) Handles MyBase.Load
    'TODO Pass this value in instead of hard coding it here
    XMLNewsFeed1.XMLSource = "http://www.salcentral.com/rss/newws.xml"
    DataGrid1.DataSource = XMLNewsFeed1.XMLDataView()
    DataGrid1.DataBind()
End Sub
```

Now let's view the Task List, which should look similar to the following:

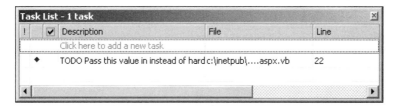

If your task list does not show the above entry then right-click your mouse on the center of the task list window and then select **Show Tasks** and **All** to make sure it's displayed correctly. As you can see when the task list is dynamically updated, it actually looks for the TODO token tag and if it finds it, it makes sure that it's listed in the Task List. To prove the point about how token tags work and naming conventions, go to your code and change TODO to TOD; the task list item is removed immediately. Now spell it correctly and it comes back again.

If a task list entry has a line number, then by double-clicking your mouse button on it you will immediately load the relevant code and be positioned on the correct line.

There are three inbuilt token tags, HACK, TODO, and UNDONE, but you can add more by using the Options main menu in VS .NET. Select **Tools, Options, Environment** then **Task List** to display the screen below:

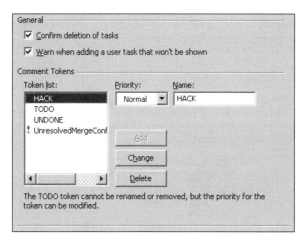

Tasks are grouped into one of four different types, each of which has a series of token tags, which are explained below:

❑ **Comment** – Tasks that have been entered within your code using token tags such as TODO, HACK and UNDONE, also additional custom token tags you enter using the above form.

❑ **Build Errors** – When you build your project, if any errors occur, for example syntax and formatting problems, then a Build Error task entry will be placed in the task list. These entries can be removed from the task list by simply fixing the error and rebuilding the solution.

❑ **User** – These are entries that have been placed in the task list by simply clicking on the Click here to add a new task option.

❑ **Shortcut** – You can highlight any single line of code within the task list by simply moving to the relevant code line, right-clicking your mouse, and selecting Add Task List Shortcut from the pop-up menu. This option allows you to quickly mark a line of code and go back to it later.

Below is a screenshot of the task list after I have entered a Task List Shortcut on one of the lines from the previous code sample:

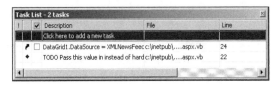

It's also worth noting that code lines that have been marked with a short cut have a blue ribbon pointer alongside them:

```
Private Sub Page_Load(ByVal sender As S
    'TODO Pass this value in instead of
    XMLNewsFeed1.XMLSource = "http://ww
    DataGrid1.DataSource = XMLNewsFeed1
    DataGrid1.DataBind()
End Sub

End Class
```

Server Explorer

The server explorer allows you to set up data connections to remote (or local) servers. You can also administer these servers performing such tasks as viewing event logs and performance counters. Below is a screenshot of a typical server explorer window. This particular screenshot also shows you a connection to a SQL Server database:

The Server Explorer acts like a mini enterprise manager, by allowing you to create tables, stored procedures, views, triggers, etc. You can also expand the properties on any table and view/amend data within your Document Window.

There are two types of database contact within the Server Explorer window:

❑ You can create a connection to a database and then use that connection within your application. Note that you only need to create a connection if you prefer to use DSN connections; if you use DSN-less connections you do not need to create a connection here. Using connection you can create ODBC connections to any support database such as Oracle, FoxPro, Access etc.

❑ You can browse down to a SQL server database and administer it from within your VS .NET application. Currently SQL Server is the only supported database administrator.

Language-Centric Features

> Again, please remember while reading this section that these features are available to ALL languages, even though we will be coding around the C# and VB .NET languages. Therefore languages such as Perl, COBOL, and JavaScript all have IntelliSense, Syntax Checking, Debugging, etc.

Language-Centric features act upon the code within the Document Window area of Visual Studio .NET. Because of the code-intensive aspects of these features, we'll explain it better by producing what we've all come to know and love, yes, the infamous `HelloWorld` project. However, this time we'll do it in relation to an ASP.NET project.

Simply create a new project, using the C# ASP.NET Web Application template and press the following button on the Solution Explorer window:

Now click on the cross icon on the left of the WebForm1.aspx file, whereby the WebForm1.aspx.cs file (associated code-behind) will appear as follows (this was covered as one of the non-language-centric features):

Now double-click on the `WebForm1.aspx.cs` file to load it.

IntelliSense

Rather than work with some example code right out of the box, let's add the following line within the `Page_Load` method:

```
Int16 iLoop;
```

Press the *CTRL* key and the *SPACEBAR* at the same time; you should be able to see a list of relevant information pop up to help you complete the line, as in this screenshot:

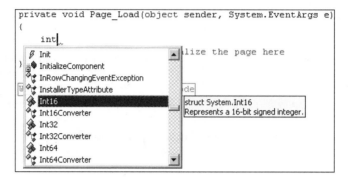

This is **IntelliSense**, the ability help you complete your code snippet. This feature is available to all languages that are fully CLS-compliant.

Error Trapping

Yes, error trapping is actually part of the .NET framework as well and therefore you can embed error trapping directly into your application no matter what language you are using. Error trapping works using exceptions; there are different exceptions for different types of errors. In the following code snippet we'll describe the basic method of using exceptions:

```
Dim iLoop As Integer
Dim sVal As String = "Hello"
Dim sTmp As String
Try
    For iLoop = 0 To Len(sVal)
        sTmp = sTmp + "<h" + iLoop.ToString + ">" + _
                   Mid(sVal, iLoop, 1) + _
                   "</h" + iLoop.ToString + ">"
    Next iLoop
    Response.Write(sTmp)
Catch ex As Exception
    Response.Write(ex.Message)
End Try
```

There are two additions in the above code to the example we've been using so far. First of all change the 1 in the ForLoop to a 0 (error will occur when using Mid) and then insert a TryCatch statement block.

The idea about TryCatch is that if any errors occur within the section of code that's encapsulated then the error is passed to the Catch part of the block for processing. When you run the above project the Mid command fails (cannot use 0 as its starting point) and then the Catch section writes the error to the web page.

Syntax Checking

Now let's type in the next line immediately below the first:

```
string sVal
```

This is not complete, but if you move your cursor off this line it should look something like the following:

```
string sVal
```

Notice the squiggle after the sVal; this states that the value entered is not understood; this feature is called Syntax Checking and is similar to the method Microsoft Word uses to check spelling within a document (if auto spell checking is turned on). Now let's complete the entire method and move on to the basics of debugging:

```
string sVal = "";
string sTmp = "";
for (int i = 1; i <= sVal.Length; i++)
{
   sTmp = sTmp + "<h" + i.ToString() + ">"
      + sVal.Substring(i-1, 1) + "</h"
      + i.ToString() + ">";
}
Response.Write(sTmp);
```

Debugging

Now press *F5* (or select **Debug** and **Start** from the menu), and the project will run. But unfortunately if you've followed my code it's already got an error in it, and the web page simply displays as blank.

So let's now debug this code; move your cursor to the 'For' part of the loop and right-click your mouse button and select **Insert Breakpoint** (pressing *F9* also works). Now run your code again by pressing *F5*.

This time the project will stop within your code as follows:

```
string sVal = "";
string sTmp = "";
for (int i = 1; i <= sVal.Length; i++)
{
    sTmp = sTmp + "<h" + i.ToString() + ">"
       + sVal.Substring(i-1, 1) + "</h"
       + i.ToString() + ">";
}
Response.Write(sTmp);
```

This is called Breakpoint debugging. To see why the problem occurred and nothing appeared on our Web Page, simply hover your mouse over the sVal variable. As you can see, it's blank, and therefore the 'for loop' simply didn't run. To prove the point pressing the *F11* key will now simply step through your code skipping over the 'for loop'.

Debugging is also capable of stepping into and out of methods and other projects, which may even be written in a different language. This is the method used to debug multiple projects with multiple languages (see the next section for multiple project debugging).

Watching

Before seeing how watching works, change the following line of code in your example:

```
string sVal = "Hello";
```

Click on any of the sTmp variable names and right-click your mouse button, then select Add Watch from the pop-up menu. You'll now see the following window appear:

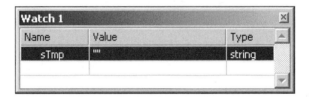

Run your project again (*F5*) and when the breakpoint has been reached, simply use the *F11* key to step through your code. As you progress, the watch window constantly gets updated with the latest value of the sTmp variable. The screenshot below shows the first repetition of the 'for loop'.

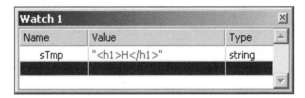

Dynamic Help

We discussed this earlier in the chapter, so to see it in action, simply double-click on one of the Keywords in your current example, say String. Then press *F1* and, as if by magic, help for the keyword String appears.

It's worth consideration that if you create your own Server Control you can actually allow dynamic help to be attached to your control in a similar way, for example the user of your control drags it onto their .aspx page, and after highlighting it simply presses *F1*. Your preformatted help page will then be displayed.

Resource Checking

This form of debugging is only available while running a project and after you have set a breakpoint, this then allows you to view certain resource windows, by using Debug then Windows menu selection. Resource checking is split into two types:

❑   Program Resource Checking

❑   Environment Resource Checking

Program Resource Checking is useful for developing in any language and allows developers to check the condition/position of their code while it is running; the resources that fall into these categories are as follows:

Feature Name	Description
Call Stack	This window allows you to view the position your code is in with relation to other procedures, methods, and programs while they are all executing. It's effectively like a paper trail showing you where you've been. See below for an example of the Hello method we've been using previously. To display the following window run your project to the breakpoint and then select **Debug, Windows,** and then **Call Stack:**  This above list can also be customized to display only entries that you're interested in, for example right-click the mouse button on the main window and then de-select (every column is selected by default) some of the columns. Another great feature of the call stack is the ability (not shown above) to double-click on any method and move instantly to that part of the code. Below is an example of what the call stack looks like once you've taken all our example code and moved it to a `Private Hello Sub` method; it now actually shows two methods in the call stack, **Hello** and **Page_Load**; the other calls are system calls only: 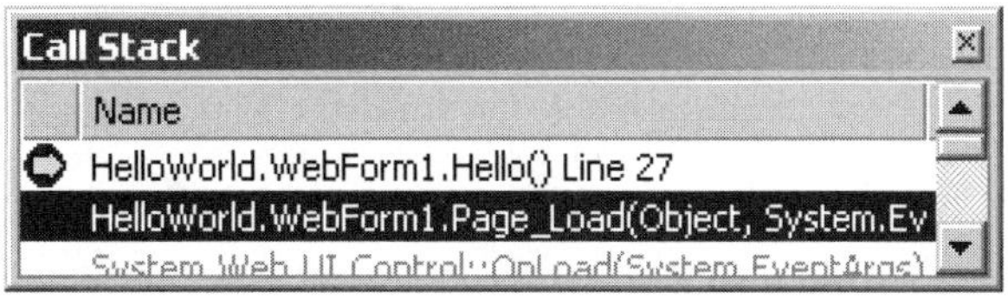

Table continued on following page

Feature Name	Description
Modules	This window shows the EXEs and DLLs loaded that are currently servicing the code that you are running:

	You can load this window by selecting Debug, Windows, then Modules.
	A benefit of this window is being able to work out what version of what DLL your actually using, moving the horizontal bar along indicates the path and version of every DLL
Dis-Assembly	The reason this window is classified as Program Resource is that it allows you to view the assembly (machine) code of every single line that your running..
	This function is a fascinating way of seeing how your code actually compiles to raw machine code rather than to MSIL:

	An interesting ability of this feature is that by seeing what the name of the Address is at the top of the window you can effectively run through different events and see exactly in what order that they are called.

Environment Resource Checking is essentially more do to with the environment that VS .NET is running under and the level of interaction it allows developers

Feature Name	Description
Memory	View sections of memory, by entering memory address pointers. This allows you to view variables in memory. Note: some languages may not give you access to these memory addresses.
Threads	With the Threads window, you can examine and control threads in the program you are debugging. A thread is a sequence of executable instructions created by a program. By default, a program has a single thread. Multithreaded programs create additional threads. One thread is active at a time. The active thread is the thread that is currently able to run. From the Threads window, you can set the active thread. In addition, you can freeze or thaw the execution of each individual thread. Freezing prevents the execution of a thread. Thawing allows it to continue. "frozen" and "thawed" are states set by the debugger.
Registers	The Registers window displays register contents. If you keep the Registers window open as you step through your program, you can see register values change as your code executes. Values that have changed recently appear in red.

Server Control IDE Features Example

News Desk Server Control

We live in a time of instant news; a famous musician can release a song on any continent and we'll all hear about it on television the same day. However, on the Internet, news is often difficult to integrate into a web site. As developers you may have to create your own web pages and constantly manually update them to reflect the latest and greatest news becoming available. Admittedly, creating your own dynamic ASP pages is always an option but shouldn't we be concentrating on the news itself rather than the technical aspects?

Manually updating your web site's news is, at best, time-consuming, and at worst, prone to errors and inconsistencies. We're going to look at the alternative to creating your own news pages and updating manually by using VS .NET to create two surprisingly simple Server Controls in an ASP.NET project to construct, extract, and display news that's held in an XML formatted file.

In addition we will be showing you some of the previously mentioned features of VS .NET in action along with the unique feature of cross-language debugging.

The XML file that we'll be reading is formatted in what is commonly know as an RSS (an acronym for Rich Site Summary) format. This is a very common type of XML-formatted file, which is a defined standard to display news feeds. You can get more information about this standard by following this pointer:

http://www.webreference.com/authoring/languages/xml/rss/1/

To change your news simply update the text in your XML file and allow the Server Control to instantly reflect your changes without having to worry about positioning or formatting your information.

By browsing on the Internet you will be able to find hundreds of other feeds and therefore should be able to quickly and easily create your own news desk. For a list of RSS feeds that can be used in the XMLNewsFeed Server Control that we're just about to create, use one of the following web sites:

- ❏ www.userland.com
- ❏ www.xmltree.com
- ❏ www.newsisfree.com
- ❏ www.syndic8.com

Cross-Language Debugging

The code used within this book is solely C#, however, within this chapter we have attempted to bring you certain features, predominantly Cross-Language Debugging, a feature that needs us to use two languages to show you how we can step from one project to another during debugging even if one is written in VB .NET (see the xmlnews project below) and the others are written in C# (see XmlNewsFeed below). Therefore, this section of the chapter will mix languages during the following example to show you debugging, and also how common features such as dynamic help can be used within both languages and the same solution.

Overview of Design

The following diagram shows the structure of the solution (three projects) we are just about to create:

The completed solution will display a web page that will format news contained in XML format in the file NewWebServices.xml.

XMLNews is the main project (VB and ASP.NET project), which will display the formatted and completed web page (WebForm1.aspx), and uses the XMLNewsFeed project to retrieve the data and XMLNewsDisplay to perform the GUI formatting of the data.

The XMLNewsFeed project contains a Server Control (XMLNewsFeed.cs) written in C#, which acts as a data retrieval system, and also contains a bitmap (XMLNewsFeed.bmp) that is used to display a neat icon on the toolbar.

The XMLNewsDisplay project is meant to act as a template for the XML file. Written in C#, it uses HTML generation to build the table on the fly at run time. In reality, the output from XMLNewsFeed can be fed into any type of control that accepts DataSets. Likewise XMLNewsDisplay could accept DataSets from any type of application or server control that can produce them, even from disparate systems such as Xenix or ICL.

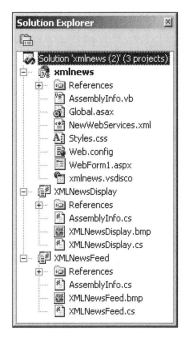

Creating the News Web Site (VB .NET)

Let's firstly create the web site that will be displaying the news (XMLNews). Start up VS .NET by running the "Microsoft Visual Studio .NET 7.0" option from your program's taskbar. Once started select File, New, Project; this will then display the following screen:

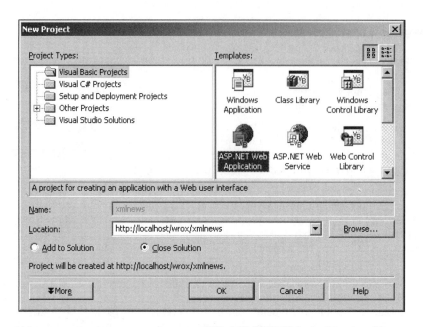

Input the project name as XMLNews and create a VB ASP.NET Web Application. Please note that we have also used a wrox sub-directory and for compatibility with our demonstration code it is certainly best to do the same. When creating a new project in other languages, the available templates will change depending on what the language actually supports.

This is probably a good time to explain a little about how VS .NET manages files on IIS. In the above example we have created the xmlnews project.

In reality what happened within the IIS application is that a Virtual Directory was created called xmlnews (see opposite). This Virtual directory would by default point towards a sub-directory of the default wwwroot directory, but you may in fact change the directory to point to another area if preferred.

Those of you who are used to ASP pages and IIS should note that there is nothing special about these virtual directories, they are simply standard IIS virtual directories with application settings on.

> **By default when ASP.NET creates a web project it now sets the authentication level to Basic; to allow this example code to work correctly you can either use the Credentials namespace or tick the anonymous tag on the xmlnews virtual directory from within IIS, using the following properties screen.**

The following screen can be displayed by right-clicking your mouse button on the xmlnews project within Microsofts Internet Information Server (IIS) and then selecting Properties:

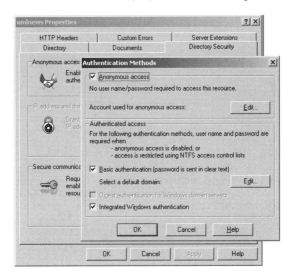

The screenshot opposite shows what your Solution Explorer menu will look like once you have created your VB project. If you cannot see the Solution Explorer then select View | Solution Explorer from the main menu.

The Solution Explorer allows you to manipulate files within the VS .NET project similarly to how you would use the Windows File system. However, right-clicking your mouse button while hovering over each file within the Solution Explorer window shows you that each file has its own series of short menus that allow you to perform different tasks:

As an example of this click on the Reference folder and right-click your mouse to see this pop-up menu

Now click on the following icon on the Solution Explorer window:

Then click on the cross hair icon on the left of the `WebForm1.aspx` file, and the `WebForm1.aspx.vb` file (associated code behind) will appear as follows (this was covered as one of the non-language-centric features):

Double-click on the `WebForm1.aspx.vb` file to load it. Then type in the following code:

```
Public Class WebForm1
    Inherits System.Web.UI.Page

[ Web Form Designer Generated Code . . . ]

    Private Sub Page_Load(ByVal sender As System.Object, _
      ByVal e As System.EventArgs) Handles MyBase.Load
        PopulateDataGrid()
    End Sub

    Private Sub PopulateDataGrid()
        'TODO Pass this value in instead of hard coding it here
        XMLNewsFeed1.XMLSource = _
                   "http://localhost/wrox/xmlnews/NewWebServices.xml"
        XMLNewsDisplay1.XMLDataSet = XMLNewsFeed1.XMLDataSet
        XMLNewsFeed1.Populate()
    End Sub

End Class
```

Now let's display the **Task List** window; we can do this by selecting **View, Other Windows,** and then **Task List** from the menu. Once the window has displayed, right-click your mouse on the window (middle) and make sure that you are viewing all Task List entries by selecting **Show Tasks** and then **All:**

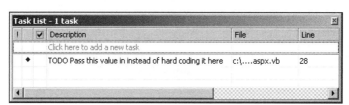

The **Task List** is displaying the above comment because is contains a Token Tag (**TODO**) at the front of a comment line within our code.

After typing the above code you'll also notice some squiggly lines appearing, this is the previously mentioned Syntax Checking feature in operation; see the screenshot below:

```
XMLNewsDisplay1.XMLDataSet = XMLNewsFeed1.XMLDataSet
```

We're now going to set up the XML data within the same project, but this XML file can also be held remotely anywhere on the Internet and as previously mentioned there are a considerable number of free sources of XML (RSS format) files that are available. To create a local file create a new item by right-clicking your mouse on the project name (XMLNews) and then select Add, **Add New Item**, then **XML File**; you need to call it NewWebServices.xml:

```xml
<?xml version="1.0" encoding="ISO-8859-1" ?>
<rss version="0.91">
  <channel>
    <title>New Web Services from SalCentral</title>
    <link>http://www.salcentral.com</link>
    <description>Your source for WSDL / SOAP Web Services from the World First
dedicated search engine</description>
    <language>en-us</language>
    <image>
      <title>SalCentral</title>
      <url>http://www.salcentral.com/public/salcsmall.gif</url>
      <link>http://www.salcentral.com</link>
      <width>129</width>
      <height>41</height>
      <description>Web Services Brokerage and Quality Assurance</description>
    </image>
    <item>
      <title>BusDataTransformation by DataConcert Inc</title>
      <link>http://www.salcentral.com/link.asp?ID=362</link>
      <description>Business Data Transformation Service. Convert business data to
or from CSV, EDI, xCBL and other XML vocabularies</description>
    </item>
    <item>
      <title>StatDogFootBallStatistics by StatDog</title>
      <link>http://www.salcentral.com/link.asp?ID=359</link>
      <description>NFL Statistics. Updated weekly Monday at 10 A.M. and Tuesday at
10 A.M</description>
    </item>
    <item>
      <title>DutchZipCodeLookup by Matthijs Hoekstra</title>
      <link>http://www.salcentral.com/link.asp?ID=357</link>
      <description>Looks up address in Netherlands from zipcode and
housenumber</description>
    </item>
    <item>
      <title>ZipToCityState by dpchiesa</title>
      <link>http://www.salcentral.com/link.asp?ID=354</link>
      <description>Retrieves valid City+State pairs for a given US Zip
Code.</description>
    </item>
    <skipHours>
      <hour>1</hour>
    </skipHours>
  </channel>
</rss>
```

The above list has been supplied by www.salcentral.com and gives a list of new Web Services available for you to consume within your .NET application. For the latest version of this file use the following link:

http://www.salcentral.com/rss/newws.xml

Looking within the XML file we typed in you can see that it simply contains an <item> repetition element for each item within the RSS formatted file; this is the same for all RSS formatted XML files.

XML News Feed Server Control (C# .NET) – XMLNewsFeed

The XML News Feed contains a Server Control that encapsulates the data being download from the XML News Source. You should now create a completely new project by selecting File, Add Project, then New Project, making sure you select C# Project then use the Web Control Library as the template but this time name it XMLNewsFeed.

Now we need to add some code to the XMLNewsFeed, by editing the code within the Server Control. You can do this by firstly renaming the WebControl.vb file to XMLNewsFeed.vb and then double clicking on the XMLNewsFeed.vb file and replacing the existing code with the following snippet:

```csharp
using System;
using System.Xml;
using System.Web.UI;
using System.Web.UI.WebControls;
using System.ComponentModel;
using System.Data;

namespace XMLNewsFeed
{
  /// <summary>
  /// Summary description for WebCustomControl1.
  /// </summary>
  [DefaultProperty("Text"),
  ToolboxData("<{0}:XMLNewsFeed runat=server></{0}:XMLNewsFeed>")]
  public class XMLNewsFeed: System.Web.UI.WebControls.WebControl
  {
    private string _text;
    private System.Data.DataSet  _xmldataset =
            new System.Data.DataSet();
    private string _xmlsource;

    [Bindable(true),
    Category("Data"),
    DefaultValue("")]
    public string XMLSource
    {
      set
      {
        try
        {
          _xmlsource = value;
        }
```

```
         catch (Exception e)
         {
           _text = "Error unable to set property [XMLSource] to that value<br>[" +
                   e.Message + "]";
         }
       }
     }

     [Bindable(true),
     Category("Data"),
     DefaultValue("")]
     public System.Data.DataSet XMLDataSet
     {
       get
       {
         return _xmldataset;
       }
     }

     [Bindable(true),
     Category("Appearance"),
     DefaultValue("")]
     public string Text
     {
       get
       {
         return _text;
       }

       set
       {
         _text = value;
       }
     }

     /// <summary>
     /// Render this control to the output parameter specified.
     /// </summary>
     /// <param name="output"> The HTML writer to write out to </param>
     protected override void Render(HtmlTextWriter output)
     {
       output.Write(Text);
     }

     public void Populate()
     {
     //TODO Change this to only load after the skip XML statement
     _xmldataset.ReadXml(oXML);
     }
   }
}
```

If you're typing the code above (rather than using our already typed demo code) you'll notice that some of the features (Language Centric) will appear, for example in the following screenshot IntelliSense kicks in as you type and shows you what the arguments for the ReadXml method are as you are typing:

```
public void Populate()
{
XmlTextReader oXML = new System.Xml.XmlTextReader(_xmlsource);
//TODO Change this to only load after the skip XML statement
_xmldataset.ReadXml(
  ▲ 1 of 8 ▼ ReadXml (string fileName, System.Data.XmlReadMode mode)
  fileName: The file name (including the path) from which to read.
```

Notice the:

```
▲ 1 of 8 ▼
```

This indicates that there are 1 to 8 different arguments or return value combinations for this method. Press the **down** arrow while in the above position to see the rest.

Stepping through the above code you'll see the following line:

```
[DefaultProperty("Text"),
  ToolboxData("<{0}:XMLNewsFeed runat=server></{0}:XMLNewsFeed>")]
  public class XMLNewsFeed: System.Web.UI.WebControls.WebControl
```

This indicates the XML tag that will be used within the HTML window when adding it to a Web Form. Next let's look a little further down the code example at the following line:

```
[Bindable(true),  Category("Appearance"), DefaultValue("")] public string Text
```

The Bindable attribute states that you want this property to appear in the properties window and the other attributes simply state where you want it to appear (Category) and what (if any) is the default value (DefaultValue).

Finally because what we've just created is a Server Control what we'll do now is place it on the toolbar along with a custom icon to improve the display. To create the icon we need to first of all create a bitmap and place a simple drawing on it, making sure that it is 16 x 16 pixels only. You can create a bitmap within VS .NET by adding a **New Item** to the XMLNewsFeed project:

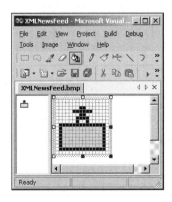

For this bitmap to be used by the Server Control as its icon for the toolbar you need to make sure that:

- ❑ The bitmap must be 16 x 16 pixels and be 256 colors

- ❑ The bitmap's name must be the same as the class name (XMLNewsFeed.bmp)

The build action property for the bitmap must be set to **Embedded Resource**. To change the properties select **View** then **Properties Window** from the **Main** Visual Studio .NET menu.

Before continuing, you now need to build the Server Control. Simply right-click your mouse button on the **XMLNewsFeed** project name, and then select **Build**.

To place this new Server Control on the toolbar, you must first of all select the **General** tab, you can in fact create a new tab if you want, but for this demonstration we'll use the one called **General**. To add your control right-click your mouse button on the main body of the **General** tab, then select **Customize Toolbox** from the pop-up menu. Server Controls come under the classification of .NET Framework components, so select the correct tab and then press the **Browse** button, search for the XMLNewsFeed.dll (in the bin directory of the XMLNewsFeed project), and add it by clicking on the checkbox and then pressing the **OK** button.

After completing these tasks your toolbox should now look as follows, with the XMLNewsFeed Server Control now able to be dragged and dropped onto any WebForm:

XML News Display Server Control (C# .NET) – XMLNewsDisplay

The XML News Display Server Control is responsible for creating the actual HTML that contains and displays the outputted XML file. Below is an example of the typical output from this server control:

Create another completely new project by selecting **File**, **Add Project**, then **New Project**, making sure you select C# Project, then use the **Web Control Library** as the template but this time name it XMLNewsDisplay.

Now we need to add some code to the XMLNewsDisplay by editing the Server Control. You can do this by firstly renaming the WebControl.cs file to XMLNewsDisplay.cs and then double-clicking on the XMLNewsDisplay.cs file and then replace the existing code with the snippet below:

```
using System;
using System.Xml;
using System.Data;
using System.Web.UI;
using System.Web.UI.WebControls;
using System.ComponentModel;
using System.Web.UI.Design;

namespace XMLNewsDisplay
{
  [
  Designer("XMLNewsDisplay.Design.XMLNewsDisplayDesigner, XMLNewsDisplay")
  ]

  [DefaultProperty("XMLDataSet"),
  ToolboxData("<{0}:XMLNewsDisplay runat=server></{0}:XMLNewsDisplay>")]
  public class XMLNewsDisplay : System.Web.UI.WebControls.WebControl
  {
    private System.Web.UI.WebControls.Unit _width;
    private string _itemheadingcolor;
```

```
private string _itemdescriptioncolor;
private string _listtitle;
private System.Data.DataSet  _xmldataset = new System.Data.DataSet();

public XMLNewsDisplay() : base (HtmlTextWriterTag.Table){}

public System.Data.DataSet XMLDataSet
{
  set  {_xmldataset = value;}
}


[Bindable(true), Category("Appearance"),
DefaultValue("")]
override public System.Web.UI.WebControls.Unit Width
{
  get  {return _width;}
  set  {_width = value;}
}


[Bindable(true), Category("Appearance"),
DefaultValue("")]
public string ItemHeadingColor
{
  get  {return _itemheadingcolor;}
  set  {_itemheadingcolor = value;}
}


[Bindable(true), Category("Appearance"),
DefaultValue("")]
public string ItemDescriptionColor
{
  get  {return _itemdescriptioncolor;}
  set  {_itemdescriptioncolor = value;}
}


[Bindable(true), Category("Appearance"),
DefaultValue("")]
public string ListTitle
{
  get {return _listtitle;}
  set  {_listtitle = value;}
}

protected override void AddAttributesToRender(HtmlTextWriter output)
{
  output.AddAttribute(HtmlTextWriterAttribute.Width,Width.Value.ToString());
  base.AddAttributesToRender(output);
}

protected override void RenderContents(HtmlTextWriter output)
{
  System.Data.DataTable _datatable = _xmldataset.Tables["item"];
  output.RenderBeginTag(HtmlTextWriterTag.Tr);
  output.RenderBeginTag(HtmlTextWriterTag.Td);
```

```
        output.Write(ListTitle);
        output.RenderEndTag();
        output.RenderEndTag();
        for (int i = 0; i < _datatable.Rows.Count; i++)
        {
            output.AddAttribute(HtmlTextWriterAttribute.Bgcolor,ItemHeadingColor);
            output.RenderBeginTag(HtmlTextWriterTag.Tr);
            output.RenderBeginTag(HtmlTextWriterTag.Td);

output.AddAttribute(HtmlTextWriterAttribute.Href,_datatable.Rows[i]["link"].ToStri
ng());
            output.RenderBeginTag(HtmlTextWriterTag.A);
            output.Write(_datatable.Rows[i]["title"]);
            output.RenderEndTag();
            output.RenderEndTag();
            output.RenderEndTag();
            output.AddAttribute(HtmlTextWriterAttribute.Bgcolor,ItemDescriptionColor);
            output.RenderBeginTag(HtmlTextWriterTag.Tr);
            output.RenderBeginTag(HtmlTextWriterTag.Td);
            output.Write(_datatable.Rows[i]["description"]);
            output.RenderEndTag();
            output.RenderEndTag();
        }
        base.RenderContents(output);
    }
  }
}

namespace XMLNewsDisplay.Design
{
  public class XMLNewsDisplayDesigner : ControlDesigner
  {
    public XMLNewsDisplayDesigner() {}

    protected override string GetEmptyDesignTimeHtml()
    {
      string text="Not visible at runtime with current settings";
      return CreatePlaceHolderDesignTimeHtml(text);
    }
  }
}
```

As for the previous project you can also create an icon and use it within this project. If you have already followed the previous example for the XMLNewsFeed project then you should now be familiar with how to build your server control and how to attach it into the **General** toolbar, follow the same example but using this XMLNewsDisplay server control.

Completing the Web XML News Web Site

You should now have three projects in your Solution Explorer that should look similar to the following screenshot:

Notice that VS .NET has allowed us to create and maintain three projects at the same time; in VS .NET, the combination of more than one project is called a **solution**. When we debug these components we will be able to step seamlessly between them even though one has been written in VB .NET and the other two have been written in C#.

To complete this web site, double-click on the `WebForm1.aspx` file, which will load the `aspx` interface. Simply drag the **XMLNewsFeed** icon off the **General** toolbar tab and onto the `WebForm1.aspx`. Then drag the **XMLNewsDisplay** icon off the **General** toolbar tab and onto the same form.

Now press the **HTML** tab at the bottom of the `WebForm1.aspx` page; this will display the HTML code, but we are specifically interested in the following two lines:

```
<%@ Register TagPrefix="cc1" Namespace="XMLNewsFeed" Assembly="XMLNewsFeed" %>
<%@ Register TagPrefix="cc2" Namespace="XMLNewsDisplay" Assembly="XMLNewsDisplay"
%>
```

The above lines were automatically generated when you dragged your Server Controls onto the web page. These controls register the Server Control to be used and also assign it a unique tag prefix or reference:

```
<cc2:xmlnewsfeed id="XMLNewsFeed1" runat="server">
</cc2:xmlnewsfeed>
<cc1:xmlnewsdisplay id="XMLNewsDisplay1" runat="server" </cc1:xmlnewsdisplay>
```

We've just created the Feed and the Display, but before we continue let's set up some default values for the properties we supplied for the XMLNewsDisplay server control. To do this simply click on the XMLNewsDisplay control (see below) that's now sitting within your WebForm1.aspx file:

Then select **View** from the menu, then **Properties Window**. You'll now see a the basic properties for your server control, including the custom ones we've input for controlling the server's color and heading.

Now enter all the default values you see on the opposite example properties window. These values will format the HTML produced to create a more professional display.

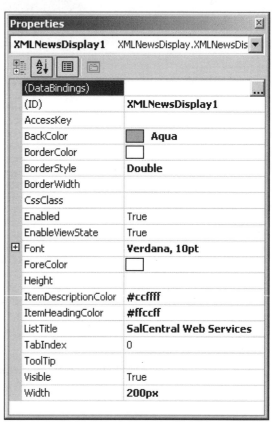

Build the **XMLNews** project (select **Build** then **XMLNews** menu option) and continue on and debug your newly created solution.

Debugging the XML News Web Site

Now for the fun part, debugging!

Edit the code behind for the **WebForm1.aspx** and place a breakpoint on the following line:

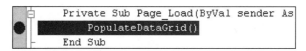

You can do this by moving your cursor to that line and then pressing *F9*. You can if preferred place a breakpoint at any point within your code including within the Server Control.

Press *F5* to run your code. After a few seconds while VS .NET creates MSIL after which the JIT compiler creates Machine Code, the following will appear, indicating that the code has stopped at that specific point:

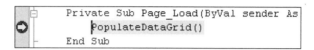

```
Private Sub Page_Load(ByVal sender As
    PopulateDataGrid()
End Sub
```

Now use the **Debug | Step Into** menu option (or whatever quick key press is assigned to the same menu, *F8* or *F11* depending on how you set up VS .NET during installation) and step through your code line by line. As you step through you will see that VS .NET allows debugging to step between projects and even into the Server Control.

As you move through these projects, stop momentarily in the XMLNewsFeed.Populate method and see what resources are available to us; select **Debug | Windows | Call Stack:**

The above entries indicate where you are in the code and also which methods and projects have led you to this point. By double-clicking on any of these lines you can instantly move to the point of entry for your currently executing code.

Reviewing the Code

Let's consider what we've done by creating this example XML News control. If you add up all the code lines in every control it totals approximately 40 lines; this in itself is unusual, as attempting to perform the same technique using ASP and JavaScript/VBScript would have probably trebled these figures.

At the start, it's not so obvious why we split the Feed (XMLNewsFeed) away from the Display (XMLNewsDisplay), but on reflection you can now create an alternative Server Control that simply has the same interface and creates a publicly available DataSet to feed into the XMLNews Display Control. This makes the control much more versatile as the feed does not even have to be from an XML file any more; you could create a Server Control to feed off a SQL Server or even an Oracle database.

Performance is definitely an issue with a component like this as you really would like to get the remote RSS XML file instantly and there is a certain amount of latency in getting the RSS XML file for every user who visits your page. One possible solution to this would be to place the XML in an application variable (which is accessible by all users, and remains in scope until the server is restarted) and use the <skipHours> element to get the XML only when a new version is available. For the sake of this simple example, we have left this ability out.

There's always the task list to remind you of course; this is an excellent feature all you need to do is display it by selecting **View, Other Windows**, then **Task List** from the VS .NET main menu, making sure the list is not filtered, and the following comments (we left these in there from the start) should be shown:

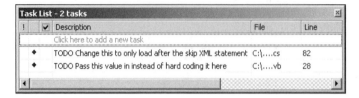

Just double-click on either one to instantly show the relevant code.

Summary

In this chapter we have looked at the role that VS .NET can play in helping us to develop our applications. Let's have a quick re-cap of some of the features of VS .NET that we covered earlier.

- ❏ VS .NET is a code maintenance application for any supported language, allowing rapid development and deployment of applications.

- ❏ Non-language-centric features are supported by all languages and not all language-centric features are supported by all languages. Syntax checking and IntelliSense are also available to new .NET languages if they decide to support them.

- ❏ The .NET Framework lets any language supporting the CLS (Common Language Specifications) use any of its base classes.

- ❏ You can load multiple projects at the same time; this is called a solution. You can also debug between multiple projects at the same time, even if they are in different languages. Debugging gives you the ability to step from one project to another irrespective of the language they are written in.

- ❏ The VS .NET interface can be limited using Enterprise Template Policy. This will allow you to restrict the options available on the interface.

- ❏ VS .NET allows you to embed your own dynamic help for Server Controls. Also, Project Management in the form of Source Safe is built into VS .NET, allowing team development within a controlled environment.

- ❏ You can add your own Server Controls to the toolbar along with neat customizations such as proprietary attributes on the property window and an icon on the toolbar. Skins allow you to have a look and feel of another application such as C++ or VB6. This allows you to have a similar interface to what you're currently used to.

- ❏ You can produce composite controls, which greatly enhance their ability. Composite controls are controls that encapsulate multiple controls, either ones you've created yourself or inbuilt controls within the same component.

- ❏ The toolbar can be used for code snippets as well as default and custom controls.

In the next chapter, we will be looking at creating a custom design-time appearance for our custom controls within Visual Studio .NET.

Professional ASP .NET Server Controls

9

Design-Time Support

In the last chapter we looked at what was involved when creating controls from within an IDE. We looked at examples using Visual Studio .NET, detailing its benefits over Notepad.

In this chapter we will discuss the use of various classes that enhance the support provided by our controls to developers working with VS .NET (although other IDEs could use the same functionality). The whole architecture is extensible, so we will start with simple examples adding little design-time support, and move on to more complex support and interaction with the IDE.

This support comes in many forms. In this chapter we'll be considering:

❑   Generating sourcecode for a control (to the ASPX page)

❑   Interacting with the `ControlBuilder` to parse the generated code

❑   Converting a control to, and from, other types

❑   Cooperation with the Property Browser

❑   Adding custom editing UI for properties and controls

❑   Using advanced services provided by the hosting environment of the control

What Does Design-Time Support Mean?

When we speak of design-time functionality we are referring to how a control or component is displayed and its behavior within an IDE. Some of the things that we may need our control to do within the design-time environment are: display itself in the toolbox, render itself on the design surface in a way that may or may not be different from run time, show events and properties in the property browser, and generate any 'helper' code the control may need.

Advanced design-time functionality is implemented from outside the component, not from within (of course, .NET provides great support for this). This means that not only is the required code outside the control class, but it can even be in another assembly. And this "Design" assembly doesn't even need to be present on the production machine in order for the controls to work properly at run time. This provides a big advantage for deployment: as you only need to distribute the "run-time" controls library you can license the "design" library separately. Of course, as with many intrinsic ASP.NET controls, any descendent custom control won't be of much use without its corresponding "Design" assembly. If you have any doubt about this, try configuring a DataGrid with templated columns and complex formatting by hand...

If you're having trouble conceptualizing this idea try thinking of the designer as a magic jacket that our component is wearing. This jacket (a **Designer**) can help our control do things such as be invisible at run time and visible at design time (so we can see it in order to work with it), convert a property value to a cohesive text string to display in the property sheet (using a **TypeConverter**), or attach a UI-based property setting mechanism to help with things such as pointing our control to an image or file that it needs.

One benefit to the "jacket" style design-time implementation is that we can change our control's design-time behavior very easily just by altering its attributes, effectively changing "jackets", leaving the actual code untouched.

A Sample Control

Throughout this chapter, we will work with two controls: WroxButton and WroxButtonBar. As you may have guessed, the last control is just a container for the buttons. We will also need a blank page to drag our controls into to play around. We will create them in a new **Class Library** project, called **WroxDesign**. Here we see only the relevant code of the WroxButton. The toolbar will be created later in the chapter, as it is more complex.

It is a very simple control, to start playing with. It just creates a label to contain the text and an image control to load the image. Then it adds these controls to the base WebControl collection of child controls:

```
public class WroxButton : WebControl
{
  protected override void CreateChildControls()
  {
    //Reset values before rendering.
    base.Controls.Clear();
    //Height depends on the button content.
    base.Height = 0;
```

```
        Image img = new Image();
        img.ImageUrl = _image;
        img.ImageAlign = ImageAlign.AbsMiddle;

        Label lbl = new Label();
        lbl.Text = _text;
        //Add a little margin around the text.
        lbl.Style.Add("padding-left", "5pt");
        lbl.Style.Add("padding-right", "5pt");

        base.Controls.Add(lbl);
        base.Controls.Add(img);
        _size.Width = base.Width;
        _size.Height = base.Height;
    }
}

    protected override void Render(HtmlTextWriter output)
    {
      EnsureChildControls();
      base.Render(output);
    }
}
```

The control has a couple of string properties, `Text` and `ImageUrl`, which set the inherited `ChildControlsCreated boolean` property to `false` in the property `set` method. When `EnsureChildControls()` is called inside the `Render` method, that setting forces a call to `CreateChildControls()`. This way we ensure that we are rebuilding the control layout every time a property changes.

> To add a custom icon to our control, all we need do is add a bitmap image of 16x16 pixels to the project, set the file's **Build Action** property to **Embedded Resource**, and give it the exact name of the control. In our case, a **WroxButton.bmp** file will do the job.

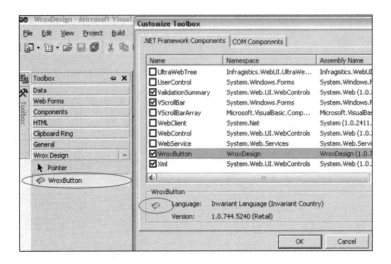

If you get tired of changing from the COM Components to the .NET Framework Components tab every time you customize your toolbox, move the registry DWORD value named DefaultTbx from HKEY_LOCAL_MACHINE\SOFTWARE\Microsoft\ VisualStudio\7.0\ToolboxPages\ActiveXControls to the .NET Framework Components folder under the same ToolboxPages folder (the picture below shows the result of this):

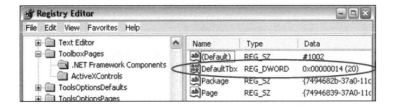

Overview of the Design-Time Architecture

The design-time support we can offer to our control's users can be categorized in three levels, and each of them also refers the amount of relative effort required to implement the functionality into our controls:

❏ **Basic**: involves setting various attributes on our control, to change their behavior without writing any custom code.

❏ **Intermediate**: in this level we use custom TypeConverters to provide conversions and custom representation of properties in the PropertyBrowser, and custom TypeEditors, to ease the process of setting complex properties of our control.

❏ **Advanced**: here we use a custom Designer, which provides greater flexibility at design time, and interacts with a ControlBuilder to recreate the control, if custom sourcecode is emitted. This level also involves integration with the IDE and the use of services provided by the host environment.

In the advanced level, there are areas that require going back to the intermediate or even the basic level to add new functionality. So don't be surprised if from time to time we need to go back to things that we've covered in an earlier section.

Basic

We have already seen in previous chapters how to apply attributes to classes (see Chapter 8). Applying them to class members is no different, except that they are located just above the member declaration (either a property, method, or event). There are a number of attributes that affect the way a control behaves. We will analyze them according to their complexity, starting with the simpler ones.

The target of the attribute is one or more values of the `AttributeTargets` enumerations (`All`, `Assembly`, `Class`, `Constructor`, `Delegate`, `Enum`, `Event`, `Field`, `Interface`, `Method`, `Module`, `Parameter`, `Property`, `ReturnValue`, `Struct`), that defines in which context the attribute is valid:

❑ **TagPrefix** – Target: Assembly

This is where the whole story begins. Every custom control on a page must have a prefix registered with the `Register` directive. This allows the page framework to locate the assembly and classes when the corresponding prefix and control tags are found in the page. The syntax is simple, providing the prefix to be used thorough the page to identify our controls, and the assembly where they are located. This attribute will typically be located in the `AssemblyInfo.cs` file:

```
[assembly: System.Web.UI.TagPrefix("WroxDesign", "wx")]
```

❑ **Description** – Target: All

This is a small block of text that shows up at the bottom of the **Property** browser when we select the property with our mouse. For example, when we select `ID` on a `Panel` control the text at the bottom of the screen reads "Programmatic name of the control". The constructor takes a string. This attribute can also be set at the class level, and is shown in the property browser when a control has a property of this class type (for example if another custom control contains a property of type `WroxButton`).

❑ **Browsable** – Target: All

This `true`/`false` attribute designates whether the element can be shown in the **Property** browser. Beware that the **Property** browser can display events too. But it will be mainly used for properties. The default value is `true`.

❑ **Category** – Target: All

Specifies the group that our element should be associated with (such as "Appearance", "Data", and so on). If our entry is not one of the default groupings, the IDE creates a new one, naming it with the value that we entered.

❑ **DefaultValue** – Target: All

Sets the default value for the element. It is hard to imagine why this attribute doesn't target only properties.

❑ **DefaultProperty** – Target: Class

Takes a string designating which property will be selected by default when displaying the object in the property browser. When a user changes the current selected control on the page designer surface, the property browser tries to select a property of the same name and type as the previous control. If it fails to do so, it looks for this default property and selects it.

❑ **DefaultEvent** – Target: Class

This has identical behavior to the previous attribute, but works for events.

❑ **MergableProperty** – Target: All

This attribute sets whether in a multi-selection scenario the property is allowed to be merged with the other objects to allow addition of all of them together. By default, it is true.

Examples:

Let's decorate our WroxButton with these attributes to see the design-time effect:

```
[DefaultProperty("Text")]
[DefaultEvent("Init")]
[Description("A custom button")]
public class WroxButton : WebControl
{
  private string _text;
  private string _image;

  [DefaultValue("My default value")]
  [Description("The text to display in the button.")]
  [Category("Custom Category")]
  [MergableProperty(false)]
  public string Text
...

  [Browsable(false)]
  public override Unit Width
```

We have overridden the base Width property to hide it from the property browser. We have also disabled the ability to edit the Text property for multiple objects simultaneously. The result looks like this:

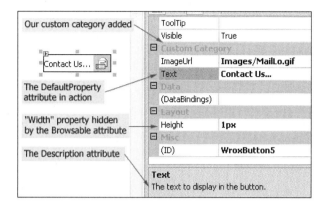

❑ **ParenthesizePropertyName** – Target: All

Tells the property browser to put parentheses around our property name, just like the DataBindings and ID properties we can see in the previous picture.

❑ **ReadOnly** – Target: All

Allows a property with get and set accessors to appear as readonly at design time. This is useful when we only want to allow a property to be modified programmatically though our code, but not at design time using the property browser.

❑ **DesignOnly** – Target: All

According to the documentation, it allows a read/write property to be set only at design time. But changing it at run time from the code-behind file works.

❑ **Bindable** – Target: All

This attribute tells the IDE the element can be bound to a valid source. Databinding is out of the scope of this chapter, (see Chapter 6) but it should suffice to say that it allows the property to be filled with the property of another component or a valid datasource (maybe a DataSet).

❑ **RefreshProperties** – Target: All

Using this attribute, we can tell the property browser how different properties affect each other. It takes an enum value, which can be All (which requeries the component for the list of properties and reloads them into the property browser), Repaint (which repaints the values of all the properties), and Default (which only repaints the changed property). This attribute is set on the property that is going to trigger the refresh. For example, we may have a calculated property (maybe a summary concatenating the WroxButton.Text and WroxButton.ImageUrl properties), and a change in any value providing this summary must trigger a repaint of it, to reflect the new value.

Tip: the property browser will actually refresh the summary value example we used, but it may take a little time to do so. If we want immediate feedback, we can use RefreshProperties.Repaint.

❑ **Editor** – Target: All

This attribute associates a custom UI editor to change the property value. This can either show a modal dialog (like the `Names` sub-property of the `Font` property in our `WroxButton`) or a drop-down dialog (like the `BackColor` property). Depending on the type of UI to display, we will see an arrow or ellipsis next to the property value. Some built-in editors include `System.Drawing.Design.ColorEditor` (associated with the `System.Drawing.Color` class), `System.ComponentModel.Design.ArrayEditor` (associated with all array-inherited classes), `System.Web.UI.Design.UrlEditor`, and its descendents (`ImageUrlEditor`, `XmlUrlEditor`, and `XslUrlEditor`, all of them in the same namespace), and so on. Associating one of these editors is very simple, and greatly increases our control usability with trivial effort.

❑ **Localizable** – Target: All

This attribute tells the hosting designer to persist the property value outside the form, inside a resource file (`.RESX`) associated with it. A special class, called `ResourceManager` is in charge of loading the resources and retrieving and setting values on them.

This actually works flawlessly for Windows Forms controls, because the Forms designer automatically adds code to the form's `InitializeComponent()` private method, calling the `ResourceManager` class's methods and setting the localized properties based on it. For example, to set a button's text property, it writes:

```
this.button1.Text = resources.GetString("button1.Text").
```

Unfortunately, this is not the case for Web Forms, and we have to both persist and load the properties we want from the corresponding resource. We will see an example of this in the advanced section.

❑ **DesignerSerializationVisibility** – Target: Method, Property

This is an `Enum` that controls what should be serialized to the ASPX page code. The value set through this attribute must be consistent with the `PersistenceMode` attribute, or nothing will be serialized at all. Possible values are:

   ❑ **Content**: serializes the content of the property instead of the property itself. This only makes sense when the property is an `ICollection` implementation or an `Array`. Serializing the property itself will serialize the item count, capacity, and other properties of the collection itself. Serializing the content will try to serialize the actual elements in it. If the property is an object and not a collection, each property of this object will be serialized. The way this content is serialized depends on the next attribute, `PersistenceMode`.

   ❑ **Visible**, which is equal to **Default**: serializes the property itself. This is the most common case. In the case of simple properties (I mean, not other objects, but `strings`, `numbers`, `booleans`, or enums), they are serialized as attributes of the control's opening tag, and the `PersistenceMode` must be `Attribute`, which is the default.

   ❑ **Hidden**: designates that the property shouldn't be serialized at all. This is very useful when we add calculated properties, or we provide our own serialization mechanism though the use of a `Designer`, as we will see in the Advanced section of this chapter.

❑ **PersistenceMode** – Target: All

Controls the way properties are serialized. Where the previous attribute controls **what** to persist, this attribute controls **how** to persist. Possible values are:

❑ **Attribute**, which is equal to **Default**: the property will be serialized as an HTML attribute of the control. When combined with `DesignerSerializationVisibility.Content` in a property whose type contains subproperties, it produces the following output, which shows the `Property-SubProperty="Value"` generated format:

```
Font-Size="8pt" Font-Names="Tahoma"
```

❑ **EncodedInnerDefaultProperty**: MSDN help is self-explanatory; "*Specifies that a property is persistable as the only inner content of this ASP.NET server control. The property value is HTML encoded before being persisted.*" We must be aware, however, that persisting the property this way will require assigning a `ControlBuilder` with the control, to perform the validation and re-building of the control.

❑ **InnerDefaultProperty**: the same as the previous one, but no encoding is performed.

❑ **InnerProperty**: the property will be persisted as a nested tag inside the control. This is the preferred setting to generate complex nested hierarchies of objects. An example of this can be found in the `DataList` and `DataGrid` controls, which generated inner tags for various styles:

```
<asp:DataGrid id="DataGrid1" runat="server" >
  <FooterStyle ForeColor="Black" BackColor="#CCCCCC" />
  <HeaderStyle Font-Bold="True" ForeColor="White" BackColor="#000084"
/>
  <PagerStyle HorizontalAlign="Center" ForeColor="Black"
BackColor="#999999" Mode="NumericPages" />
  <SelectedItemStyle Font-Bold="True" ForeColor="White"
BackColor="#008A8C" />
  <AlternatingItemStyle BackColor="#DCDCDC" />
  <ItemStyle ForeColor="Black" BackColor="#EEEEEE" />
</asp:DataGrid>
```

However, this setting requires us to have a `ControlBuilder` associated with the control, to recreate the control structure. We cover how to do this later in the advanced section.

Examples:

We will add a calculated property to the control:

```
[Category("Custom Category")]
[DesignerSerializationVisibility(DesignerSerializationVisibility.Hidden)]
[ReadOnly(true)]
public string CalculatedValue
{
  get { return String.Format("{0} ({1})", _text, _image); }
  set { }
}
```

The property `set` accesor does nothing, but is there just to show that even when it is a read/write property it will be grayed in the property browser. As the value is based on the other properties, we don't want its value to be persisted to the page code (`DesignerSerializationVisibility.Hidden`). We will add a new attribute to the `Text` property:

```
[RefreshProperties(RefreshProperties.Repaint)]
public string Text
```

This will make any changes to this property perform a repaint of all the other properties, giving instant feedback in the summary property. We will also add an attribute to the `WroxButton.ImageUrl` property declaration too:

```
[Category("Custom Category")]
[Editor(typeof(ImageUrlEditor), typeof(UITypeEditor))]
public string ImageUrl
```

Let us override the `Font` property to change the way it is persisted:

```
[PersistenceMode(PersistenceMode.InnerProperty)]
public override FontInfo Font
{
  get { return base.Font; }
}
```

The persisted code generated for the `WroxButton` control is:

```
<wx:wroxbutton id="btnWrox"
    style="Z-INDEX: 103; LEFT: 485px; POSITION: absolute; TOP: 97px"
    runat="server" Width="94px" Height="1px"
    BorderWidth="1pt" BorderColor="Black" BorderStyle="Solid"
    Text="Contact Us... " ImageUrl="Images/MailLo.gif">
  <Font Size="8pt" Names="Tahoma" Bold="True"></Font>
</wx:wroxbutton>
```

> Note how the **Font** property is now serialized differently. (It used to be a **Font-Size="8pt"** attribute.) This is the effect of **PersistenceMode**.

❑   **ParseChildren** – Target: Class

Specifies whether the page parser should parse the inner tags and try to set control properties with them. It is `true` by default, so if we add inner tags that are not mapped to properties of our control, the control building process will fail. This can be used in conjunction with the `PersistenceMode` and `DesignerSerializationVisibility` to persist and reload complex properties to and from the page code. When we provide a custom `ControlBuilder`, this attribute will usually be set to `false`, to allow the builder to do its work parsing the tags and rebuilding the control.

Design-Time Attributes and Inheritance

When we derive a control from a base class that has design-time attributes, our control inherits the design-time functionality of its parent, just like with inheritable methods and properties. If the parent class's implementation of the design-time attributes is sufficient for our control we do not need to reapply them. It is still possible to apply more attributes or override the ones inherited from the base class.

To do so, we must first override the property, and re-apply the changed attributes or add the new ones. Most of the properties in the base classes `WebControl` and `Control` are marked as virtual, allowing us to change their behavior. For example, if we wanted to hide the `Height` property of a `WebControl`-inherited custom control from the Property Browser (maybe because it is calculated from the content rather than set by the developer), we would write the following code:

```
[Browsable(false)]
public override Unit Height
{
  get { return base.Height; }
  set { base.Height = value; }
}
```

We could have omitted the **override** keyword, but this has a side effect, and it has to do with OO programming. When we inherit a class, we gain all the base class functionality. From this point, our control can be used either with a reference to the parent type or our own type. This is so because the interface (the properties, methods, and events) of our control now includes both.

For example, our `WroxButton` inherits from `WebControl`, and as such, it can be **up-cast** to it:

```
//Some code in the aspx page hosting our control
//Up-cast to the parent interface
WebControl control = this.WroxButton1;

//access though the parent type interface
control.Width = new Unit("120", UnitType.Pixel);

//access though our control interface
WroxButton1.Width = new Unit("110", UnitType.Pixel);
```

As we have *overridden* the base `Width` property, accessing it though either interface will result in the same code being invoked: our control's code. If we hadn't added the `override` keyword, the compiler would issue a warning:

```
'WroxDesign.WroxButton.Width' hides inherited member
'System.Web.UI.WebControls.WebControl.Width'. To make the current member override
that implementation, add the override keyword. Otherwise add the new keyword.
```

What this warning is saying is that if we access the property though the parent class interface (the first case), the parent type code will be called, not ours. Adding the `new` keyword will make this intention and behavior explicit, and will avoid the compiler warning, although I doubt this is the usual case.

Intermediate

In this level we start to actually write our own code. Whenever the declarative functionality provided by the basic level is not enough, we can start to leverage the rich extensibility infrastructure built in the framework and the VS IDE.

We have already seen how to create `ControlBuilders`, and use the `ControlBuilder` attribute to associate it with a control. They are part of this intermediate level of support, and generally are one of the first steps to take towards increasing design-time support, as parsing the control's tags representation is usually the starting point.

There are different degrees of complexity in this level too, and we are going to work with the most common uses of `TypeConverters` and `TypeEditors`, which go beyond `ControlBuilders` and add many useful features. They also offer some more advanced services that be exploited, however, and they will be analyzed later in the advanced section of the chapter.

Custom TypeConverters

A type converter is useful for a number of things at design time. It will allow for conversion from a given data type to another data type (usually `string` to `value` conversions) or perform some sort of design-time validation. In the IDE's property browser, we can have a type converter represent a property value as text to the user and convert it to the needed type behind the scenes for our code to use. Most of the types in .NET (`String`, `Int32`, and so on) have default type converters that provide string-to-value conversions and validation but we can override those or create our own if they are insufficient for our purposes.

One of the most useful built-in converters is the `EnumConverter`, which provides the `DropDown` list we see in the property browser when we set properties whose type is an enumeration, such as a control's `BorderStyle` property. We will get this converter for free for all our `Enums`.

> We can find the default type converters in the `System.ComponentModel` namespace.

As with the other design-time subjects we have seen in this chapter, the implementation of a type converter is not attached to any UI functionality so we can actually use this functionality within Windows Forms as well!

There are many ways to customize a type converter, and it will be up to us to decide which members of the base class we are going to override. The functionality provided by a type converter can be divided into four areas:

❑ **Conversions**: The most common conversion will be performed to and from a `string` representation, which is the format the property browser uses. The `string` representation is also used to persist and recover control properties in the page sourcecode.

❑ **Standard Values**: These provide a way to display a list of valid values in the property browser. This is used when the list is not based on an `Enum`. The values vary from hardcoded values to database-driven lists; it's up to us.

❑ **Subproperties**: These methods allow us to return a filtered list of properties for the object. For example, we may want to show in the property browser only those that have been marked with the `DesignOnly` attribute, or any other. We can also filter by the type of the property. This is only used in advanced scenarios.

❑ **Object creation and code persistence**: These methods assist the client (that is, the property browser) in the process of creating an instance of the type, and more importantly, they are responsible for persisting to and from sourcecode in the designer. This is primarily used in conjunction with the Windows Forms designer to control the automatic code generation. Because the ASP.NET Server Controls are not persisted to actual sourcecode, but to an XML representation of it, this functionality is not used. The object responsible for persistence of our Server Controls is the control designer attached to them, as we will see later in the advanced section.

The first two categories are the kind of features we will add for an intermediate level of design time support.

Examples:

We will use the WroxButton we have already built to test a new converter. For that purpose, we will create a new class named WebControlSize, which will contain the height and width units for a given control:

```
[TypeConverter(typeof(WebControlSizeConverter))]
[Description("The representation of a size, with [Height, Width] string
representation")]
public class WebControlSize
{
  private Unit _width;
  private Unit _height;

  public WebControlSize(Unit height, Unit width)
  {
    _height = height;
    _width = width;
  }
  public Unit Width
  {
    get { return _width; }
    set { _width = value; }
  }
  public Unit Height
  {
    get { return _height; }
    set { _height = value; }
  }
}
```

Now we will change the WroxButton to contain a property of this type. First we will add a private variable to contain a reference:

```
private WebControlSize _size =
  new WebControlSize(new Unit(0), new Unit(0));
```

We will override the Height and Width properties to add a ChildControlsCreated = false instruction on the property set, the same as we have already done for the Text and ImageUrl properties. This forces a call to CreateChildControls() before rendering the new dimensions. In this place we must initialize the WebControlSize:

```
    _size.Width = base.Width;
    _size.Height = base.Height;
```

And finally the property itself:

```
[Category("Layout")]
[DesignerSerializationVisibility(DesignerSerializationVisibility.Hidden)]
[RefreshProperties(RefreshProperties.Repaint)]
public WebControlSize ButtonSize
{
  get { return _size; }
  set
  {
    _size = value;
    base.Height = _size.Height;
    base.Width = _size.Width;
  }
}
```

Please note how we are using the attributes we saw in the **Basic** section to control this property's design-time appearance. We have put it in the Layout category so that it appears just above the Height and Width properties. DesignerSerializationVisibility.Hidden avoids generating sourcecode for this property, as it is a calculated value. The RefreshProperties.Repaint is necessary to reflect the change in the property browser immediately.

Conversions

Now we move on and create the type converter for the WebControlSize class. Note that we have already added the [TypeConverter(typeof(WebControlSizeConverter))] attribute to it. Our custom converter must derive from an existing TypeConverter-derived class. In this case we will just inherit the base TypeConverter:

```
public class WebControlSizeConverter : TypeConverter
{
  public WebControlSizeConverter()
  {
  }
```

As a convention, we should always name the converter with the name of the control to which it is attached plus the word "Converter". This way we make explicit the purpose and use of this class.

Now, we have the following methods to override:

❑   **CanConvertFrom**: This specifies which data types the converter can convert from.

❑   **ConvertFrom**: This is the method that actually implements the conversion.

❑   **CanConvertTo**: This specifies which data types the converter can convert to.

❑   **ConvertTo**: This is the method that implements the actual conversion.

❑   **IsValid**: Overriding this method is optional. As the intrinsic control's properties already work raising exceptions (try to set the BackColor property to an invalid string), we can rely on these exceptions to abort property changes in the ConvertFrom method.

The first thing we will do before delving into the overridden methods is to add a couple of private helper methods to perform the conversion to and from strings, which will be the most used conversion:

```
private string ToString(object value)
{
  WebControlSize size = value as WebControlSize;
  return String.Format("{0}, {1}", size.Height, size.Width);
}
```

We just return the string value of both the `Height` and `Width` properties of the value passed. We first cast it to our `WebControlSize` type:

```
private WebControlSize FromString(object value)
{
  string[] values = ((string)value).Split(',');
  if (values.Length != 2) throw new ArgumentException("Could not convert the
value");;
  try
  {
    Unit h = new Unit(values[0]);
    Unit w = new Unit(values[1]);
    return new WebControlSize(h, w);
  }
  catch
  {
    throw new ArgumentException("Could not convert the value");
  }
}
```

As our converter always implements the conversion, we expect a `string` in the format we produce, otherwise we'll raise an exception. If we succeed, we return the new object instance from the received values.

The client (the property browser) will first query the `CanConvert*` methods. If it receives a `true` value it will call the actual `Convert*` method. This is why we check the source type in one method and the destination type in the other, for equality with the `string` type, which is the one we actually support. If they are not a `string` type, we call the corresponding base method, just to give the base converter a chance to try:

```
public override bool CanConvertFrom(
    ITypeDescriptorContext context,
    Type sourceType)
{
    if (sourceType == typeof(string)) return true;
    return base.CanConvertFrom(context, sourceType);
}

public override object ConvertFrom(
    ITypeDescriptorContext context,
    CultureInfo culture, object value)
{
```

```
      if (value is string) return FromString(value);
      return base.ConvertFrom(context, culture, value);
    }

    public override bool CanConvertTo(
      ITypeDescriptorContext context,
      Type destinationType)
    {
      if (destinationType == typeof(string)) return true;
      return base.CanConvertTo(context, destinationType);
    }

    public override object ConvertTo(
      ITypeDescriptorContext context,
      CultureInfo culture, object value,
      Type destinationType)
    {
      if (destinationType == typeof(string))
        return ToString(value);
      return base.ConvertTo(context, culture, value, destinationType);
    }
```

> **It is good OO programming practice to always give the base classes from which we inherit a chance to handle a message we are not going to support.**

The run-time result achieved is:

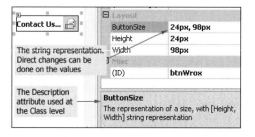

We have seen the `ITypeDescriptorContext` interface as a parameter to various methods, and it contains a reference to the context in which the conversion is being executed. Relevant properties are:

❑ **Container**: this property, of type `IContainer` is a reference to the parent host where the control is. This interface contains only one property, `Components`, which is the collection of components actually residing in the page. We can use it to enable or disable certain conversions based on the presence of some other control, or even to directly change a property on some other component in the page.

Directly changing other components' properties, however, is not a very good idea, although at first it would seem so. We will see in the advanced section the issues involved with doing this, which concern primarily notifications not being sent to the environment signaling the changes. So, although we effectively change the property, and it gets properly persisted to the page source, we don't see any change in the actual instance of the control on the design surface.

To test this behavior, we can just change the `ConvertTo` method:

```
if (destinationType == typeof(string))
{
  foreach (IComponent comp in context.Container.Components)
    if (comp is Label)
      ((Label)comp).Text = "WebControlSize Changed!!";
  return ToString(value);
}
```

This code changes every label in the page every time the `ButtonSize` property is converted to its `string` representation. If we select any `label`, we will see in the property browser the changed property, but the `label` instance in the design surface remains unchanged.

❑ **Instance**: contains a reference to the object whose property is being edited. In our case, it is the reference to our `WroxButton` control. Of course we have to cast it to our type. Changing properties on this object doesn't cause the effect we saw in the previous case. This is because the change is taking place in the same object being monitored by the property browser, although a `RefreshProperties` attribute on any changed properties will help to speed up the process of updating the property browser.

> When multiple objects are selected, and editing of the property is allowed (the default behavior) in this scenario, the **Instance** property of the context will be an array of the selected objects.

❑ **PropertyDescriptor**: this is the main class used by the property browser to interact with object instances and properties. Instead of changing and assigning values directly, all the communication goes though this object. It is a description of the property instance, and contains the following useful properties:

❑ **ComponentType**: contains a `System.Type` object describing the component that contains this property. This property contains the same type that is returned by calling `context.Instance.GetType()`.

❑ **Converter**: gets a reference to this converter type.

❑ **PropertyType**: contains a `System.Type` object describing the current property being changed, in our case, the type `WebControlSize`.

❑ **Common attributes as properties**: all the common attributes, especially the ones we saw in the Basic section, are converted to properties for easy access to their value. For example, we have `IsLocalizable`, `IsReadOnly`, `IsBrowsable`, `SerializationVisibility`, and so on as properties.

Methods:

❑ **GetValue**: gets the current value for the property

❑ **SetValue**: changes the property value

This class will be analyzed in more detail in the advanced section, because it provides some needed services to the hosting environment.

The other parameter, `CultureInfo` can be used to provide localized strings to for the object during conversion.

Standard Values

Standard values represent a list of possible values for a property, and are displayed by the property browser as a drop-down list. It's the kind of list we see for Enum values.

To provide custom lists, we have to override three methods:

❑ **GetStandardValuesSupported**: a `boolean` method designating whether this converter provides standard values.

❑ **GetStandardValuesExclusive**: tells the property browser if the property value must be one of the list values.

❑ **GetStandardValues**: returns an object of type `StandardValuesCollection` containing the values to display. The constructor of this class recieves an `ICollection` object with the values, which will typically be an array.

To demonstrate this functionality, we will associate a new type converter to the Text property of our WroxButton control. This converter will provide the list of Publishers in the Pubs database (distributed with the VS IDE). This is enough to show the flexibility of this feature.

To increase the performance of the retrieval, it will be performed only once, the first time the list is accessed. This list will be shared (static in C#) among the type converter instances. A single entry point to retrieve the property will first check if it has already been loaded. This is called a **Singleton** design pattern:

```
public class PublisherListConverter : TypeConverter
{
  public PublisherListConverter()
  {
  }

  //Shared list of publishers
  private static StandardValuesCollection _publisher;
  //Change to point to your pubs database
  private static string _connection = @"data source=DEVMOVIL\NETSDK;initial
catalog=pubs;password=;user id=sa;";

  //The Singleton pattern to access the single list instance
  private StandardValuesCollection ListInstance()
  {
    if (_publisher == null)
    {
      DataSet ds = new DataSet();
      SqlDataAdapter ad = new SqlDataAdapter(
        "SELECT pub_name FROM publishers", _connection);
      ad.Fill(ds);
```

After filling the `DataSet` we need to transform the `DataRowCollection` object into an array of values, so we iterate the collection and get the string representation of each one:

```
    //Build an array and pass it to the
    //StandardValuesCollection constructor
    string[] pubs = new string[ds.Tables[0].Rows.Count];
    for (int i = 0; i < pubs.Length; i++)
      pubs[i] = ds.Tables[0].Rows[i][0].ToString();
    _publisher = new StandardValuesCollection(pubs);
  }
  //Return the instance
  return _publisher;
}
```

Now we override the methods:

```
public override bool GetStandardValuesSupported(
  ITypeDescriptorContext context)
{
  return true;
}

public override bool GetStandardValuesExclusive(
  ITypeDescriptorContext context)
{
  // Return false to allow not listed values.
  return true;
}

public override StandardValuesCollection GetStandardValues(
  ITypeDescriptorContext context)
{
  return ListInstance();
}
```

That's it! Now the result is:

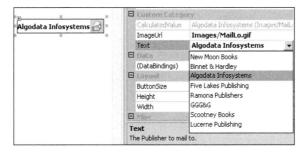

> We will typically associate a **TypeConverter** with our control at the class level. This way, it's not necessary to set this attribute for each property that uses our control to get the right converter.

The `TypeConverter` is a stateless class, so we shouldn't save values received in any method as private variables. That's why we receive the `ITypeDescriptorContext` in every method. It allows the host to share a single instance of this class, instead of creating a converter object for each control to convert.

> **Only one instance of the `TypeConverter` is created for the type to convert. The instance is shared among all the controls of the same type. So we shouldn't persist any value related to the context at the class level.**

Custom TypeEditors

In some situations, the value-to-string conversion that allows a property to be displayed as text in the property browser might not be enough. Imagine life without the color browser for things such as background color or the browser for image URLs. How many times have we needed one of those? Well, with `TypeEditors` we can save our control user's time tracking down these mishaps.
We have already seen some intrinsic `TypeEditors`, and we have seen that they are custom UI for the developer to assign properties easily.

Just as with `TypeConverters`, and almost everything in the extensible architecture of the Framework and IDE, creating a new type editor involves inheriting a base, and overriding desired members.

The base type, `UITypeEditor` is located in the `System.Drawing.Design` namespace, and is very simple. We can override:

❑ **EditValue**: this where the main action takes place.

❑ **GetEditStyle**: lets the property browser know about the editing support we will provide, and it will draw an ellipsis button (if we return `UITypeEditorEditStyle.Modal`), a drop-down arrow (if we return `UITypeEditorEditStyle.DropDown`) or nothing at all (if set it to `UITypeEditorEditStyle.None`).

❑ **GetPaintValueSupported**: tells the property browser whether it should call the `PaintValue` method. This one and the next are optional.

❑ **PaintValue**: called if we returned `true` in the previous method. Allows us to paint a custom representation in the property browser, much like the `Font.Name` subproperty does.

A Modal Editor

A modal editor is just a Windows Form that is displayed when the developer clicks the ellipsis button added to the property browser. We will add a type editor to the `WebControlSize` class, which contains information about the width and height of a control. We will put it inside the `Design` namespace:

```
namespace WroxDesign.Design
{
  public class WebControlSizeEditor : UITypeEditor
  {
    public override UITypeEditorEditStyle GetEditStyle(ITypeDescriptorContext
context)
    {
      return UITypeEditorEditStyle.Modal;
    }
```

```
        public override object EditValue(ITypeDescriptorContext context,
          IServiceProvider provider, object value)
      {
        //Always return a valid value.
        object retvalue = value;

        IWindowsFormsEditorService srv = null;

        //Get the forms editor service from the provider,
        //to display the form.
        if (provider != null)
          srv = (IWindowsFormsEditorService)
        provider.GetService(typeof(IWindowsFormsEditorService));

        if (srv != null)
        {
          WebControlSizeForm form = new WebControlSizeForm();
          form.CurrentSize = (WebControlSize)value;
          if (srv.ShowDialog(form) == DialogResult.OK)
            return form.CurrentSize;
        }

        return retvalue;

      }
    }
  }
```

There is little code, but there are a couple interfaces we haven't seen yet. All interaction between the type editor and the IDE, such as displaying dialog boxes or showing a drop-down list should be done through the services provided by the environment. It would have been valid to just call the form.ShowDialog() method, but as we will need to use the service infrastructure as we move on to more advanced features, and to implement a DropDown editor, we will use it now.

The host, VS, provides a number of services, as we will see in the advanced section, later. We request services from the environment calling the GetService method on an IServiceProvider object. This is one of the objects we receive in the EditValue method. The GetService method recieves the type of service requested. We cast it to the IWindowsFormsEditorService that is responsible for managing forms interaction.

We check if the provider argument is not null, because the Visual Studio .NET documentation points out that it may be absent. We can also obtain the service from the ITypeDescriptorContext, as it is also an IServiceProvider implementer. But to keep their functions separated, we will use the provider argument.

IWindowsFormsEditorService provides the following methods:

- **ShowDialog**: recieves the Form to display in modal form. We can check the DialogResult after.

- **DropDownControl**: we will use this method in our next editor. It recieves a Windows Forms control, and drops down it in the property browser.

- **CloseDropDown**: closes a dropped-down control.

337

We have already seen the `ITypeDescriptorContext` interface and we know we can get additional information about the property being edited, the component it belongs to, and so on.

The main editing work is done in the form itself. We added a property to it, `CurrentSize`, to pass around the value to edit and the result. This way, the form can be initialized with the current value, prior to chages. We created the `retvalue` variable to always return a valid value. Just in case the developer doesn't accept the changes made in the form, we will return the original value. Otherwise, the updated `CurrentSize` property on the form will be returned. This is how the form should look:

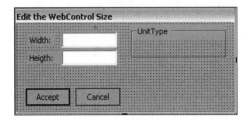

Note that we haven't hardcoded the `UnitType` enumeration. It is not a new idea, but remember: avoid hardcoding whenever possible!

The trick for loading the actual `enum` options is done in the form `Load` event handler:

```
private void WebControlSizeForm_Load(object sender, System.EventArgs e)
{
  string[] values = Enum.GetNames(typeof(UnitType));
```

This line retrieves a `string` array with all the valid values for the `Enum`. Next we just set some default values:

```
int x = 10;    //Default left margin inside the group
int y = 20;    //Default height of each option
int sel = 0;   //The index of the selected option

System.Windows.Forms.RadioButton btn;
```

Now we iterate the values, creating a new `RadioButton` for each one. Its text is set to the enum value, and its `Y` location is increased to put one option above the previous one:

```
for (int i = 0; i < values.Length; i ++)
{
  btn = new System.Windows.Forms.RadioButton();
  btn.Location = new Point(x, y * (i + 1));
  btn.Text = values[i];
```

The Unit class Type property returns a reference to the UnitType enum currently used. Its string representation, the ToString() method call, is the same as the corresponding element name retrieved with the Enum.GetNames method. We check this while we iterate the names, and when we find a match, we save the index:

```
      if (btn.Text == _size.Height.Type.ToString()) sel = i;
      grpUnit.Controls.Add(btn);
    }

  grpUnit.Height = y * values.Length + y * 2;
  this.Height = grpUnit.Height + 40;
  ((System.Windows.Forms.RadioButton)grpUnit.Controls[sel]).Checked = true;

  txtHeight.Text = _size.Height.Value.ToString();
  txtWidth.Text = _size.Width.Value.ToString();
}
```

After adding the RadioButtons to the group, setting its height and the form's, we initialize the selected option and the textboxes with the values received.

The Accept button code just iterates the controls in the group looking for the Checked one, and tries to recreate the Unit instances based on the selected values and UnitType. If it succeeds, it creates the new WebControlSize object based on them, and closes the form. The DialogResult is automatically OK for the calling code, because we have set it in the DialogResult property for the button:

```
private void btnAccept_Click(object sender, System.EventArgs e)
{
  try
  {
    System.Windows.Forms.RadioButton btn = null;
    foreach (System.Windows.Forms.RadioButton current in grpUnit.Controls)
      if (current.Checked)
      {
        btn = current;
        break;
      }

    UnitType type = (UnitType)Enum.Parse(typeof(UnitType), btn.Text);
    Unit h = new Unit(int.Parse(txtHeight.Text), type);
    Unit w = new Unit(int.Parse(txtWidth.Text), type);
    _size = new WebControlSize(h, w);
    Close();
  }
  catch
  {
    throw new ArgumentException("The values are invalid!");
  }
}

private void btnCancel_Click(object sender, System.EventArgs e)
{
  Close();
}
```

```
internal WebControlSize CurrentSize
{
  get { return _size; }
  set { _size = value; }
}
```

Now we can compile the entire project. We don't need to apply the Editor attribute to the WroxButton.ButtonSize property since it is already associated in the class definition. Now the property looks like:

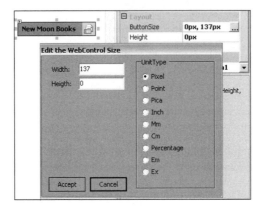

An ellipsis button has been added and now the RadioButtons have been populated. We have anchored the Accept and Cancel buttons to the left and bottom margins so they remain at the bottom of the form.

When the developer accepts this dialog, the new value is passed back to the TypeEditor, which in turn returns it to the property browser, which refreshes the value.

> **The full Windows Forms programming model can be used to create the editor UI, and the only limit is your imagination.**

This was a simple modal editor, but has shown the concept. The editor can receive more data about the object being edited, besides the current property. This information can be taken from the ITypeDescriptorContext passed to the EditValue method. We will see more of this in the Advanced section.

A DropDown Editor

A drop-down editor, by contrast, is useful for simpler tasks. Where the Modal editor can show several modal forms without loosing control, trying to do so in a drop-down editor will cause it to be closed. This is the very nature of a drop-down control. It must be the only control with the focus, all the time.

> **A DropDown editor is just a Windows Forms UserControl.**

As such, it isn't supposed to be either a **big** control taking up all the space available, or an overly complicated UI. If we need something more complicated than the Color editor, which contains three tabs and is a good reference to compare our editors to, we should go for a modal editor. Even the Windows Forms FontEditor is modal, although its UI isn't too complex to fit in a drop-down editor.

The built-in Color editor used for web color properties doesn't provide a mechanism to select custom colors, changing the alpha, red, green, and blue components. We will build a custom Color editor, which allows this, and additionally provides a way to call the built-in editor.

As we have just done for the modal editor, we will create a new class, and almost clone the code from it:

```
public class ColorTypeEditor : UITypeEditor
{
  public override UITypeEditorEditStyle GetEditStyle(ITypeDescriptorContext
context)
  {
    return UITypeEditorEditStyle.DropDown;
  }
}
```

This is the code that configures the property browser to display the drop-down arrow:

```
public override object EditValue(ITypeDescriptorContext context,
  IServiceProvider provider, object value)
{
  object retvalue = value;
  IWindowsFormsEditorService srv = null;

  //Get the forms editor service from the provider,
  //to display the form.
  if (provider != null)
    srv = (IWindowsFormsEditorService)
  provider.GetService(typeof(IWindowsFormsEditorService));

  if (srv != null)
  {
    ColorTypeEditorControl editor =
    new ColorTypeEditorControl((System.Drawing.Color)value);
    srv.DropDownControl(editor);
    return editor.SelectedColor;
  }

  return retvalue;
}
}
```

The only change is where we create the editor control, and we pass the current color to its constructor. Then, we call the IWindowsFormsEditorService.DropDownControl method that receives the control and displays it.

A drop-down control doesn't have the concept of a `DialogResult`. Whenever a change is made, it is always accepted, when it is closed. This is the control's layout:

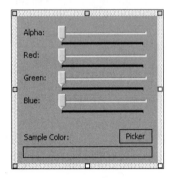

The panel at the bottom will be used to display the color, and the **Picker** button shows the default color editor. The `TrackBar` controls have a minimum value of 0 and a maximum of 255, representing the corresponding component of a color's value.

The control's code is almost trivial – important sections include the constructor:

```
//Variable keeping the current color selection. It is initialized to black.
private Color _color = Color.Black;

public ColorTypeEditorControl(Color colorToEdit)
{
    // This call is required by the Windows.Forms Form Designer.
    InitializeComponent();

    //Initialize controls.
    _color = colorToEdit;
    trkAlpha.Value = _color.A;
    trkBlue.Value = _color.B;
    trkGreen.Value = _color.G;
    trkRed.Value = _color.R;
    pnlSample.BackColor = _color;

    //Attach handlers to controls.
    trkAlpha.ValueChanged += new EventHandler(OnColorChanged);
    trkBlue.ValueChanged += new EventHandler(OnColorChanged);
    trkGreen.ValueChanged += new EventHandler(OnColorChanged);
    trkRed.ValueChanged += new EventHandler(OnColorChanged);
}
```

We are redirecting all the `ValueChanged` events to the same handler, as we have to recreate a color when any component changes:

```
private void OnColorChanged(object sender, EventArgs e)
{
    _color = Color.FromArgb(trkAlpha.Value,
        trkRed.Value, trkGreen.Value, trkBlue.Value);
    pnlSample.BackColor = _color;
}
```

```
private void btnPicker_Click(object sender, System.EventArgs e)
{
  ColorDialog dlg = new ColorDialog();
  dlg.Color = _color;
  if (dlg.ShowDialog() == DialogResult.OK) _color = dlg.Color;
}

internal Color SelectedColor
{
  get { return _color; }
}
```

In the `btnPicker_Click` event, we just initialize and display a new `ColorDialog`. Doing so causes the drop-down editor to close, but as the focus has passed to this modal dialog, it will still acomplish the property change.

We have to attach it to the `BackColor` property of our `WroxButton`. We have to override the property to apply the new attribute:

```
[Editor(typeof(ColorTypeEditor), typeof(UITypeEditor))]
public override System.Drawing.Color BackColor
{
  get { return base.BackColor; }
  set { base.BackColor = value; }
}
```

And that's it! Lets look at the design-time support added:

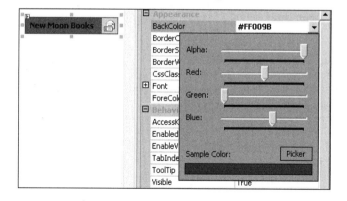

We must apply a `[ToolboxItem(false)]` attribute to the `UserControl` we have created. As it is a custom control, not doing so will make it appear in the list of components when the developer customizes the toolbox.

Custom Painting

Now we will add a couple of overrides to the drop-down editor just created, to display a visual representation of the `WroxButton.Text` property with the `BackColor` selected, instead of the number representation of the color. Add the following code to `ControlTypeEditor`:

```
public override bool GetPaintValueSupported(ITypeDescriptorContext context)
{
    return true;
}

/// <summary>
/// Paint your custom drawing in the output Graphics object recieved.
/// </summary>
public override void PaintValue(PaintValueEventArgs e)
{
    WroxButton button = e.Context.Instance as WroxButton;

    //Fills the left rectangle with a color.
    e.Graphics.FillRegion(new SolidBrush(button.BackColor), \
       new Region(e.Bounds));

    e.Graphics.DrawString("ab", new Font("Tahoma", 8,
       FontStyle.Regular |
       (button.Font.Bold ? FontStyle.Bold : FontStyle.Regular) |
       (button.Font.Italic ? FontStyle.Italic : FontStyle.Regular) |
       (button.Font.Underline ? FontStyle.Underline : FontStyle.Regular)), new
    SolidBrush(button.ForeColor), e.Bounds);
}
```

We are just filling the little box next to the property with the actual color selected, just like the built-in color editor does. This rectangle is delimited by the Bounds property of the PaintValueEventArgs argument received.

After that, we draw a string with the Tahoma font, using the style set in the button. The button instance is retrieved from the argument's Context.Instance property. Again, the e.Context property is an ITypeDescriptorContext object, so we'd better get used to it!

We are performing inline if statements where the first (boolean) expression is evaluated and then either the first or second expression is returned, depending on whether the first expression evaluated to true or false, respectively. More advanced drawing is possible, although there is such a small space that it won't be possible to put much information there.

Here's what we have achieved:

Here we see our custom painted rectangle. It shows how the text will look over the selected background color, with the selected ForeColor.

Advanced

Advanced support is provided in two areas:

❑ **Designer**: this is a special object that is responsible for interacting with the page designer to represent and persist our control in a customized way.

❑ **Environment services**: involves integrating with the services provided by the environment or host. We have already seen a simple example retrieving an `IWindowsFormEditorService` from the `IServiceProvider` instance.

Custom Designers

Again, a custom designer is a class that inherits the base `ControlDesigner` class and overrides the desired methods. We will start with a very simple designer for our `WroxButton`, and analyze available methods as we go:

```
public class WroxButtonDesigner : ControlDesigner
{
  public WroxButtonDesigner()
  {
  }

  public override string GetDesignTimeHtml()
  {
    //Get a typed reference to the button being designed.
    WroxButton wb = (WroxButton) base.Component;

    Panel pnl = new Panel();
    //Make it look just as the button control.
    pnl.CopyBaseAttributes(wb);
    pnl.Controls.Add(wb);
    //Add a dotted border and adjust the new size.
    pnl.BorderStyle = BorderStyle.Dotted;
    pnl.BorderWidth = new Unit(2, UnitType.Point);
    pnl.Height = new Unit(pnl.Height.Value + 4);
    pnl.Width  = new Unit(pnl.Width.Value + 4);
    //Return the rendered string.
    return GetRenderHtml(pnl);
  }

  /// <summary>
  /// Provides the string representation of a rendered control.
  /// </summary>
  /// <param name="control">The control to render.</param>
  /// <returns>The HTML representing the control.</returns>
  private string GetRenderHtml(Control control)
  {
    StringWriter text = new StringWriter();
    HtmlTextWriter writer = new HtmlTextWriter(text);
    control.RenderControl(writer);
    return text.ToString();
  }
}
```

We have created a private helper method to perform the rendering and return a string from a control. The RenderControl method expects an HtmlTextWriter, which we have created based on a StringWriter, which uses a StringBuilder internally and provides the TextWriter interface functionality. This is where the rendered HTML resides after calling RenderControl.

The important method here is the overriden GetDesignTimeHtml(). This method returns a representation of the object to show in the design surface. This can be different from the run-time representation of the object, and usually is. We have simply added a surrounding panel control with the same attributes as the WroxButton it is designing, and a dotted border. We increase the panel width and height taking into account the additional border, to let the button fit perfectly inside it. A reference to the designed component is obtained from the base class's Component property. The result looks like this:

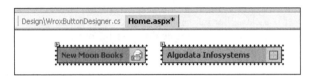

We could have completely changed the representation; it's up to us. A good example of this is the way a DataGrid displays itself in the designer, adding sample rows. We can use the rendering techique we want, including manual string contatenation of HTML code. We will now add code to change the representation when the control is first dragged onto the surface, that is, when there's nothing to display yet:

```
protected override string GetEmptyDesignTimeHtml()
{
   //Render design time warning if there's nothing to display.
   string text= "Please set the Text or ImageUrl to initialize the button.";
   return CreatePlaceHolderDesignTimeHtml(text);
}
```

This override returns a custom representation for the object when it is empty. We call the base class CreatePlaceHolderDesignTimeHtml, which creates a gray panel displaying the text we pass to it. We will add a call to GetEmptyDesignTimeHtml in the GetDesignTimeHtml, when we find an empty WroxButton:

```
public override string GetDesignTimeHtml()
{
   WroxButton wb = (WroxButton) base.Component;

   if (wb.Text == string.Empty &&
     wb.ImageUrl == string.Empty)
     return GetEmptyDesignTimeHtml();
```

When the button is dragged to the design surface, we will see:

We can also provide a customized error when the control fails to be displayed overriding the
`GetErrorDesignTimeHtml` method:

```
protected override string GetErrorDesignTimeHtml(Exception e)
{
  string text = string.Format("{0}{1}{2}{3}",
    "There was an error and the control can't be displayed:",
    "<BR>", "Exception: ", e.Message);

  return CreatePlaceHolderDesignTimeHtml(text);
}
```

In fact, it is just a helper method, and must be explicitly called if we want to use it. An unhandled
exception won't call this method, so we must carefully catch possible exceptions:

```
public override string GetDesignTimeHtml()
{
  try
  {
    WroxButton wb = (WroxButton) base.Component;

    if (wb.Text == string.Empty &&
      wb.ImageUrl == string.Empty)
      return GetEmptyDesignTimeHtml();

    Panel pnl = new Panel();
    pnl.CopyBaseAttributes(wb);
    pnl.Controls.Add(wb);
    pnl.BorderStyle = BorderStyle.Dotted;
    pnl.BorderWidth = new Unit(2, UnitType.Point);
    pnl.Height = new Unit(pnl.Height.Value + 4);
    pnl.Width  = new Unit(pnl.Width.Value + 4);
    //Simulate an exception being thrown
    throw new InvalidOperationException
      ("My custom exception test.");
    return GetRenderHtml(pnl);
  }
  catch (Exception e)
  {
    return GetErrorDesignTimeHtml(e);
  }
}
```

We have added a `try...catch` block around the design-time HTML generation to avoid unhandled exceptions. When we catch an exception, we call the overriden helper method `GetErrorDesignTimeHtml`. We have deliberately thrown an exception, to see the results:

When generating very complex design-time HTML code, we may want to force the environment to wait until we finish our job. To do so, we override the `DesignTimeHtmlRequiresLoadComplete` property and return `true` in the property `get`. We can also override the following methods to react to specific changes in the control:

❑ **OnComponentChanged**

❑ **OnSetParent**: occurs when the parent of our control changes, either when it is placed inside another control or when it is taken out of it

❑ **OnBindingsCollectionChanged**

❑ **OnControlResize**

Persistence and Interaction with the ControlBuilder

If the design-time attributtes on the properties aren't enough for our source representation purposes, we can generate or own sourcecode representation of component properties. However, generating custom sourcecode also requires better interaction with a `ControlBuilder`, which will be responsible for parsing this code and rebuilding the control from that. We will need a more complex example to show this interaction, so we are going to build a `WroxToolBar` that will contain several `WroxButtons`.

> When we provide custom parsing and persistence of child controls, we have to use the **ParseChildren** and **PersistChildren** attributes to disable the default behavior, which sets both to **true**.

Our toolbar will contain the font, color, and other formatting elements. So we will only need to persist the button's `Text`, `ImageUrl`, and `ID` attributtes, as the other attributtes will be "inherited" (in HTML/CSS context, that is, when it is rendered) from the toolbar's format. We will only see the relevant code:

```
[Designer(typeof(WroxToolBarDesigner))]
[ControlBuilder(typeof(WroxToolBarControlBuilder))]
[ParseChildren(false)]
[PersistChildren(false)]
public class WroxToolBar : WebControl, INamingContainer
{
    private ArrayList _buttons = new ArrayList();
```

The toolbar implements `INamingContainer` to avoid naming conflicts between controls. We keep references to the buttons in the _buttons `ArrayList`.

```
protected override void CreateChildControls()
{
  base.Controls.Clear();
  //Height depends on the content.
  base.Height = 0;

  foreach (WroxButton btn in _buttons)
  {
    base.Controls.Add(btn);
  }
}
```

The toolbar just adds the buttons to its collection of `Controls`:

```
protected override void Render(HtmlTextWriter output)
{
  EnsureChildControls();
  base.Render(output);
}

[Browsable(false)]
[DesignerSerializationVisibility(
  DesignerSerializationVisibility.Hidden)]
public ArrayList Buttons
{
  get { return _buttons; }
  set
  {
    _buttons = value;
    ChildControlsCreated = false;
  }
}
}
```

The serialization visibility must be set to avoid the default type converter for the `ArrayList` to persist a string representation of it, which will be "`(Collection)`". This is the default behavior, and our control will fail to be parsed if it finds that value, as an `ArrayList` can't be rebuilt from it. We also reset the `ChildControlsCreated` property to force a new rendering:

```
protected override void AddParsedSubObject(Object obj)
{
  if (obj is WroxButton)
  {
    _buttons.Add(obj as WroxButton);
    ChildControlsCreated = false;
  }
}
```

This method is very important. It is called whenever an inner object has been succesfully parsed by the associated `ControlBuilder` (or the default builder if we don't use a custom one). We only allow `WroxButtons` to be added to our control.

Here we see a configured toolbar and an empty one, at design time:

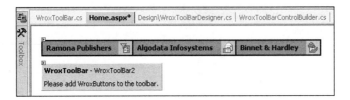

Now the `ControlBuilder`:

```
public class WroxToolBarControlBuilder : ControlBuilder
{
  public WroxToolBarControlBuilder()
  {
  }

  public override Type GetChildControlType(
    String tagName, IDictionary attributes)
  {
    if (String.Compare(tagName, "button", true) == 0)
      return typeof(WroxButton);
    return null;
  }

  public override bool HasBody()
  {
    return true;
  }
}
```

As we have already seen in the chapter about `ControlBuilders` (Chapter 7), the `GetChildControlType` determines what child controls to parse. The type returned from this method is filled with properties by the page parsing and is passed down to the toolbar `AddParsedSubObject`. We expect a "button" tag name. We don't need to append the registered prefix for our assembly ("`wx:`"), because we are manually parsing and generating the persisted code. The `tagName` we check for can be anything we want, as our own designer is generating it:

```
public class WroxToolBarDesigner : ControlDesigner
{
  public override string GetPersistInnerHtml()
  {
    StringWriter text = new StringWriter();
    HtmlTextWriter writer = new HtmlTextWriter(text);

    WroxToolBar tbr = Component as WroxToolBar;
```

```
      writer.WriteFullBeginTag("buttons");
      foreach (WroxButton btn in tbr.Buttons)
      {
        //We won't persist other attributes, which will be copied
        //from the toolbar settings.
        writer.WriteBeginTag("button");
        writer.WriteAttribute("ID", btn.ID);
        writer.WriteAttribute("Text", btn.Text);
        writer.WriteAttribute("ImageUrl", btn.ImageUrl);
        writer.Write(" />");
      }
      writer.WriteEndTag("buttons");


      return text.ToString();
    }
```

It is important to see how flexible this custom persistence is. We can generate anything we want, and using the `HtmlTextWriter` makes it extremely easy to create the hierarchy we need.
Note that we are only persisting as attributes of the <button> tag the ID, Text, and ImageUrl attributes of inner `WroxButtons`. We also show how to enclose elements in custom tags (<buttons>). This tag is ignored by the `ControlBuilder` in the `GetChildControlType` method.

```
    public override string GetDesignTimeHtml()
    {
      try
      {
        WroxToolBar wb = (WroxToolBar) base.Component;
        if (wb.Buttons.Count == 0)
          return GetEmptyDesignTimeHtml();

        //Returns just the same runtime layout.
        return base.GetDesignTimeHtml();
      }
      catch (Exception e)
      {
        return GetErrorDesignTimeHtml(e);
      }
    }
```

We are not changing the design-time representation of the toolbar, but we trap any possible errors here and display the placeholder if there's nothing to display. The other methods, `GetEmptyDesignTimeHtml` and `GetErrorDesignTimeHtml` are exactly the same as the `WroxButtonDesigner`'s.

Now we have a complete interaction between the elements of our control:

❑ The `Designer` traverses the collection and generates the custom persistence code.

❑ The `ControlBuilder` watches the tags, ignoring everything except the <button> tags, for which it returns the correct `WroxButton` type. The page parser fills any properties found and passes this object to the `WroxToolBar.AddParsedSubObject` method.

❑ Finally, with the whole object built, the `Designer` returns its design-time representation, and has full access to it in its inherited `Component` property.

351

This process can be recursive, if the control `Type` we return has a `ControlBuilder` associated itself. We still don't have an easy way of adding and removing buttons, but to take a look and test the control, we can directly write some sourcecode like this:

```
<wx:wroxtoolbar id="WroxToolBar1" style="Z-INDEX: 104; LEFT: 17px;
   POSITION: absolute; TOP: 22px"
   runat="server" Width="462px" Height="2px" ForeColor="#000000"
   Font-Bold="True" Font-Names="Tahoma" Font-Size="8pt"
   BackColor="#9999FF" BorderWidth="1pt"
   BorderColor="Black" BorderStyle="Double">
   <buttons>
     <button ID="btnWrox1" Text="Ramona Publishers"
ImageUrl="Images/FilterFormLo.gif" />
     <button ID="btnWrox2" Text="Algodata Infosystems"
        ImageUrl="Images/MailLo.gif" />
     <button ID="btnWrox3" Text="Binnet & Hardley"
        ImageUrl="Images/OpenWebLo.gif" />
   </buttons>
</wx:wroxtoolbar>
```

The result, as we saw earlier, looks like this:

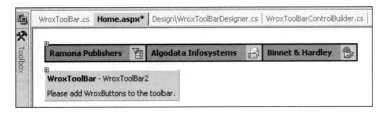

Providing Shortcuts to Common Operations: DesignerVerbs

Designer verbs are shown by the IDE as items in the pop-up menu displayed for our control, and as links in a small panel added on top of the description panel at the bottom of the property browser:

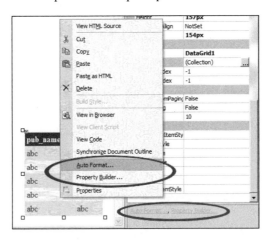

Here we see the **Auto Format** and **Property Builder** "verbs" added to the IDE when we right-click a `DataGrid`. A verb is a delegate, which is called when the corresponding item is clicked. The designer associated with a control is given a chance to add these verbs to the IDE when its `Verbs` property is retrieved. We have to override this property to provide our handlers. Each verb is an object of type `DesignerVerb`, which takes a string description and a `System.EventHandler` delegate, pointing to the method to be called when the verb is selected.

Let us add the following code to the `WroxToolBarDesigner` class:

```
public override DesignerVerbCollection Verbs
{
  get
  {
    DesignerVerb[] verbs = new DesignerVerb[]
      { new DesignerVerb("Wrox Format...", new System.EventHandler(OnWroxFormat))
};
    return new DesignerVerbCollection(verbs);
  }
}
```

We must return an array of `DesignerVerb` objects, so we construct the array in the same line. The `EventHandler` delegate points to the following method:

```
public void OnWroxFormat(object sender, EventArgs e)
{
  WroxToolBar wb = Component as WroxToolBar;

  //Apply a formatting style.
  wb.BackColor = Color.LightSkyBlue;
  wb.BorderColor = Color.Black;
  wb.Font.Name = "Tahoma";
  wb.Font.Size = new FontUnit("8pt");
  wb.ForeColor = Color.White;
  wb.BorderStyle = BorderStyle.Solid;
  wb.BorderWidth = new Unit(1, UnitType.Point);
  //Notify the environment we have changed the component.
  RaiseComponentChanged(null, null, null);
  UpdateDesignTimeHtml();
}
```

In this method we set some formatting options. We just access the `Component` property and modify it accordingly. However, all these changes being made directly on the object will not be reflected in the persisted code or the property browser until we call `RaiseComponentChanged`. We can try commenting that line and we will see how the design-time representation reflects the new format, but the property browser and the persisted code in the page don't change.

`RaiseComponentChanged` recieves a `MemberDescriptor` object containing the changed member. This will typically be a `PropertyDescriptor`, which is a descendent of it, but in our case we just pass `null`, telling the designer that it isn't important what specific property has changed. We will see more about this parameter and the notification mechanism in a moment. The other two parameters specify the old and new value. We pass `null` as we are updating multiple properties.

Here's what we have achieved:

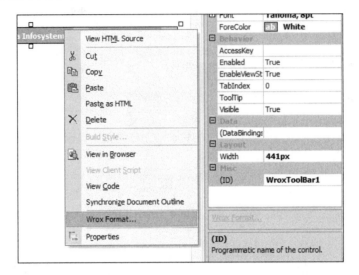

Now we can add a UI for adding buttons to the toolbar:

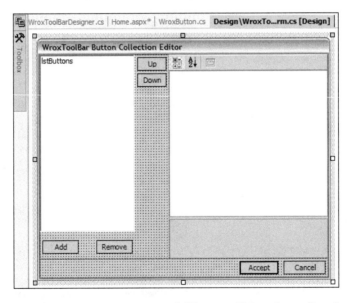

The key component is the PropertyGrid control. We can add it to the toolbox by customizing it and locating the control in the list. It provides the same control we see in the property browser. The new functionality available in the ListBox allows the code for this form to be trivial:

```
private ArrayList _buttons;

public WroxToolBarButtonsForm(ArrayList Buttons)
{
  InitializeComponent();
  _buttons = Buttons;
}
```

The current buttons in the toolbar will be passed to the constructor:

```
private void WroxToolBarButtons_Load(object sender, System.EventArgs e)
{
  foreach (object obj in _buttons)
        lstButtons.Items.Add(obj);
}
```

When the form loads, we just add the buttons in the list directly to the Items property of the ListBox:

```
private void lstButtons_SelectedIndexChanged(
  object sender, System.EventArgs e)
{
  propGrid.SelectedObject = lstButtons.SelectedItem;
}
```

When we assign the SelectedObject property, it shows all the object properties and allows direct editing:

```
private void btnAdd_Click(object sender, System.EventArgs e)
{
  int i = lstButtons.Items.Add(new WroxButton());
  lstButtons.SelectedIndex = i;
}

private void btnRemove_Click(object sender, System.EventArgs e)
{
  lstButtons.Items.Remove(lstButtons.SelectedItem);
  propGrid.SelectedObject = null;
}

private void btnUp_Click(object sender, System.EventArgs e)
{
  object selected = lstButtons.SelectedItem;
  int idx = lstButtons.SelectedIndex;
  if (selected != null)
  {
    lstButtons.Items.Remove(selected);
    lstButtons.Items.Insert(idx - 1, selected);
  }
}
```

```
private void btnDown_Click(object sender, System.EventArgs e)
{
  object selected = lstButtons.SelectedItem;
  int idx = lstButtons.SelectedIndex;
  if (selected != null)
  {
    lstButtons.Items.Remove(selected);
    lstButtons.Items.Insert(idx, selected);
  }
}
```

Up and **Down** methods remove the element from the list and insert it in the new position. Finally, we return a new `ArrayList` based on the items in the list.

```
public ArrayList Buttons
{
  get { return new ArrayList(lstButtons.Items); }
}
```

To associate a new verb to edit the buttons we just add the following code to the toolbar designer:

```
public void OnEditButtons(object sender, EventArgs e)
{
  WroxToolBar wb = Component as WroxToolBar;
  WroxToolBarButtonsForm form = new WroxToolBarButtonsForm(wb.Buttons);

  if (form.ShowDialog() == System.Windows.Forms.DialogResult.OK)
  {
    wb.Buttons = form.Buttons;
    RaiseComponentChanged(null, null, null);
    UpdateDesignTimeHtml();
  }
}
```

This method will display the form, and change the `Buttons` property of the toolbar accordingly. Let us change the `Verbs` property too:

```
public override DesignerVerbCollection Verbs
{
  get
  {
    DesignerVerb[] verbs = new DesignerVerb[] {
      new DesignerVerb("Wrox Format...", new System.EventHandler(OnWroxFormat)),
      new DesignerVerb("Edit Buttons...", new
System.EventHandler(OnEditButtons))};
    return new DesignerVerbCollection(verbs);
  }
}
```

We have added a new verb to the array, and this is the result:

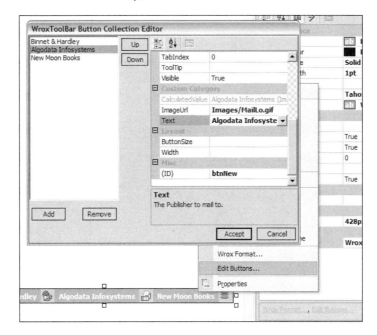

This is a collage actually, because we won't be able so see at the same time the popup menu (which is displaying our new designer verbs) and the modal form. It's just to save space... when we accept the dialog, the buttons are displayed in the toolbar.

Advanced Interaction with the Property Browser

When we saw the `TypeConverter` class, we saw that one of its features was to provide **subproperties**. To understand this functionality, it is neccesary to take a closer look at the property browser. When an object is selected (that is, assigned as the selected object of the property grid, as we just saw), the property browser asks the `TypeConverter` for a collection of `PropertyDescriptor` objects, which are a complete description of a property and provide methods for retrieving and setting the property value (see the section on Custom `TypeContervers`, where we analyzed the `ITypeDescriptorContext` interface, which contains a `PropertyDescriptor` property)

If we don't override the default behavior on a custom converter, a property descriptor for each property will be returned, and displayed in the property browser. We can change this behavior, by overriding a couple methods in a custom type converter.

The previous sample is a good place to start. The `WroxToolBarButtonsForm` displays the selected button properties in the property grid. It is **very** important to realize that this control is just **the same** control that makes the property browser. So every change we make to the way properties are displayed will affect both the custom form and the property browser. When a `WroxButton` is selected in the editor form, all the properties are displayed. This should not be the case, as inside our toolbar, we only care about the `ID`, `Text`, and `ImageUrl` properties. All the others are useless as they are inherited from the parent control, and aren't even persisted with our designer. What we need is to filter the properties.

Filtering properties, or providing custom ones, involves overriding the `GetPropertiesSupported` and `GetProperties` methods. As we can see, the methods follow the same design pattern as the `GetStandardValuesSupported` and `GetStandardValues` methods we saw, and they behave the same way. The first method is queried to check the support, and the second method is called if the result was `true`:

```
public class WroxButtonConverter : TypeConverter
{
  public WroxButtonConverter()
  {
  }
  public virtual bool GetPropertiesSupported(
    ITypeDescriptorContext context)
  {
    return true;
  }
  public virtual PropertyDescriptorCollection GetProperties(
    ITypeDescriptorContext context, object value,
    Attribute[] attributes)
  {
  }
}
```

The `GetProperties` parameters are:

- **ITypeDescriptorContext context**: this object is the same we have already seen.

- **object value**: this is the current object being converted. This is the same as the `context.Instance` property.

- **Attribute[] attributes**: the attributes the client (the property browser) wants the properties filtered by. When the request comes from the property browser, this parameter will contain the `BrowsableAttribute` with a value of `true`, to retrieve only browsable properties.

To see how this works, let us rewrite the default behavior. Attach the type converter to the `WroxButton` control adding the attribute `[TypeConverter(typeof(WroxButtonConverter))]` to it, and write this code in the converter `GetProperties` method:

```
return TypeDescriptor.GetProperties(context.Instance,
  new Attribute[] { new BrowsableAttribute(true) });
```

That's exactly what the default converter does. We use the `TypeDescriptor`, which is the main class to work with the descriptors. It provides static methods to get a component's associated `TypeConverter`, `TypeEditor`, `EventDescriptors` and `PropertyDescriptors`.

Two methods, `TypeDescriptor.GetDefaultEvent` and `TypeDescriptor.GetDefaultProperty` are used by the property browser to automatically select the default member we set though the corresponding `Default*` attribute (see the *Basic* section, earlier in the chapter).

We use the `GetProperties` method of this class, which has a number of overloads, receiving an object, a type, and optionally an array of attributes to use as filter. For example, let's return just the properties that have our `ColorTypeEditor` attached:

```
//Only Color properties with our editor!!
return TypeDescriptor.GetProperties(context.Instance,
   new Attribute[] { new EditorAttribute(typeof(ColorTypeEditor),
typeof(UITypeEditor)) });
```

At design time, when we select a `WroxButton` control, we now see the following properties:

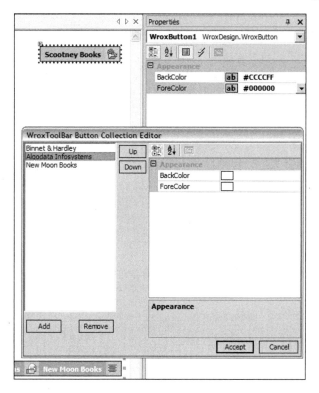

Here we see the property browser in the background showing the properties of the selected `WroxButton`. At the same time, we selected the **Edit Button...** verb on the toolbar to display the editor. We can see how the change affected both! Of course it makes no sense to hide all the properties of a `WroxButton` just because inside a toolbar they can't be used. So we will use a custom attribute to mark properties to be displayed in the editor:

```
public class ToolBarEditableAttribute : Attribute
{
  public ToolBarEditableAttribute()
  {
  }
}
```

We don't need any code in it, as it is just a marker. Now we can add the attribute to the ID, Text, and ImageUrl properties of the control:

```
[ToolBarEditable()]
public override string ID
{
  get { return base.ID; }
  set { base.ID = value; }
}
```

We have overriden the ID property to apply the attribute. Now the actual work is performed in the GetProperties method in the WroxButtonConverter class:

```
public override PropertyDescriptorCollection GetProperties(
  ITypeDescriptorContext context, object value,
  Attribute[] attributes)
{
  //If we are outside the host designer, we are in a custom editor
  if (context.Container == null)
        return TypeDescriptor.GetProperties(context.Instance,
    new Attribute[] { new ToolBarEditableAttribute() });

  //Otherwise, return the solicited members
  return TypeDescriptor.GetProperties(context.Instance, attributes);
}
```

We check the context argument, which will contain a reference to the host designer only if we are outside our custom buttons editor form. If we are not inside a custom editor, we return all the properties matching the attributes solicited, just as the default converter would do. What we achieved is different property "views" depending on the presence of the container. We can provide more advanced filtering reacting to different containers.

TypeDescriptor and the PropertyDescriptor are useful in other areas too. When we set property values through the PropertyDescriptor.SetValue method the environment is automatically notified of the change. Notifying the environment is very important, as it triggers not only the update of the design-time representation of the controls, but also the persistence mechanism.
As an example, we will change the code in the color editor we built, and change directly the component's BackColor:

```
private IComponent _component;
public ColorTypeEditorControl(Color colorToEdit, WebControl component)
```

We need the component reference in the constructor, to change it later in the OnColorChanged method, called every time the value is changed (either the alpha, red, green, or blue values). We have to change the EditValue method in the ColorTypeEditor to reflect this change in the constructor. We will pass the context Instance to it:

```
private void OnColorChanged(object sender, EventArgs e)
{
  _color = Color.FromArgb(trkAlpha.Value,
    trkRed.Value, trkGreen.Value, trkBlue.Value);
  pnlSample.BackColor = _color;
  _component.BackColor = _color;
}
```

After doing this, we will see that the button isn't refreshed. Further, after leaving the editor, we see the new value painted next to the property value, but the button remains with the old color! This has happened because we have lost sync between the object instances and the persisted value. To remain in sync, we can use the `PropertyDescriptor` for the property and set the value though it. Change the previous code to:

```
private void OnColorChanged(object sender, EventArgs e)
{
  _color = Color.FromArgb(trkAlpha.Value,
    trkRed.Value, trkGreen.Value, trkBlue.Value);
  pnlSample.BackColor = _color;
  //_component.BackColor = _color;
  PropertyDescriptorCollection col =
    TypeDescriptor.GetProperties(_component);
  col["BackColor"].SetValue(_component, _color);
}
```

We first retrieve the collection of properties for the object. Then we access the property by name and use the `SetValue` method to change it. Of course we could rewrite the two lines to fit into just one statement:

```
TypeDescriptor.GetProperties(_component)["BackColor"].SetValue(_component,
_color);
```

The effect is that the button reflects the change inmediately, and the value is persisted to the page code too:

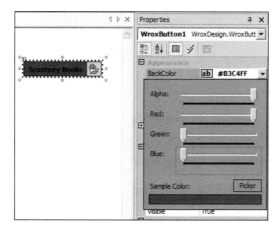

Note that the custom painted rectangle next to the property value isn't updated. That is because we haven't formally finished editing the value. When we leave the editor it will be redrawn.

Now that we know how to use `TypeDescriptor`, let's change the **Picker** button's code to use a great color editor! (I wonder why this is not used to change a web control's color?):

```
private void btnPicker_Click(object sender, System.EventArgs e)
{
  TypeConverter tc = TypeDescriptor.GetConverter(_color);
  string res = System.Web.UI.Design.ColorBuilder.BuildColor(
    _component, this, string.Empty);

  if (res != string.Empty && res != null)
    _color = (Color)tc.ConvertFromString(res);
}
```

We first retrieve the type converter for the `Color` object. Then we use the `ControlBuilder` class, which recieves the component being edited, the owner control, and an initial value, and returns a `string` with the selected color. If we have a valid value, we use the converter to transform the string back into the color instance. This is the dialog shown:

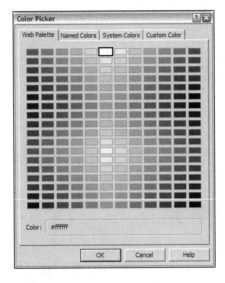

This MEGA color picker has everything! The Custom Color tab sheet even provides what our `ColorTypeEditor` does, bar update the control instantly.

Using Services from the Hosting Environment

The IDE provides services to components at design time. The key method to retrieve services is `GetService`:

```
object GetService(Type serviceType)
```

This method is implemented in the `ITypeDescriptorContext` interface, which is passed to various methods we have seen, and the `ComponentDesigner` class, which is the base class for all our designers. Working with a service involves passing the type of service needed, casting the result to the service, and using methods and properties on this object. We have already seen how to use the `IWindowsFormsEditorService`.

IComponentChangeService

This service allows a component to subscribe to changes in other components, or to fire its own events to the host. It allows us to add and remove event handlers for the `ComponentAdded`, `ComponentAdding`, `ComponentChanged`, `ComponentChanging`, `ComponentRemoved`, `ComponentRemoving`, and `ComponentRename` events. Event functionality is self-explanatory and is fired for every component in the designer. Each of them recieves an event argument that we can use to check additional data about the event:

❑   `ComponentAdded`, `ComponentAdding`, `ComponentRemoved`, `ComponentRemoving`: `ComponentEventArgs`

The argument class has a `Component` property to use. It references the object affected.

❑   `ComponentChanging`: `ComponentChangingEventArgs`

The argument has a `Component` property and a `Member` property, which is the `MemberDescriptor` (usually a `PropertyDescriptor`, if the change is on a property) describing the element being changed. This is called before the change takes place.

❑   `ComponentChanged`: `ComponentChangedEventArgs`

We also have a `Component` and a `Member` property. We also receive `NewValue` and `OldValue` as objects, representing the change.

❑   `ComponentRename`: `ComponentRenameEventArgs`

Recieves `Component`, `NewName`, and `OldName`.

This service also provides two methods to raise `ComponentChanged` and `ComponentChanging`: `OnComponentChanged` and `OnComponentChanging`. They receive the same arguments that are thereafter propagated though the event as properties of the `EventArgs` class. We already know how to get a `PropertyDescriptor` for a property in an object using the `TypeDescriptor` class.

As an example, we will create a `Validator`-like control that has a reference to another control on the form. But unlike the validators built upon the `BaseValidator` class (`RequiredFieldValidator`, `RangeValidator`, and so on.), we are going to be smarter: they don't synchronize changes in the `ID` property of the referenced control to validate, and so they may throw a run-time exception in that case. We won't loose that change, and will use the `IComponentChangeService` to achieve it.

Let us create a very simple control, which will only display the related control's `ID` property:

```
public class WroxStyler : WebControl
{
    //Give it a default value.
    private string _related = "Wrox Styler";

    public WroxStyler()
    {
    }

    [Category("Wrox")]
    [TypeConverter(typeof(WroxButtonConverter))]
    public string RelatedButtonID
    {
```

```
      get { return _related; }
      set { _related = value; }
  }

  protected override void Render(HtmlTextWriter output)
  {
    base.Controls.Clear();
    Label lbl = new Label();
    lbl.Text = _related;
    base.Controls.Add(lbl);
        base.Render(output);
  }
}
```

The notification work is performed in the type converter:

```
public class WroxStylerConverter : TypeConverter
{
  //Hold references to WroxStyler instances.
  private ArrayList _stylers = new ArrayList();

  public WroxStylerConverter()
  {
  }

  public override bool GetStandardValuesSupported(
    ITypeDescriptorContext context)
  {
    if (!_stylers.Contains(context.Instance))
      _stylers.Add(context.Instance);
    return true;
  }
```

As we already know, the converter instance will be shared among all the instances of WroxStyler in the page. So we will need to keep all their references for later use. We are sure that GetStandardValuesSupported will always be queried by the current instance of WroxStyler, so we take advantage of that and check if we have already added it to our list:

```
public override bool GetStandardValuesExclusive(
  ITypeDescriptorContext context)
{
  return true;
}
```

We will only allow the selection via the list to avoid typing mistakes. Now we build an array containing all the WroxButtons IDs found on the page, to display the list to select values from:

```
public override StandardValuesCollection GetStandardValues(
  ITypeDescriptorContext context)
{
  System.Collections.ArrayList list =
    new System.Collections.ArrayList();
```

```
   foreach (IComponent comp in context.Container.Components)
   {
     if (comp is WroxButton) list.Add(((WroxButton)comp).ID);
   }

   IComponentChangeService svc = context.GetService(
     typeof(IComponentChangeService)) as IComponentChangeService;

   svc.ComponentRename +=
     new ComponentRenameEventHandler(OnRename);
   svc.ComponentRemoved +=
     new ComponentEventHandler(OnRemove);
   return new StandardValuesCollection(list);
}
```

We retrieved the service and attached our handlers to it before returning the list of buttons:

```
private void OnRemove(object sender, ComponentEventArgs e)
{
   if (_stylers.Contains(e.Component))
     _stylers.Remove(e.Component);
}
```

We must remove the component from our list when it is deleted from the design surface. This will be called because we used the service provided by the host:

```
private void OnRename(object sender, ComponentRenameEventArgs e)
{
   if (e.Component is WroxButton)
     foreach (WroxStyler st in _stylers)
       if (e.OldName == st.RelatedButtonID)
         TypeDescriptor.GetProperties(st)
           ["RelatedButtonID"].SetValue(st, e.NewName);
   }
}
```

We first check the type of component being renamed. This is important because this method will be called for all components being renamed. Then we traverse our list of stylers and check whether they are pointing to the renamed component. Then, we use the `PropertyDescriptor` of the property to change the value. Again, if we try to change the property directly, the control will not be properly updated. This is what we've created:

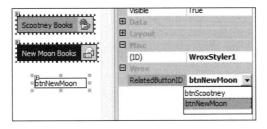

Now the `RelatedButtonID` property will be updated automatically whenever the "source" control's ID is changed. We can easily inherit the validator controls and add this functionality.

IReferenceService

This service allows us to regain a reference to an object from its name. It is useful when we have related controls on the page and want to access them having only their ID.

We just have to pass the control name to the `GetReference` method, and we will get the object, if it is found.

For example, we can copy the related button's format for the `WroxStyler` we created. To do so we will associate a designer, which will retrieve the properties from the referenced `WroxButton`. We will only change the design-time representation. The format will not be persisted in this example:

```
public class WroxStylerDesigner : ControlDesigner
{
  public WroxStylerDesigner()
  {
  }

  public override string GetDesignTimeHtml()
  {
    WroxStyler st = (WroxStyler) base.Component;

    if (st.RelatedButtonID != string.Empty)
    {
      IReferenceService svc =
        GetService(typeof(IReferenceService)) as IReferenceService;
      WroxButton button =
        svc.GetReference(st.RelatedButtonID) as WroxButton;
      //Was the button found?
      if (button != null)
      {
        st.CopyBaseAttributes(button);
        st.Font.CopyFrom(button.Font);
        st.BackColor = button.BackColor;
        st.BorderColor = button.BorderColor;
        st.BorderStyle = button.BorderStyle;
        st.BorderWidth = button.BorderWidth;
        st.ForeColor = button.ForeColor;
      }
    }
    return base.GetDesignTimeHtml();
  }
}
```

We can easily imagine a more useful scenario inverting the responsibilities of these two objects. We can make `WroxStyler` contain all the formatting for `WroxButtons`. Those buttons could be associated with the styler and get the formatting automatically. Of course the styler would be hidden at run time, setting its `Visible` property to `false`.

> There seems to be a bug in the `FontInfo.CopyFrom(FontInfo)` method we used to transfer font attributes from one control to another. The documentation says that this method overrides all the settings in the destination control, but actually the copying only occurs for values that are changed from the default values. For example, if we have a control **A** with `Font.Bold=true` (changed from the default value `false`), and we copy the font from another control **B** with the default value for this property, the attribute will not be changed. So we will have all the font properties from the **B** plus all our previous values in the object **A** that were not changed from the default values in the **B** object. (That was difficult to explain!)

IDictionaryService

When working with design-time elements, usually we will need to persist some values, such as loaded lists, flags, and so on, that should be shared among the controls on the page, even if they are not of the same type (in which case we can easily use class-level variables in objects which are shared, as we did in the `WroxStylerConverter` to hold a list of those controls).

This service provides a mechanism to save and retrieve values from a store that lasts for the whole life of the page designer. It is accessible from designer classes only, not from type converters, and provides:

- ❑ `GetKey`: given an object, returns the key associated with it
- ❑ `GetValue`: returns the object with the required key
- ❑ `SetValue`: saves an object to the service

ISelectionService

If we want to allow changes for multiple controls simultaneously, we can use this service to retrieve the selected objects. It also provides methods to change the current selected objects, and so on. Let's see the available features:

Properties:

- ❑ `PrimarySelection`: when multiple objects are selected, one of them is the primary selected object. Use this property to retrieve it.
- ❑ `SelectionCount`: the count of selected objects.

Methods:

- ❑ `GetComponentSelected`: indicates whether the object we pass is currently selected
- ❑ `GetSelectedComponents`: and `ICollection` with the selected objects
- ❑ `SetSelectedComponents`: changes the selected objects

Events:

- ❑ `SelectionChanged`: receives notification every time the selection changes
- ❑ `SelectionChanging`: occurs before the selection changes

Events should be used sparingly, because they can cause a large performance impact during design time.

IDesignerHost

This service provides access to the hosting designer. Although this is primarily used by the Windows Forms designer, there are some features we can use in an ASP.NET scenario:

❑ Loading: this property tells us if the designer is currently loading. This typically is true while the designer is querying the various controls on the form to render on the design surface. While this is happening, we won't have access to the control's Site property, which won't be set yet.

❑ Container.Components: provides access to all the components on the page.

❑ GetDesigner: if we provide an object to the method, it will return the designer associated with it. We can manipulate another control's designer using this method.

❑ GetService: this interface implements the IServiceProvider interface, so we can get other services from this method too.

❑ **Transaction-related methods**: inside the designer, transactions are units of actions that enable undo/redo functionality. These services are primarily focused on Windows Forms, where the code being generated is intimately related with these operations. In ASP.NET controls, there is no code generator, and the designer is responsible for the persistence mechanism. Although the documentation doesn't say anything about it, and it should be possible to undo multiple operations performed on a custom control (say the "Wrox Format..." action we created for the toolbar control) using these "transactions", this currently doesn't work as expected.

❑ **Service authoring-related**: we can provide our own custom services inside the IDE. This interface provides methods to add and remove them from the host designer.

Deployment Options

We can use the alternative attributes constructors that take strings instead of Type objects. This applies to almost every design-time attribute. This allows the object to compile and run even if the "Design" assemblies are not present in the machine. This is very important when downsizing distributable run-time assemblies, and additionaly makes it possible to have different licensing schemas depending on the amount of design time support desired.

Debugging the Control Designers

To fully debug the classes we write, we have to go to the Class Library project properties, select Configuration Properties | Debugging, and point the startup application to the VS .NET IDE executable, typically:

```
C:\Program Files\Microsoft Visual Studio.NET\Common7\IDE\devenv.exe
```

Now we can run the project, and a new Visual Studio .NET instance will launch. We open the same solution we are working on, and now all the design-time functionality can be fully debugged.

Summary

Providing good design-time support is fundamental to the success of our custom control. It allows for greater developer productivity, and makes handling complex tasks a breeze.

We have seen how to use design-time attributes to provide a **basic** level of support, and how to go beyond that to Intermediate and Advanced levels.

In the **intermediate** level we saw how a control is associated with a `TypeConverter` to provide various services to the controls, such as conversions, standard values, and subproperties. We also learned how to build a custom `TypeEditor`, which allows the user to set properties in a friendly UI, integrated in the property browser.

The **advanced** level involved creating a custom `Designer`, and we saw how intimately related it is to the `ControlBuilder` class. We also added common tasks to the pop-up menu of our control by using `DesignerVerbs`, a very straightforward way to route IDE requests, to our designer class.

Now that the interaction with the design time environment is exposed in Visual Srudio .NET, we can provide a high level of integration with the IDE. We learned how the `PropertyDescriptor` interacts with the property browser and how to filter the list of properties.

Every component in the design surface has a chance to use services provided by the host. The `IDesignerHost` interface provides the `GetService` method to get objects that can do work on our behalf. We used the `IWindowsFormsEditorService` to display modal forms and to drop down a control inside the property browser. `IComponentChangeService` allowed us to notify changes on our controls and to receive notifications of modifications in the other components in the design surface and we have taken a look at the `ISelectionService` interface.

Most of the functionality we learned thorough the chapter isn't only related to ASP.NET Server Controls, and applies equally to Windows Forms User Controls, except for the the parsing and HTML code generation. The service infrastructure is primarily provided by the `System.ComponentModel` namespace, which is used on both platforms.

As we hope you can now appreciate, all these features make Visual Studio .NET a great environment to develop components for, with great design-time support.

Professional ASP .NET Server Controls

10

Deploying and Licensing Server Controls

In all of the previous chapters in this book we've concentrated on creating functional Server Controls that meet a specific requirement. Once you've got to the stage where you've created a fully functional server control that you can feel proud of, you will need to consider deploying and licensing your control. Compared to "classic" ASP, packaging and deployment of your server controls is quite simple. With support for "XCOPY" deployment, you can literally drop your control onto a machine and it will work, instead of having to learn to master the infamous Registry.

In this section, we will review the various scenarios for deployment and consider protecting our intellectual investment by making use of the licensing features that the .NET Framework provides for us.

Deploying Server Controls

Once you've developed and compiled your Server Control, the result is a `.dll` file saved in the `/bin` directory of the web application that you're working on. This `.dll` can then be distributed so that others may make use of your control. Let's take a look at how we can do this.

The easiest and simplest way to deploy an assembly is to use XCOPY deployment (or drag-and-drop as it's known these days). Simply take the assembly that contains your control, and copy it into the `\bin` directory in the application root of the application that requires your control. All that the user then needs to do to use your control is reference your assembly in their ASPX file or `web.config` file. The following pseudo-code shows this in action – though this is something that should be familiar by this stage:

```
<%@ Register TagPrefix="Wrox" NameSpace="WroxCode" Assembly="WroxCode" %>
...
<Wrox:TestControl id="MyFirstControl" TestAttribute="Hello" runat="Server"/>
```

This method of deployment, known as private deployment, is the recommended standard for most situations. However, there are sometimes situations where you may wish to deploy just one copy of your control, rather than five in separate application directories. For example, a corporate intranet with various different applications hosted on one web server in different application directories, but all of which rely on one control. In this situation, we could consider a different method of deployment.

Working with the Global Assembly Cache

The alternative to having to deploy a copy of our control into the \bin directory of every web application on your web server is to place a copy of our control in the **Global Assembly Cache** (GAC). The GAC is a central repository for system-wide controls and components that can be accessed by any application on a particular machine. If we were to make an alteration to our server control and wish to deploy it, copying the new version of the control into each \bin directory would be a time-consuming process. Instead, we could deploy it into the Global Assembly Cache. There's a bit more to it compared to XCOPY deployment, so let's take a closer look.

Firstly, here's what the GAC offers us as developers:

❑ A common location for all of our custom controls and assemblies.

❑ Side-by-side versioning – a bonus feature of the .NET Framework is that it allows us to have multiple versions of any assembly running side by side, which is useful for situations when you create a new version of a control with different functionality designed for new applications, but still have applications relying on the older version of the control.

❑ Increased file security due to the location of the GAC (within the \WINNT directory). Access to this folder is strictly controlled by an Access Control List, and the default permission is to deny anyone with less than Administrative privileges from being able to alter any of the contents of this directory, thereby giving our controls an extra layer of protection from the errant user.

❑ Additional location that the CLR can search to ascertain if the assembly requested resides on the machine.

Note that once you've installed an assembly into the GAC that you cannot XCOPY the application directory to reproduce or install your application onto a separate system without also moving the assembly that's in the GAC.

Before installing an assembly in the GAC, we must first assign a **Strong Name** to our assembly.

It's worth clarifying the terminology we're using here for a moment – an Assembly is a container for our compiled server controls, and consists of four parts. One part is called the Manifest, and contains the metadata describing various features of the assembly, including versioning and security features. Another part contains the MSIL code that is the compiled version of our control. The remaining parts of the assembly contain type metadata and resources.

Introducing Strong-Named Assemblies

A strong name is the .NET way of ensuring uniqueness for our assemblies, and is based on the concept of public key cryptography. The public-private key pair that is used to assign a strong name to an assembly ensures that if someone else attempts to generate the same assembly name as we generated, they will fail – the private key will be different, hence the strong name of the assembly will be different.

Once a strong name is applied to an assembly, we can feel safer in the knowledge that if our control has been tampered with in any way since we created it, the .NET security checks will be able to flag this up. Also, subsequent versions of your assembly that you create will bear your mark – the publisher of an assembly leaves a stamp on it, so if anyone else were to attempt to create an altered version of your control and attempt to distribute it in your name, they will be caught out.

A strong name consists of several items:

- ❑ The simple text name of the assembly
- ❑ The version number of the assembly
- ❑ Culture Information (if provided)
- ❑ A public key
- ❑ A digital signature

The easiest way to explain this process is by example. Let's run through how to sign an assembly containing an extremely simple server control.

Here's our control:

```
using System;
using System.Web.UI;

namespace SampleServerControlNameSpace{

  public class SampleServerControl : Control{

    protected override void Render(HtmlTextWriter output)
    {

      output.Write("<h2>This is our simple server control.</h2>");
    }
  }
}
```

As you can see, nothing too special here, but then we're not overly concerned with the functionality of our control – we just want to see how we can deploy it.

Versioning Your Controls

The .NET Framework supports a very useful feature called side-by-side execution, meaning that we can have assemblies with the same name registered on our machine, but with different version numbers. In order to take advantage of this, we need to assign a version number to our control. Note that this is handled internally by Visual Studio .NET, but if you're running from command line, you'll need to get familiar with this method.

Version information is stored in sets of four numbers representing the major version, the minor version, the build number, and the revision, in the following format:

```
<major version>.<minor version>.<build number>.<revision>
```

The Common Language Runtime first checks the major and minor version numbers when checking to see if an assembly is the correct version. These two numbers must match that of the required assembly for it to be deemed compatible. If these two numbers match, but the build number is different, then as long as the build number is greater than that required by the application, then it is assumed that the assembly is backwards-compatible with the expected version.

To add a version number to our assembly, we need to add one line of code to our control just after the `using` statements:

```
[assembly:AssemblyVersionAttribute("1.0.0.0")]
```

You'd obviously amend the version number as appropriate to your situation.

Culture Information

The .NET Framework gives us the ability to encode culture-specific information into our assemblies, including the language, sublanguage, country or region, calendar, and cultural conventions, by using the `CultureInfo` class. Culture information is encoded using two values – the first is called the culture information, and specifies the language, for example, en for English. The second value is the subculture information, and specifies the country, so en-US is US English, whereas en-GB is British English.

You can assign culture information with the following syntax:

```
[assembly:AssemblyCultureAttribute("en-US")]
```

> These codes are based on the RFC 1766 standard, the details of which can be found at http://www.ietf.org/rfc/rfc1766.txt.

We can refer to two types of culture. One is a `neutral` culture, which is where just the two lowercase culture code is used. The other type is a specific culture, which is when both the culture code and the subculture are specified.

We won't be looking into how this subject in too much detail since globalization is a vast topic worthy of much more coverage than we can provide in this section.

> There's a good article on this topic available on C# Today (www.csharptoday.com), called Globalization in C#, published October 16, 2001, by Matthew Reynolds.

Creating a Key Pair

The first step in signing an assembly with a strong name is to create a public-private cryptographic key pair. All you have to do to create a key pair (for sake of argument, let's call it `MyKeyPair.snk`) is type the following command:

```
sn -k MyKeyPair.snk
```

> *`sn.exe` is available as part of the .NET Framework. Note that all `sn.exe` options are case-sensitive, so take care when typing them.*

The resulting file contains both the public and the private key in a pair.

You can extract the public half of the pair, which would be useful when delay-signing assemblies (see following section).

The key pair must be stored in the correct location for naming to work. If you are planning on assigning a strong name from the command prompt, the pair must be placed in the same directory as the binary (the `.dll`), whereas if you want to assign a strong name from within Visual Studio .NET, the key pair must reside in the same location as the solution file.

> Note that once a control is signed, the `.snk` file is no longer necessary, and can be removed from the application directory. Accidentally distributing your `.snk` file with your application would give your customers a copy of both your public and private keys.

Signing an Assembly

We then need to assign the key pair to the assembly, either using assembly attributes to insert strong name information into your code, or the Assembly Linker (`al.exe`). There is a third way of signing an assembly, delay-signing, which is a slightly different scenario that we will also look at.

If we're signing an assembly using attributes, we need to add either the `AssemblyKeyFileAttribute` (for keys that are stored in a file, like the pair we just created) or the `AssemblyKeyNameAttribute` (when the key pair is stored in a key container within the Cryptographic Service Provider (CSP)), to our control and specify the name of the key pair file. (The CSP is a key repository that can be managed across a machine, a network, or the Internet.) Once the attribute has been added to our control, the strong name will be generated when the assembly is compiled.

In the case of our example control, we need to add the following highlighted lines of code:

```
using System;
using System.Web.UI;
using System.Reflection;

[assembly:AssemblyKeyFileAttribute("MyKeyPair.snk")]

namespace SampleServerControlNameSpace{

  public class SampleServerControl : Control{
```

```
      protected override void Render(HtmlTextWriter output){

        output.Write("<h2>This is our simple server control.</h2>");
      }
    }
  }
```

The assembly statement must be the first statement in the file after the using statements. All we need to do now to sign our control is compile it in exactly the same way that we've done previously.

Before we move on, let's consider the two other ways we can sign our assembly. The second method is to use the Assembly Linker. This is the tool that comes in useful if you're creating modules instead of library files. We're not going to go into this in detail, but if you're familiar with creating modules, you can strong-name your controls by typing the following command at the command prompt:

al /out:MyAssembly.dll MyServerControlModule.netmodule /keyfile:MyKeyPair.snk

The final way to sign an assembly is to delay-sign it. This partially signs the assembly by making use of the public key portion of the key pair, then just before shipping, the assembly has to be fully-signed with the actual strong name. This is likely to be a scenario used in large development organizations, where access to the full pair is likely to be controlled and restricted to only certain individuals.

In order to separate out the public key, you would have to type:

sn -p MyKeyPair.snk MyPublicKey.snk

You would then have to add the following lines into the assembly (again, these rely on the System.Reflection namespace, so don't forget to import it with a using statement):

```
[assembly:AssemblyKeyFileAttribute("MyPublicKey.snk")]
[assembly:AssemblyDelaySignAttribute(true)]
```

The compiler will insert the public key into the manifest of our assembly, leaving room for the full strong name signature.

While our assembly has yet to be signed by a full key pair, it doesn't actually have a valid strong name signature. The public key attachment means that other assemblies that reference our assembly can obtain the key necessary, but the assembly will fail verification. In order to bypass this, you need to turn off verification with the following command:

sn -Vr MyAssembly.dll

Finally, when all testing is complete and the assembly is almost ready to ship, the assembly must be fully signed by the key holder:

sn -R MyAssembly.dll MyKeyPair.snk

If your organization has a licensing department, then this is the sort of thing it would handle.

So, our assembly is now signed using one of the three methods described above. We can take a look at what's been added to our assembly using the ILDASM tool, supplied as part of the .NET Framework, which gives us a look inside compiled assemblies to see the intermediate language code and the metadata that's stored in the assembly manifest. It's simple to work – just navigate to the folder containing the assemblies you want to look at and type:

```
ildasm MyAssembly.dll
```

A window will pop up with some collapsible nodes in it – we're going to take a quick look at the assembly manifest, which is where the public key is stored. Double-click on the MANIFEST node and you should see the following:

Notice the `.publickey` section – this is what we've added to our assembly. You might want to check out the differences yourself by comparing a non-strong-named assembly with a strong-named assembly. You'll also notice `.publickeytoken` statements referring to other assemblies – every public key also has an associated public key token, which is automatically generated from the full public key as a sort of shorthand representation of our public key.

Adding a Control to the GAC

There are two ways we can add a control to the GAC – the first is by using the Global Assembly Cache tool (`gacutil.exe`), and the other is by using the Windows Installer 2.0.

Using the GAC, all we need to type is:

```
gacutil -I MyAssembly.dll
```

And that's it – our control is now added to the GAC. Made a mistake? Want to remove a control?

```
gacutil -u MyAssembly.dll
```

So, how do we know it's worked? Let's throw together a quick web application consisting of an ASPX page and a `web.config` file and see if we can display our control.

> **Note: make sure you create the ASPX in an application directory that has no trace of our signed control in it to make sure you're accessing the copy in the GAC, not a local copy.**

The `web.config` is where we reference our control. You'll need to have handy the public key token of our control, which is stored in the GAC. Make sure your `web.config` has at least the following code in it:

```
<configuration>
  <system.web>
    <compilation>
      <assemblies>
    <add assembly="MySignedServerControl, PublicKeyToken=ac8f5d659200afbf"/>
      </assemblies>
    </compilation>
  </system.web>
</configuration>
```

Make sure you substitute your `PublicKeyToken` for the value shown above. Moving on, we now need an ASPX page. The simple ASPX page shown below isn't actually going to do much beyond display our control on the screen. Let's have a quick look at the code:

```
<%@ Page language="c#" AutoEventWireup="true" %>
<%@ Register TagPrefix="wrox" Namespace="SampleServerControlNameSpace"
Assembly="MySampleServerControl" %>

<html>

<head>
  <title>Sample Server Control</title>
</head>

<body>
  <form id="Form1" method="post" runat="server">
    <wrox:SampleServerControl id="TestControl1" runat="server" />
  </form>
</body>
</html>
```

If we go ahead and run this code, we should see the following:

We can be more specific with the information supplied in our `web.config` file in that we can specify a version number or specific cultural variant of our control, which is useful when working with multiple versions of a control side by side. To do this, we can add extra attributes to the statement:

```
<add assembly="MySampleServerControl, version=1.0.3300.0,
                    Culture=en-UK, PublicKeyToken=ac8f5d659200afbf"/>
```

Introduction to Licensing

The other half of the problem of distributing and deploying an ASP.NET server control is how you sell it. Well, the .NET Framework has managed to solve a lot of problems, but you're still going to have to sell the control the old-fashioned way: through a catalog, component vendor, or from your web site. But the .NET Framework, however, does offer great built-in support for licensing.

In this section, we will see how to protect our intellectual investment by making use of the licensing features that the .NET Framework provides for us. We'll look at how we can achieve this both from the perspective of a Visual Studio .NET environment, and also from the perspective of someone who just runs the .NET Framework without having a copy of Visual Studio .NET. Before we go on to look at the process of creating licensed controls, let's understand what licensing is and how important licensing is to creating ASP.NET server controls.

Understanding Licensing

Licensing refers to the process of providing a mechanism for verifying that a consumer of the control has the proper permissions to utilize and build applications using that control. Most Windows users are familiar with the idea of registering software, with shrink-wrapped software requiring the long string of strange letters and numbers (the software **key**) printed on the back of the CD case. Entering any string of random letters, however, isn't sufficient – the program **verifies** that the key is valid.

Recently, verifying the key has been supplemented by **validating** the key. Because people have gotten used to sharing their software keys, thinking, "Why should I pay for a copy of Office 2000 when my employer leaves the CD lying around?" So, some time during (or after) the registration process, the key will be validated, this time against a list of keys (which may be available online) that are already registered. If the key is already found in this list, the vendor will typically inform the application that the key is now **invalid**, and if there is a legitimate reason for attempting to register the same key twice (say if a system has to be reformatted), then the situation has to be resolved over the telephone.

Finally, we're all familiar with the idea of trying demonstration (or trial) software – downloaded from a web site, and either licensed for a short period of time (typically, 30 days), or with limited features. In this case, a valid key also contains enough information for the application to determine whether certain features should be enabled or disabled, and how long the key has been valid.

Why Would I Want to Use Licenses for Server Controls?

In the case of server controls, you specifically have two sorts of licensing to consider. First, you will want to make sure that someone who is using your control to develop applications has a valid license. Note that I did not say that they have paid for your control. Licensing is completely separate from payment. A typical scenario, however, would be that you or your company would like to make money selling your controls. In that case, you will find that the .NET Framework provides much better licensing support than any of the previous Microsoft products. There are any number of charging models you may wish to employ. But you won't only need to employ licensing if server controls are your end product.

Consider, for example, the case of a fictional small company, SnakeNET, which is developing a revolutionary ASP.NET-based portal solution. It has decided to sell customized portals to small business, and, to reduce the cost of development, it will implement all the functionality through the use of sophisticated server controls. The controls themselves are not for sale – instead, SnakeNET is selling the **result** – the portal itself, which would be co-located at its preferred application service provider. SnakeNET, however, wants to use licensing for several reasons:

❑ SnakeNET will spend a significant amount of time and energy building their controls. They would like to ensure that only company employees can use their controls. SnakeNET doesn't want a disgruntled employee sending out "free" copies of their work, or the casual "borrowing" of one of their controls for a personal web site. This would be an example of *design-time licensing* – the license ensures that the control **user** is permitted to use the control.

❑ SnakeNET's current ISP is great, but they had a bad experience with their previous provider, BlackBallWebHosting. BlackBallWeb offered services to its other customers based on code it was hosting for SnakeNET. This resulted in a lengthy court case and a substantial judgment in favor of SnakeNET – which is of course being used to pay for the next generation portal system, now the venture capital funding has dried up. SnakeNET would like to ensure that its controls are only used in portal solutions that it has sold. This would be an example of *run-time licensing* – that is, after the control has been deployed, it can verify that the user is valid.

❑ Finally, SnakeNET has several controls for advertising and message boards that it would like to charge for, based on usage, so it can ensure that if one of their customer's portal solutions becomes the next Yahoo, for instance, the customer's fee can be adjusted appropriately. This is another example of run-time licensing, but incorporates "metering" – adjusting the server controls' license validation logic to take into consideration the run-time environment.

In short, licensing can provide a number of benefits regardless of whether you are selling your control or not. It is a crucial part of ensuring that your control is being used appropriately – but it's up to you to decide if "appropriately" is simply a matter of signing an agreement, making a one-time payment, usage, or metered access.

Licensing Models

Licensing your controls allows you to determine how, and by whom, your control may be used. In some cases, licensing your control might be a completely optional step – as, for instance, if you are planning to post the control and the source files to a site like GotDotNet.com for other developers to use. In other cases licensing will play a major role in the initial design and implementation of your control. But don't assume that because you are not selling your control, licensing does not apply to you – as in the case of SnakeNET, licensing can be an invaluable way to protect the intellectual property of your work in many ways, beyond simply receiving financial compensation.

Common Types of Licensing-Models:

❑   Free (including public domain, freeware, and demonstration software)

❑   Source-inclusive (including GNU Public License, open source, Apache License)

❑   For purchase (including one-time fee, fee and support, shareware)

❑   Run-time licensing (for example, per-CPU, per-user)

❑   Metered (per-hit, per-registered-user)

❑   Subscription

Using Licensing in .NET

Developing controls (ActiveX Controls) in previous versions of Windows was a complicated process. Since Licensing was a late addition to the COM runtime, it required some clever hacks to correctly create licensed classes. This, fortunately, has been fixed in the .NET Framework, which was designed with licensing in mind. In the .NET Framework, licensing is designed into the runtime. All classes are instantiated the same way, whether or not they are licensed. Simply calling "new Foo()" causes the runtime to use the proper validation scheme specified by the creator of Foo. The piece that holds licensing together in .NET is the LicenseManager.

LicenseManager class

The LicenseManager class is an important part of the sophisticated licensing mechanism provided by the .NET Framework. Whenever an instance of a licensed class is created, it is the LicenseManager class that accesses the proper validation mechanism for the control or component.

Let's identify the steps involved in creating a licensed control:

❑   Firstly, we need to mark the class that we want to license, with a license provider. To accomplish this, we need to adorn the class with a LicenseProvider attribute. This attribute allows us to specify the type of validation that occurs.

❑ Secondly, we need to invoke the Validate method of the LicenseManager class. If the nominated LicenseProvider cannot find a valid license, this will throw a System.ComponentModel.LicenseException.

❑ Finally we clean up the license by invoking its Dispose method, and disposing of any local references to the license, when the licensed class is no longer needed. We can do this from within the class's own dispose method, or from the finalize method, if we don't mind waiting for the garbage collector to get around to cleaning up our object.

Now that we have seen the steps involved in creating licensed controls, let's consider an example of creating a simple licensed control

Creating a Simple Licensed Class

As an example, let's build a simple C# server control that takes advantage of the .NET Framework support for licensing:

```csharp
//MyLinkControl.cs
using System;
using System.Web.UI;
using System.Web.UI.WebControls;
using System.ComponentModel;

namespace Wrox
{
  [LicenseProvider(typeof(LicFileLicenseProvider))]

  public class MyLinkControl : Control
  {
    private License license = null;

    public MyLinkControl()
    {
      license = LicenseManager.Validate(typeof(MyLinkControl), this);
    }

    protected override void Render(HtmlTextWriter output)
    {
      output.Write("<a href='http://www.wrox.com'>This is the link to wrox
              site</a>");
    }

    public new void Dispose()
    {
      if (license != null)
      {
        license.Dispose();
        license = null;
      }
    }
  }
}
```

The first thing to notice is the attribute adorning the class. The `LicenseProvider` attribute takes a `Type` parameter identifying the class that implements the actual licensing validation. For the purposes of this sample, we're making use of the `LicFileLicenseProvider`, which is provided as part of the .NET framework. The base `LicFileLicenseProvider` is the only license provider that ships with the .NET Framework. `LicFileLicenseProvider`, like COM's licensing model, relies on design-time `.LIC` files, which identify licensed classes. When compiled, the licenses are automatically embedded into the resulting assembly. It is important to understand that the design-time `.LIC` files are required only when compiling the licensed classes. Once the license is embedded into the assembly, then they are no longer needed. We'll look at how we can provide our own licensing logic, by writing our own `LicenseProvider`, later in the chapter:

```
[LicenseProviderAttribute(typeof(LicFileLicenseProvider))]
   public class MyLinkControl : Control
   {
```

We add a private field holding a `System.ComponentModel.License` class, and initialize it to `null`:

```
   private License license = null;
```

Next, in our class constructor, we use the static `Validate` method of the `LicenseManager` class to validate that the user of our class has a valid license. We pass in a `Type` object representing this class (which allows the `LicenseManager` to look up which `LicenseProvider` looks after licensing for the class), and a reference to the object being created. If the user does have a valid license, the method will return a valid instance of the `System.ComponentModel.License` class, and then we store that instance in the private variable:

```
   public MyLinkControl()
   {
     license = LicenseManager.Validate(typeof(MyLinkControl), this);
   }
```

Next we override the `Render` method and use the `Write` method of the `HtmlTextWriter` object to write the text to the screen:

```
   protected override void Render(HtmlTextWriter output)
   {
     output.Write("<
         a href='http://www.wrox.com'>This is a link to the Wrox site</a>");
   }
```

In this case, since this is a server control and we don't want resources hanging around in memory, we implement the `Dispose()` method to clean up the `License` reference:

```
   public override void Dispose()
   {
     if (license != null)
     {
       license.Dispose();
       license = null;
     }
   }
 }
```

That's it – we've created a licensed class. Now that we have created the licensed class, let's look at the steps involved in consuming this class.

What about the License?

If you try to use the above licensed class in a client application, you'll find it will fail at run time with a `System.ComponentModel.LicenseException`. This is because the license file that our license provider is looking for does not exist, and therefore the `LicenseManager`'s `Validate` method will fail. To fix this, we need to add a design-time license file for the licensed class.

The `LicFileLicenseProvider` looks for a file named `"[namespace].[class].LIC"` in the same directory as the licensed class. In our case, since we have not enclosed our class in a namespace, we will simply name the file as `Wrox.MyLinkControl.LIC`.

Once we have created the `.LIC` file, we can now compile our licensed class by using the following command in the command prompt:

```
csc /t:library /out:SimpleLicensedClass.dll SimpleLicensedClass.cs
```

As we've seen, creating a licensed class is not that difficult. But the default mechanism shipped with the .NET Framework – the `LicFileLicenseProvider` class – is a rather simple implementation. Its chief advantage is that it is very similar to the way in which licensing has worked with VB6, and should be relatively easy for Windows Form control developers to use.

Simple schemes like `.LIC` files can't make very many assumptions about the environment in which they will run, since it is really up to the consumer of the licensed class to decide how they will use the control. But for ASP.NET Server Controls, we can make some assumptions about our run-time environment, and that opens the possibility for doing all sorts of interesting validation tests. For example, rather than read the registry or a file for licensing, you could provide a web service that your controls could query to get valid licenses. The control could hold onto the license. In the following section, we will see what it takes to create licensed ASP.NET server controls.

Using Licensed Server Controls

Now that we've added licensing to our server control, let's go about using it in a different project. This time we will utilize Visual Studio .NET to create an ASP.NET web application that can be used to host our hyperlink server control. By using Visual Studio.NET to create the client application, we can also explore the design-time support provided by Visual Studio.NET for consuming server controls. We will refer to this project as the `MyLinkControlHost`. Using a licensed server control is almost as easy as using an unlicensed server control. This is a radical change from previous Microsoft development environments, where consuming a licensed control required a lot of little tricks to work correctly.

In Visual Studio .NET, we can add our previously created hyperlink control to the Toolbox. To accomplish this, we need to perform the following.

❑   Right-click on the Toolbox and select **Customize Toolbox...**

❑   Select **.NET Framework Components** tab and click **Browse...**

❑   Navigate to the path of the assembly that we have created previously and add the assembly

Once you complete the above steps, you can see that our hyperlink control is added to the Toolbox. Now we can just drag and drop the hyperlink control onto the design editor similar to the way we normally do with built-in controls. If you drag and drop the hyperlink control onto the design time editor, Visual Studio .NET automatically creates a file called `licenses.licx`, which looks like the following:

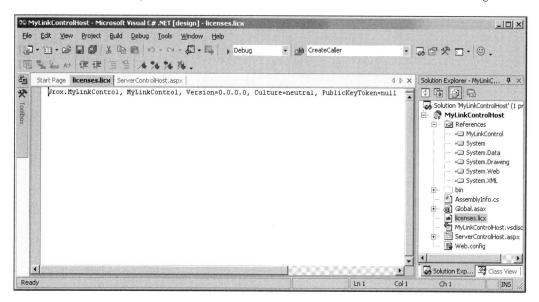

As you can see from the above screenshot, the `licenses.licx` file contains just a listing of the fully qualified (assembly-qualified) name of the class, followed by the type of the licensed class.

If you build the project, the license will be extracted from the licensed class and inserted into the resulting application. So, now you have built an application hosting a licensed class – but what about the license itself? You don't, of course, have to distribute the actual `.LIC` file with your resulting application. Instead, if the `LicFileLicenseProvider` can't find a `.LIC` file at run time, it looks for the key embedded in the running application.

Advanced Licensing Topics

In both of the examples above, we used the .NET Framework's included `LicFileLicenseProvider`. Although simple to use, it's not very sophisticated. It only checks for the presence of a valid `.LIC` file; if you wished to provide different levels of licensing, you could not accomplish that with the `LicFileLicenseProvider`. For instance, if you wished to charge based on the number of processors in the server, you would need to implement your own `LicenseProvider`.

Custom LicenseProviders

To create a custom `LicenseProvider`, a class must inherit from `LicenseProvider` and then override the `IsKeyValid` and `GetLicense` methods. In the following example, we will create a custom license provider class that allows us to control the usage of a licensed class based on the number of system processors present. We will also create a custom license (by inheriting from `System.ComponentModel.License`), which will allow us to add additional properties and methods to the classes utilizing the license provider:

```
using System;
using System.ComponentModel;
using System.ComponentModel.Design;
using System.IO;

namespace CustomLicenseProvider {

  public class ProcessorLicense : License {

    private ProcessorLicenseProvider owner;
    private string key;
    private int validProcCount;

    public ProcessorLicense(ProcessorLicenseProvider owner, string key) {
      this.owner = owner;
      this.key = key;
      this.validProcCount = Int32.Parse(key.Substring(key.IndexOf(',') + 1));
    }

    public override string LicenseKey {
      get {
        return key;
      }
    }

    public int ValidProcCount {
      get {
        return validProcCount;
      }
    }

    public override void Dispose() {
    }
  }

  public class ProcessorLicenseProvider : LicenseProvider {

   protected virtual bool IsKeyValid(string key, Type type) {
    if (key != null)
    {
      uint procCount = 1;

      int validProcCount = Int32.Parse(key.Substring(key.IndexOf(',') + 1));

      return (procCount <= validProcCount &&
                        key.StartsWith(string.Format("{0} is a licensed
                                                component.",type.FullName)));
      }
      return false;
    }

public override License GetLicense(LicenseContext context, Type type, object
instance, bool allowExceptions) {
```

```
        ProcessorLicense lic = null;

    if (context != null) {
     if (context.UsageMode == LicenseUsageMode.Runtime) {
      string key = context.GetSavedLicenseKey(type, null);
      if (key != null && IsKeyValid(key, type)) {
       lic = new ProcessorLicense(this, key);
      }
     }
    }

    if (lic == null) {
     //Build up the path where the .LIC file
     string modulePath = null;
     //Try and locate the file for the assembly
     if (context != null) {
      ITypeResolutionService resolver =
                         (ITypeResolutionService)context.GetService
                                 (typeof(ITypeResolutionService));
      if (resolver != null) {
       modulePath = resolver.GetPathOfAssembly(type.Assembly.GetName());
      }

      if (modulePath == null) modulePath = type.Module.FullyQualifiedName;

      string moduleDir = Path.GetDirectoryName(modulePath);
      string licenseFile = moduleDir + "\\" + type.FullName + ".lic";

     if (File.Exists(licenseFile)) {
      Stream licStream = new FileStream(licenseFile, FileMode.Open,
                                FileAccess.Read, FileShare.Read);
      StreamReader sr = new StreamReader(licStream);
      string s = sr.ReadLine();
      sr.Close();

      if (IsKeyValid(s, type)) {
       lic = new ProcessorLicense(this, s);
      }
     }

      if (lic != null) {
       context.SetSavedLicenseKey(type, lic.LicenseKey);
      }
     }
    }
    return lic;
   }
  }
}
```

Let's walk through the above lines of code. We start by declaring the `ProcessorLicense` class that is derived from the `License` class:

```
public class ProcessorLicense : License {
```

In this line, we specify the type of the licensing provider that is going to utilize this custom license. We also declare variables that can hold the license key as well as the number of system processors:

```
private ProcessorLicenseProvider owner;
private string key;
private int validProcCount;
```

In the constructor, we determine the number of processors from the license key:

```
public ProcessorLicense(ProcessorLicenseProvider owner, string key) {
  this.owner = owner;
  this.key = key;
  this.validProcCount = Int32.Parse(key.Substring(key.IndexOf(',') + 1));
}
```

By overriding the LicenseKey property, we can get the license key granted to this component at run time:

```
public override string LicenseKey {
  get {
    return key;
  }
}

public int ValidProcCount {
  get {
    return validProcCount;
  }
}

public override void Dispose() {
}
```

As we already discussed, to be able to create a custom licensed provider, we need to inherit from LicenseProvider class:

```
public class ProcessorLicenseProvider : LicenseProvider
  {
```

In this case, since we want to control the licensing based on the number of processors, we override the IsKeyValid method by providing custom validation logic:

```
protected virtual bool IsKeyValid(string key, Type type) {
  if (key != null)
  {
```

The next section is where we would find out the number of processors in system in which the licensed control is hosted. For reasons of brevity, we assume the number of processors to always be one:

```
uint procCount = 1;
```

The following lines of code allow us to extract the individual elements in the license key. For example, if the license key is "SimpleLicensedClass is a licensed component.,2", the following line of code will return 2, meaning that the license is valid for 2 processors. We store the returned value into a local variable:

```
int validProcCount = Int32.Parse(key.Substring(key.IndexOf(',') + 1));
```

In the following statement, we check to see the following conditions:

- ❏ If the number of processors is less than or equal to the allowed number of processors
- ❏ If the license key starts with the string that is formed by concatenating the name of the type and the literal " is a licensed component."

If both of the above conditions return true, we then return true to indicate that the license key is valid:

```
        return (procCount <= validProcCount &&
                        key.StartsWith(string.Format("{0} is a licensed
                                        component.",type.FullName)));
    }
    return false;
}
```

In the GetLicense method, we provide the implementation to return a license for the instance of the component:

```
public override License GetLicense(LicenseContext context, Type type, object
instance, bool allowExceptions) {
```

We start by declaring an object of type ProcessorLicense:

```
        ProcessorLicense lic = null;
```

Here we check the Licensecontext to see if we can use the licensed context in this case. If no context is provided, we do nothing:

```
        if (context != null) {
```

The UsageMode property of LicenseContext allows us to determine whether the control is in design time or run time. And if the control is in run time, we retrieve the saved licensed key for the specified type by invoking the GetSavedLicenseKey method:

```
            if (context.UsageMode == LicenseUsageMode.Runtime) {
              string key = context.GetSavedLicenseKey(type, null);
```

Once we get the license key, we can invoke the IsKeyValid method to verify if the key is valid. If the key is valid, we create a new instance of the custom license class ProcessorLicense passing to its constructor the current object and the key as arguments:

```
if (key != null && IsKeyValid(key, type)) {
 lic = new ProcessorLicense(this, key);
 }
}
```

If the control is in design-time mode, we retrieve the key from the .LIC file by using the following lines of code:

```
if (lic == null) {
//Build up the path where the .LIC file
string modulePath = null;
//Try and locate the file for the assembly
if (context != null) {
```

Here we call the GetService method of LicenseContext class to get reference to the ITypeResolutionService interface:

```
ITypeResolutionService resolver =
(ITypeResolutionService)context.GetService(typeof(ITypeResolutionService));
```

Once we have reference to an object of type ITypeResolutionService, we can very easily get the path of the currently executing assembly:

```
if (resolver != null) {
 modulePath = resolver.GetPathOfAssembly(type.Assembly.GetName());
 }

if (modulePath == null) modulePath = type.Module.FullyQualifiedName;
```

To get the directory name alone from the entire path, we call the static method GetDirectoryName of Path class and build the path of the .LIC file:

```
string moduleDir = Path.GetDirectoryName(modulePath);
string licenseFile = moduleDir + "\\" + type.FullName + ".lic";
```

Once we have the full path of the file including the name of the file, we can check if the file exists by invoking the Exists method of File class. And if the file is present, we then read the contents of the file into a local variable:

```
if (File.Exists(licenseFile)) {
Stream licStream = new FileStream(licenseFile, FileMode.Open,
                                    FileAccess.Read, FileShare.Read);
StreamReader sr = new StreamReader(licStream);
string s = sr.ReadLine();
sr.Close();
```

If the key is valid, we create a new instance of the custom license class `ProcessorLicense`:

```
if (IsKeyValid(s, type)) {
  lic = new ProcessorLicense(this, s);
  }
 }
```

Finally, we set the license key for the specified type by invoking the `SetSavedLicenseKey` method:

```
if (lic != null) {
  context.SetSavedLicenseKey(type, lic.LicenseKey);
  }
 }
 }
   return lic;
  }
 }
}
```

Summary

Deployment is a big topic, and there's much more to it than we've been able to cover in this chapter, but hopefully some of the concepts will be much clearer now. In this chapter, we started off by discussing how we deploy our ASP.NET server controls, both using drag-and-drop from one machine to another, and also by strong-naming our controls and adding them to the Global Assembly Cache. We then moved on to discussing the need for licensing, detailing the steps required for creating licensed server controls. We saw how we could create a licensed ASP.NET server control and then saw for ourselves how to consume it from an ASP.NET web application. Finally we discussed the procedures involved in creating a custom license provider class.

In the next chapter, we'll take a look at a sample ASP.NET application that relies on Server Controls.

Professional ASP .NET Server Controls

11

Case Study

So far in this book, we've covered the details of ASP.NET Server Controls, focussing on custom controls, with some mention of user controls, and composite controls. We've learned what they are, and considered event models, custom properties, templating, databinding, custom control builders, state management, control distribution, and control designers. Whew! Now comes the moment of truth. It's plain to see how incredible this technology is, but when would we actually use it? So many controls that we need are already built. In addition, much of the functionality that we need is usually specific to only one project, isn't it? That might have been true in the Windows DNA days, but now, by combining the facets of Server Controls, we can come up with a solution that is truly reusable. Think of Server Controls as if they were a precious gem: a gem has facets, or sides, that unless cut properly ruin the beauty of the product. We need to be able to use each of the facets of Server Controls to the proper degree, in order to come up with something reusable. Before we delve into how, let's take a look at what we'll cover in this chapter:

- ❑ The Code-Behind model

- ❑ When to use a Custom Control, rather than a User Control

- ❑ Custom Events

- ❑ Managing State

- ❑ Up-level/Down-level browser detection

- ❑ Rendering Controls

- ❑ Custom Properties

This chapter will tackle the various aspects of Server Controls in a somewhat different manner from the rest of the book. The challenge in learning any new technology is not "biting off more than you can chew". Each of the previous chapters has covered its specific topic in detail, illustrating its points with simple examples so as not to cloud our understanding. In this chapter we will be doing something different. The purpose of a Case Study is not just to bring everything together, but also to provide a more "real-world" example of how the technology would actually be used in the field.

> The code for this case study, along with the code for the rest of the book, is available for download from www.wrox.com.

Enter the Code-Behind Model

In previous chapters, server-side code was produced in the page, or **in-line**. While that approach provides a simple and clear implementation, an approach that you will no doubt implement in your scenarios is the **code-behind** model. Code-behind means that the server-side code is not placed in the ASPX page, but in a separate class file that is linked to your ASPX page. This means that code can effectively be separated from layout (HTML). The advantages of the code-behind model are obvious; a developer can be used for their strengths (developing server-side code), and graphic artists can be used for theirs (developing HTML and graphics). Both can peacefully co-exist, without the code being mangled by WYSIWYG editors. In addition, pages can be re-skinned, while keeping the same server-side code file, or perhaps even share the same file! Another benefit is that the code-behind page is compiled separately and on the fly.

Implementing the code-behind model is relatively simple. The class must derive from `System.Web.UI.Page`, as in the class declaration example below:

```
public class testclass : System.Web.UI.Page
```

It's not absolutely necessary to fully qualify the name, but it's a good habit to get in to. The ASPX page must also specify the class file that it will use. The following Visual Studio .NET generated code, illustrates the point:

```
<%@ Page language="c#" Codebehind="HomePage.aspx.cs" AutoEventWireup="false" %>
```

The `CodeBehind` attribute is not always necessary. The .NET framework does not require it to be present it unless the name of the code-behind file is anything other than the assumed names of *pagename*.aspx.cs (or *pagename*.aspx.vb in the case of a Visual Basic class file). Our page will not use a code-behind class file because we have no code that the page will execute (other than using our custom and user controls). The other attribute, `AutoEventWireup`, is important to us, since it can drastically affect the page being rendered. We'll talk more about it in our case study's home page.

> *It is worth noting that Visual Studio .NET will have some difficulty accepting the fact that you are not using a code-behind class file. When you compile and debug, you'll have to click past a few prompts to convince it otherwise.*

To Custom Control or to User Control? That is the Question...

Should you use a custom control or a user control? This will likely be a constant point of turmoil for the meticulous architect for some time to come. It may be advantageous to review Chapter 1 for more detailed information on considerations of performance, development time, and functionality. Put briefly, if you would typically place it in an ASPX page, but will use the same layout often (such as a navigation bar that is the same on every page) place it in a user control, since you can take advantage of fragment caching. If it will be complex and require more functionality, use a custom control.

Case Study: Wrox Travel – An Overview

A travel company would like to build an application that allows its clients to perform operations using their browsers that would traditionally be performed by Travel Agents.

The application (Wrox Travel) requires authentication of a username-password combination, then provides quick access to important URLs via menus, and a counter that lists the number of users that have visited the site.

As Windows DNA developers we've done this a thousand times. That's the problem. We should have done it once and reused it! As .NET developers, that's no longer an issue. Let's look at each of the items we're going to provide in greater detail.

Architectural Decisions

Earlier, we touched on the problem with a login control; namely, it's difficult to reuse. However, let's break it down into its main components. Our authentication requires us to validate a username-password pair against a database and provide a means of verifying that someone is logged in. Finally, we need to terminate the opportunity for further attempts if the user exceeds the set maximum number of attempts. This control will also be placed in various locations on key pages, so coding it into the page is not an option.

Think back to the n-tier days. It didn't always make sense, or wasn't always possible to completely separate data, business logic, and presentation. After all, what's the point of calling an ASP component from ASP, which calls a business component, which calls a data component, which only wraps ADO, which makes the database call? Data components fell by the wayside. After all, doesn't ADO sufficiently wrap data handling? If you don't believe me, try using Visual C++ to create an OLE DB consumer.

Since we're building a reusable login component, let's keep all practical functionality flexible, while trying to anticipate any reasonably foreseeable functionality. A custom control for authenticating and producing a response should do the trick. We'll use custom properties for the maximum number of login attempts, custom events for a validation response, and methods for requesting authentication, and login status. In the real world, we would probably do the actual data calls in custom data classes, but since we are only doing one data call in the entire example, let's keep it simple.

Layout will be implemented in a user control that will 'wrap' our custom control. The user control will be responsible for any validation, UI layout, and actually securing the page. In addition, it allows us to drop it into any page that requires authentication. One of the best features, is that it takes all of the features that will likely change from one application to another, out of our custom control. That leaves our control to do what it does best: authenticate without being aware of the UI.

In some instances, the custom control may require a UI. After all, our custom control can inherit from System.Web.UI.WebControls.WebControl, so it must serve a purpose. The hit counter is a prime example of an instance where we would create a UI. We must be careful not to hard-code too much of the UI into the control, though. We'll display only the count, and allow the users to set any display properties themselves, thereby allowing it to be used in any application, simply by being dropped in.

Earlier in the book we were shown how to overload the constructor with a base class of the type of HTML element we would like to render. With it comes all of the functionality of that class, including styles. We'll overload our constructor with a paragraph tag.

To provide the quick link menu functionality, we'll implement a simple row of anchor tags that will resolve to our links for down-level browsers. For up-level browsers, we'll display a much more rich context menu, that looks and feels much like Office XP, and Visual Studio .NET.

> **Uplevel browsers are ones that support a higher level of functionality, such as ECMA script and stylesheets, for example Microsoft's Internet Explorer 5 and 6. Down-level browsers do not, such as earlier Netscape and Internet Explorer versions.**

It will render all the HTML, style tags, and client script necessary to display, hide, control hover appearance, and so on. To do this, we'll have to detect whether the user has an up-level or down-level browser.

Login Custom Control

Create a new Visual Studio .NET web control library project, or open a new instance of Notepad and save the file as Login.cs. First, we'll need to make our declarations:

```
using System;
using System.Web.UI;
using System.Web.UI.WebControls;
using System.ComponentModel;
using System.Data;
using System.Data.SqlClient;
```

As mentioned earlier, we're not complicating this example with unnecessary code, but we would likely place the data calls in a separate class, hence not requiring the above declarations. Since we know that our travel company is strictly using Microsoft SQL Server, we can use the System.Data.SqlClient namespace; otherwise, we'd use System.Data.OleDb.

Although we could still use OLE DB, using the SQL Server-specific class will allow us to use the more powerful performance and features of SQL Server in our application.

We'll define our namespace as `Wrox.WebControlLibrary`, which all of our classes will share, since they're in the same assembly. Our default property is `RetryAttempts`, followed by a prototype for our tag.

The `DefaultProperty` class attribute determines which attribute receives focus in the properties window by default. The `ToolboxData` attribute determines what the underlying HTML will look like when the tool is dragged from the toolbox and dropped onto the code editor. `{0}` represents a token that will be replaced by the tag prefix selected in the ASPX page:

```
namespace WroxWebControlLibrary
{
  [DefaultProperty("RetryAttempts"),
    ToolboxData ("<{0}:Login runat=server></{0}:Login>")]
```

This class will derive from `Control`, since we will not be rendering a UI in this example:

```
public class Login : Control
{
```

Our member variables will be used internally for our properties and for the state we retrieve:

```
private int retryattempts;
private string connectionstring;
private string loggedinuserid;
private int currentattempt;
```

Notice that we are using lower case here. Microsoft generally recommends using Pascal case (first letter of every word capitalized), but for member variables, it typically tends to use the same name as the property but in lower case, although that is frowned upon elsewhere. In addition, there should be no underscores (which if it weren't for DBA's we'd never use anyway).

Events

The event model is illustrated in the sequence diagram below:

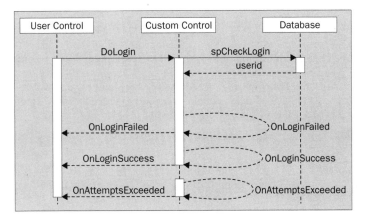

The User Control will call the `DoLogin` method of the custom Server Control. That control will make the database call to the `spCheckLogin` procedure, and either call `OnLoginFailed`, `OnLoginSucceeded`, or `OnAttemptsExceeded`. The user control will in turn implement the desired events.

Events are declared. For more information, see Chapter 3. Remember, these events declared below will actually be delegated to their `OnEventName` handlers. .NET events are based on having delegates connect events to their handlers. Event handler `LoginFail`, for instance, is the delegate that will handle the event, and it implicitly supplies an `EventArgs` class to hold the event data, which adds slightly more overhead. We're also providing a category and description for each event:

```
[Category("Action"),
Description("Raised when the RetryAttempts are exceeded")]
public event EventHandler AttemptsExceeded;

[Category("Action"),
Description("Raised when the user is not authenticated")]
public event EventHandler LoginFailed;

[Category("Action"),
Description("Raised when the user passes authentication")]
public event EventHandler LoginSucceeded;
```

An alternative, more efficient, yet vastly more complicated method, in which the event is explicitly defined, is shown below:

```
private static readonly object LoginSuccessEvent = new object();
public event EventHandler LoginSuccess
{
  add
  {
    Events.AddHandler(LoginSuccessEvent, value);
  }
  remove
  {
    Events.RemoveHandler(LoginSuccessEvent, value);
  }
}
```

The events are raised with a call to their `OnEventName` protected method. This custom control will be used in our `SiteLogin` user control to follow shortly. One point to note is that since we set `AutoEventWireup` to `false` in `SiteLogin.ascx.cs.`, and registered the `OnLoginFail`, `OnLoginSuccess`, and `OnAttemptsExceeded` ourselves, we don't have to worry about any possible illegal values, such as `null`s, in the functions below. A good practice to follow is to do the usual "sanity checks" especially if wiring the events manually is an issue.

```
protected void OnLoginSucceeded()
{
  LoginSucceeded(this, new EventArgs());
}
```

```
  protected void OnLoginFailed()
  {
    LoginFailed(this, new EventArgs());
  }

  protected void OnAttemptsExceeded()
  {
    AttemptsExceeded(this, new EventArgs());
  }
```

Custom Properties and Methods Implementation

Since our control will connect to the database, we need to retrieve the `ConnectionString`. It makes sense to group this property under `Data`. In the real world, we would probably have many pages that access the same database, so we would probably access the connection string from the `Web.Config` file. Again, for simplicity's sake, we'll just make it a property. The `RetryAttempts` property will represent the maximum number of times a user can attempt to log in:

```
[Bindable(true),
Category("Behavior")]
public int RetryAttempts
{
  get
  {
    return retryattempts;
  }

  set
  {
    retryattempts = value;
  }
}

[Bindable(true),
Category("Data")]
public string ConnectionString
{
  get
  {
    return connectionstring;
  }

  set
  {
    connectionstring = value;
  }
}
```

The above properties will appear in the properties window below. Note that the `ConnectionString` property is located under the `Data` category, and `RetryAttempts` appears under `Behavior` as we specified above. We'll set `RetryAttempts` to 2 and `Connectionstring` to :

```
"Data Source=localhost;Initial Catalog=dotNet;Integrated Security=SSPI".
```

We could also have specified the SQL provider, user ID, and password if we'd wanted to:

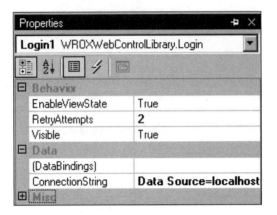

Our custom control will provide two methods: `DoLogin` and `IsLoggedIn`. `DoLogin` accepts an already validated username and password. As long as this attempt is within the maximum number of allowed attempts, it checks the database for the presence of the username-password pair. If it is found, it raises the `OnLoginSuccess` event, if not it raises `OnLoginFail`. If the maximum number of attempts has been exceeded, `OnAttemptsExceeded` is raised. This simple implementation obscures the data layer by using a stored procedure. Of course, more complex authentication could also be implemented, by raising more detailed events, perhaps specifying whether the user did not exist, or the password was incorrect:

> *Note that in this case, Microsoft recommends using "camel case" for method parameters, which capitalizes the first character in every word of the variable name, except for the first one. We also should capitalize abbreviations of two characters or less.*

```
public void DoLogin(string userID, string password)
{
  //We only get the number of retryattempts chances
  if (currentattempt > retryattempts)
  {
    OnAttemptsExceeded();
  }
  else
  {
    SqlConnection conn = new SqlConnection(connectionstring);
    conn.Open();

    /*We'll call the SQL stored procedure that returns the userid if
    the userid/password pair match what is in the database*/

  string sql="exec spCheckLogin '" + userID + "', '" + password + "'";

    SqlCommand cmd = new SqlCommand(sql, conn);

    string ReturnedValue = (string)cmd.ExecuteScalar();

    conn.Close();
```

```
      //If it is in the database, success!
      if (ReturnedValue != null)
      {
        loggedinuserid = userID;
        OnLoginSucceeded();
      }
      else
      {
        //Failed this time
        OnLoginFailed();
      }

      ++currentattempt;
  }
}
```

`IsLoggedIn` simply compares a given username with the one currently logged in:

```
public bool IsLoggedIn(string userID)
{
  if (UserID == loggedinuserid)
    return true;
  else
    return false;
}
```

State Management

The heart of our control requires us to maintain certain key pieces of information, such as the currently logged in user's ID, and how many attempts the user has made so far to log in. We do this by overriding two key methods. `SaveViewState` and `LoadViewState` that are protected methods of the `System.Web.UI.Control` class, which can be used to save the control's properties. You would typically access state through `Control.ViewState`. However in this instance, we don't want to save properties, but other special data. In our case, neither the current login attempt, nor the logged in user ID are stored as properties, but we need to save their current information for the next time the page posts back.

We can use `SaveViewState` by returning the `CurrentAttempt` and `LoggedInUserID` in an object array. `SaveViewState` saves the returned object for the next time the page posts back.

We use `LoadViewState` to read back out `CurrentAttempt` and `LoggedInUserID` array and casting them back into our private variables:

```
protected override object SaveViewState()
{
  if (currentattempt == 0)
    currentattempt = 1;

  object [] State = new object[2];

  State[0] = currentattempt;
  State[1] = loggedinuserid;
```

```
    return (object)State;
  }

  protected override void LoadViewState(object state)
  {
    object[] SavedState = (object[])state;
    currentattempt = (int) SavedState[0];
    loggedinuserid = (string) SavedState[1];
  }
```

Compile it into a DLL called `WroxWebControlLibrary.dll` either using a Visual Studio .NET Web Control Library (shown below), or by typing:

csc /t:library /out d:\wrox\WroxWebControlLibrary.dll /r:System.Web.dll Login.cs.

We'll add more classes to this assembly later:

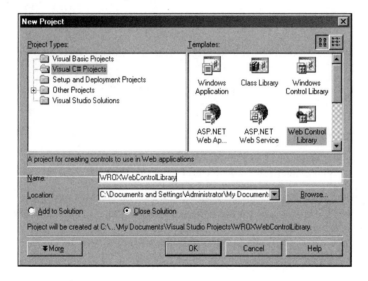

Login User Control

Create a new .NET ASP web application in Visual Studio .NET called WroxTravel as shown below:

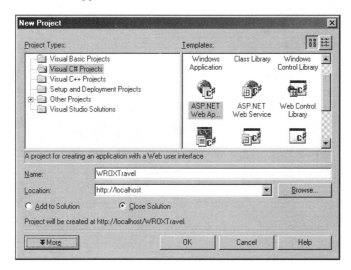

The Server Control is included in our custom control. As we mentioned at the outset, we'll be using the code-behind model. This page is called "SiteLogin.ascx", so we'll create a code-behind page as "SiteLogin.ascx.cs". If you are using Visual Studio .NET this code will be generated for you automatically.

Ultimately, we want our login user control to look like this, while wrapping the functionality of our custom control:

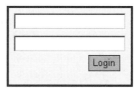

We'll add the custom Server Control we just created to this page. Its namespace is "WroxWebControlLibrary", and we compiled it to WroxWebControlLibrary.dll. Drop the DLL into the bin directory of our new WroxTravel ASP.NET web application. When we finish our WroxWebControlLibrary, we can do a release compile, and add it to the Global Assembly Cache (GAC):

```
<%@ Control Language="c#" AutoEventWireup="false"
          Codebehind="SiteLogin.ascx.cs" Inherits="WroxTravel.SiteLogin"%>
<%@ Register TagPrefix="wrox" Namespace="Wrox.WebControlLibrary"
                             Assembly="WroxWebControlLibrary" %>
```

The user control's layout is fairly simple. The majority of the code to follow contains styles, fonts, sizes, and so on, that are only to attain the look that we wanted, and was primarily generated by the design tools of Visual Studio .NET. First, we specify that we're targeting the schema for Internet Explorer 5:

```
<meta name="vs_targetSchema"
                content="http://schemas.microsoft.com/intellisense/ie5">

<DIV style="BORDER-RIGHT: #000084 thin solid; BORDER-TOP: #000084 thin solid;
BORDER-LEFT: #000084 thin solid; WIDTH: 173px; BORDER-BOTTOM: #000084 thin solid;
POSITION: relative; HEIGHT: 107px; BACKGROUND-COLOR: #f7f7f7"
ms_positioning="GridLayout">
```

It consists of two `asp:TextBox` controls. One will contain the `TextMode = "Password"` attribute, which will mark it as a `password` box, displaying asterisks instead of what we actually type:

```
<asp:TextBox style="Z-INDEX: 101; LEFT: 7px; POSITION: absolute; TOP: 7px"
                            tabIndex="1" id="UserID" runat="server">
</asp:TextBox>

<asp:TextBox id="Password" style="Z-INDEX: 102; LEFT: 7px; POSITION:
    absolute; TOP: 37px" runat="server" TextMode="Password" tabIndex="2">
</asp:TextBox>
```

We'll also add an `asp:Label` control, a `RequiredFieldValidator` for each of the textbox controls, and a button to submit the form:

```
<asp:Label id="Label1" style="Z-INDEX: 103; LEFT: 10px;
                POSITION: absolute; TOP: 69px" runat="server"
                Width="97px" Height="19px" Font-Names="Arial"
                Font-Size="XX-Small">
</asp:Label>
 

<asp:RequiredFieldValidator id="RequiredFieldValidator1"
                style="Z-INDEX: 104; LEFT: 5px; POSITION: absolute;
                TOP: 61px" runat="server" ErrorMessage="UserID Required"
                Font-Names="Arial" Font-Size="XX-Small"
ControlToValidate="UserID">
  </asp:RequiredFieldValidator>

<asp:RequiredFieldValidator id="RequiredFieldValidator2"
                style="Z-INDEX: 105; LEFT: 5px; POSITION: absolute;
                TOP: 76px" runat="server" ErrorMessage="Password Required"
                Font-Names="Arial" Font-Size="XX-Small"
                ControlToValidate="Password">
  </asp:RequiredFieldValidator>

<asp:Button style="BORDER-RIGHT: #000084 1px solid;
                BORDER-TOP: #000084 1px solid; LEFT: 110px;
                BORDER-LEFT: #000084 1px solid;
                BORDER-BOTTOM: #000084 1px solid;
                POSITION: absolute; TOP: 63px; BACKGROUND-COLOR: #adaed6"
                id="Button1" runat="server" Text="Login" accessKey="l"
                tabIndex="3">
  </asp:Button>
</DIV>
```

Finally, we'll add our `wrox:Login` control to the page, and set its `ConnectionString` and `RetryAttempts` properties as attributes (or via the **Properties** window as we saw earlier). Let's allow two unsuccessful attempts at login before we lock users out on the third try:

```
<P>
  <wrox:Login id="Login1" runat="server"
                 ConnectionString="Data Source=localhost;
                 Initial Catalog=dotNet;Integrated Security=SSPI"
                 RetryAttempts="2">
  </wrox:Login>
</P>
```

Now that we have our layout ASCX file, it's time to write our code-behind class file. Remember, in an ASPX file, the class must derive from `System.Web.UI.Page`. In a user control, it must derive from `System.Web.UI.UserControl`, which will provide us access to the same context and visual inheritance that we would in an ASPX page. Our project namespace is `WroxTravel`, and although Visual Studio .NET automatically imports the `System.Data`, `System.Drawing`, and `System.Web.UI.HtmlControls`, in our case, we don't need them, so they've been removed:

```
namespace WroxTravel
{
  using System;
  using System.Web;
  using System.Web.UI.WebControls;

  public abstract class SiteLogin : System.Web.UI.UserControl
  {
```

The controls are declared so that we can use the IDs we specified in the layout file in our code. They should be declared as `protected`, since declaring them otherwise will cause ASP.NET to attempt to de-reference a `null` object, thus causing a run-time error:

```
    protected System.Web.UI.WebControls.TextBox UserID;
    protected System.Web.UI.WebControls.TextBox Password;
    protected System.Web.UI.WebControls.Button Button1;
    protected System.Web.UI.WebControls.RequiredFieldValidator
                               RequiredFieldValidator1;
    protected System.Web.UI.WebControls.RequiredFieldValidator
                               RequiredFieldValidator2;
    protected Wrox.WebControlLibrary.Login Login1;
    protected System.Web.UI.WebControls.Label Label1;

    public SiteLogin()
    {
      this.Init += new System.EventHandler(Page_Init);
    }
```

We also touched on the fact that `AutoEventWireup` is critical when using Server Controls. Setting `AutoEventWireup` to `false` requires us to code our events as follows, because we are telling the compiler not to attempt to wire them up:

```
private void Page_Load(object sender, System.EventArgs e)
{
  Login1.LoginFailed += new EventHandler(Login1_OnLoginFailed);
  Login1.LoginSucceeded += new EventHandler(Login1_OnLoginSucceeded);
  Login1.AttemptsExceeded += new EventHandler(Login1_OnAttemptsExceeded);
}
```

ASP.NET will not attempt to use the default OnEventName(object sender, System.EventArgs e) call to wire our events. An alternative and simpler method is to set the AutoEventWireup to true, and remove the three lines of code above from the Page_Load event. ASP.NET in effect is guessing that we are going to use the standard naming convention, which we do, so it wires the events up for us. Had we tried to wire it up ourselves and set AutoEventWireup to true, the events would have fired twice.

> A word of caution; if you choose to wire your events up yourself, be sure to set the **AutoEventWireup to false,** as failing to do so will cause your events to fire twice (once when ASP.NET tried to wire it, and once when you wired it).

The next section of code is auto-generated by the Visual Studio .NET Web Forms Designer. It's pretty adamant that we should leave it alone, so we'll do that. In essence all they are doing here is wiring their own events for the page load and button click events:

```
private void Page_Init(object sender, EventArgs e)
{
  InitializeComponent();
}

#region Web Form Designer generated code
///     Required method for Designer support - do not modify
///     the contents of this method with the code editor.
/// </summary>
private void InitializeComponent()
{
  this.Button1.Click += new System.EventHandler(this.Button1_Click);
  this.Load += new System.EventHandler(this.Page_Load);

}
#endregion
```

We'll use the OnLoginFailed, OnLoginSucceed, and OnAttemptsExceeded events we created in our custom Server Control, to display a message to the user in our user control.

When the username-password pair do not match an entry in the database, the OnLoginFail event fires. We'll use that event to set our label text to display a "Login Failed" message to the user. An example of what we'd expect to see is below:

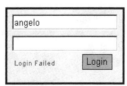

```
protected void Login1_OnLoginFailed(object sender, System.EventArgs e)
{
  Label1.Text = "Login Failed";
  Label1.ForeColor = System.Drawing.Color.Red;
}
```

The OnLoginSucceeded event fires when a username-password pair matches a record in the database, in which case, we will hide the UserID and Password textboxes (since we don't need them any more) and display a green "**Logged In**" message in the middle of our control. We need to set the EnableClientScript property to false, in order to avoid problems when a successful login occurs, in that case, we don't need validation, and blank boxes are OK (in fact they are hidden). An example of what we'd expect to see is as follows:

Logged In

```
protected void Login1_OnLoginSucceeded(object sender, System.EventArgs e)
{
  RequiredFieldValidator1.EnableClientScript = false;
  RequiredFieldValidator2.EnableClientScript = false;
  Label1.ForeColor = System.Drawing.Color.Green;
  Label1.Font.Name = "Arial Black";
  Label1.Font.Size = 8;
  Label1.Style.Add("top","35px");
  Label1.Style.Add("left","50px");
  Label1.Width = 150;
  Label1.Text = "Logged In";
  UserID.Visible=false;
  Password.Visible=false;
  Button1.Visible=false;
}
```

The OnAttemptsExceeded event fires when we have called DoLogin more than the number of times specified in LoginAttempts. An example of what we'd expect to see is as follows:

**Login Attempts
Exceeded Maximum
Allowed**

```
protected void Login1_OnAttemptsExceeded(object sender, System.EventArgs e)
{
  RequiredFieldValidator1.EnableClientScript = false;
  RequiredFieldValidator2.EnableClientScript = false;
  Label1.ForeColor = System.Drawing.Color.Red;
  Label1.Font.Name = "Arial Black";
```

```
    Label1.Font.Size = 8;
    Label1.Text = "Login Attempts Exceeded Maximum Allowed";
    Label1.Style.Add("top","25px");
    Label1.Width = 150;
    UserID.Visible=false;
    Password.Visible=false;
    Button1.Visible=false;
  }
```

The work is actually done when we press our Login button. It calls DoLogin and passes the value of the UserID and Password textboxes:

```
    private void Button1_Click(object sender, System.EventArgs e)
    {
      Login1.DoLogin(UserID.Text,Password.Text);
    }
  }
```

That's it! We now have a complete login system! Implementing it in a page is simply a matter of dropping it into that page. We'll prove this when we create our home page. We would probably want to create a public method that will make the IsLoggedIn method of our custom Server Control available to the web form through reflection.

Hit Counter Custom Control

The idea behind a hit counter is simple. In the days of ASP, we could simply create an Application variable, increment it each page load, then Response.Write it to the screen as seen below:

```
<% Application("HitCount") = CInt(Application("HitCount")) + 1%>
<P>Visitors: <%Response.Write(Application("HitCount")%></P>
```

Taking it a step further, if we wanted to do the same thing in an MTS COM+ component using VB, we would do it as follows:

```
Dim objContext as ObjectContext
Dim objApplication as ASPTypeLibrary.Application
Dim objRespose as ASPTypeLibrary.Response

Set objContext = GetObjectContext()
Set objApplication = objContext("Application")
Set objRespose = objContext("Response")
objApplication("HitCount") = CInt(objApplication("HitCount")) + 1

objResponse.Write objApplication("HitCount")

Set objResponse = Nothing
Set objApplication = Nothing
Set objContext = Nothing
```

Essentially that's the same way we'll do it in .NET. We'll access the `HitCount` application variable through the `Context` class. We'll create a new class called `HitCounter.cs` that we'll add to our `WroxWebControlLibrary` project.

We'll begin by importing the classes we need, and setting the namespace and default property. Since `Count` is our only property, we'll set it as the default:

```
using System;
using System.Web.UI;
using System.Web.UI.WebControls;
using System.ComponentModel;

namespace Wrox.WebControlLibrary
{
   [DefaultProperty("Count"),
     ToolboxData("<{0}:HitCounter runat=server></{0}:HitCounter>")]
```

It would be nice to have a hit counter that we could drop on any page and be self-contained yet fit in with any look and feel. Our hit counter will simply display the number of hits the page has received in an <A> tag. This is a good tag to choose, since down-level browsers support it, and it can be affected by style sheets, or set in the properties window of a web form as shown:

This time, we'll derive the class from `System.Web.UI.WebControl`, since we are going to display a UI. You'll probably notice immediately that we're using the constructor to derive our control from the <A> tag. This will allow us to inherit all of the other attributes of an <A> tag, such as `font`, `color`, and all other styles, allowing us to fit into any look and feel:

```
public class HitCounter : System.Web.UI.WebControls.WebControl
{

   //Constructor
   public HitCounter(): base (HtmlTextWriterTag.A)
   {
   }
```

We have a single property, Count. It is read-only; hence we only need the get part of the code. We cast the contents of the HitCount application variable to an integer and return it:

```
public int Count
{
  get
  {
    return (int)Context.Application["HitCount"];
  }
}
```

We can simply cast the contents of HitCount into an integer without worrying about a run-time error, because we did our validating in the OnInit event we'll look at next. If the variable does not exist, it is set to 0. If it does exist, we'll just increment it by one.

The important thing we should understand about the following code is that we need the Context class to get to the application variables. This is part of the System.Web.UI.Control class. We don't need to import it directly, since our class is derived from System.Web.UI.WebControl, which in turn is derived from System.Web.UI.Control:

```
protected override void OnInit(EventArgs e)
{
  int count = 0;

  if (Context.Application["HitCount"]!= null)
          count = (int)Context.Application["HitCount"];

  Context.Application["HitCount"] = ++count;
}
```

The final output will produce HTML like the following:

```
<A>4</A>
```

Since we derived from System.Web.UI.WebControl, we have access to the RenderContents method that we can override and use to display our control. We could accomplish the same thing by overriding Render, which is part of System.Web.UI.Control, but RenderContents provides us with the ability to call some utility methods for allowing us to render child controls, and so on. We're not using any of those in our control, but it's good practice to use RenderContents when deriving from System.Web.UI.WebControl. Since our constructor specified that our base is an <A> tag, we can also simply output.Write our Count, and it will be placed between <A> tags:

```
protected override void RenderContents(HtmlTextWriter output)
{
  output.Write(Count);
  base.RenderContents(output);
}
```

Context Menu Custom Control

Both the login control and hit counter offered various ways of allowing us to sidestep placing presentation directly into code. The login control accomplished that by using a user control to handle that for us. The hit counter did the same through the sheer simplicity of using a <P> tag, which even down-level browsers support. The context menu we'll create is a little different. It is much more complex, and relies heavily on UI support to function. You may have noticed that when you drag certain Server Controls onto a web form in Visual Studio .NET, the exposed properties in the properties window will vary depending on the target browser schema of the form. Up-level browsers provide a much richer UI, which is fine if you are simply omitting styles in down-level browsers, but if your entire control depends on an up-level browser, this is a real concern.

We could avoid the browser concern by going back to the server each time the user right-clicks, or hovers over the menu items, and displaying some complicated table scheme back to the browser, but is that realistic? A better approach can be seen by the RequiredFieldValidator example in Chapter 3. Notice that in up-level browsers, script is rendered, while on down-level browsers the form is posted to the server for validation.

We'll discuss exactly what the criteria for distinguishing up-level browsers are a little later on. We'll also take a look at how Microsoft implements up-level/down-level checking in its Server Controls. For now, you just need to know that they represent varied levels of higher-level support.

The up-level version of our context menu looks as follows:

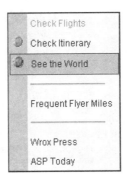

The down-level version looks as follows:

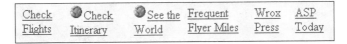

Since it is so UI-centric, we'll derive it from the System.Web.UI.WebControls.WebControl class. We'll call our context menu ContextMenuXP, since we'll try to emulate the look and feel of Office XP and Visual Studio .NET. We'll add it to our WroxWebControlLibrary as well, and name the class ContextMenuXP.cs.

We have only one property, called XmlFile, which we'll make the default. We want the tag to be rendered <prefix:ContextMenuXP>, so we'll set the ToolboxData attribute accordingly:

```
using System;
using System.Web;
using System.Web.UI;
using System.Web.UI.WebControls;
using System.ComponentModel;
using System.Xml;

namespace Wrox.WebControlLibrary
{
  [DefaultProperty("XMLFile"),
  ToolboxData("<{0}:ContextMenuXP runat=server></{0}:ContextMenuXP>")]

  public class ContextMenuXP : System.Web.UI.WebControls.WebControl
  {
```

The links contained in our context menu will likely vary from page to page. Rather than creating a complex hierarchy of properties and methods to populate the control, we'll use an XML file in the following schema:

```
<?xml version="1.0" standalone="yes" ?>

<contextmenu>
  <item disabled="true">
    <id>cmFlights</id>
    <text>Check Flights</text>
    <url>http://www.microsoft.com</url>
    <image></image>
  </item>
  <item>
    <id>cmItinerary</id>
    <text>Check Itinerary</text>
    <url>http://www.wrox2.com</url>
    <image>images/.kastroulis.com/angelo/bio.htm</image>
  </item>
  <item>
    <id>cmWorld</id>
    <text>See the World</text>
    <url>http://www.kastroulis.com/angelo</url>
    <image>images/folder.gif</image>
  </item>
  <item></item>
  <item>
    <id>cmMiles</id>
    <text>C Sharp Today</text>
    <url>http://www.csharptoday.com</url>
    <image></image>
  </item>
  <item>
    <id>cmPub</id>
```

```
      <text>Wrox Press</text>
      <url>http://www.wrox.com</url>
      <image></image>
    </item>
    <item>
      <id>cmASP</id>
      <text>ASP Today</text>
      <url>http://www.asptoday.com</url>
      <image></image>
    </item>
  </contextmenu>
```

We need one top-level element, which in our case is `<contextmenu>`, but can be named anything you'd like. The same cannot be said for any other tags in the file. They are all case-sensitive and are required, with some exceptions. Here's a list of the elements and their respective functions:

- ❑   `<item>` – will equate to one item in the context menu for up-level browsers, or anchor tag for down-level browsers. Any `<item>` elements without child elements will be considered to be separators in the context menu, and ignored in the down-level version. If a `disabled="true"` attribute exists, the item is grayed out in the context menu.

- ❑   `<id>` – is only needed in the up-level context menu. It allows a mechanism to call through client script in case you should ever want to access the menu items yourself, in the web form.

- ❑   `<text>` – is what appears in the context menu, or between anchor tags.

- ❑   `<url>` – is the location that the page will navigate to. The down-level version will navigate the window to that location, while the up-level version will open a new window in that location.

- ❑   `<image>` – is the location of an image that is placed in front of the link in the down-level version, or in the context menu in the up-level version.

Typically, a performance penalty is taken when reading often from a flat file. Since XML can be contained in a flat file, and will potentially be accessed on every page, a concern may be raised as to whether or not a performance penalty will be taken. This concern may be laid to rest, since the XML file will be cached by the web server, especially if you are using IIS.

Our `XmlFile` property will contain the filename of the XML file used to populate the control. The file should be placed in the same folder as the web form.

```
    private string xmlfile;

    [Bindable(true),
    Category("Data")]
    public string XMLFile
    {
      get
      {
        return xmlfile;
      }
```

```
    set
    {
      xmlfile = value;
    }
  }
```

While `Render` will work just as well as `RenderContents` in our case, we'll stick with the better practice of using `RenderContents` with our `WebControl` class. We needed to import the `System.Web` namespace so that we could have access to the `HttpBrowserCapabilities` object through `Context.Request.Browser`.

Up-Level and Down-Level Browsers

As we touched on previously, browsers that support the following criteria are usually considered **Up-level**:

- ❑ ECMAScript version 1.2
- ❑ HTML version 4.0
- ❑ The Microsoft Document Object Model (MSDOM)
- ❑ Cascading Style Sheets (CSS)

Down-level browsers and client devices support only the following:

- ❑ HTML version 3.2

A more concise definition can gained by examining the `BaseValidator.DetermineUplevelRender` method, as it will render an up-level version if the client browser supports the Microsoft DOM version 4.0 or higher, and any version of ECMAScript.

We'll use the same criteria for our control. We'll create a `RenderUplevel` method, and `RenderDownlevel` method for each case. We can test the results of this by setting the `ClientTarget` attribute in our @Page directive of our home page to `downlevel`, and removing it for up-level.

The directive may look like this for down-level targets (or testing):

```
<%@ Page language="c#" AutoEventWireup="false" ClientTarget="downlevel" %>
```

Or like this for up-level targets (assuming you are using an up-level browser to view the page):

```
<%@ Page language="c#" AutoEventWireup="false" %>
```

We'll detect the browser and route to the appropriate method as seen below:

```
protected override void RenderContents(HtmlTextWriter output)
{
  HttpBrowserCapabilities browsecap = Context.Request.Browser;

  if (browsecap.MSDomVersion.Major > 4 && browsecap.EcmaScriptVersion.Major > 0)
    RenderUplevel(output);
  else
    RenderDownLevel(output);
}
```

Our down-level version is fairly simple. The XML is returned by a `GetXMLNodes()` private utility method. A one row table is created with each anchor and image (if one exists) ID placed in a table data tag. The code will not render separators, as our up-level version does, so we'll ignore the blank `<item>` elements:

```
private void RenderDownLevel(HtmlTextWriter output)
{
  XmlNodeList nodes = GetXMLNodes();

  output.RenderBeginTag(HtmlTextWriterTag.Table);
  output.RenderBeginTag(HtmlTextWriterTag.Tr);

  foreach(XmlNode node in nodes)
  {
    if (node.HasChildNodes) //ignore blank items
    {
      output.RenderBeginTag(HtmlTextWriterTag.Td);

      if (node.SelectSingleNode("image").InnerText != "")
      {
        output.AddAttribute(HtmlTextWriterAttribute.Src,
node.SelectSingleNode("image").InnerText);
        output.RenderBeginTag(HtmlTextWriterTag.Img);
        output.RenderEndTag(); //image
      }

      output.AddAttribute(HtmlTextWriterAttribute.Href,
node.SelectSingleNode("url").InnerText);
      output.RenderBeginTag(HtmlTextWriterTag.A);
      output.Write(node.SelectSingleNode("text").InnerText);
      output.RenderEndTag(); //anchor

      output.RenderEndTag(); //td
    }

  }
  output.RenderEndTag(); //tr
  output.RenderEndTag(); //table
}
```

Our up-level version is vastly more complex than our down-level version. We'll begin by rendering our client-side script to capture our right-click, show and hide our context menu, and highlight and un-highlight the item we hover over. It will probably be easiest to use the design tools in Visual Studio .NET (or your favorite HTML editor) to create a simple HTML page that contains the script and styles we'll use. We'll need functions to hide the context menu, display it, and control mouse-over and click events as we just said, but we'll also need styles to control the appearance of the menu. The menu will be simply composed of `<DIV>` and `<TABLE>` tags that we'll move to the mouse location when a right-click occurs. Each menu item will be a `<TABLE>` inside the main `<TABLE>`. It'll take some time to write the script, styles, and layout, and whittle it out to the bare necessities, so the final product is listed overleaf:

```
private void RenderUplevel(HtmlTextWriter output)
{
  output.AddAttribute("language","javascript");
  output.RenderBeginTag(HtmlTextWriterTag.Script);
  output.WriteLine("document.oncontextmenu =
                        Item_show;document.body.onmouseup = Item_hide;");
  output.WriteLine("function Item_show(eButton){");
  output.WriteLine("if (window.event.srcElement.tagName != 'INPUT'){");
  output.WriteLine("var rightedge =
                           document.body.clientWidth-event.clientX;");
  output.WriteLine("var bottomedge =
                           document.body.clientHeight-event.clientY;");
  output.WriteLine("CMENU = document.getElementById('divContextMenu');");
  output.WriteLine("if (rightedge < CMENU.offsetWidth){");
  output.WriteLine(
                      "CMENU.style.left = document.body.scrollLeft +
                                event.clientX - CMENU.offsetWidth;}");
  output.WriteLine("else");
  output.WriteLine(
                      "{CMENU.style.left = document.body.scrollLeft +
                                           event.clientX;}");
  output.WriteLine("if (bottomedge < CMENU.offsetHeight)");
  output.WriteLine(
                      "{CMENU.style.top = document.body.scrollTop +
                             event.clientY - CMENU.offsetHeight;}");
  output.WriteLine("else");
  output.WriteLine(
                      "{CMENU.style.top = document.body.scrollTop +
                                          event.clientY;}");
  output.WriteLine("CMENU.style.visibility = 'visible';");
  output.WriteLine("return false;}}");
  output.WriteLine("function Item_hide(){");
  output.WriteLine("for (i=0; i < document.all.length; i++){");
  output.WriteLine("if (document.all(i).className == 'MenuFrame'){");
  output.WriteLine("document.all(i).style.visibility = 'hidden';}}}");
  output.WriteLine("function MenuItem_onmouseover(){");
  output.WriteLine("var eButton = window.event.srcElement;");
  output.WriteLine("eButton = GetRealElement(eButton);");
  output.WriteLine("if (document.all(eButton.id).className != 'disabled')");
  output.WriteLine("{eButton.className = 'MenuHighlighted';");
  output.WriteLine("eButton.children(0).children(0).children(0).className =
                                             'ImageOver';}}");
  output.WriteLine("function MenuItem_onmouseout(){");
  output.WriteLine("var eButton = window.event.srcElement;");
  output.WriteLine("eButton = GetRealElement(eButton);");
  output.WriteLine("if (document.all(eButton.id).className != 'disabled')");
  output.WriteLine("{eButton.className = '';");
  output.WriteLine("eButton.children(0).children(0).children(0).className =
                                             'MenuImage';}}");
  output.WriteLine("function GetRealElement(el){");
  output.WriteLine("if (el.tagName == 'TD')");
  output.WriteLine("{return
                        el.parentElement.parentElement.parentElement;}");
  output.WriteLine("else if (el.tagName == 'IMG')");
  output.WriteLine("{return
            el.parentElement.parentElement.parentElement.parentElement;}");
  output.WriteLine("else{return el;}}");
  output.RenderEndTag(); //script
```

You may have noticed that in Visual Studio .NET or Office XP, a context menu has a gray margin that images appear in, but are slightly discolored. As the mouse is moved over the menu item, the image becomes clear, slightly offset, and a dropshadow is added. Separators do not extend the complete length of the menu. The highlighting is a blue box with a dark blue border. Let's make our control look just like that. We'd also like to add some of the 'bells and whistles' that Office XP's menus provide. If you look closely, when you hover over a menu item, it becomes more vivid, slides slightly up and to the left, and a slight dropshadow occurs. To do this, we use Internet Explorer's filters. Remember, this is for up-level browsers, so we can use anything Internet Explorer has to offer. We won't get too in depth with filters here, but a filter would appear in the style tag something like this (this one makes the item slightly transparent):

```
progid:DXImageTransform.Microsoft.Alpha(opacity=75);
```

Let's begin rendering our style tag, which will contain classes for normal appearance, highlighted appearance, disabled appearance, separator appearance, the gray left image margin, and the dropshadow for highlighted images:

```
output.RenderBeginTag(HtmlTextWriterTag.Style);

output.WriteLine(".MenuItem{");
output.WriteLine("BORDER-TOP:     rgb(102,102,102) 1px outset;");
output.WriteLine("BORDER-RIGHT:    rgb(102,102,102) 1px outset;");
output.WriteLine("BORDER-LEFT:     rgb(204,200,193) 2px outset;");
output.WriteLine("BORDER-BOTTOM:  rgb(102,102,102) 1px outset;");
output.WriteLine("POSITION:       absolute;");
output.WriteLine("BACKGROUND-COLOR:  rgb(249,248,247);");
output.WriteLine("WIDTH:          150px;}");

output.WriteLine(".MenuItem TABLE {");
output.WriteLine("FONT-FAMILY:    Arial;");
output.WriteLine("FONT-SIZE:      9pt;");
output.WriteLine("BORDER:         0px;");
output.WriteLine("WIDTH:          100%;");
output.WriteLine("TEXT-ALIGN:     left;");
output.WriteLine("PADDING:        4px;");
output.WriteLine("CURSOR:         default;");
output.WriteLine("background-color:  rgb(249,248,247);");
output.WriteLine("HEIGHT:         25px;}");

output.WriteLine(".MenuItem .disabled{");
output.WriteLine("FILTER:         gray;");
output.WriteLine("COLOR:          graytext;}");

output.WriteLine(".sep1{");
output.WriteLine("PADDING-LEFT:    4px;");
output.WriteLine("Align:          right;");
output.WriteLine("width:          13px;");
output.WriteLine("color:          rgb(204,200,193);");
output.WriteLine("background-color:  rgb(180,180,180); ");
output.WriteLine("FILTER:
progid:DXImageTransform.Microsoft.Alpha(opacity=75);}");
```

```
output.WriteLine(".sep2{");
output.WriteLine("PADDING-LEFT:     4px;");
output.WriteLine("Align:        right;");
output.WriteLine("width:        100px;}");

output.WriteLine(".MenuItem .ImageOver{");
output.WriteLine("filter:        progid:DXImageTransform.Microsoft.Shadow(
                              color=black, Direction=135, Strength=1);");
output.WriteLine("left:         -1px;");
output.WriteLine("top:          -1px;");
output.WriteLine("position:       relative;}");

output.WriteLine(".MenuItem .MenuHighlighted{");
output.WriteLine("color:        black;");
output.WriteLine("background:     rgb(182,189,210);");
output.WriteLine("border:        1px solid rgb(10,36,106);");
output.WriteLine("Padding:        3px;");
output.WriteLine("Padding-left:    4px;}");

output.WriteLine(".MenuItem .MenuImage{");
output.WriteLine("background-color:  rgb(180,180,180);");
output.WriteLine("border-color:    rgb(180,180,180);");
output.WriteLine("FILTER:
                 progid:DXImageTransform.Microsoft.Alpha(opacity=75);}");
output.RenderEndTag();
```

Here's where the actual work begins. As mentioned earlier, our context menu is actually a
<TABLE> inside of a <DIV> that is hidden and moved around. We'll initialize some of the appearance
that is common to all styles and use our utility function to get the XML nodes for us:

```
output.AddAttribute(HtmlTextWriterAttribute.Id, "divContextMenu");
output.AddAttribute(HtmlTextWriterAttribute.Height, "92");
output.AddAttribute(HtmlTextWriterAttribute.Width, "150");
output.AddAttribute(HtmlTextWriterAttribute.Class, "MenuFrame");
output.AddStyleAttribute("position", "absolute");
output.AddStyleAttribute("visibility", "hidden");
output.AddStyleAttribute("z-index", "5000000");
output.RenderBeginTag(HtmlTextWriterTag.Div);

output.AddAttribute("onselectstart", "return false");
output.AddAttribute(HtmlTextWriterAttribute.Id, "MenuTable");
output.AddAttribute(HtmlTextWriterAttribute.Class, "MenuItem");
output.AddAttribute(HtmlTextWriterAttribute.Border, "0");
output.AddAttribute(HtmlTextWriterAttribute.Cellspacing, "0");
output.AddAttribute(HtmlTextWriterAttribute.Cellpadding, "0");
output.RenderBeginTag(HtmlTextWriterTag.Table);
output.RenderBeginTag(HtmlTextWriterTag.Tr);

output.AddAttribute(HtmlTextWriterAttribute.Nowrap,"");
output.AddAttribute(HtmlTextWriterAttribute.Id, "MenuContainer");
output.RenderBeginTag(HtmlTextWriterTag.Td);

XmlNodeList nodes = GetXMLNodes();
```

If an `<item>` contains child elements, it is not a separator, so we need to render the table for each menu item, including any client script events that need to be bound, styles, and images:

```
foreach(XmlNode node in nodes)
{
  if (node.HasChildNodes)
  {
    output.AddAttribute(HtmlTextWriterAttribute.Onclick,
                        "javascript:window.open('" +
                        node.SelectSingleNode("url").InnerText + "')");
    output.AddAttribute("onmouseover", "MenuItem_onmouseover()");
    output.AddAttribute("onmouseout", "MenuItem_onmouseout()");
    output.AddAttribute(
        HtmlTextWriterAttribute.Id, oNode.SelectSingleNode("id").InnerText);
    output.AddAttribute(HtmlTextWriterAttribute.Border, "0");
    output.AddAttribute(HtmlTextWriterAttribute.Cellpadding, "0");
    output.AddAttribute(HtmlTextWriterAttribute.Cellspacing, "0");
    output.RenderBeginTag(HtmlTextWriterTag.Table);

    try
    {
    if (oNode.Attributes.GetNamedItem("disabled").ToString() != "")
    {
      output.AddAttribute(HtmlTextWriterAttribute.Class, "disabled");
    }
    }
    catch(System.Exception nodedoesntexist)
    {
       /*We won't rethrow this exception,
    because it's ok not to have a disabled attribute*/
    }

    output.RenderBeginTag(HtmlTextWriterTag.Tr);
    output.AddAttribute(HtmlTextWriterAttribute.Width, "16");
    output.AddAttribute(HtmlTextWriterAttribute.Class, "MenuImage");
    output.RenderBeginTag(HtmlTextWriterTag.Td);

    if (node.SelectSingleNode("image").InnerText != "")
    {
      output.AddAttribute(HtmlTextWriterAttribute.Src,
                          node.SelectSingleNode("image").InnerText);
      output.AddAttribute(HtmlTextWriterAttribute.Width, "16");
      output.AddAttribute(HtmlTextWriterAttribute.Border, "0");
      output.RenderBeginTag(HtmlTextWriterTag.Img);
      output.RenderEndTag(); //img

    }

    output.RenderEndTag(); //td

    output.RenderBeginTag(HtmlTextWriterTag.Td);
    output.Write(node.SelectSingleNode("text").InnerText);
    output.RenderEndTag(); //td
    output.RenderEndTag(); //tr
    output.RenderEndTag(); //table

    }
```

If it is a separator, all we need to do is create a table with a horizontal rule and appropriate styles attached:

```
else //It's a separator..
{
  output.AddAttribute(HtmlTextWriterAttribute.Border, "0");
  output.AddAttribute(HtmlTextWriterAttribute.Cellpadding, "0");
  output.AddAttribute(HtmlTextWriterAttribute.Cellspacing, "0");
  output.RenderBeginTag(HtmlTextWriterTag.Table);
  output.RenderBeginTag(HtmlTextWriterTag.Tr);

  output.AddAttribute(HtmlTextWriterAttribute.Class, "sep1");
  output.RenderBeginTag(HtmlTextWriterTag.Td);
  output.RenderEndTag();

  output.AddAttribute(HtmlTextWriterAttribute.Class, "sep2");
  output.RenderBeginTag(HtmlTextWriterTag.Td);
  output.RenderBeginTag(HtmlTextWriterTag.Hr);
  output.RenderEndTag(); //hr
  output.RenderEndTag(); //td

  output.RenderEndTag(); //tr
  output.RenderEndTag(); //table
    }
  }
```

Finally, close out the main table that contains all of the sub-tables:

```
  output.RenderEndTag(); //td
  output.RenderEndTag(); //tr
  output.RenderEndTag(); //table
  output.RenderEndTag(); //div
}
```

GetXMLNodes is a utility function that we visited earlier in the book:

Notice that we are using an XmlTextReader, because we can get higher performance out of an explicitly created forward-only, read-only reader. We can also guarantee that the XML will be read synchronously.

```
private XmlNodeList GetXMLNodes()
{
  string RawCurrentPath =
                    System.Web.HttpContext.Current.Request.PhysicalPath;
  int LastPos = RawCurrentPath.LastIndexOf("\\");
  int TotalChars = RawCurrentPath.Length;
  int RemoveTotal = RotalChars - LastPos - 1;

  string XMLPath = RawCurrentPath.Remove(LastPos+1,RemoveTotal)+ XMLFile;
  XmlDataDocument XMLDoc = new XmlDataDocument();
  XmlTextReader reader = new XmlTextReader(XMLPath);

  XMLDoc.Load(reader);
  XmlNodeList nodes = XMLDoc.GetElementsByTagName("item");
  return nodes;
}
```

Putting It All Together

Finally, we arrive to the home page, the page that glues all of our stuff together. We'll place our User Controls, and Server Controls on this page. The layout and code to follow demonstrate the cleanness of this page. We don't need any server-side code at all, here, to implement our Server Controls and User Controls.

The up-level version looks as follows (of course, we only developed the hit counter, context menu, and login controls):

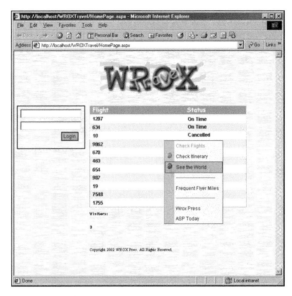

The down-level version looks like this:

Registering our User Control and Server Control library is a snap:

```
<%@ Register TagPrefix="wrox" Namespace="Wrox.WebControlLibrary"
                      Assembly="WroxWebControlLibrary" %>
<%@ Register TagPrefix="uc1" TagName="SiteLogin" Src="SiteLogin.ascx" %>
<%@ Page language="c#" AutoEventWireUp="false"%>
```

For reference, this is the layout HTML for our page. Most of it was generated using Microsoft Visual
Studio .NET:

```
<!DOCTYPE HTML PUBLIC "-//W3C//DTD HTML 4.0 Transitional//EN" >
<HTML>
  <HEAD>
    <meta content="C#" name="CODE_LANGUAGE">
    <meta content="JavaScript (ECMAScript)" name="vs_defaultClientScript">
    <meta content="http://schemas.microsoft.com/intellisense/ie5"
                                   name="vs_targetSchema">
  </HEAD>
  <body bgColor="#f7f7f7" MS_POSITIONING="GridLayout">
    <form id="Form1" method="post" runat="server">
      <TABLE style="Z-INDEX: 104; LEFT: 5px; WIDTH: 606px;
             POSITION: absolute; TOP: 4px; HEIGHT: 472px" cellSpacing="1"
             cellPadding="1" width="606" border="0">
        <TR>
          <TD style="HEIGHT: 109px" bgColor="#f7f7f7">
          </TD>
          <TD style="HEIGHT: 109px" bgColor="#f7f7f7">
            <IMG alt="" src="/WroxTravel/images/wroxtravellogo.gif">
          </TD>
        </TR>
        <TR>
          <TD style="HEIGHT: 245px" vAlign="top" align="left"
                                    bgColor="#f7f7f7">
            <uc1:sitelogin id="SiteLogin1" runat="server">
            </uc1:sitelogin>
          </TD>
          <TD style="HEIGHT: 245px" bgColor="#f7f7f7">
            <IMG alt="" src="/WroxTravel/images/1.gif">
          </TD>
        </TR>
        <TR>
          <TD bgColor="#f7f7f7">
          </TD>
          <TD bgColor="#f7f7f7">
            <P>
              <wrox:contextmenuxp id="ContextMenuXP1" runat="server"
                                   XMLFile="contextmenu.xml">
              </wrox:contextmenuxp>
            </P>
            <P>
```

```
            <asp:label id="Label1" runat="server" Font-Names="Arial Black"
                        Font-Size="XX-Small">Visitors: </asp:label>
            <wrox:hitcounter id="HitCounter1" runat="server"
                        Font-Names="Arial Black" Font-Size="XX-Small">
            </wrox:hitcounter>
            <br>
            <asp:label id="Label2" runat="server"
                        Font-Size="XX-Small"
               >Copyright 2002 Wrox Press. All Rights Reserved.</asp:label>
          </P>
        </TD>
      </TR>
    </TABLE>
  </form>
  </body>
</HTML>
```

> Remember, we often need to use all of the tools in our toolbox to reach an effective
> product. Technologies may fit into our current task at hand, but our task should never
> fit into a technology.

Summary

In this chapter, we've used **Custom Server Controls** to develop several Controls that show us how to:

❑   Develop Custom Events

❑   Develop Custom Properties

❑   Render both UI and UI-less Controls

❑   Detect Up-level and Down-level browsers to enrich our controls

The code that we've developed in this chapter can be expanded on in a variety of ways – we could have used Templating to handle style issues, reused controls developed elsewhere in the book to enrich the user experience, or added databinding functionality to increase the example's flexibility and depth. Custom Control Builders could have been use to add additional functionality.

Due to the constraints of keeping our examples clean and clear we've not done any of this, but it might prove beneficial to spend a few minutes thinking about ways in which our project could be expanded through this application of this, and other technologies.

Professional ASP .NET Server Controls

Index

A Guide to the Index

The index is arranged hierarchically, in alphabetical order, with symbols preceding the letter A. Most second-level entries and many third-level entries also occur as first-level entries. This is to ensure that users will find the information they require however they choose to search for it.

Symbols

.ASPX page
    converting into valid .ASCX file, 25
    writing code-behind class files, 405
.NET Framework
    event model, 75
        consuming an event, 77
        defining an event, 77
        delegates, 76
        naming conventions, 82
        raising an event, 77
    ILDASM tool
        looking inside assemblies, 377
    licensing, 381
    side-by-side execution, 374
.SLN suffix, 284
.SUO suffix, 284
@Control directive
    attributes, 23
    attributes not supported, 25
@Import directive
    import the System.Reflection namespace, 24
@Page directive
    AutoEventWireup attribute, 405
    CodeBehind attribute, 394
@Register directive
    defining the TagPrefix, TagName, and Src, 24
\bin directory
    deploying Server Controls, 371
__doPostBack function, 89, 91
__VIEWSTATE, 108, 109, 110
    Base64 decoding, 128
    information contained in StateBag, 108
    securing, 128
    storing proper data in ViewState, 126
    type of data stored within, 127
    using 3DES, 130
    values encoded in a Base64 format, 127

A

ActiveX Controls property, HttpBrowserCapabilities class, 67
AddAttribute method, HtmlTextWriter class, 42, 46, 57
AddAttributesToRender method, WebControl class, 51, 54, 56, 185, 186
AddParsedSubObject method, WebControl class, 350
AddStyleAttribute method, HtmlTextWriter class, 42, 46
AdRotator control
    Rich Controls, 14
AllowWhitespaceLiterals method, ControlBuilder class, 245
    methods acts as property, 247
    simple example, 240
    true and false values, 240
AllowWhitespaceLiterals method, HyperLinkControlBuilder class, 254
AllowWhitespaceLiterals method, LabelControlBuilder class, 254
AllowWhitespaceLiterals method, PlaceHolderControlBuilder class, 254
AllowWhitespaceLiterals method, TableCellControlBuilder class, 254
AlternatingItemTemplate element
    shopping cart custom databound control, 213
AppendLiteralString method, ControlBuilder class, 245, 248, 249
    example, 248
    filtering, 249, 251
    modifies state of ControlBuilder, 247
    parameters, 248
    passed literal text between controls, 261
    passes literal string from page parser to ControlBuilder, 248
AppendSubBuilder method, ControlBuilder class, 245
    classes overriding, 258
    method modifies the state of the ControlBuilder, 247

AppendSubBuilder method, LiteralControlBuilder class, 261
  camnnot be used to substitute alternative ControlBuilder, 259
  override generates System.Web.HttpException, 258
  purpose, 258
application and session state
  accessing variables, 130
  exposing to server controls, 131
application state variables
  exposing to a server control, 131
    creating a read / write application property, 133
ApplyStyle method, WebControl class, 176
ArrayList
  defining as data source for control, 141
ASP applications
  migrating to ASP.NET architecture, 11
ASP.NET architecture, 10
  compared to DNA framework, 11
  compared to traditional ASP, 11
  features, 11
  Server Controls, 12
    types, 13
  Web Forms, 11
ASP.NET pages
  code behind mechanism, 139
  separation of presentation from logic, 139
ASP.NET projects
  authentication level set to Basic, 301
<asp:Button> control
  syntax, 12
  wiring to event handler, 13
ASP:DataGrid
  List Controls, 13
<asp:DropDownMenu> control, 130
<asp:Label> controls
  adding to login user control, 404
ASP:ListBox
  List Controls, 13
<asp:TextBox> controls
  adding to login user control, 404
Assembly Linker, 375, 376
AssemblyKeyFileAttribute class, System.Reflection namespace, 375
Attribute attribute, 325
AttributeTargets enumeration, System namespace, 321
AutoEventWireup attribute, @Control directive, 23
AutoEventWireup attribute, @Page directive
  setting to false, 405
  setting to true, 406

B

BackColor property, WebControl class, 15
base controls
  handling events in, 92
Base64 decoding, 128
BaseDataList class, System.Web.UI.WebControls namespace, 206
  IsBindableType method, 206
BaseValidator class, System.Web.UI.WebControls namespace
  DetermineRenderUplevel method, 414

Bindable attribute, 323
<body> tags, 25
boxes
  convention used in this book, 4
Browsable attribute, 321
Browser property, HttpBrowserCapabilities class, 67
Browser property, HttpRequest class, 62, 66
bubbling events, 96
  defined, 96
Build Errors task, 289
Button class, System.Web.UI.WebControls namespace
  instantiating, 12
<button> tag, 351

C

Calendar control
  Rich Controls, 14
CanConvertFrom method, 330
CanConvertTo method, 330
cascading style sheets
  allows separation of HTML content from presentation, 174
  syntax for accessing styles, 175
case study, 393
Category attribute, 321
cellpadding property, TableStyle class, 181
cellspacing property, TableStyle class, 181
ChildControlsCreated property, Control class, 200, 201
ChildControlsCreated property, WebControl class, 349
ClassName attribute, @Control directive, 23
ClearChildViewState method, Control class, 125
Click event
  event handler, 13
Click event, EventHandler delegate
  event definition, 77
client-side validation techniques
  limitations, 64
ClientTarget property, Page class, 68
Clipboard Ring tab, 286
CloseControl method, ControlBuilder class, 244, 249, 252
  displays properties of base class, 252
  properties displayed, 253
CloseDownControl method, IWindowsFormsEditorService interface, 337
ClrVersion property, HttpBrowserCapabilities class, 67
CLS
  compilers that adhere to, 277
CodeBehind attribute, @Page directive, 394
code-behind class files
  writing, 405
code-behind model, 394
  code separated from layout, 394
    benefits, 394
  implementing, 394
ColorTypeEditor
  EditValue method, 360
ColumnSpan Property, TableCell class, 163
CommandEventArgs class, System.Web.UI.WebControls, 96, 98
Comment task, 289

Common Language Specification
see CLS.
CompareValidator control
description, 65
Validation Controls, 13
CompilerOptions attribute, @Control directive, 23
compilers
CLS adherent, 277
ComponentType property, 333
Composite Control creation, 32
example, 33
implements the INamingContainer interface:, 37
overriding of the CreateChildControls method, 37
naming conflicts, 32
composite controls
creating in Toolbox, 286
Server Controls, 14
consuming an event, 77
adding an event handler, 78
contained controls
bubbling events, 96
event handling, 92, 93
Container property, 332
containers
control that the defined template(s) get added to, 145
Content attribute, 324
Context property, Control class, 410
Control class, System.Web.UI namespace, 12
assumed if container class not specified, 155
base class that controls inherit from, 9
ChildControlsCreated property, 200, 201
Context property, 410
CreateChildControls method, 32, 37, 96, 116, 121, 122, 124, 149, 152, 163, 177, 182, 199
Custom Server Control inherits from, 28
DataBind method, 153, 199
DataBinding event, 169
deriving from, 397
EnableViewState property, 126
extended by WebControl class, 15
importing, 28
LoadViewState method, 110, 401
NamingContainer property, 169
OnBubbleEvent method, 97
OnDataBinding method, 199
properties and methods affecting ViewState, 124
RaiseBubbleEvent method, 97
Render method, 43, 96, 113, 410
RenderControl method, 346
SaveViewState method, 110, 401
ShowGoodies class inherits from, 132
ViewState property, 109, 401
ControlBuilder class, System.Web.UI namespace, 362
AllowWhiteSpaceLiterals method, 245
simple example, 240
AppendLiteralString method, 244, 245, 249, 261
AppendSubBuilder method, 245
classes overriding, 258
classes derived from, 254
CloseControl method, 244, 249, 252
properties displayed, 253
CreateBuilderFromType method
cannot be overridden, 269
defining interaction between page parser and controler, 237
deriving classes from, 240

facilitates parsing customization, 237
filtering, 243
GetChildControlType method, 244, 249, 261, 266, 350
practical reason to override, 265
prototype, 265
gives parsing help to page parser, 239
HasBody method, 251
hierarchies of controls, 240
HtmlDecodeLiterals method, 245
classes overriding, 255
Init method, 244, 246, 248
methods acting as properties, 247
NeedsTagInnerText method, 244, 249
true and false values, 261
OnAppendToParentBuilder method, 244, 249
unifies hierarchy of control builders, 268
overriding methods, 238
overview, 239
persistence and interaction with, 348
SetTagInnerText method, 244, 249, 261
cannot be used as filter, 262
supports creation of LiteralControl class, 239
ControlBuilderAttribute class, System.Web.UI namespace, 266
associates ControlBuild instance with custom control, 242
elements exposed, 242
specifying control builder class, 240
ControlDesigner class, System.Web.UI.Design namespace, 345
Component property, 353
CreatePlaceHolderDesignTimeHtml method, 346
GetDesignTimeHtml method, 346
GetEmptyDesignTimeHtml method, 346, 351
GetErrorDesignTimeHtml method, 347, 351
OnBindingsCollectionChanged method, 348
OnComponentChanged method, 348
OnControlResize method, 348
OnSetParent method, 348
RaiseComponentChanged method, 353
ControlStyle property, WebControl class, 174, 181
accessing styles declaratively, 175
overwriting, 187
ControlType property, ControlBuilder class, 253
conventions used in this book, 4
Conversion methods, type converters, 328
Converter property, 333
ConvertFrom method, 330
converting .ASPX page
into valid .ASCX file, 25
ConvertTo method, 330
Cookies property, HttpBrowserCapabilities class, 67
CopyFrom method, Style class, 176, 181
Crawler property, HttpBrowserCapabilities class, 67
CreateBuilderFromType method, ControlBuilder class
cannot be overridden, 269
CreateChildControls method, Control class, 116, 121, 122, 163, 177, 199
creating a composite control, 32
events in contained controls, 96
modifying, 152
overriding, 37, 149, 201
populating child control values, 124
update the attributes for our table control, 182
CreateChildControls method, DBDropDown custom control, 218

CreateChildControls method, shopping cart custom databound control, 209
CreateControlHierarchy method, 199
  DBDropDown custom control, 218, 219
  shopping cart advanced custom databound control, 229
  shopping cart custom databound control, 210
  using, 202
CreatePlaceHolderDesignTimeHtml method, ControlDesigner class, 346
Cross Languge Debugging, 298
Cryptographic Service Provider
  see CSP.
CSP
  key repository, 375
CultureInfo class, System.Globalization namespace
  encoding cultural information, 374
Current property, IEnumerator interface, 208
custom control builder
  class derived from ControlBuilder class, 238
  controls that utilize, 238
Custom Controls
  compared to User Controls, 19, 395
    reusability, 19
  custom DataBound controls, 191
    creating advanced templated control, 223
    creating simple control, 214
    creating simple templated control, 206
  DbListItem custom control, 214
  integration with Visual Studio. NET toolbox., 14
  Server Controls, 14
custom DataBound controls, 191
  creating advanced templated control, 223
  creating simple control, 214
  creating simple templated control, 206
  DBDropDown custom control, 216
  setup instructions, 194
  shopping cart advanced custom databound control, 223
  shopping cart custom databound control, 207
custom designers
  advanced interaction with the property browser, 357
  class inherits ControlDesigner, 345
  persistence and interaction with ControlBuilder, 348
  providing shortcuts to common operations - designer verbs, 352
Custom EventArgs and delegates, 80
  naming, 82
  WebForm1.aspx, 81
custom mobile controls
  benefits of using, 61
  device detection and customized rendering, 62
    advantages of Mobile Controls, 63
    limitations of Mobile Controls, 64
    using device specific filters, 62
    using MobileCapabilities class, 62
custom painting, 343
Custom Server Control creation, 26
  OurFirstControl.cs, 27
  setting properties, 28
  using Control in a page
    by hand, 30
    using VS.NET, 30
      referencing from toolbox, 31
  VS.NET integration, 26
custom style class
  creating, 184
    deriving from Style class, 184

custom type converters, 328
  Conversions, 330
  Standard Values, 334
    methods to be overridden, 334
custom TypeEditors, 336
  custom painting, 343
  DropDown editor, 340
  Modal Editor, 336
customer support, 5
CustomValidator control
  description, 65
  Validation Controls, 13

D

Daily Special control
  build control hierarchy, 159
  create class for header template, 167
  design, 156
  exposing style elements as top level properties, 181
DAP.TDL template
  VS.NET IDE uses by default, 280
DataBind method, Control class, 153, 199
DataBind method, Page class, 195
  using DropDownList control in Web Form, 195
DataBind method, ShoppingCartItem container class, 212
DataBinder class, System.Web.UI namespace, 203
  GetPropertyValue method, 199, 203
  DBDropDown custom control, 220
DataBinding event, Control class, 169
DataBound controls
  custom DataBound controls, 191
    creating advanced templated control, 223
    creating simple control, 214
    creating simple templated control, 206
  essential issues, 198
  simple DataBound controls, 192
    creating simple control, 214
    DataGrid controls, 192
  table of methods, 199
  templated DataBound controls, 192
    creating advanced templated control, 223
    creating simple templated control, 206
    DataList control, 192
    Repeater control, 192
  using, 192
DataBound simple controls, 192
  creating simple control, 214
  DataGrid controls, 192
  extracting values from data source, 203
DataBound templated controls, 192
  create DataItem property on container class, 150, 207
  creating advanced templated control, 223
  creating control hierarchy, 201
  creating simple templated control, 206
  DataList control, 192
  Repeater control, 192
DataGrid controls, 192
  display in designer, 346
DataItem property, DataListItem class, 197
  DataList control and, 197
  ItemTemplate element and, 197
DataItem property, ShoppingCartItem container class, 207, 212

DataList control, 140, 192
DataItem property, DataListItem class, 197
DataListItem container, 144
defining the item templates, 140
ItemTemplate element and, 197
rendering content
use of HTML tables, 143
using in Web Form, 196
**DataListItem class, System.Web.UI.WebControls
namespace, 197**
DataItem property, 197
DataListItem container, 144
DataMember property, DropDownList control, 193
**DataProductField property, shopping cart advanced
custom databound control, 228**
**DataSource property, DBDropDown custom control,
216**
DataSource property, DropDownList control, 193
using DropDownList control in Web Form, 195
**DataSource property, shopping cart custom databound
control, 208**
SqlDataReader class, System.Data.SqlClient
namespace, 213
**DataTextField property, DBDropDown custom control,
216, 220**
using DBDropDown custom control in Web Form, 221
DataTextField property, DropDownList control, 193
using DropDownList control in Web Form, 195
**DataValueField property, DBDropDown custom control,
216, 220**
using DBDropDown custom control in Web Form, 221
DataValueField property, DropDownList control, 193
using DropDownList control in Web Form, 195
DBDropDown custom control, 216
CreateChildControls method, 218
CreateControlHierarchy method, 218, 219
DataSource property, 216
DataTextField property, 216, 220
DataValueField property, 216, 220
GetPropertyValue method, DataBinder class, 220
IPostBackDataHandler interface, 217
IsTrackingViewState property, 218
LoadViewState method, 220
OnDataBinding method, 218
Render method, 220
SaveViewState method, 220
<select> element, 220
SelectedIndexChanged event, 217
using in Web Form, 221
DbListItem custom control, 214
Selected property, 214
Text property, 214
Value property, 214
Debug attribute, @Control directive, 23
Debugging, 276
control designers, 368
multi language, 281
debugging multiple projects
project management, 281
debugging the control designers, 368
DefaultEvent attribute, 322
DefaultProperty attribute, 322
**DefaultPropertyAttribute class,
System.ComponentModel namespace, 397**
DefaultValue attribute, 321
delay-signing, 375, 376

delegates
declaring, 76
EventHandler delegate, 76
multicast deleagates, 76
object oriented and type safe, 76
deploying Server Controls, 371
adding a control to GAC, 377
compared to traditional ASP, 371
referencing assembly, 371
strong named assemblies
creating a key pair, 375
strong-named assemblies, 373
culture information, 374
signing an assembly, 375
versioning controls, 374
working with GAC, 372
XCOPY deployment, 371
Description attribute, 321
Description attribute, @Control directive, 23
design time architecture, 320
advanced level, 320
designers, 345
environment services, 345
services from hosting environment, 362
basic level, 320
attributes, 321
design time attributes and inheritance, 326
intermediate level, 320, 327
custom type converters, 328
custom TypeEditors, 336
design time suppport, 317
advanced, 318
classes, 317
sample control, 318
designer verbs, 352
DesignerSerializationVisibility attribute, 324
**DesignerVerb class, System.ComponentModel.Design
namespace, 353**
DesignOnly attribute, 323
detecting browser capabilities, 66
HttpBrowserCapabilities class, System.Web
namespace, 66
RequiredFieldvalidator control, 70
using ClientTarget property to affect output of Server
Control, 68
**DetermineRenderUplevel method, BaseValidator class,
414**
Dispose method, LicenseManager class, 382, 383
dispose phase
Server Control life-cycle, 17
<DIV> element, 415, 418
DNA framework
ASP.NET architecture compared to, 11
Document Window, 276
DownLevel
ClientTarget property, Page class, 69
Downlevel browsers
description, 396
supports, 66
drag and drop
see also XCOPY deployment.
Server Control deployment, 371
DrawString method, Graphics class, 383
DropDown editor
custom color editor example, 341
defined, 341
focus, 340

DropDownControl method,
  IWindowsFormsEditorService interface, 337, 341
DropDownList class, System.Web.UI.WebControls
  namespace, 20, 38
  SelectedIndexChanged event, 20
  DataMember property, 193
  DataSource property, 193
  DataTextField property, 193
  DataValueField property, 193
DropDownList control, 192
  description, 192
  using in Web Form, 194
DummyDataSource class
  DummyDataSourceEnumerator class, 208
  IEnumerable interface, 207
  shopping cart custom databound control, 207
DummyDataSourceEnumerator class
  IEnumerator interface, 208
  shopping cart custom databound control, 208
Dynamic Help, 276, 294
Dynamic Help & Search, 276
  customizing help information, 287
    example, 287
dynamic templates
  event bubbling, 174
  implementing ITemplate interface
    DynamicTemplate.cs, 167
    DynamicTemplateHost.aspx, 169
    web.config file, 170
  loading templates, 171
    DailySpecialAdminHeader.ascx, 172
    DailySpecialHeaderTemplate.ascx, 172
    DynamicTemplateHost.aspx, 172
  template rendering, 174

E

Editor attribute, 324
EditValue method, ColorTypeEditor, 360
EditValue method, UITypeEditor class
  overriding, 336
EnableViewState attribute, @Control directive, 23
EnableViewState property, Control class, 124
  set to false to disable, 126
EnableViewStateMAC property, Page class
  set to true, 129
  ViewState and security, 128
EncodedInnerDefaultProperty attribute, 325
Enterprise Template Policy, 278
Enum class, System namespace
  GetNames method, 339
Environment Resource Checking, 296
errata, 5
error trapping, 276, 292
  TryCatch, 292
event bubbling, 174
event definition, 77
  Click event, EventHandler delegate, 77
  raising an event, 77
event handling
  in base controls, 92
  overriding the OnEvent method, 92
  shopping cart advanced custom databound control,
    224
event model
  login custom control, Wrox Travel, 397

event sample, 78
  WebForm1.aspx.cs, 79
EventArgs class, System namespace, 13, 76, 363
  base class for all custom event arguments classes,
    76
  create a new class that derives from, 80
  derive custom event arguments from, 97
EventHandler delegate, System namespace, 78, 79
  designer verbs, 353
  parameters, 76
events, 75
  .NET Framework, 75
  bubbling events, 96
  consuming, 77
  custom EventArgs and delegates, 80
    naming, 82
  defining, 77
  delegated to OnEventName handlers, 398
  delegates, 76
  example, 78
  handling events in base controls, 92
  in contained controls, 93
  in server controls, 83
    inheritance and containment, 92
    postback, 83
ExecuteReader method, SqlCommand class, 57
Exists method, File class, 390
Explicit attribute, @Control directive, 23

F

FChildrenAsProperties property, ControlBuilder class,
  253
feedback, 5
File class, System.IO namespace
  Exists method, 390
filtering
  AppendLiteralString method, ControlBuilder class,
    249, 250, 251
  Replace method, String class, 250, 251
FIsNonParserAccessor property, ControlBuilder class,
  253
Font property, WebControl class, 15
fonts
  convention used in this book, 4
ForeColor property, WebControl class, 15
<form> tags, 25
Frames property, HttpBrowserCapabilities class, 67

G

GAC
  adding control to, 377
    using GAC tool, 377
    using Windows Installer 2.0, 377, 378
  adding Custom Controls to, 19
  benefits to developers, 372
  working with, 372
GetChildControlType method, ControlBuilder class,
  244, 266, 350
  page parser determines nature of control, 248
  passed the tag name and attributes of a child control,
    261
  practical reason to override, 265
  prototype, 265

GetDefaultEvent method, TypeDescriptor class, 358
GetDefaultProperty method, TypeDescriptor class, 358
GetDesignTimeHtml method, ControlDesigner class, 346
GetDirectoryName method, Path Class, 390
GetEditStyle method, UITypeEditor class
    overriding, 336
GetEmptyDesignTimeHtml method, ControlDesigner class, 346, 351
GetErrorDesignTimeHtml method, ControlDesigner class, 347, 351
GetLicense method, LicenseProvider class, 389
    overriding, 385
GetName method, SqlDataReader class, 57
GetNames method, Enum class, 339
GetPaintValueSupported method, UITypeEditor class
    overriding, 336
GetProperties method, TypeConverter class, 358, 360
    parameters, 358
GetProperties method, TypeDescriptor class, 199, 359
    extracting information about control properties, 205
GetPropertiesSupported method, TypeConverter class, 358
GetPropertyValue method, DataBinder class, 199
    DataBinder class, 203
    DBDropDown custom control, 220
GetService method, IServiceProvider interface, 337
GetService method, LicenseContext class, 390
GetStandardValues method, 334
GetStandardValues method, TypeConverter class, 358
GetStandardValuesExclusive method, 334
GetStandardValuesSupported method, 334, 364
GetValue property, 333
Global Assembly Cache
    see GAC.
global.asax file, 131
Graphics class, System.Drawing namespace
    DrawString method, 383

H

HACK token tag, 289
HasAspCode property, ControlBuilder class, 253
HasBody method, ControlBuilder class, 251
    methods acts as property, 247
HasChildViewState property, Control class, 125
help from Wrox, 5
Hidden attribute, 324
hidden form fields
    ViewState, 108
hosting environment services, 362
    debugging the control designers, 368
    deployment options, 368
    IComponentChangeService interface
        events, 363
    IDictionaryService interface, 367
    IReferenceService interface, 366
HTML elements
    <button> element, 351
    <DIV> element, 415, 418
    <html> tags, 25
    <id> element, 413
    element, 413
    <item> element, 413, 419
    <ItemTemplate> element, 140
    <li> element, 143
    <pre> elements, 241, 242
    <TABLE> element, 415, 418
    <text> element, 413
    <UL> element, 143
    <url> element, 413
HTML Server Controls, 14
<html> tags, 25
    attributes not supported, 25
HtmlDecode method, HttpUtility class, 256
HtmlDecodeLiterals method, ControlBuilder class, 245, 260
    classes overriding, 255
    methods acts as property, 247
    TextBoxControlBuilder class overrides, 257
HtmlDecodeLiterals method, ListItemControlBuilder class, 255
HtmlDecodeLiterals method, TextBoxControlBuilder class, 255, 259
HtmlEncode method, HttpUtility class, 256
HtmlTextWriter class, System.Web.UI namespace, 41, 351
    AddAttribute method, 46, 57
    AddStyleAttribute method, 46
    benefits of using, 61
    HTML styles used for rendering, 46
    important methods, 42
    passed as an argument in Render method, Control class, 44
    Render method, 383
    RenderBeginTag method, 47
    RenderEndTag method, 47, 59
    using utility methods for Server Control creation, 45
        advantages, 45
    Write method, 43, 47, 133
HtmlTextWriterAttribute enumeration, System.Web.UI namespace
    exposes all HTML tags, 46
    Href attribute, 54
HtmlTextWriterStyle enumeration, System.Web.UI namespace, 46
HttpBrowserCapabilities class, System.Web namespace, 42, 414
    detecting browser capabilities, 66
    functionality of browser capabilities component encapsulated, 66
    table of properties, 67
HttpException class, System.Web namespace
    generated by AppendSubBuilder method, LiteralControlBuilder class, 258
HttpRequest class, System.Web namespace
    Browser property, 62, 66
HttpUtility class, System.Web namespace
    HtmlDecode method, 256
    HtmlEncode method, 256
HyperLinkControlBuilder class, System.Web.UI.WebControls namespace
    AllowWhitespaceLiterals method, 254
    derived from ControlBuilder class, 254

I

ICollection interface, System.Collection namespace
compared to IEnumerator interface, 208
IComponentChangeService interface,
System.ComponentModel.Design namespace, 363
creating Validator-like control, 363
OnComponentChanged method, 363
OnComponentChanging method, 363
IContainer interface, System.ComponentModel
namespace
Components property, 332
<id> element, 413
ID property, ControlBuilder class, 253
IDE, 273
see also VS.NET, 273
IDictionaryService interface,
System.ComponentModel.Design namespace, 367
IEnumerable interface, System.Collection namespace
DummyDataSource class, 207
IEnumerator interface, System.Collection namespace
compared to ICollection interface, 208
compared to IList interface, 208
Current property, 208
DummyDataSourceEnumerator class, 208
MoveNext method, 208
IIS
VS.NET management of files, 300
ILDASM tool
looking inside assemblies, 377
Manifest mode, 377
IList interface, System.Collection namespace
compared to IEnumerator interface, 208
<image> element, 413
INamingContainer interface, System.Web.UI
namespace
events in contained controls, 96
implementing, 145, 148
marker interface, 146
marks start of new naming scope, 146
providing new naming context for templates and
controls, 163
ShoppingCartItem container class, 226
when to implement, 32
InDesigner property, ControlBuilder class, 253
inheritance, 92
events defined in base controls, 92
inherited controls, 92
Inherits attribute, @Control directive, 23
Init method, ControlBuilder class, 244
initialization by page parser, 244
parameters, 247
start tag information provided by page parser, 248
virtual method, 246
initialize phase
Server Control life-cycle, 16
inner HTML elements
treatment of, 146
InnerDefaultProperty attribute, 325
InnerProperty attribute, 325
Instance property, 333
Instance property, ITypeDescriptorContext interface,
344
InstantiateIn method, ITemplate interface, 144, 153,
167

Integrated Development Environment
see IDE.
Intellisense, 276, 291
shows arguments for ReadXml method, 306
intrinsic controls
autonomous to the application in which they reside,
130
IPostBackDataHandler interface, System.Web.UI
namespace, 84, 86
DBDropDown custom control, 217
implementing, 100
LoadPostData method, 17, 84, 88, 217
RaisePostDataChangedEvent method, 17, 84, 88,
217
working with events related to changed data in the
control, 92
IPostBackEventHandler interface, System.Web.UI
namespace, 89
implementing, 100
RaisePostBackEvent method, 89, 91
specifying control ID, 92
working with events caused by an action on the
control that resulted in the page being posted back,
92
IReferenceService interface,
System.ComponentModel.Design namespace, 366
GetReference method, 366
IsBindableType method, BaseDataList class, 206
ISelectionService interface,
System.ComponentModel.Design namespace, 368
properties, methods and events, 367
IServiceProvider interface, System namespace, 337
GetService method, 337
IsKeyValid method, LicenseProvider class, 389
overriding, 385, 388
IsPostBack property, Page class, 196
IsTrackingViewState property, DBDropDown custom
control, 218
IsValid method, 330
<item> element, 413, 419
ItemCommand event, shopping cart advanced custom
databound control, 227
ItemCreated event, shopping cart advanced custom
databound control, 227
ItemDataBound event, shopping cart advanced custom
databound control, 227
ITemplate interface, System.Web.UI namespace
implementing, 167
InstantiateIn method, 144, 153, 167
templated controls creation, 144
Items property, ListBox class, 355
ItemTemplate element, 140
DataItem property, DataListItem class, 197
DataList control and, 197
shopping cart custom databound control, 213
ITypeDescriptorContext interface,
System.ComponentModel namespace, 332, 336,
337, 344
Instance property, 344
ITypeResolutionService interface,
System.ComponentModel.Design namespace, 390
IWindowsFormsEditorService interface,
System.Windows.Forms.Design namespace, 337
DropDownControl method, 341

J

JIT compiler, 275

K

key pairs
assigning to assembly, 375
AssemblyKeyFileAttribute class, 375

L

Label class, System.Web.UI.WebControls namespace, 122
Text property, 122
LabelControlBuilder class, System.Web.UI.WebControls namespace
AllowWhitespaceLiterals method, 254
Language attribute, @Control directive, 23
<li> element, 143
licence class creation, 382
License class, System.ComponentModel namespace
creating custom license class, 385
LicenseKey property, 388
LicenseContext class, System.ComponentModel namespace, 389
GetService method, 390
SetSavedLicenseKey method, 391
UsageMode property, 389
LicenseException class, System.ComponentModel namespace, 382, 384
LicenseKey property, Licence class
overriding, 388
LicenseManager class, System.ComponentModel namespace
Dispose method, 382, 383
licensing in .NET Framework, 381
Validate method, 382, 383, 384
LicenseProvider class creation, 385
declaring ProcessorLicense class, 387
inheriting from LicenseProvider class, 388
LicenseProvider class, System.ComponentModel namespace
GetLicense method, 385, 389
IsKeyValid method, 385, 389
LicenseProviderAttribute class, System.ComponentModel namespace, 381
licensing, 379
in .NET, 381
licensing models, 381
common types of, 381
reasons for licensing Server Controls, 380
SnakeNET example, 380
understanding, 379
using licensed server controls, 384
LicFileLicenseProvider class, System.ComponentModel namespace, 383, 384
not very sophisticated, 385
LinkButtonControlBuilder class, System.Web.UI.WebControls namespace
AllowWhitespaceLiterals method, 254

ListBox class, System.Web.UI.WebControls namespace
Items property, 355
ListItemControlBuilder class, System.Web.UI.WebControls namespace
HtmlDecodeLiterals method, 255
Literal class, System.Web.UI.WebControls namespace
AppendSubBuilder method overrides, 258
LiteralControl class, System.Web.UI namespace, 239
encapsulates text not requiring server-side processing, 239
using to add HTML table, 122
LiteralControlBuilder class, 258
System.Web.UI.WebControls namespace
AppendSubBuilder method overrides, 258
load phase
Server Control life-cycle, 17
load view state phase
Server Control life-cycle, 16
Load ViewState execution phase
server control execution lifecycle, 110
LoadPostData method, IPostBackDataHandler interface, 17, 84, 88, 217
implementing, 101
postData parameter, 99
postDataKey parameter, 86, 89
LoadTemplate method, TemplateControl class, 172
performance considerations, 173
LoadViewState method, Control class, 110, 125
LoadViewState method, DBDropDown custom control, 220
LoadViewState method, WebControl class, 15
Localizable attribute, 324

M

managing state, 107
postback events, 107
ViewState, 107
marker interface, 146
MemberDescriptor class, System.ComponentModel namespace, 353
Memory
Environment Resource Checking, 297
<MENUCONSTRAINTS> element, 279
MergableProperty attribute, 322
MergeStyle method, WebControl class, 176
MergeWith method, Style class, 176
Microsoft Message Queue
see MSMQ.
mobile controls, 14, 61
rapid growth of mobile device market, 61
Mobile Internet toolkit
web.config file
adding new device, 62
entries added after installing, 62
Mobile Internet Toolkit, 61
<mobile:Image> control, 63
<mobile:List> control, 62
MobileCapabilities class, System.Web.UI.MobileControls namespace, 62
Modal Editor, 336

MouseEventArgs class, System.Windows.Forms namespace
 naming conventions, 82
MouseEventHandler delegate, System.Windows.Forms namespace
 naming conventions, 82
MoveNext method, IEnumerator interface, 208
MS Mobile Controls
 device independant, 61
MSDomVersion property, HttpBrowserCapabilities class, 67
MSMQ, 11
multi language debugging, 281
multicast deleagates, 76

N

NameValueCollection class, System.Collections.Specialized namespace, 99
naming conventions, 82
 table of event parts, 82
NamingContainer property, Control class, 169
NamingContainerType property, ControlBuilder class, 253
NeedsTagInnerText method, ControlBuilder class, 244, 249
 methods acts as property, 247
 true and false values, 261
News Desk Server Control, 297
 completing the Web XML News Web Site, 311
 Cross Languge Debugging, 298
 debugging the Web XML News web site, 312
 News Web Site
  creating as VB ASP.NET Web Application, 299
 overview of design, 299
  XMLNews, 299
  XMLNewsDisplay project, 299
  XMLNewsFeed project, 299
 reviewing the code, 313
 XML News Display Server Control, (C# .NET), 308
  XMLNewsDisplay project, 308
  XMLNewsFeed project, 310
 XML News Feed Server Control
  build Server Control, 307
  creating in C# .NET, 304
  XMLNewsFeed, 304
Next method, Random class, 122, 265
Notepad
 lack of support when coding, 275

O

Object class, System namespace, 13, 76
Object creation and code persistence methods, type converters, 329
<object> element, 12
observers, 75
Office XP menus, 417
OnAppendToParentBuilder method, ControlBuilder class, 244, 249
 defined, 268
 method modifies the state of the ControlBuilder, 247
 unifies hierarchy of control builders, 269

OnBindingsCollectionChanged method, ControlDesigner class
 overriding, 348
OnBubbleEvent method, Control class, 97
OnBubbleEvent method, shopping cart advanced custom databound control, 228
OnBubbleEvent method, ShoppingCartItem container class, 226
OnComponentChanged method, ControlDesigner class
 overriding, 348
OnComponentChanged method, IComponentChangeService interface, 363
OnComponentChanging method, IComponentChangeService interface, 363
OnControlResize method, ControlDesigner class
 overriding, 348
OnDataBinding method, Control class, 199
 implementing override of method, 200
OnDataBinding method, DBDropDown custom control, 218
OnDataBinding method, shopping cart custom databound control, 209
OnItemCreated method, shopping cart advanced custom databound control, 229
OnItemDataBound method, shopping cart advanced custom databound control, 229
OnSetParent method, ControlDesigner class
 overriding, 348

P

p2p (programmer to programmer)
 lists suitable for this book, 6
 web site, 6
Page class, System.Web.UI namespace
 ClientTarget property, 68
 code-behind model
  class must derive from, 394
 DataBind method, 195
 EnableViewStateMAC property, 128
 IsPostBack property, 196
 writing code-behind class file
  ASPX file, 405
page parser
 actions taken for child controls, 245
 defining interaction with controler, 237
 determines whether tag is associated with specific control, 244
 determines whether text between tags needs processing, 244
 initialization of ControlBuilder class, 244
 parsing custom controls, 237
 processing a parent control, 239
 providing literal text to ControlBuilder, 244
 queries custom control for opening and closing tags, 244
 runat attribute, 237
PaintValue method, UITypeEditor class
 overriding, 336
Panel class, System.Web.UI.WebControls namespace, 149
 provides lightweight control to act as container, 149
ParenthesizePropertyName attribute, 323
ParseChildren attribute, 326, 348

ParseChildrenAttribute class, System.Web.UI
    namespace, 146
    allows template to be specified in HTML, 148
    treating inner HTML elements, 146
Parser property, ControlBuilder class, 253
Password Change control, 86
    PasswordChange.cs
        extending, 89
    PasswordChangeComposite.cs, 94
    using containment, 94
Path Class, System.IO namespace
    GetDirectoryName method, 390
PersistChildren attribute, 348
PersistenceMode attribute, 324
persisting attributes
    <button> tag, 351
PlaceHolderControlBuilder class,
    System.Web.UI.WebControls namespace
    AllowWhitespaceLiterals method, 254
Policy Templates
    see also Template Policy.
    customization, 278
    <MENUCONSTRAINTS> element, 279
post back data handling
    postDataKey parameter, 86
postback
    responding to events and data, 83
        __doPostBack function, 89, 91
        EventBox.cs, 84
        form data, 83
        PasswordChange.cs, 86
            extending, 89
        post back data handling, 86
        ViewState, 107
postback change notification sending phase
    Server Control life-cycle, 17
postback data
    handling by ViewState, 109
postback data processing phase
    Server Control life-cycle, 17
postback event handling phase
    Server Control life-cycle, 17
postback interfaces
    provide for identifying and raising different types of
        events, 92
postDataKey parameter, LoadPostData method, 89, 99
    Nameattribute of server control, 86
<pre> elements, 241, 242
prerender phase
    Server Control life-cycle, 17
Program Resource Checking
    Call Stack, 294
    Dis-Assembly, 296
    Modules, 296
    two types, 294
programming languages
    common interface, 273
    common requirements, 273
    two high level areas of functionality, 275
Projects
    Solution Explorer, 283
PropertyDescriptor class, System.ComponentModel
    namespace, 353
    example of using, 203
    extracting information about control properties, 203
    SetValue method, 360, 361
PropertyDescriptor property, 333

PropertyGrid class, System.Windows.Forms
    namespace
    SelectedObject property, 355
PropertyGrid control
    add to toolbox, 354
PublicKeyToken, 378

R

RaiseBubbleEvent method, Control class, 97
RaiseComponentChanged method, ControlDesigner
    class, 353
RaisePostBackEvent method, IPostBackEventHandler
    interface, 91
    eventArgument parameter, 91
RaisePostDataChangedEvent method,
    IPostBackDataHandler interface, 17, 84, 88, 217
    calling OnEvent method, 84
raising an event, 77
    EventArgs class used as second argument, 77
Random class, System namespace, 122
    Next method, 122, 265
RangeValidator control
    description, 65
Read method, SqlDataReader class, 58
ReadOnly attribute, 323
references to web sites
    p2p, 6
RefreshProperties attribute, 323
Registers
    Environment Resource Checking, 297
RegularExpressionValidator control
    description, 65
Render method, Control class, 43, 96, 410
    HtmlTextWriter object passed as an argument, 44
    overriding, 43, 113
Render method, DBDropDown custom control, 220
Render method, HtmlTextWriter class
    overriding, 383
Render method, WebControl class, 15, 51
render phase
    Server Control life-cycle, 17
RenderBeginTag method, HtmlTextWriter class, 42, 47
RenderBeginTag method, WebControl class, 51
RenderContents method, WebControl class, 51, 54,
    185, 414
    overriding, 410
    specify contents to be rendered, 57
RenderControl method, Control class, 346
RenderEndTag method, HtmlTextWriter class, 42, 47,
    59
RenderEndTag method, WebControl class, 51
rendering
    compared to containment, 93
    definition, 42
rendering Server Controls, 41
Repeater control, 140, 192
    consuming in a Web Form, 140
    creating an HTML unordered list, 141, 143
    names of templates, 143
    rendering content, 143
    RepeaterItem container, 144
RepeaterItem container, 144
Replace method, String class
    filtering, 250, 251, 263

RequiredFieldValidator class,
    System.Web.UI.MobileControls namespace, 404
RequiredFieldValidator control
    adding to textbox controls, 404
    description, 65
    detecting browser capabilities, 70
    Validation Controls, 13
Resource Checking, 276, 294
Revision Control technology, 281
Rich Controls, 12, 14
runat attribute, 237

S

sample code
    downloading, 5
save state phase
    Server Control life-cycle, 17
Save ViewState execution phase
    server control execution lifecycle, 110
SaveViewState method, Control class, 110, 125
SaveViewState method, DBDropDown custom control,
    220
SaveViewState method, WebControl class, 15
security
    see also ViewState and security.
    strong-naming, 373
<select> element
    DBDropDown custom control, 220
    List Controls, 13
Selected property, DbListItem custom control, 214
SelectedIndexChanged event, DBDropDown custom
    control, 217
    using DBDropDown custom control in Web Form, 221
SelectedIndexChanged event, DropDownList class, 20
SelectedObject property, PropertyGrid class, 355
SelectSingleNode method, XmlDocument class, 161
SelectSingleNode method, XmlNode class, 161
Server Component development, 281
Server Control based architecture, 9
    base classes, 9
Server Control creation
    complex control creation example, 56
        exposing public properties, 56
    exposing attributes as properties, 48
        HyperLink property, 50
    invoking Write method, HtmlTextWriter class, 43
    using the utility methods of the HtmlTextWriter class,
        45
        specifying font size and color, 46
    using the WebControl class for control creation, 51
    when should we create our own, 18
    writing the markup content directly, 43
        compiling, 44
        consume that control in an ASP.NET page, 44
        derive from base class Control, 43
Server Control execution lifecycle
    Load ViewState execution phase, 110
    phases, 110
    Save ViewState execution phase, 110
Server Control IDE features example
    News Desk Server Control, 297
Server Control Model, 15
    base classes derived from, 15
    class hierarchy, 15
    life-cycle, 16

Server Controls, 12
    ability to specify the layout, 139
    <asp:Button> control, 12
    base classes, 12
    compared to User Controls, 18
    custom controls, 14
        custom DataBound controls, 191
    deploying, 371
    exposing application and session state, 131
    exposing application state variables to, 131
        creating a read / write application property, 133
    exposing session state variables to, 134
    events, 83
    managing state, 107
    performance considerations, 19
    referring to programmatically, 13
    registering, 422
    rendering, 41
    types, 13
    UI functionality, 12
    when should we create our own, 18
Server Explorer, 276, 290
    two types of database contact, 291
server-side validation techniques
    limitations, 64
session state variables
    exposing to a server control, 134
session state variables accessing
    see application and session state variables
        accessing.
SetSavedLicenseKey method, LicenseContext class,
    391
SetTagInnerText method, ControlBuilder class, 244,
    249, 261
    cannot be used as filter, 262
    method modifies the state of the ControlBuilder, 247
SetValue method, PropertyDescriptor class, 360, 361
SetValue property, 333
shopping cart advanced custom databound control,
    223
    CreateControlHierarchy method, 229
    DataProductField property, 228
    event handling, 224
    ItemCommand event, 227
    ItemCreated event, 227
    ItemDataBound event, 227
    OnBubbleEvent method, 228
    OnItemCreated method, 229
    OnItemDataBound method, 229
    shopping cart loader, 224
    ShoppingCartCommandEventArgs class, 224
    ShoppingCartCommandEventHandler delegate, 224
    ShoppingCartItem container class, 225
    ShoppingCartItemEventArgs class, 224
    ShoppingCartItemEventHandler delegate, 224
    TrackViewState method, 231
    using in Web Form, 231
shopping cart custom databound control, 207
    CreateChildControls method, 209
    CreateControlHierarchy method, 210
    DataSource property, 208
        SqlDataReader class, System.Data.SqlClient
            namespace, 213
    defining templates, 212
        AlternatingItemTemplate element, 213
        ItemTemplate element, 213
    DummyDataSource class, 207
        DummyDataSourceEnumerator class, 208

shopping cart custom databound control (continued)
OnBataBinding method, 209
ShoppingCartItem container class, 207
using in Web Form, 212
SqlDataReader class, System.Data.SqlClient
namespace, 212
shopping cart loader, 98
CartLoader.cs, 99
ProductDetail.aspx, 104
shopping cart advanced custom databound control,
224
ShoppingCartCommandEventArgs class
shopping cart advanced custom databound control,
224
ShoppingCartCommandEventHandler delegate
shopping cart advanced custom databound control,
224
ShoppingCartItem container class
DataBind method, 212
DataItem property, 207, 212
INamingContainer interface, System.Web.UI
namespace, 226
OnBubbleEvent method, 226
shopping cart advanced custom databound control,
225
shopping cart custom databound control, 207
TableRow class, System.Web.UI.WebControls
namespace, 225
ShoppingCartItemEventArgs class
shopping cart advanced custom databound control,
224
ShoppingCartItemEventHandler delegate
shopping cart advanced custom databound control,
224
Shortcut task, 290
**ShowDialog method, IWindowsFormsEditorService
interface, 337**
side-by-side execution, 374
signing an assembly, 375
Assembly Linker, 376
delay-signing, 376
using attributes, 375
simple DataBound controls
see DataBound simple controls.
SnakeNET example
licensing Server Controls, 380
Solution Explorer, 276, 283
manipulating files within the VS .NET project, 301
Projects, 283
Solutions, 283
Solution Items, 284
Solutions
combination of more than two projects, 311
Solution Explorer, 283
SqlCommand class, System.Data.SqlClient namespace
create instance of, 57
ExecuteReader method, 57
**SqlConnection class, System.Data.SqlClient
namespace, 57**
**SqlDataReader class, System.Data.SqlClient
namespace, 57**
DataSource property, shopping cart custom
databound control, 213
GetName method, 57
Read method,, 58
using DBDropDown custom control in Web Form, 221

using shopping cart custom databound control in Web
Form, 212
Src attribute, @Control directive, 23
Standard Values methods, type converters, 328
state management, 107
application and session state variables accessing,
130
mechanics of ViewState, 109
ViewState and performance, 125
ViewState and security, 127
StateBag, 108
STAThreadAttribute class, System namespace, 238
Strict attribute, @Control directive, 23
String class, System namespace
Replace method, 250, 251
filtering, 263
StringWriter class, System.IO namespace, 346
strong-named assemblies
example, 373
made up of, 373
security, 373
**Style class, System.Web.UI.WebControls namespace,
174**
CopyFrom method, 176, 181
custom style class derives from, 184
MergeWith method, 176
Style property, WebControl class, 174
allows the simple addition of named style attributes,
176
style sheets, 174
styles
creating custom style class
StyledDailySpecials.aspx, 184
StyledDailySpecials.aspx (excerpt), 186
StyledDailySpecials.cs (DailySpecialStyle class), 184
StyledDailySpecials.cs (excerpts), 185
exposing style elements as top level properties, 181
extending DailySpecials control, 181
StyledDailySpecials.aspx, 183
StyledDailySpecials.cs (excerpts), 182
exposing styles as properties, 177
StyledSimpleRepeater.cs, 177
working with, 175
applying declaratively, 175
applying programatically, 175
Subproperty methods, type converters, 328
support from Wrox, 5
syntax checking, 276, 293, 302
System namespace
Enum class, 339
EventArgs class, 13, 76
EventHandler delegate, 78, 79, 353
IServiceProvider interface, 337
Object class, 13, 76
Random class, 122
STAThreadAttribute class, 238
Type class, 333
System.Collections.Specialized namespace
NameValueCollection class, 99
System.ComponentModel namespace
DefaultPropertyAttribute class, 397
importing, 28
ITypeDescriptorContext interface, 336, 344
License class, 383
LicenseContext class, 389, 390
LicenseException class, 382, 384
LicenseManager class, 381

System.ComponentModel namespace (continued)
LicenseProviderAttribute class, 381
LicFileLicenseProvider class, 383, 384
MemberDescriptor class, 353
PropertyDescriptor class, 203, 353
TypeConverter class, 336, 357
TypeDescriptor class, 203
System.ComponentModel.Design namespace
DesignerVerb class, 353
ISelectionService interface, 367, 368
ITypeResolutionService interface, 390
System.Data namespace
importing, 56
System.Data.SqlClient namespace, 396
importing, 56
SqlCommand class, 57
SqlConnection class, 57
SqlDataReader class, 57
System.Diagnostics namespace
Trace class, 246
System.Drawing namespace
automatically imported by Visual Studio .NET, 405
Graphics class, 383
System.Drawing.Design namespace
UITypeEditor class, 336
System.Globalization namespace
CultureInfo class, 374
System.IO namespace
File class, 390
Path Class, 390
StringWriter class, 346
System.Reflection namespace, 24
AssemblyKeyFileAttribute class, 375
importing with a Using statement, 376
System.Web namespace
HttpBrowserCapabilities class, 42, 414
importing, 414
System.Web.UI namespace
Control class, 9, 12, 149, 155, 401
ControlBuilder class, 237
ControlBuilderAttribute class, 266
DataBinder class, 203
HtmlTextWriter class, 41, 351
HtmlTextWriterStyle enumeration, 46
INamingContainer interface, 32, 145, 148
IpostBackDataHandler interface, 17
IPostBackDataHandler interface, 84, 86
IPostBackEventHandler interface, 89
ITemplate interface, 144
LiteralControl class, 239
ParseChildrenAttribute class, 146
TemplateContainerAttribute class, 145, 151, 155
TemplateControl class, 172
ToolboxDataAttribute class, 397
System.Web.UI.Design namespace
ControlDesigner class, 345
System.Web.UI.HtmlControls namespace
automatically imported by Visual Studio .NET, 405
System.Web.UI.MobileControls namespace
MobileCapabilities class:, 62
RequiredFieldvalidator class, 404
System.Web.UI.WebControls namespace
BaseDataList class, 206
Button class, 12
classes derived from ControlBuilder class, 254
classes overriding HtmlDecodeLiterals method, 255

CommandEventArgs class, 96
DataListItem class, 197
DropDownList class, 20
Panel class, 149
Style class, 174
TableCell class, 163
TableItemStyle class, 181
TableRow class, 225
TextBoxControlBuilder class, 255
UnitType enumeration, 339
WebControl class, 9, 12, 146, 148
System.Windows.Forms namespace
MouseEventArgs class, 80
System.Windows.Forms.Design namespace
IWindowsFormsEditorService interface, 337
System.Xml namespace
importing, 157
XmlDocument class, 161
XmlNode class, 161
System.Xml.dll file
adding reference to, 157
System.Xml.Serialization namespace
XMLElementAttribute class, 238

T

<TABLE> element, 415, 418
TableCell class, System.Web.UI.WebControls
namespace
ColumnSpan Property, 163
TableCellControlBuilder class,
System.Web.UI.WebControls namespacee
AllowWhitespaceLiterals method, 254
TableItemStyle class, System.Web.UI.WebControls
namespace, 181
TableRow class, System.Web.UI.WebControls
namespace
ShoppingCartItem container class, 225
TableStyle class, System.Web.UI.WebControls
namespace, 181
cellpadding property, 181
cellspacing property, 181
TagName property, ControlBuilder class, 253
TagPrefix attribute, 321
Task List, 276, 288
displaying, 302
project management, 281
Show Tasks, 302
token tag, 288
types, 289
Template Policy, 281
see also Policy Templates.
template projects, 278
TemplateContainerAttribute class, System.Web.UI
namespace, 155
applying to ItemTemplate property, 146
decorating template properties, 157
decorating templates, 151
defining container type, 145
TemplateControl class, System.Web.UI namespace
LoadTemplate method, 172
templated controls, 139
containers, 144
defined, 145
separate classes, 145

templated controls (continued)
creating, 144
DataList control, 140
defining the various templates, 140
HTML tags
definitions, 139
names of templates, 143
rendering content, 143
Repeater control, 140
requirements for working with examples, 141
templated controls creation, 144
advanced, 156
CreateItem method, 161, 163
Daily Special control, 156
DailySpecials.aspx, 164
DailySpecials.cs, 157
DailySpecials.xml, 157
basic
SimpleRepeater2Host.aspx, 154
SimpleRepeaterHost.aspx, 149
SuperSimpleRepeater.cs, 147
SuperSimpleRepeater2.cs, 150
data bound templated controls, 206, 223
dynamic templates, 167
implementing ITemplate interface, 167
ITemplate interface, 144
recap of basic steps, 147
rendering header template, 153
SimpleRepeaterHost.aspx
RepeatCount attribute, 149
template property definition, 144
templates can share containers, 145
templated DataBound controls
see DataBound templated controls.
text boxes
convention used in this book, 4
Text property, DbListItem custom control, 214
Text property, Label class, 122
<text> element, 413
**TextBox class, System.Web.UI.WebControls
namespace**
creating a custom class, 256, 257
**TextBoxControlBuilder class,
System.Web.UI.WebControls namespace**
creating a custom class, 256
HtmlDecodeLiterals method, 255, 259
Threads
Environment Resource Checking, 297
TODO token tag, 289, 302
token tags, 288
Toolbox, 276
Clipboard Ring tab, 286
creating composite controls, 286
creating custom toolbox tabs, 286
**ToolboxDataAttribute class, System.Web.UI
namespace, 397**
setting, 411
Trace class, System.Diagnostics namespace
WriteLine method, 246
TrackViewState method, Control class, 125
**TrackViewState method, shopping cart advanced
custom databound control, 231**
TryCatch, 292
Type class, System namespace, 333
type converters
conversions example, 330
example, 329

functionality, 328
methods that can be overridden, 330
**TypeConverter class, System.ComponentModel
namespace, 336**
GetProperties method, 358, 360
GetPropertiesSupported method, 358
GetStandardValues method, 358
GetStandardValuesSupported method, 358
provides subproperties, 357
**TypeDescriptor class, System.ComponentModel
namespace**
example of using, 203
extracting information about control properties, 203
GetDefaultEvent method, 358
GetDefaultProperty method, 358
GetProperties method, 199, 205, 359

U

UI controls, 12
UI functionality, 12
compared to other HTML controls, 12
**UITypeEditor class, System.Drawing.Design
namespace, 336**
overriding methods, 336
<UL> element, 143
UNDONE token tag, 289
**UnitType enumeration, System.Web.UI.WebControls
namespace, 339**
up-casting, 327
UpLevel
ClientTarget property, Page class, 69
Uplevel browsers
description, 396
supports, 66
<url> element, 413
UsageMode property, LicenseContext class, 389
User Control creation, 20
compared to Web Form creation, 20
converting to User Control, 25
DropDownList control, 20
UserControlExample.ascx, 21
User Controls
compared to custom control, 395
compared to Server Controls, 18
limited in scope, 26
registering, 422
Server Controls, 14
uses, advantages and drawbacks, 18
User task, 290
UserControl class, System.Web.UI namespace
writing code-behind class file, 405

V

**Validate method, LicenseManager class, 381, 383,
384**
validation controls, 12, 13
classes in ASP.NET object model, 65
limitations of current validation techniques, 64
Value property, DbListItem custom control, 214
versioning controls, 374

ViewState, 107
    compared to
        application and session state, 112
        cookies, 112
        HTML hidden form control, 111
    hidden form fields, 108
    in a clustered environment, 111
    introduction, 108
        persistence of property values across postback events,
            108
    mechanics, 109
        property of Control class, 109
        server control execution lifecycle, 110
    performance, 125
    populating child control values, 124
    StateBag, 108
ViewState and security, 127
    __VIEWSTATE
        values encoded in a Base64 format, 127
    transfer data over SSL protocol, 130
    using 3DES encryption, 129
    using EnableViewStateMAC property, Page class, 128
ViewState client performance, 127
    size of _VIEWSTATE field, 127
ViewState property, Control class, 109
    accessing state, 401
    information held in name-value pairs, 109
ViewState server performance, 125
    disabling ViewState, 126
    security, 127
    server resources, 127
    storing proper data in ViewState, 126
ViewState with composite controls, 116
    building server control, 117
        property statements, 121
        SlotMachine.cs, 117
    SlotMachine.dll file, 117
ViewState with simple controls, 112
    building server control, 113
        property declarations, 114
    creating ASP.NET web form, 115
ViewStateIgnoresCase property, Control class, 124
Visible attribute, 324
Visual Studio .NET
    adding hyperlink control to Toolbox, 384
    Add Reference wizard
        System.Xml.dll file, 157
    advantages, 274
    building controls, 273
    cross language debugging, 298
    Custom Server Control integration, 26
    design time support, 9
    interoperability, 274
    managing files on IIS, 300
    namespaces automatically imported, 405
    non language specific, 275
    Property Window
        Category properties, 28
    Toolbox, Custom Controls, 14
    versioning controls, 374
Visual Studio .NET IDE, 274
    creating a solution, 311
    creating an icon for Server Control, 306, 307
    customizing using template policy, 278
        DAP.TDL template, 280
        Enterprise Template Policy, 278
        example, 279
        template projects, 278

    design time architecture
        intermediate level, 327
    design time suppport, 317
    features, 275
        language centric, 276
        non language centric, 276
    language-centric features, 291
        debugging, 293
        Dynamic Help, 294
        error trapping, 292
        Intellisense, 291, 306
        Resource Checking, 294
        syntax checking, 293
        watching, 294
    look and feel, 277
    multi language debugging, 281
    non language-centric features, 282
        Document Window, 285
        Dynamic Help & Search, 287
        Server Explorer, 290
        Solution Explorer, 282
        Task List, 288
        Toolbox, 285
    project management, 281
    shared development environment, 277
        CLS compilers, 277

W

WarningLevel attribute, @Control directive, 23
watching, 276, 294
Web Form Controls, 13
Web Forms
    consuming a Repeater control, 140
    using DataList control in Web Form, 196
    using DBDropDown custom control in Web Form, 221
    using DropDownList control in Web Form, 194
    using shopping cart advanced custom databound
        control in Web Form, 231
    using shopping cart custom databound control in Web
        Form, 212
        SqlDataReader class, System.Data.SqlClient
            namespace, 212
web.config file
    access connection string from, 399
    adding new device, 62
    entries added after installing Mobile Internet toolkit,
        62
    setting up filters, 63
**WebControl class, System.Web.UI.WebControls
namespace, 148**
    AddAttributesToRender method, 51, 54, 56, 185,
        186
    AddParsedSubObject method, 350
    ApplyStyle method, 176
    BackColor property, 15
    base class that controls inherit from, 9
    Button and LinkButton derived from, 268
    ChildControlsCreated property, 349
    context menu derives from, 411
    ControlStyle property, 174, 187
    deriving from, 100
    deriving HitCounter class from, 409
    Font property, 15
    ForeColor property, 15
    LoadViewState method, 15
    MergeStyle method, 176

WebControl class, System.Web.UI.WebControls namespace (continued)
Render method, 15, 51
RenderContents method, 51, 54, 186, 410, 414
RenderEndTag method, 51
SaveViewState method, 15
Style property, 174, 176
UI functionality, 12
using for Server Control creation, 51
Windows authentication
modify the web.config file to enable login as Windows user, 170
Write method, HtmlTextWriter class, 43, 47, 133
WriteAttribute method, HtmlTextWriter class, 42
WriteBeginTag method, HtmlTextWriter class, 42
WriteEndTag method, HtmlTextWriter class, 42
WriteLine method, Trace class, 246
Wrox support, 5
WROX Travel case study, 393, 395
architectural decisions, 395
browser links, 396
reusable login component, 395
WebControl class, 396
context menu custom control, 411
list of elements and their functions, 413
Uplevel and Down Level browsers, 414
hit counter custom control, 408

Context class, 410
deriving class from WebControl class, 409
login custom control, 396
class derives from Control class, 397
custom properties and methods implementation, 399
declaring events, 398
event model, 397
state management, 401
System.Data.SqlClient namespace, 396
login user control, 403
code-behind model used, 403
layout, 403
putting it all together, 421
downlevel version, 421
uplevel version, 421

X

XCOPY deployment
deploying Server Controls, 371
XmlDocument class, System.Xml namespace
SelectSingleNode method, 161
XMLElementAttribute class, System.Xml.Serialization namespace, 238
XmlNode class, System.Xml namespace
SelectSingleNode method, 161

Notes

Notes

Notes

Notes

Notes

wrox

Programmer to Programmer™

Wrox writes books for you. Any suggestions, or ideas about how you want
information given in your ideal book will be studied by our team.
Your comments are always valued at Wrox.

Free phone in USA 800-USE-WROX
Fax (312) 893 8001

UK Tel.: (0121) 687 4100   Fax: (0121) 687 4101

Professional ASP.NET Server Controls – Registration Card

Name _____

Address _____

_____

_____

City _____ State/Region _____

Country _____ Postcode/Zip _____

E-Mail _____

Occupation _____

How did you hear about this book?

☐ Book review (name) _____

☐ Advertisement (name) _____

☐ Recommendation _____

☐ Catalog _____

☐ Other _____

Where did you buy this book?

☐ Bookstore (name) _____ City _____

☐ Computer store (name) _____

☐ Mail order _____

☐ Other _____

What influenced you in the purchase of this book?

☐ Cover Design   ☐ Contents   ☐ Other (please specify):

_____

How did you rate the overall content of this book?

☐ Excellent   ☐ Good   ☐ Average   ☐ Poor

What did you find most useful about this book? _____

_____

What did you find least useful about this book? _____

_____

Please add any additional comments. _____

_____

What other subjects will you buy a computer book on soon?

_____

What is the best computer book you have used this year?

_____

Note: This information will only be used to keep you updated
about new Wrox Press titles and will not be used for
any other purpose or passed to any other third party.

wrox

Programmer to Programmer™

Note: If you post the bounce back card below in the UK, please send it to:

Wrox Press Limited, Arden House, 1102 Warwick Road,
Acocks Green, Birmingham B27 6HB. UK.

Computer Book Publishers